SPUDASMATA 98

SPUDASMATA

Studien zur Klassischen Philologie und ihren Grenzgebieten
Begründet von Hildebrecht Hommel und Ernst Zinn
Herausgegeben von Gottfried Kiefner und Ulrich Köpf

Band 98

ANASTASIOS D. NIKOLOPOULOS

Ovidius Polytropos

2004

GEORG OLMS VERLAG HILDESHEIM · ZÜRICH · NEW YORK

ANASTASIOS D. NIKOLOPOULOS

Ovidius Polytropos

Metanarrative in
Ovid's *Metamorphoses*

2004

GEORG OLMS VERLAG HILDESHEIM · ZÜRICH · NEW YORK

Das Werk ist urheberrechtlich geschützt.
Jede Verwertung außerhalb der engen Grenzen
des Urheberrechtsgesetzes ist ohne Zustimmung
des Verlages unzulässig und strafbar.
Das gilt insbesondere für Vervielfältigungen,
Übersetzungen, Mikroverfilmungen
und die Einspeicherung und Verarbeitung
in elektronischen Systemen.

Bibliografische Information Der Deutschen Bibliothek
Die Deutsche Bibliothek verzeichnet diese Publikation
in der Deutschen Nationalbibliografie; detaillierte bibliografische Daten
sind im Internet über *http://dnb.ddb.de* abrufbar.

Bibliographic information published by Die Deutsche Bibliothek
Die Deutsche Bibliothek lists this publication in the
Deutsche Nationalbibliografie; detailed bibliographic data are available
in the Internet at *http://dnb.ddb.de*.

∞ ISO 9706
© Georg Olms Verlag AG, Hildesheim 2004
www.olms.de
Alle Rechte vorbehalten
Printed in Germany
Umschlagentwurf: Irina Rasimus, Köln
Gedruckt auf säurefreiem und alterungsbeständigem Papier
Herstellung: Hanf Buch- und Mediendruck, 64319 Pfungstadt
ISSN 0548-9705
ISBN 3-487-12745-8

To Michael Winterbottom
and Persephone Antoniou
upon their retirement
σῆμα ἀριφραδές

Contents

Contents	5
List of Tables	8
Acknowledgements	9
I Introduction	11
I.1 The Study of Narrative	11
I.2 Genette's Narratological Model	12
I.3 Narratology and Classical Epic	15
I.3.1 Homer	15
I.3.2 Hellenistic and Latin Epic	17
I.4 Ideology	19
I.5 Bakhtinian Polyphony	24
I.6 Feminism	27
I.7 Metadiegesis: The Object of this Study	31
Appendix	38
II Time	41
II.1 Time and Narrative	41
II.2 Temporal Macro-Analysis	41
II.2.1 Order	41
II.2.1.1 Analeptic Metanarrative	44
II.2.2 Duration / Speed	47
II.2.3 Frequency	50
II.3 Temporal Micro-Analysis	51
II.3.1 Order	51
II.3.2 Duration / Speed	54
II.3.2.1 Summary	54
II.3.2.2 Scene	57
II.3.2.3 Ellipsis	59
II.3.2.4 Pause	60
II.3.3 Frequency	63
II.4 Conclusions	66
III Mode	69
III.1 Mode	69

III.2 Distance	70
III.2.1 Narratized Discourse	71
III.2.2 Transposed Discourse	73
III.2.3 Directly Reported Discourse	77
III.3 Focalisation	87
III.3.1 Zero Focalisation	90
III.3.2 Internal Focalisation	92
III.4 Voice Usurpation	98
III.5 Conclusions	100
IV Voice	103
IV.1 Voice: A Complex Category	103
IV.2 Can the Written Text Speak?	104
IV.3 Vox vs. Littera	106
IV.4 Time of Narrating	107
IV.5 Narrative Level	108
IV.6 Meta-metadiegetic narrative	117
IV.7 Relation to Story	118
IV.8 Function and Motivation	121
IV.9 Conclusions	132
V Towards a Pragmatics of Narrative Voice	135
V.1 Feminist Narratology: Moving Forward Or Backward?	135
V.2 Feminist Narratology: The Story	137
V.3 Female Narrators	141
V.3.1 The Literary Background	141
V.3.2 Ovidian Female Narrrators: Numbers and Narratees	142
V.3.3 Ovidian Female Narrators: Thematics	146
V.3.3.1 Love in the Tales of the Minyeides	146
V.3.3.2 Rape	147
V.3.4 Female Narrators and Patriarchal Order	155
V.3.5 Ovide en Travestie?	160
V.4 Sexuality	161
V.5 Age	165
V.6 Class	170
V.7 Conclusions	175

VI Extra-narrative functions of the narrators	179
VI. 1 Extra-narrative functions of the narrator	179
VI.2 Directing Function of the Intradiegetic Narrators	180
VI.3 Communicative Function of the Intradiegetic Narrators	185
VI.4 Testimonial Function of the Intradiegetic Narrators	185
VI.5 Ideological Function of the Narrator	195
VI.5.1 Ideological Function in Ancient (Epic) Narrative before Ovid	196
VI.5.2 'Augustanism': the (dominant) ideology	199
VI.6 Ideological Function of the Intradiegetic Narrators	201
VI.6.1 Judgement	202
VI.6.2 Explanation	211
VI.6.3 Generalisation	218
VI.7 Conclusions	221
VII Intradiegetic Narratees	225
VII.1 The Study of the Narratee	225
VII.2 Signals of the Narratee	226
VII.3 Classification of the Narratees	239
VII.4 Function of the Narratees	248
VII.4.1 Function of Mediation	248
VII.4.2 Function of Characterisation	251
VII.4.3 Other Functions	254
VII.5 Conclusions	254
VIII General Conclusions	257
Bibliography	263
General Index	291

List of Tables

Transposed Discourse in Metanarrative	74
Attributive Discourse	113
Position of Attributive Discourse	116
Relation of Metadiegesis to Diegesis	126
Female Narrators	143
Erotic Tales by Female Narrators	147
Rape-stories by Female Narrators	152
Narrators Explicitly Designated as Elderly	165
Directing Function (of the Narrator)	180
Testimonial Function (of the Narrator)	185
Implicit Signs of the Narratee	228
Parenthesis in Metanarrative	235
Diegetic Roles of Narratees	239
The Narratees' Familiarity with Metadiegesis	244
Reactions of the Narratees	249

Acknowledgements

> There is one glory of the sun, and another glory of the moon, and
> another glory of the stars; indeed star differs from star in glory.
> *1 Cor.*15.41

This book is a slightly altered and corrected version of the dissertation which I submitted for the degree of D.Phil. in 2001 at the University of Oxford. The research was generously funded by the Alexander S. Onassis Public Benefit Foundation, the British Academy Humanities Research Board and my dear parents, Dimitris and Chryse. I am deeply indebted to Prof. Köpf and Dr. Kiefner, for including my dissertation in the series of "Spudasmata".

During my years at Oxford as a member of Corpus Christi College (1994-1998) I benefited from the moderate criticism and constant support of my supervisor, Dr Stephen Harrison. In times of troubled anxiety my college advisor Prof. Michael Winterbottom has been a sweet comforter and Fr Michael Piret a calm mediator of grace. The Choir of Magdalen College provided me with abundant inspiration and a model of industrious devotion.

The efficient and serviceable staff of the Oxford Libraries, the Ashmolean, the Bodleian and the Taylorian as well as the Library of Corpus Christi College, the University Library and the Classics Library at Cambridge, the Bibliothèque Nationale de Paris, the Blegen Library and the Faculty Library in Athens also deserve my gratitude for making my research an easier and more fulfilling task. Last, but not least, I should thank my examiners, Prof. Denis Feeney, Philip Hardie, and Irene de Jong, as well as Dr. Angus Bowie for their engagement and encouragement.

I Introduction

I.1 The Study Of Narrative

—So much for what is said (*logoi*). We must next consider its expression (*lexis*). When that is done we shall have covered the whole subject of what is to be said and how.

—I don't understand what you mean.

—You ought to; but perhaps you'll know better if I put it like this. Everything that fable-tellers or poets say is a narrative of past or present or future.

—Of course.

—And they execute it either by simple narrative or by narrative conveyed by imitation (*mimesis*) or by both.

—I should like a clearer account of that too, please. (...)

—Now it is narrative both when he makes the various speeches and in the passages between the speeches.

—Of course.

These are the instituting words of narratology in the Third Book of Plato's *Republic* (392c6-393b8),[1] establishing the question of narrative voice at the very heart of the inquiry into the *how* of the narrative act.[2]

But let us take first things first: what is narrative? It can be defined as "the semiotic representation of a series of events meaningfully connected in a temporal and causal way."[3] This means that the Parthenon frieze or a mime is also a narrative, even though they are constructed using only visual images and gestures respectively, without having recourse to the linguistic system of signs. Literary narrative, on the other hand, is an exclusively linguistic phenomenon defined by the presence of a narrator or teller and a verbal (oral or written) text;[4] a receiver or narratee should be added to make the narrative situation complete.

Narrative may of course be approached from a wide variety of angles and theoretical viewpoints: historically, thematically, archetypally, deconstructively, to name but a few. What exactly does it mean to study

---

[1] The translation is that of D. A. Russell in Russell 1972: 61.
[2] The Platonic passage is discussed by Genette 1972: 184 and de Jong 1987: 2-5. See most recently Kirby 1991.
[3] Onega 1996: 3.
[4] Onega 1996: 4.

a (literary) narrative narratologically? If narrative is a semiotic representation of a series of events, one level of analysis will examine the events represented and communicated [the thematic aspect of narratology]; another level will examine the structure of the representation, the *how* of narration in Socrates' terms [the formal aspect of narratology]. It is on this formal aspect of narratology that this dissertation will focus. This entails that any problems encountered in the descriptive analysis will naturally be of a formal nature.

Theorists of narrative often differ when it comes to defining these levels of analysis: some distinguish two, while others speak of three or four. For the purpose of this dissertation a bipartite framework of vertical analysis of narrative will be assumed as sufficient: text and story. *Text* is the finite and structured set of linguistic signs in which an agent relates a story; *story* is the signified of the narrative text. Following Genette's practice, however, unless a distinction between the two levels of analysis is explicitly made in a particular context, *narrative* in this dissertation will be used in the restricted sense of narrative *text*.[5]

I.2 Genette's Narratological Model

The theoretical model followed in this dissertation is mainly the one developed by Gérard Genette. Almost thirty years have passed since the publication of Genette's *Narrative Discourse* in *Figures III*, the book in which he first presented his narratological model.[6] It was an extremely influential work, presenting a systematic theoretical framework for the analysis of what Genette himself calls the "constant literary forms" existing or conceivable in all kinds of narrative. All three topics that have dominated narratological discussions and analyses are covered in that "Essay in Method", as it was subtitled: time in its threefold aspect of *order*, *duration*, and *frequency*; and also *mood* (including *focalisation*) and *voice*. It is natural that a model which had such a huge impact would be used in various ways: others have been inspired by individual aspects, while others have chosen to follow in detail the entire theoretical approach of Genette.

---

[5] Genette 1980: 27.
[6] Genette 1972. *Discours du récit* appeared in English in 1980. This was followed by Genette 1983, which appeared in English in 1988, and most recently the article Genette 1990.

Genette's model is not the only one available. An important alternative, more influential in German-speaking academic circles, was developed by Franz K. Stanzel.[7] His approach is not so strictly structuralist as Genette's: he constantly searches for a gradation and illustrates his model by means of a circle of narrative situations whereas Genette uses tables with discrete categories based on binary oppositions. Stanzel is synthetical and places himself in relation to general theory and a large corpus of texts whereas Genette is analytical and systematically refers to Proust's *À la Recherche du Temps Perdu* in order to illustrate his categories.[8] The disadvantage of Stanzel's model is that it leaves out of consideration time and, most importantly for our purposes, the notion of narrative level.

Another important difference between Genette an the other narratologists is that he sticks to the mechanics of the text, avoiding interpretation as much as possible. Booth has explicitly criticized him for neglecting to explore the function of the techniques identified and studied in *Narrative Discourse*, while others like Chatman and Rimmon-Kenan left the field of structural description and entered hermeneutics without commenting on Genette's practice.[9] This is symptomatic of the shift in priorities towards historical and ideological questions or issues of gender and sexuality in recent literary theory and criticism, which led to rejection of narratology, according to Mieke Bal.[10] In light of these developments applications of narratology, like the present dissertation, may seem naive, implying "an unwarranted acceptance of imperfect theories."[11] I believe, however, (a) that despite a great number of articles published in the last two decades, Ovid's *Metamorphoses* has not been exhaustively explored with the help of narratology, and (b) that an accurate narratological description is a prerequisite for political and ideological criticism. Besides, even Mieke Bal (1997) or Susana Onega and J. A. García Landa (1996), who view this development of adding an

---

[7] Stanzel 1985.
[8] See Cohn 1981: 158-161. A comparison of Stanzel and Genette can also be found in Bal 1986, who argues that Stanzel never took up the challenge of structuralism while Genette did but then gave up.
[9] Florin 1996: 18.
[10] Bal 1997: 13.
[11] Bal 1997: 13.

ideological, psychoanalytic, feminist etc. dimension to narratological analysis as necessary or at least possible, admit that the original structuralist core of the discipline is still valuable and valid to a large extent, while those who, like Ingeborg Hoesterey (1992), hail the advent of a new era in which "the specter of formalism so often associated with narratological pursuits is about to vanish" look back to the narratology of the 70s and 80s as the "classical period" of the discipline.

I find that Seymour Chatman's claim that instead of annulling the structuralist project "deconstruction presupposes structuralist efforts to understand the complex codes amidst which we live and cannot itself exist apart from them" is still valid.[12] That essay of 1988 also included a warning about the surreptitious reintroduction into poetics, and narratology in particular, of interpretation, which is inherently alien to a project that ultimately aims at identifying and describing the universal distinctive characteristics of narrative.[13] As Mieke Bal laments in the 'Preface to the Second Edition' of her *Narratology*, "it seems that with the growth of the study of narrative, interest in what makes narratives 'be' or 'come across' as narrative has only declined."[14]

Before clarifying the specific aims of my research in the fifiteen books of *Metamorphoses*, a narrative in hexameters composed by P. Ovidius Naso during his final decade in Rome, which roughly coincides with the first decade of the Christian era, it will be useful to review the narratological work that has already been done in the broader field of classical studies.[15] Narratology has become better known and more widely practised among classicists than other contemporary approaches. Its theoretical framework allows for relatively straightforward, practical studies of how stories are presented and of the general principles underlying narrative texts, including modern fiction as well as the epics, histories, and "romances" that constitute major genres of Greek and Latin literature.

---

[12] Chatman 1988: 10.
[13] Chatman 1988: 15
[14] Bal 1997: xiv.
[15] Aristotle (*Po*.6, 1449b21) refers to epic poetry as ἡ ἐν ἑξαμέτροις μιμητική.

I.3 Narratology and Classical Epic
I.3.1 Homer
It was not until the late 1980s that the first systematic narratological descriptions of classical texts were published in English. Given Homer's prime position in the canon both ancient and modern, it is not surprising that two of the earliest efforts concerned the epics that have always been attibuted to the legendary bard. De Jong 1987 proposed a "systematic and refined analysis of the presentation of the story" in the *Iliad* only, "by using the narratological model" developed by her supervisor M. Bal "as a heuristic device to tackle existing problems of interpretation or signal new ones."[16] Three years later Scott Richardson with *The Homeric Narrator* attempted to sketch the portrait of what he called "the Homeric narrator," amalgamating two theoretically distinct narrative voices, the narrator of the *Iliad* and that of the *Odyssey*. His study used "the tools offered by Genette and Chatman, among others, to come to terms with the extradiegetic-heterodiegetic narrator" of the two poems.

Homer's case clearly illustrates two basic problems of narratological studies. First, the pluralism of theoretical models. They are, of course, related, cover a lot of common ground and may be combined to a certain extent. Yet, their multiplicity may prove confusing, especially when the same taxonomic categories have different names in the various theories. It can also complicate comparative studies of narrative texts if the primary analyses are based on a variety of models. Second, the specific emphasis of each study. This, in turn, is determined by a variety of factors; besides the model itself, the researcher's own interests and idiosyncrasies or the text's dominant narrative strategies play an important role. To come back to the two studies discussed here, de Jong's emphasis is on narrative as action ("presentation") and is therefore interested in agents ("narrators and focalizers") not in personas, like Richardson. The latter focuses on the issue of narrative voice and is interested in other aspects of narrative technique, like time (summary, pause, order) or the presentation of discourse (speech) primarily as factors that determine the degree of the narrator's presence. This special emphasis also explains his coverage of extra-narrative

---

[16] De Jong 1987: xii.

functions performed by the narrator, such as "commentary" and moments of "self-consciousness".

De Jong's study is further characterized by an attempt to bridge traditional classical scholarship and modern literary theory, a trend that is still popular among classicists. For instance, the first chapter is dedicated to the *status quaestionis* concerning the presentation of the story in the *Iliad*. The discussion mainly revolves around the polarity objectivity-subjectivity and the dramatic quality of Homeric narrative. Concluding that all previous analysis of the presentation of the story in the *Iliad* based on this distinction "has been superficial and far from comprehensive," De Jong suggests narratology may prove a more adequate analytical tool.[17] In the concluding chapter, however, Bal's model is not appreciated as a third way of overcoming the traditional dichotomies straightaway. Instead, at first it merely "enables us to see in a very clear way the serious shortcomings of the time-honoured dogma of Homeric objectivity".[18] This naturally implies that the opposite, subjectivity, would be an apposite, if inadequate, description of Homeric narrative style. Reading further on, however, we discover that narratological analysis has indeed forced upon us a *tertium aliquid*, which De Jong thinks "is best characterized as *multiple*."[19]

Richardson also tried to provide links of a different sort. His several examples and quotations from modern novels suggested above all that most narrative techniques are transhistorical and transcultural but also that Homer is just as sophisticated as many modern classics. His idea, however, has not found many followers with the exception of Don Fowler in his celebrated article on "Deviant Focalisation in Virgil's *Aeneid*."[20] Gian Biagio Conte is probably expressing the view of many classicists and at the same time their lack of interest in modern narratives, when he pontificates that "as a literary form, the novel is only remotely comparable with the epic even if many authors have oversimplified by considering it the last stage in the development of the classical epic."[21]

---

[17] De Jong 1987: 27.
[18] De Jong 1987: 221.
[19] De Jong 1987: 227.
[20] Fowler 1990.
[21] Conte 1986: 155 n.10.

I.3.2 Hellenistic and Latin epic

Massimo Fusillo has been the leading Italian classicist in the application of narratology to classical texts. To the best of my knowledge, Fusillo 1985 is the first published narratological study of a classical text.[22] The model used is essentially the one developed by Genette with special emphasis on the manipulation of time in Apollonius' epic; hence the title. Only pages 347-96 discuss issues of focalisation and voice. This emphasis has made it seem poorer in comparison with De Jong's but, in a sense, it is more comprehensive.

This concentration of critical effort on point of view/focalisation, one of the most controversial theoretical issues and the most interesting narratological concept in the eyes of many classicists, is also evident in the case of Vergilian studies. For instance, the only book-length narratological analysis of the *Aeneid* is dedicated to the "point of view and modes of narration" in the poem.[23] Further references may be found in Fowler 1990. Besides a new name (deviant) for an already recognized type of focalisation according to Bal's model (implicit embedded), the article's main interest lies in its tentative exploration of the ideological parameters and repercussions of focalisation. Although investigation of "*enforced* focalisation shifts" is suggested as "one way of looking at the way that cultural hegemony [i.e. ideology][24] is imposed through language," the critic, in fact, pursues a different line of research into possible cases of "deviant focalisation", a rather recondite aspect of the poem's dialogics –the Bakhtinian term appears in his conclusions.[25] The implicit nature of this type of focalisation activates the reader/critic

---

[22] He has also published a narratological study of the Greek Romance (Fusillo 1989). The second chapter appeared in English as Fusillo 1988.
[23] Bonfanti 1985. See also Segal 1981, and most recently Smith 1999.
[24] Hegemony is a key term in Italian Marxist Antonio Gramsci's thought. "Gramsci normally uses the word hegemony to mean the ways in which a governing power wins consent to its rule from those it subjugates" (Eagleton 1991: 112). Hegemony is a broader category than ideology, but Don Fowler's reference to *enforcement* seems to render the two terms semantically coextensive. This relaxed usage is perhaps legitimated by Gramsci's own occasional use of *hegemony* "to cover both consent and coercion together" (Eagleton, *ibid.*).
[25] Fowler 1990: 47.

to an extent that is not usually encouraged by narrative theory.[26] Fowler rejoices in this potential for interpretative disagreement, even though he expresses his own preference for a dialogic *Aeneid* that challenges monolithic Augustan order.[27]

The term "ideology" only appears once in Genette's *essai de méthode*. In the last section of the chapter on narrative voice, he offers his reader a quick tour of the narrator's functions broadly based on R. Jakobson's model of linguistic communication. One of these is providing an authoritative commentary on the action, for which the label "ideological function" is suggested. As M. Bal observes, "it would be naïve to suppose that only argumentative parts of the text communicate ideology."[28] These differ from the strictly narrative and descriptive sections because they provide the narratee with explicit information on the taken-for-granted assumptions, beliefs and value-systems of the story. Explicitness and clarity of presentation do not, however, entail straightforward application. The narrator may make such statements only to contradict them or treat them ironically in narrative proper.

Both Richardson's and Fusillo's analyses include sections on the ideological function of the narrator. The former concludes that such comments, generally limited to evaluative adjectives and a few generalisations, are rarely made by the Homeric "narrator *in propria persona*; they are, rather, expressed by the characters themselves as well as by the structure, the themes, and the subject matter."[29] Apollonius does not score higher, however, with only three passages from Book Four, two apostrophes (445-9 and 1673-7) and one generalisation (1165-7) overtly performing an ideological function.[30] It is not only the material but also the scope of its discussion which is limited. Neither of the two pioneers makes any serious effort to compare these overt comments with the ideology implicit in the presentation of the story.

---

[26] Bal 1997: xiv.
[27] Fowler 1990: 57.
[28] Bal 1997: 34.
[29] Richardson 1990: 165-6.
[30] Fusillo 1985: 378-80.

I.4 Ideology

The aim of all semiotic studies is to analyse the universe of signs or else the structure and function of semiotic systems. The premise of semiology is that there is no need to refer to socio-historical context to comprehend a semiotic system (e.g. myth), insofar as what is of crucial importance is not so much what texts mean as how they mean.[31] Since ideological meaning is radically contextual in nature, semiology has neglected the 'practico-social' force of ideology in favour of an analysis of its formal structure. But, as Michael Gardiner reminds us, the power of ideology is not simply a matter of the formal structure of ideological discourses; it is crucially a matter of what is said.[32]

Marxism, on the other hand, is not a theory of semiosis. It is a global theory of society and thus also of ideology as a social product. Indeed, ideological analysis has been the appropriate designation for the critical "method" specific to Marxism. From the Marxist point of view, as expressed by Frederick Jameson, "Marxism subsumes other interpretive modes or systems; or to put it in methodological terms, (...) the limits of the latter can always be overcome, and their positive findings retained, by a radical historicizing of their mental operations."[33] From the semiologist's point of view, represented e.g. by Alexandros Lagopoulos, Marxism offers "the general and indispensable context for the study of semiosis, and the general concepts to be used in the domain of semiotics, and reveals the structuring axes of the semiotic systems."[34] Unlike contemporary French post-structuralists and deconstructionists, like Derrida, who have targeted their polemic against hermeneutic or interpretive activity, negating the reference to reality and the referential function of discourse, there are theorists from both sides who urge for a synthesis of Marxism with semiotics.[35]

This is not an easy task. Tzouma 1996 has shown the deficiencies of previous efforts, Lucien Goldmann's in particular. In the third part of her dissertation, however, she offers her own views on the reconciliation

---

[31] Gardiner 1992: 149, where references to good critiques of sructuralism along these general lines can be found.
[32] Gardiner 1992: 151.
[33] Jameson 1981:.47.
[34] Lagopoulos 1996: 493-94.
[35] Lagopoulos 1996: 494. See also Lagopoulos 1971 and 1988.

of Marxism and semiotics in what she calls a double reading, starting with a semiotic approach on the level of the text's formal structure, and continuing with an interpretation of its interconnection with reality, i.e. a description of its ideological function.[36] In turn, this "double reading" is articulated on two levels: (a) the level of signifiers and (b) the level of signifieds. With regard to the first, which is the main focus of our research, she sees the ideology of the text as reflected in the deviations from the norm of chronological representation —she is particularly interested in the category of texts with an explicit historical context, to which the *Met.* (and Latin epics in general) largely belong.[37] In particular, she recognizes three possible deviations: (a) collapsing the distance between narrative and narrated time, e.g. through what Genette has called *metalepsis*; (b) disturbing the chronological order of the narrated events through *homodiegetic anachronies*; and (c) disorganizing the paratactic sequence of narration from a certain past to present time through *heterodiegetic anachronies*, e.g. the celebrated technique of "mise en abyme".[38]

Narratology emerged as a structuralist-semiotic project and has been reluctant to consider such contextual, or rather extra-textual, parameters such as the socio-historical circumstances of a narrative's production and reception. One of the few efforts to consider ideology from a narratological point of view is Hamon 1983.[39] His major premise for the study of ideology from a truly semiotic or poetic point of view, is that one should not study the ideology "of the" text (in its "relationship to the text") but rather the "ideological effect" of the text as a relationship inscribed in the text and constructed by it.[40] Where is this "ideological effect" to be sought? Hamon sees ideology as intervening in the differential semantic definition of the actants of the utterance (i.e. the narrators), as in the knowledge they have of things (i.e. focalisation), their programmes of manipulation and reciprocal persuasion, or the evaluations that they make of narrative states or programmes (i.e.

---

[36] Τζούμα 1991: 151-207.
[37] She admits, however, that her list is not exhaustive.
[38] Τζούμα 1991: 162-65. Tambling 1991 makes similar observations in ch.7.
[39] Hamon 1983. Hamon's book on the same subject (Hamon 1984) is listed in the select bibliography of Τζούμα 1991 but not referred to in the body of her text.
[40] Hamon 1983: 95.

judgements and other forms of narratorial commentary). It is on this last aspect that Hamon focuses in the main part of his essay: "The ideological point is to be considered as the intrusion or surfacing in a text of knowledge, of a normative competence of the narrator (or of an evaluating character) distributing at this intersection positivities or negativities, successes and failures, conformities and deviances, excesses and lacks, dominants or hierarchical subordinations, something as acceptable or unacceptable, suitable or unsuitable, and so forth."[41] Most relevant to our purposes is his observation about the origin of evaluations in a narrative: it can be diversified, i.e. shared among several narrators and focalizing characters, or monopolized by a single narrator-focalizer.[42] Although Hamon does not refer to Genette's narrative theory, his views are broadly reconcilable with the latter's model, as the bracketed paraphrases in Genettean terminology suggest.

Until about ten years ago European and American classicists hardly ever talked about ideology. The work of Simon Goldhill (e.g. 1990), Josiah Ober (1989), or the recent collection edited by Boegehold and Scafuro 1994 on the Greek side, and that of Wallace-Hadrill (e.g. 1987), Feeney (1991 and 1992), Hinds (1992) on the Latin side has put the word on the map of classical studies.[43] The characteristic use of the term by most classicists derives from the source Ober explicitly acknowledges, the enormously influential writings of M. I. Finley, who in turn relies heavily on the sociology of Weber.[44] Ober's definition of ideology is set forth as number 3 of his "Premises and Methods": "Each member of any given community makes assumptions about human nature and behavior, has opinions on morality and ethics, and holds some general political principles; those assumptions, opinions, and principles which are common to the great majority of those members are best described as ideology."[45]

The notion of norm is clearly important for any consideration of ideology and literature. Ideology and its filtering work can be perceived

---

[41] Hamon 1983: 102. Narratorial intrusions are also presented as ideologically charged in Tambling 1991: 33.
[42] Hamon 1983: 107.
[43] See Fowler 1994: 252
[44] Rose 1997: 155.
[45] Ober 1989.38.

in the gap between a constructed model which acts as a norm and a given. In Gian Biagio Conte's view, "the ideology to be constructed by the critique should be wholly embodied in the structural form of the work and should also be detectable (as part of the code) within literature's routes to signification."[46] His essay on the interpretation of Vergil's *Aeneid* illustrates plainly his method, by presenting the poem against the background of the ideologically charged norm of Latin epic.[47] In his view, the Latin epic norm "establishes that the substance of its contents should, in particular, be identified with the supremacy of the state as an embodiment of heroic action."[48] Attempting to construct the Latin epic norm on the basis of the surviving fragments of Naevius' *Punica* and Ennius' *Annales*, he observes that "in the Latin epic, an event –in itself empirical and arbitrary– becomes the motivated (justified) sign of a sense that is easily expressible as a general maxim."[49] In the identification of *sententiae* as the locus *par excellence* of the text's ideological function Conte's views coincide with those of Genette 1972.[50]

Legislation also represents an ideologically charged norm with textual form. Ovid's relation to the Augustan legislation in the *Amores* and particularly the *Ars Amatoria* has been the subject of careful investigation since the publication of Stroh 1979. He presented Ovid as "constantly making fun of the sexual standards the legislation enjoined, yet always leaving himself an escape route against the charge of openly encouraging disobedience to the law." His poetry, moreover, may be placed against a background of political discontent and dissent. In particular it is interesting to observe the protests against the marital laws by members of the equestrian order to which Ovid himself belonged; these protests resulted in A.D. 9 in modification, if not repeal of the laws.[51] Wallace-Hadrill 1985 considers this kind of interpretation as rather naive, and suggests relegating Augustus' moral legislation to the social and political order which he imposed as a whole, i.e. sexual control as a product or corollary of social control. Consequently, Ovid's rejection of Augustus'

---

[46] Conte 1986: 98; see also 149.
[47] Conte 1986: ch.5.
[48] Conte 1986: 144.
[49] Conte 1986: 146.
[50] See Genette 1972: 262-63.
[51] Wallace-Hadrill 1985: 181-2.

sexual order must be seen as a rejection of the social and political order he tried to restore after the political confusions of the previous decades. Furthermore, the poets' attitudes to sexual affairs carry implications of their view of Augustus' own role in society.[52]

Phillips 1983 contends that "Ovid's problem lay in the combination of an otherwise tolerable eroticism with a religious outlook antithetical to acceptable norms as defined in other Augustan authors."[53] In other words, the norm of Augustanism is to be constructed from material derived from Vergil, Horace and Livy, leaving out anything that seems idiosyncratic even in these authors. These authors "have in their various ways expressed belief in divinity which communicates to mortals and intervenes in their affairs. Various combinations of interventions with mortal actions have produced a quasi-dialectic of Roman history which divinity has led to the Augustan era. Thus (...) the Augustan religious revival, via its attempts to recover the spirit of early Rome, would play on deeply rooted feelings of cosmic order. History, death and suffering all had meaning in the cycles of history."[54] By contrast, "although Ovid also offers a numinous universe, that universe and its animating forces offer neither explanation nor solace. No larger meaning exists either in individual experience or historical vista."[55]

Generally speaking, the narrative's ideology is also present in indirect free discourse and interior monologue (or "stream of consciousness").[56] These are techniques unknown to classical literature.[57] They are, however, related to the issue of point of view in narrative (or *focalisation*). It is on this aspect of narrative (in particular, implicit embedded focalisation) that Fowler 1990 focused. That a narrative's ideology can be traced in its strategies of focalisation is not a novelty in narratology. In a study of point of view in fiction that was originally published in Russian in 1970, Boris Uspensky had already recognised that focalisation has an ideological facet.[58] This "consists of 'a general system of viewing

---

[52] See Wallace-Hadrill 1982.
[53] Phillips 1983: 801.
[54] Phillips 1983: 805.
[55] Phillips 1983: 812.
[56] Tambling 1991: 46.
[57] See the discussion in chapter III.1.
[58] Uspensky 1973.

the world conceptually', in accordance with which the events and characters of the story are evaluated."[59] Naturally, in texts with more than one levels of narration or variable focalisation, we need to set ourselves the question: does the ideology of the external narrator-focalizer coincide with that of the other narrators and/or focalizors? If not, what is their relation? For, in this case there are two options: (a) either the secondary-focalizers' ideologies that deviate from the primary narrator-focalizer's standard are at least implicitly (or even explicitly) censured, or (b) there is a juxtaposition of different ideological positions without any overt adjudication between them.[60] Implicit in all this is a broad definition of ideology as "a function of the relation of an utterance to its social context," the normal meaning of the word in critical linguistics.[61] This means that it is not limited to a body of ideas serving to sustain relations of domination, even less so to specifically false ideas which help to legitimate a dominant political power (in our case, the post-Actium Augustan regime).

I.5 Bakhtinian Polyphony

Language is never a one-sided, ideologically neutral entity, except perhaps when it is codified through a process of abstraction. Literary language, in particular, is stratified and plural. This is the major tenet and contribution of Bakhtinian thought to the theoretical discussion on the essence of the literary phenomenon. M. Bakhtin regarded this multiple stratification as conditioned by literary genres and their idiosyncratic particularities. In his view, several linguistic features (lexical, semantic or syntactic) become inextricably associated with particular types of text, whether literary or not.

The use of *polyphony*, i.e. the co-presence of more than one dialect, whether social or literary, in a text, is characteristic of prose and is a defining feature of the most accomplished and productive form of prose, the novel. "This for Bakhtin is one way of expressing the novel's general spirit of indeterminacy, process, inconclusiveness, *unfinalisability*,

---

[59] Rimmon-Kenan 1983: 81, quoting Uspensky 1973: 8.
[60] Toolan 1988: 74 with reference to the work of M. Bakhtin.
[61] See Eagleton 1991: 9 and Simpson 1993: 5.

to use one of his key terms."[62] By contrast, there is little room for polyphony in poetry; only the "lower" genres of poetry –satire, comedy, etc.– can accommodate it. This does not mean that it has not found its way into the so-called serious (*gravis*) genres, like epic, which have incorporated polyphony mainly through the words spoken by the characters. This is only one of the ways that plurilinguism is represented in literature and the novel in particular. Literary and social dialects with diverse ideological perspectives may be parodically embedded in the normally authoritative and uniform voice of the main narrator, creating a hybrid construction with double tone and style (*dialogism*). Bakhtin takes care to draw the line between this kind of embedding which commonly has a humorous effect and the incorporation of another particularized narrative voice as the main narrator of the novel.

Bakhtin's essays on polyphony and dialogics were written in the late 1930s but were only published in 1975 and three years later became available in the West through a French translation. Apparently, therefore, Genette's taxonomy of narrative voices was developed independently (there is no reference to Bakhtin in the bibliography of Genette 1972 and the later Genette 1983 acknowledges only another work of the Russian theorist). Despite their genetic independence both Bakhtin's and Genette's theoretical investigations were focused on the novel. For the former it was the work of Rabelais, Cervantes[63] and Dostoyevsky that epitomised the qualities of the novel, while Genette's model of narrative poetics is systematically exemplified, constructed and tested through reference to Proust's *A la Recherche du Temps Perdu*, a milestone of French modernism.[64]

So the first question that arises is whether two theories developed more or less on the basis of novels, apparently in order to describe their stylistic particularities, can be profitably employed to analyse a poem like the *Metamorphoses*. Whether one accepts Ovid's long narrative poem as epic or not, Bakhtin does allow for polyphony in poetry, at least in the

---

[62] Bakhtin 1981: 7.
[63] Bakhtin 1981: 132: "Cervante's *Don Quixote* realizes in itself, in extraordinary depth and breadth, all the artistic possibilities of heteroglot and internally dialogised novelistic discourse."
[64] Genette 1972: 68: "J' avoue ma répugnance, ou mon incapacité, à choisir entre ces deux systèmes de défense apparemment incompatibles."

mode that is our object and category of analysis, viz. narratives attributed to characters of the main story. Nevertheless, Bakhtin's theoretical analyses, and especially his essay on "Poetic and Novelistic Discourse", emphasize that true linguistic pluralism is difficult to attain in verse. Therefore, one thing that we must establish before appealing to Bakhtin's ideas on polyphony is that Ovid has achieved some sort of linguistic diversity in his representation of his character's narratives, whether in hybrid or pure form.

Examining the narratives of Achelous **[17]**, Orpheus **[21]** and Pythagoras, Barchiesi 1989 argues that internal narrators in the *Met.* are not differentiated by an individual narrative style and lexical particularities; their distinctiveness lies in the type of narrative that they represent.[65] In other words, given the limited variety of narrative styles and types that could be convincingly employed by the extradiegetic narrator 'Ovid', the use of internal narrators gave our poet the opportunity to present his readers with an encyclopaedia of narrative forms, as they could be accommodated in hexameter verse. Thus the *Met.* become not only a universal chronicle *ab origine mundi / ad mea tempora* (1.3-4), but also a history of narrative forms and contexts from Olympus to Italy, from *Palatia caeli* (1.176) to "the deep woods that grow in the valley of Aricia" (15.488), from Homer's *Odyssey* and Lucilius' *Satires* to Vergil's *Aeneid*.[66]

Barchiesi's thesis, however, poses a methodological question that needs to be addressed and satisfactorily answered: what is the semantic and paradigmatic scope of the term "type of narrative" or "narrative form". Barchiesi's original conception is more akin to that of "literary genre" (heroic epic, didactic) or "literary school", essentially Callimachean vs. non-Callimachean, to which anti- and post-Callimachean could perhaps be added.[67] Since the choice of literary genre

---

[65] Barchiesi 1989. Pythagoras' speech, which illustrates the genre of didactic hexameter poetry (cf. 15.479 *instructo pectore*) was not examined in this dissertation because it does not conform with the notion of narrative that has prevailed in our choice of material, even though it contains some narrative sections, like the succession of the four seasons (15.201-13).
[66] See Galinsky 1996: 262.
[67] Is Ovid's *Met.* a Callimachean poem? Hopkinson 1988: 85 cautiously suggests that *Met.* gives a better impression of the overall effect of the *Aetia* than either Propertius' fourth Book of elegies or the *Fasti*, as it is also "made up of diverse episodes linked by a

was related to aesthetic allegiance, it does not appear necessary to pursue a clearer distinction and definition of Barchiesi's terms of analysis. His selective corpus of material also points in the same direction.

Ovid's choice to write in hexameters makes impossible the accurate reproduction and representation of literary genres other than epic, a genre with two main types in Graeco-Roman antiquity, heroic and didactic. For genre at that stage of literary history is generally defined by a certain and "relatively stable",[68] though not necessarily static, combination of form and content, which expresses a basic attitude and gives shape as well as a certain semantic and evaluative significance to a text.[69] What can be parodied in hexameters is this attitude of the literary subject, characteristic of each genre, which is conveyed e.g. through choices on the lexical level. It will become clear, however, that even this broad working definition of generic parody in the *Met.* is rather inadequate. The problem is that unless we are able to detect and appreciate the generic context of the metanarrative's intertextual references it is often easier to talk of types of story, which may or may not have had specific generic associations. This would also align our approach to the question of polyphony with the narratological frame of our research.

I.6 Feminism

Lillian E. Doherty (1995) has firmly put female listeners and narrators on the agenda of classical studies. The theoretical foundation of her analysis "consists of two pillars: reader-response theory and narratology. Of the two, reader-response theory clearly is the more pervasive one."[70] Her use of narratological concepts is, however, wider and wilder, as de

---

common theme," while producing a general impression of "organic unity rather than of unstructured chaos" through careful arrangement of the individual episodes. See also Lyne 1984 and Knox 1986: 65-83.
[68] Bakhtin 1986: 60.
[69] Bakhtin 1986: 5: [Authors] do not construct their works with inanimate elements, with bricks, but with forms which already have a heavy semantic value, which are full of significance. For an ethical conception of genre developed by a classicist see Ford 1992: 22-3.
[70] De Jong 1998: 463.

Jong has pointed out.[71] From a feminist point of view, her very intention to establish a narrative hierarchy (chapter 5), let alone her conclusion that the (male) epic narrator and Odysseus are the apex of the hierarchy in the *Odyssey*, while broadly acceptable from the narratological point of view is suspect in terms of feminist critique. As de Jong appreciates, this is not unprecedented in feminist studies of classical texts.[72] In a book intended "to be a part of a conversation between feminist theory and the classics," Nancy Rabinowitz seems to argue that women are given important roles on the stage only in order for their dangerous sides to be fully exposed.[73]

She further admits that differences between the discourses of classics and feminist theory have made conversation between them highly problematic. "For example, the scholarly tone is essential in classical philology. The discipline's rules of research include exhaustive reviewing of everything that has been thought or said about one's subject. The dominant mode of research in classics is in the grip of an almost total empiricism and rooted in a form of textual study that purports to be value free, because it is based on a supposedly neutral philology."[74] For the last twenty-five years there has been consistent attention to women in antiquity, and there is by now a substantial body of work in that subfield. Moreover, by now women classicists have published enough, at least on Ovid, to render obsolete Rabinowitz's remark that the review of previous scholarship is yet another patriarchal aspect of classics.[75]

Much more important and almost impossible to overcome is the second problem identified by Rabinowitz, i.e. that "for the most part classics does come back to cultures dominated by men. As a result, feminism in classics has devoted much attention to decoding the images of women in works by men, a study with its own serious problems."[76] In the early 1990s a serious debate arose among feminist classical scholars about the validity of using male-authored, canonical texts. Phyllis Culham (1990) argues that women's lived reality in antiquity would be

---

[71] De Jong 1998: 466.
[72] De Jong 1998: 463.
[73] Rabinowitz 1993a: ix.
[74] Rabinowitz 1993: 3-4.
[75] Rabinowitz 1993: 8.
[76] Rabinowitz 1993: 10.

better recovered by reading female authors when possible and by paying close attention to material culture. Richlin, on the other hand, maintains that, even in discussing male writers of antiquity, we are not excluding women since all the events depicted and attitudes voiced in canonical texts "bear on the lives of the women who heard [Ovid's] poems and live(d) in the sign system that produced the canon."[77]

A fruitful framework for the discussion of women in male-authored texts was introduced by Alice Jardine (1985). She coined the term *gynesis* to describe the textualization of 'woman' within poststructuralist and postmodern discourses.[78] In other words, *gynesis* focuses on woman as a 'writing-effect' even in male-authored texts. Gold 1993 is the only feminist study in classics that adopts the perspective provided by the notion of *gynesis* in order to analyze Propertius and others who wrote elegy in Rome of the first century B.C. In her view, they were reacting in this way "to the clearly developed but already collapsing moralistic patriarchal value system of that society."[79] Gold argues that Propertius denies the feminine (Cynthia) a fixed identity and puts himself (*ego*, the elegiac persona) into play as the feminine. In this way, she thinks that the poet destabilizes the traditionally assigned male and female roles.

The dialogue on the depiction of women in Roman elegy had started earlier with contributions by Judith Hallett and particularly Maria Wyke.[80] Hallett 1973 "suggested that male Roman love elegists such as Catullus and Propertius adopted a 'counter-culture' persona which repudiated the socially prescribed patterns of behavior for males and females of the Roman elite."[81] Gutzwiller and Michelini 1991, however, contend that the Roman poets used the subversive Hellenistic view of traditional gender roles, which valued the female more positively than in earlier time, in order to "effect a covert reversion to the masculine ethos," reasserting traditional male dominance.[82]

---

[77] Richlin 1992: 159.
[78] It is not a "modernist notion" as Rabinowitz 1993: 13 suggests, probably influenced by the subtitle of Jardine's book.
[79] Gold 1993: 77.
[80] Hallett 1973 and Wyke 1987, 1987a, 1989, and 1994. See also the most recent contribution by Flaschenriem 1998.
[81] Gold 1993: 90.
[82] Gutzwiller 1991: 76.

Wyke 1994 remains faithful to the view she argued in earlier articles (e.g. 1989) that "it is not the concern of elegiac poetry to upgrade the political position of women, only to portray the male narrator as alienated from positions of power and to differentiate him from other, socially responsible male types."[83] For her the female is employed in the text only as a means of defining the male. Even though she admits that the erotic system presented by Propertian elegy is "unorthodox", she thinks it irrelevant to "the purposes of the elegiac discourse of love" to ask whether its political charge is oppositional or integrational, resisting or reproducing the hegemonic gender roles of Augustan Rome.[84]

Of particular interest to our study of oral metanarrative in the *Met.* is the discussion of Propertius' Fourth Book, where women like Arethusa, Tarpeia, Acanthis, Cynthia and Cornelia are elaborately represented and even speak. In Wyke's view, a key to this Propertian novelty is offered as part of the programmatic opening to the book. In poem 4.2 a new first-person narrator, the statue of Vertumnus, declares his capacity to take on diverse shapes, including that of a *non dura puella* ("a none too prudish girl" 4.2.23).[85] To analyze Propertius' representation of women she draws on Froma Zeitlin's work on Attic drama, where male authors put on stage female characters who were played by male actors.[86] Zeitlin concludes that "in the end, tragedy arrives at closures that generally reassert male, often paternal (or civic), structures of authority, but before that the work of the drama is to open up the masculine view of the universe." Similarly, Wyke maintains that none of the women in Propertius' Fourth Book can be regarded as speaking for or acting for herself. "Even when the elegiac poet gives a point of view and a voice to female characters, he still exercises discursive mastery over them, and their actions and utterances are still

---

[83] Wyke 1989: 42.
[84] Wyke 1994: 119. In p.120 she refers to Kennedy 1993: 34-39, who suggests that conclusions on the question are not self-evident but depend on the individual reader's way of generating and emphasizing conradictions.
[85] Wyke 1994: 122 [the translation is from G. P. Goold's Loeb edition cf. Wyke's rendering as "a soft girl"]. On PROP.4.2 see most recently Lindheim 1998, who argues that Vertumnus' shifting costumes questions the very constitution of gender.
[86] Zeitlin 1996: ch. 8.

designed to put the 'masculine' [i.e. the poet's prior self-representation as the male *ego*] into play as problematic."[87]

Feminist narratology is a sub-field of post-structuralist or contextualist narratology with its own story, which will be sketched at the beginning of chapter 5. What is important to note here is that the pioneering studies in feminist narratology by Susan Lanser and Robyn Warhol have ignored Jardine's *gynesis*. In keeping with the feminist principle of privileging speaking and hearing, as opposed to the patriarchal valuation of specularity, vision, the objectifying gaze, Lanser's version of feminist narratology has been much concerned with women finding a voice, and with women's "other voices".[88] Her aim is to show how far her **women writers** more or less radically challenge patriarchal traditions in the novel, patriarchal valuations of their work, and, above all, patriarchal conceptions of the narrative voice. And "she does so precisely by reinstating or maintaining terms of reference –authority, subjectivity, narratorial hegemony, originality, totalisation, the monologic voice– that have developed within and are surely fundamental to patriarchal ideology."[89]

I.7 Metadiegesis: the object of this study

The particular object of our study is the narrative device of *metadiegesis*. *Diegesis*, the Platonic term for the pure and simple narrative of events,[90] was reintroduced into critical discourse by Souriau and was used by Genette to designate "the universe of the first narrative".[91] *Metadiegesis* is, therefore, the universe of the second narrative or *metanarrative*, the narrative within the (first) narrative. *Metadiegetic narrative* is an articulation of the most essential property of all narrative: by telling the story of another narrative, the first narrative achieves its fundamental theme and at the same time is reflected in this image of itself. It becomes

---

[87] Wyke 1994: 123.
[88] Lanser 1992.
[89] Gibson 1996: 158.
[90] *Rep.*394c1-2: δι' ἀπαγγελίας αὐτοῦ τοῦ ποιητοῦ ("the poet's own report").
[91] Genette 1980: 228n.41. The notion of "first narrative" has proved controversial among Genette's critics and difficult to apply to texts like the *Metamorphoses* but I hope it is sufficiently self-explanatory.

metanarrative, in the sense that *metalanguage* is a language in which one speaks of another language. In order to avoid confusion with the use of *metanarrative* to designate comments made by the narrator with regard to the act of narrating, more often than not I will refer to *metanarrative* as *metadiegetic narrative* or *second-(third- etc.) level narrative*. "Any event a narrative recounts is at a diegetic level immediately higher than the level at which the narrating act producing this narrative is placed."[92] Genette did not restrict the notion of intradiegetic narration to representations of oral narrative. It may be a written text, such as a letter, or a dream, or even a non-verbal representation (most often visual) as long as it is converted into verbal narrative by the narrator (e.g. the ecphrasis of 'Arianna abandonata' in Catullus 64) or, more rarely, by having another character describe it. This dissertation has the self-imposed limitation of focusing on 'oral' intradiegetic narration.[93]

Second-degree narrative is a form which goes back to the very origins of epic poetry. It has been part of the epic narrator's apparatus from as early as the *Iliad* (mainly 6.155-95, 9.438-95, 527-99, 24.602-17) and the *Odyssey*, most notably in Odysseus' *Apologoi* to the Phaeacians in Books 9-12. The self-awareness of the gesture of embedding, however, was bound to be more appealing and crucial to Hellenistic poets and their poetics. Much indebted to Alexandrian techniques in more than one way, Ovid's *Metamorphoses* shows an impressive range of narrative voices: divine artists, like the Muses, heroes and anonymous people, men (e.g. Cephalus) and women (e.g. Minyeids), young (Iole) and old (Alcmene). The act of narrating is clearly an important theme of the poem. Narration is no longer exclusively associated with identification, as in the *Odyssey*; it is used for various purposes: to seduce, to demonstrate, to console, to while away time, to inform, to entertain, to compete, even to put someone to sleep. Indeed it is so pervasive that it is difficult to study the poem without reference to it. Of course, one of the reasons we chose the *Met.* for this study of metanarrative was the fact that narration plays such an important role in the poem.[94]

---

[92] Genette 1980: 228.
[93] The narrative 'ecphrases' of the *Met.* were examined in my unpublished M.St. Dissertation, "Some Aspects of Ecphrasis in Post-Vergilian Epic" (University of Oxford 1995).
[94] See Barchiesi 1997: 121-2.

Another reason was, of course, the lack of a systematic study of metanarrative in the poem. Pursuing an investigation of the characteristics of a distinctly Ovidian narrative aesthetic, scholarship has frequently had recourse to two comparative methods. Scholars focused on metadiegetic narratives that appear to be paired by virtue of their proximity on the syntagmatic axis of the poem's structure or by their thematic similarity, and attempting to distinguish between paradigms of the bad and the good poem, according to an assumed theory of Ovidian poetics.[95] Alternatively they explored the relationship between second-level narrative and its immediate diegetic context or another diegetic narrative of similar content, attempting to distinguish between the voice of the external and the internal narrator.[96] The latter question is not new; it was, in fact, already asked by Peters *num poeta conatus sit ad sententias moresque eius qui narret narrationem fingere an solum variandi causa tribuerit, ceterum eodem modo narraverit ac se ipse loquatur*.[97] However, as Keith implicitly suggested, commenting on the shortcomings of Solodow 1988, the only accurate and reliable method of seeking an answer to this old problem would be "an exhaustive examination of every embedded [read: metadiegetic] narrative and all of the first-layer [read: diegetic] narrative of the poet".[98] It is the first part of this project that the present dissertation aims to cover for the first time. Each of the six chapters of the dissertation addresses a particular aspect of the 37 metanarratives that constitute the corpus established for the purposes of this study.

A comparison with the most recent listing of internal narrators in the *Met.*, Appendix A to Wheeler 1999, proves how theoretical principles and personal interpretation of narratological problems posed by the text can influence even the material studied. The story of Marsyas, narrated by an unidentified narrator to an unidentified audience responding to Niobe's tragedy in free indirect discourse (Wheeler), will be discussed in the chapter on mode (chapter 3). The other three instances of metanarrative included in Wheeler's catalogue, Ajax's (13.5-122) and Ulysses' (13.128-381) speeches in front of the Achaean generals and army, as well as Pythagoras' exposition of his theory of vegetarianism,

---

[95] See Hofmann 1985.
[96] See Nagle 1983 and Keith 1992.
[97] Peters 1908: 96.
[98] Keith 1992: 4.

metensomatosis, and general mutability (15.75-478) have been excluded on the grounds that although they contain certain narrative sections, there is no sustained narrative, as defined in section 2 above.[99]

It is perhaps legitimate to call intradiegetic narrators all characters in a narrative speaking in *oratio recta*, as de Jong did in her classic narratological study of the *Iliad*. Moreover, a distinction between narrative proper and other kinds of speech attributed to characters in a narrative text may be useless in practical terms. In other words, when it comes to such questions of practical criticism as the differentiation between the voice of the external narrator (Ovid) and his surrogates, character-narrators and character-speakers, the distinction may not be valid. Nelles has even argued that using the term 'narrator' for all speakers is a strategically necessary extension.[100] There is, however, at least one aspect essential to narrative that is absent from other types of discourse, namely temporality. It is no coincidence that this is largely absent (or at least there is no particular section devoted to its study) in de Jong's analysis of the *Iliad*. A comparative study of storytelling and non-storytelling character discourse in the *Met.* and other narrative texts would clarify the practical side of the issue.

The presentation of our narratological analysis of Ovidian metanarrative follows the structure of Genette's model: first Time (Chapter II), then Mode (Chapter III) and finally Voice (Chapters V-VI). An alternative would be to present each story in order of textual appearance. Scott Richardson, for example, offers in an Appendix a narratological commentary, as it were, of *Odyssey* 5.315-443 as a complement to his category-focused chapters in the main body of his book.[101] In his view, it is a way to counterbalance the disadvantage of fragmentation of the particular metanarratives, which is even greater in a study like his, which having a broader textual corpus to cover, has to resort to statistics and illustrative examples. The present dissertation, however, aims at exhaustive description. Therefore, we have tried to discuss every single instance of the aspects of narrative technique covered by Genette's model, not just illustrate it with clear-cut examples

---

[99] The debate between Ajax and Ulysses has been analysed in narratological terms by Musgrove 1991.
[100] Nelles 1997: 125.
[101] Richardson 1990: 201-207.

and discuss the more problematic cases. At the very least we have tried to list all the relevant passages in Tables.

Chapter II is dedicated to the temporal relations between story and narrative. They are analyzed under the three categories introduced by Genette: order, duration/speed and frequency. Since metanarratives in the *Met.* are inserted within the extradiegetic narrator's story, they have to be studied from a dual perspective. First, we have to consider how metanarratives function in the temporal structure of diegetic narrative. As the extradiegetic narrator has set himself the task of unfolding the world's history of metamorphosis from its creation onwards, metanarratives are helpful in filling chronological gaps or solving problems created by the lack of precise chronological localisation of certain stories or their temporal concurrence. In terms of narrative speed we will see how metanarratives contribute to the alternation between summary and scene. Metanarrative also modulates iterative narrative into singulative. Both tendencies contribute to the Ovidian poetics of the individual episode. The second part of the chapter is dedicated to the study of the internal temporal strategies and structures of the 37 metanarratives, in an effort to establish the major trends and their function.

In Chapter III we turn to the organisation of narrative information and the study of its two major aspects: distance and focalisation. Distance is examined with reference to the representation of speech in the metanarratives. Narratised, transposed, directly reported, and pseudo-directly reported discourse are examined in terms of quantity and function. Even though direct speech is very common, the intradiegetic narrators are made capable of using it in a sophisticated and meaningful way, e.g. through intertextual echoes, careful positioning and selection of the speaking characters. Focalisation in Genette's model is also predominantly a matter of quantity. While zero focalisation is frequent even in homodiegetic narratives, internal focalisation is skilfully used in small parts of narrative text to achieve a special effect. Occasionally, however, Ovid carelessly presents intradiegetic narrators as possessing knowledge only he could have. This phenomenon is not observed here for the first time, but it is studied from a new perspective.

Chapter IV deals with the problematic notion of voice. After a presentation of the term's various uses in narratological studies we concentrate on its Genettean conception as an umbrella-term for the study of all traces of the narrative instance in the narrative text itself: time, person and level, narrator and narratee. This chapter is further limited to the relation of narrated to narrative time, of narrator to narrative and of metadiegetic to diegetic narrative. Narrators rarely limit themselves to the presentation of the events. Apart from narrating, they usually perform up to four further functions: directing, communicative, testimonial, and ideological or interpretative. The ways in which the 37 intradiegetic narrators perform these functions are studied in chapter VI. Particular emphasis is put on the testimonial and the ideological function, not only because they are frequently performed, but also because both the issue of fictionality and the poem's ideological position have been central to recent Ovidian studies.

For the reasons explained in the introduction to chapter 5, feminism has opened up the question of the relevance of such concrete aspects of the narrator as gender to the study of narrative voice. Gender, sexuality, age, and class are introduced as pragmatic factors of potential differentiation among the intradiegetic narrators. Their influence is mainly examined with regard to the metanarrative's thematics and ideology. These categories prove useful for a more accurate description of the narrators. It is certainly important that there are so many female narrators, a markedly homosexual narrator, and several elderly and low-class narrators. Our aim is to shed light on the various ways this variety of character-narrators contributes to the poem's encyclopaedic presentation of the narrative act throughout the ages, without adopting a particularly feminist or theoretical approach to the sociology of literature.[102]

The final aspect of narrative voice, i.e. the narratee, is reserved for chapter VII. After a thorough examination of the various signs of 'you' in the 37 metanarratives and a presentation of their various types, we proceed with the classification of the intradiegetic narratees according to (a) their other diegetic roles, (b) the degree to which they are affected and influenced by the narrative, (c) the degree of their indispensability,

---

[102] "It is obviously possible to count women, describe them, even explain women's behaviour without taking a feminist perspective or a theoretical one" (Rabinowitz 1993: 2-3).

and (d) the degree of their familiarity with the metanarrative, the events and the characters involved. Finally, we examine the various functions of the narratees, with particular emphasis on their role as models for the reader.

Chapter 8 contains some general conclusions and previous theories about Ovidian metadiegesis are discussed in the light of the narratological analysis.

Appendix
Intradiegetic Narrators and Narratees in the *Metamorphoses*
(after Appendix A to Wheeler 1999)

Narrator	Narratee(s)	Story/Subject	Lines (number)
1. Jupiter	Olympian gods	Lycaon	1.209-243 (35)
2. Mercury	Argus	Syrinx	1.689-700 (12)
3. Crow	Raven	Cecropides, Coronis, Nyctimene	2.549-95 (47)
4. Acoetes	Pentheus	Bacchus & Lydian Sailors	3.582-691 (110)
5. Minyeid	Minyeides & domestic slaves	Pyramus & Thisbe	4.55-166 (112)
6. Leuconoe	Minyeides & domestic slaves	a. Mars and Venus b. Phoebus, Leucothoe, & Clytie	4.169-270 (102)
7. Alcithoe	Minyeides & domestic slaves	a. Catalogue of tales b. Salmacis & Hermaphroditus	4.276-388 (113)
8. Perseus	Court of Cepheus	Neptune & Medusa	4.793-803 (11)
9. Muse	Minerva	a. Pyreneus b. Muses vs. Pierides	5.269-93 (35) 5.300-678 (379)
10. Pierides	Nymphs, Muses	Gigantomachy	5.326-31 (6)
11. Calliope	Nymphs, Pierides, other Muses	Hymn to Ceres	5.341-661 (321)
12. Arethusa	Ceres	Arethusa	5.575-641

			(67)
13. Anonymous Lydian	Unidentified Audience in Lydia	Trip to Lycia: Lycian farmers	6.317-81 (65)
14. Lycian guide	Narrator 13	Lycian farmers	6.331-81 (51)
15. Aeacus	Cephalus, sons of Pallas, sons of Aeacus	Plague on Aegina; Myrmidons	7.518-660 (143)
16. Cephalus	Phocus, sons of Pallas	Procris, hound, and spear	7.690-793, 796-862 (171)
17. Achelous	Theseus, Pirithous, Lelex	a. Echinades, Perimele	8.577-610 (34)
		b. Proteus, Mnestra, Erysichthon	8.728-878 (151)
		c. Combat with Hercules	8.879-84, 9.4-88 (91)
18. Lelex	Theseus, Pirithous, Achelous	Philemon & Baucis	8.618-724 (107)
19. Alcmene	Iole	Birth of Hercules	9.281-323 (43)
20. Iole	Alcmene	Dryope	9.326-93 (68)
21. Orpheus	Trees, birds, and beasts	a. Ganymede	10.155-61 (7)
		b. Hyacinthus	10.162-219 (58)
		c. Cerastae	10.220-37 (18)
		d. Propoetides	10.238-42 (5)
		e. Pygmalion	10.243-97 (55)
		f. Myrrha	10.298-502 (205)
		g. Adonis	10.503-739 (237)
22. Venus	Adonis	Atalanta &	10.560-707

23. Ceyx	Peleus & companions	Hippomenes Chione & Daedalion	(148) 11.291-345 (55)
24. Onetor	Ceyx, Peleus & companions	Wolf	11.352-78 (27)
25. An old man	An old man	Aesacus & Hesperia	11.751-95 (45)
26. Nestor	Achilles & Achaeans	a. Caeneus, Lapiths against Centaurs	12.182-535 (247)
		b. Periclymenus and Hercules	12.542-76 (35)
27. Anius	Anchises, Aeneas & Trojans	Daughters of Anius	13.644-74 (31)
28. Galatea	Scylla & Nymphs	Galatea, Acis, & Polyphemus	13.750-897 (148)
29. Glaucus	Scylla	Glaucus	13.917-65 (49)
30. Sibyl	Aeneas	Sibyl and Pheobus	14.130-53 (24)
31. Achaemenides	Macareus, Aeneas & Trojans	Polyphemus	14.167-220 (54)
32. Macareus	Achaemenides, Aeneas & Trojans	Travels with Ulysses	14.233-440 (208)
33. Circe's maid	Macareus	Picus, Canens & Circe	14.318-434 (127)
34. Diomedes	Venulus	Companions of Diomedes	14.464-511 (48)
35. Vertumnus	Pomona	Iphis & Anaxarete	14.695-764 (70)
36. An old man	Numa	Foundation of Croton	15.12-57 (46)
37. Hippolytus	Egeria	Hippolytus	15.493-546 (54)

II Time

II.1 Time and Narrative
One of the most apparent attributes of all discourse (linguistic text), whether oral or written, is its linearity. The sounds that make up words that in turn make up utterances follow one another in linear progression. Pauses between these sequences are also significant, normally defining the meaningful segments. As a mode of discourse, narration or story-telling is also a linear sequence in time; it cannot exist outside time and time is unavoidably inscribed in narrative. The most influential theorist of narrative from a temporal perspective is Gerard Genette, who isolates three aspects of temporal manipulation[1] or articulation in the movement from story to text, i.e. from the perceived sequence of events to their semiotic representation through language:

    1 **Order**: this refers to the relations between the assumed sequence of events in the story and their actual order of presentation in the text.

    2 **Duration / Speed**: this concerns the relations between the extent of time that events are supposed to have actually taken up and the amount of text devoted to presenting those same events.

    3 **Frequency**: how often something happens in the story compared with how often it is narrated in the text.

This chapter will be devoted to the study of time. Metanarratives in the *Met.* will be first examined in their temporal relations of order, duration, and frequency within diegesis, i.e. the extradiegetic narrator's account of metamorphosis through history from the world's creation to his own times. Then the temporal structure of the individual stories will come into focus.

II.2 Temporal Macro-Analysis
II.2.1 Order
Any departures in the order of presentation in the text from the order in which events evidently occurred in the story are termed by Genette

---

[1] On manipulation see Bal 1997: 79.

anachronies. For such a confrontation between the ordering of events in the story and their sequence in the text we need data, either explicit, for example, in the tenses of the verbs in the text, or deducible from indirect indications with our sense of everyday logic. "The issue of chronology is not a tool to decide literary quality. Narratology, in general, helps understanding, not evaluation. Nor is there a direct relation between chronological play and intellectual complexity."[2] For even elementary forms of storytelling, such as children's stories, contain anachronies.

On the whole, however, such deviations from the logical sequence of events may contribute to intense reading. "In order not to lose the thread it is necessary to keep an eye on the sequential ordering and the very effort forces one to reflect also on other elements and aspects."[3] Furthermore, violating the illusion that the story is played out before our eyes, anachronies are an abrupt reminder that we depend on the narrator to supply us with reports of the incidents as and when he will.[4]

With the exception of prophecy,[5] the weather forecast and live description of sports events, the events represented through narrative are normally assumed to have happened before they are narrated. This means that metadiegetic narrative constitutes an anachrony with regard to diegetic time, in particular one involving movement back in time or **analepsis**. The metanarrative act itself, the moment of speech within the primary narrator's discourse, is simply part of the chronological story; but the events presented in the metanarrative are either anterior or posterior to the events on the primary level. Although the question which time can or should be considered primary can be problematic when the relationship between text and story is complicated, "is in itself not particularly significant; what is relevant is to place the various time units in relation to each other." [6]

All 37 metanarratives that form the corpus of metanarratives constituted for the purposes of this dissertation are analeptic. This does not mean that there are no prophecies in the *Met.* that could qualify as

---

[2] Bal 1997: 83.
[3] Bal 1997: 82.
[4] Richardson 1990: 90.
[5] On prophecy in ancient epic see Moore 1921.
[6] Bal 1997: 88.

proleptic narratives. Themis' prophecy (9.403-17) and Helenos' prophecy quoted by Pythagoras in Book 15 (439-49) are the two instances that have considerable length and some coherence. The former concerns the fate of Callirhoe's sons but also gives a résumé of the expedition of the Seven against Thebes, a myth often presented in epic, while the latter culminates with Rome's universal power under Augustus and the *princeps'* deification (15.446-49): *hanc alii proceres per saecula longa potentem,/sed dominam rerum de sanguine natus Iuli /efficiet: quo cum tellus erit usa, fruentur /aetheriae sedes, caelumque erit exitus illi.* ("Other leaders will raise it to power, through the long years, but one, born of Julus' line, will make it mistress of the world. When the earth has enjoyed his presence, the realms of heaven will enjoy him too, and the sky will be his final destination."). The small number of prophecies in the *Met.* is a striking difference from Vergil's *Aeneid*, a poem which also presents a view of world history as a progression of events that moves towards the glory of Augustan Rome.

Helenus' prophecy is obviously connected with this teleological perspective. Indeed, it contributes enormously to the structural function of Pythagoras' speech within the poem. According to a recent article by Philip Hardie, the speech of Pythagoras both "introduces a philosophical section at a climactic point of the *Metamorphoses*", and "associates that philosophical doctrine with material on the history of Rome, preluding the Roman stories in the last part of 15." [7] Themis' prophecy is also relevant to the theme of Rome's slow progression (*per saecula longa*) towards greatness. In an earlier article, Philipe Hardie had argued that "the tragic story of Cadmus and Thebes in *Metamorphoses* 3 and 4 is constructed with constant reference to the great epic of Rome, Virgil's *Aeneid*."[8] There he referred to the Theban theme of the decoration on the cup presented to Aeneas by Anius and described by the extradiegetic narrator (13.681-99) as another instance of the association of Thebes and Rome in the poem. He overlooked, however, the fratricidal war foretold by Themis: *fientque pares in vulnere fratres* (9.405), even though he

---

[7] Hardie 1995: 206. On Pythagoras' speech as part of the poem's philosophical frame see also *ibid.*, p. 210-11. It is irrelevant to our discussion here whether Hardie 1995: 213 (with n.45) is right that Augustus' apotheosis is not immune to the suspicion of mutability while Ovid's translation to heavens escapes from the law of universal change.
[8] Hardie 1990: 225.

observes that "by the time of Lucan the analogy between the fratricides and civil wars of Thebes and Rome is well established."[9]

Unlike most prophecies in the *Aeneid*, the fulfillment of Themis' and Helenus' words is not narrated elsewhere in the poem, even though it seems to be taken for granted. Helenus' prophecy was indeed mentioned in the extradiegetic narrator's account of Aeneas' voyage to Italy: *inde futurorum certi, quae cuncta fideli / Priamides Helenus monitu praedixerat, intrant / Sicaniam* (13.722-24 "From Helenus, one of Priam's sons, they learned their future fortunes, and when all had been faithfully revealed to them by his prophecies, they then moved on to Sicily"). Pythagoras' reference to Helenus' prophecy is an internal analepsis. Its content is also partly analeptic with regard to the diegesis at this point; only the reference to Augustus' deification lies outside the poem's chronology (external analepsis), but could be a fact for readers in the author's lifetime, since he outlived the *princeps*. So, there is no discrepancy between prophecy and reality, despite the conventional disclaimers used by Pythagoras: *sic dicere vates / faticinaeque ferunt sortes*) and Helenus (15.435-36 "This, they say, is what the prophets predict, this is foretold by the oracles that reveal the fates.") Indeed, the postponed disclosure of Helenus' prophecy may be a reference to historical reality. It was the outstanding Pythagorean at first century B. C. Rome, Nigidius Figulus, that was credited with a prophecy that Augustus would rule the world.[10]

II.2.1.1 Analeptic Metanarrative

G. Genette describes anachronies with regard to two parameters: reach (cf. Bal's **distance**) and extent (cf. Bal's **span**). The former concerns the chronological distance of metadiegesis from the present moment in the primary story, while the latter refers to the anachrony's duration. Thus we can distinguish between **external** and **internal** analepses, depending on whether their span is included in the primary narrative or not; if the anachrony begins outside the primary time extent and ends within it, we call it **mixed**. This latter type is particularly common in Apollonius' epic,

---

[9] Hardie 1990: 225.
[10] On Nigidius Figulus see Liebeschuetz 1979: 130-1.

"where in fact the integration and contextualisation within the primary narrative of all the elements external to it predominate."[11]

With regard to its extent, an anachrony can be **complete** or **partial** (Bal: *incomplete*). It is complete if the reach and the extent of the anachrony coincide exactly, i.e. if its end coincides with the very moment the primary story began (if external) or was disrupted (if internal). A classical example of complete anachrony occurs "in the tradition of beginning *in medias res*, where the narrative begins in the middle of the story and the preceding events are then recalled in their totality".[12] Both the *Odyssey* and the *Aeneid* belong to this tradition; indeed, they constitute two of its cornerstones.

The *Metamorphoses*, on the other hand, have opted for an *ab ovo* narrative, typical of the annalistic mode of epic and historiography. The beginning of the story coincides with the creation of the world and its end with the end of the poem's composition some time during Augustus' paternal government: *terra sub Augusto est; pater est et rector* (15.860).[13] This entails that all analepses in the poem are internal with regard to its large temporal scale. With regard to their extent, the closest we get to a complete analepsis are the narratives of Odysseus' two companions that are saved by Aeneas **[31 & 32]**, a tribute to their Homeric and Vergilian models: Odysseus' metanarrative in *Od*.9-12 and Achaemenides' metanarrative in *Aen*.3.613-91.

The situation was described in essentially the same way, though in different terms, by Solodow. His impression was that "the numerous inserts and the several story-telling parties (...) have the effect of making unclear which event followed which." As he admits, that was also Ludwig's view of the matter back in 1965, who claimed that the poem generally fails to give "the impression of a deliberate forward motion."[14] Although I do not wish to contest the essential truth of this description I would like to point out that chronological order was not an inherent characteristic of the mass of stories that make up Greek mythology. On

---

[11] Fusillo 1985: 24.
[12] Bal 1997: 93.
[13] *Contra* Solodow 1988: 17; although it is true that the deification of Julius Caesar, which occurred one year before the poet's birth, is the last metamorphosis in the poem, the narrator's presence and the reference to Augustus' rule point to a later date.
[14] The quotations are from Solodow 1988: 29.

the contrary, such organisation was the result of the systematic efforts of mythographers active mainly in the postclassical period. Even the only substantial work representing the results of this intense activity that has come down to us, the *Library* of a certain Apollodorus, has not achieved absolute chronological order.[15] Therefore, Boillat's suggestion that Ovid included in the *Met.* so many metanarratives because it was a convenient way of including stories that had not been inscribed in the traditional chronology of myth is in principle plausible.[16] And such cases as the exotic tales narrated by the Minyades (e.g. Pyramus and Thisbe **[5]**) and Lelex (Baucis and Philemon **[18]**) or sung by Orpheus (Pygmalion **[21e]**, Myrrha **[21f]**) lend credence to this theory. But the vast majority of the stories told by intradiegetic narrators could easily be ascribed an exact position in mythical chronology, which limits the interpretative power of Boillat's theory.

A further complication of order arises from the frequent aetiological conclusion of the metamorphic stories, which often includes a statement introduced with *nunc quoque* v.sim. In a sense this covers the often huge or indeterminate temporal gap between the narrative levels, but more than once sounds awkward in the mouth of the intradiegetic narrator. A notorious case is Perseus' conclusion of the story about Medusa's snaky hair. The problem is not, however, impossible to overcome: We can either understand with Haupt that Ovid means the *gorgoneion* on Minerva's *aegis*, which according to Vergil (*Aen.*8.435-8) was forged by the Cyclopes, so that Minerva could "bear the snakes she made" even before Medusa's beheading by Perseus.[17] "Alternatively, since Perseus completed his required task [as a narrator] at [5.] 801, we could close the quotes there and assign these final lines to the poet-speaker, who brings us up to the present to end the book," a solution proposed by Anderson in his commentary.

A further factor that is used by Genette in order to describe and classify anachronies is whether they belong to the same story-line as the primary story. The latter, a rather vague and elusive concept in Genettian narratology, is better understood in this case as the immediate narrative

---

[15] Graf 1993: 193.
[16] Boillat 1976: 119-20
[17] See further Marahrens 1971: 78-80.

context of the anachronies, especially in the case of a narrative that lacks a central story-line like the *Met.*. Anachronies are accordingly labeled **homodiegetic** and **heterodiegetic**. M. Fusillo seems to be right in observing that homodiegetic anachronies are rare in ancient epic because of its preference for linear and progressive unfolding of the primary story.[18] Already commoner in the *Aeneid*, homodiegetic analepses become very frequent in the modern novel.[19]

Given that the *Met.* both lack a main story-line and has frequent anachronies, it would not be surprising if it contained more homodiegetic analeptic metanarrative than the average ancient epic. Out of 37 analeptic metanarratives that occur in the *Met.* there are thirteen that help the reader/narratee fill gaps in his/her knowledge about the primary story. To a large extent, the point of contact is the intradiegetic narrator. This means that most homodiegetic analeptic metanarratives are ascribed to homodiegetic narrators: Jupiter [1], the Crow [3], Acoetes [4], Perseus [8], a Muse [9a and to a certain extent 9b], Ceyx [23], Achaemenides [31] and Macareus [32] are the most obvious. None of them repeats events that have already been narrated; their function is to supplement the gaps in the primary narrative. These temporal *ellipses* are only recognizable retrospectively, i.e. only after we have read the metanarrative.[20] This type of analepsis is not so much a contribution to dense narrative texture; its main function is to offer an insight into a character, normally that of the intradiegetic narrator.

II.2.2 Duration / Speed

Investigations into the relationship between the amount of time covered by the events of a story and the amount involved in their narration go back to the 1920s. They have not always been successful, however, mainly because of the elusiveness of this aspect of narrative time, in particular the lack of an obvious and safe standard of measurement. The most reliable and relevant is probably the amount of textual space allocated to each event. This should be indicative of the emphasis given

---

[18] Fusillo 1985: 25.
[19] Fusillo 1985: 26.
[20] See Toolan 1988: 53.

to each event, in particular when compared with the pace at which other events of the story are narrated.

Traditionally an alternation between **summary** (when narrative duration is less than what reality would lead us to expect) and **scene** (when narrative time approximates story time) used to be the aim on the assumption that the excess in either direction, too fast or too slow, would be unpleasant for the reader. The extreme ends were identified by Genette as **ellipsis** (a break in temporal continuity) and **pause** (whenever narrative time continues but story time has stopped, e.g. a description focalized by the narrator).

From a macro-analytic perspective, metanarrative is the very epitome of scene, because it is a piece of narrative discourse reported verbatim. It may be interesting, however, to explore its distribution in the primary narrative. This would give us a clue to its function with regard to narrative speed in the overall structure of the poem.

[1] is part of a more or less scenic episode of the type 'Divine Assembly'.

[2] is part of a scenic narrative of how Argus was put out of the way.

[3] follows a summary exposition of the tale about Apollo's love for Coronis and is followed by a summary which shifts to a pause when Ovid described Apollo's reaction to the news reported by the Raven.

[4] comes after a summary rather than scenic (despite the simile) narrative of the Bacchic orgy that followed Pentheus' warning speech. The passage from summary to scenic narrative is effected through the verbatim reported answer of the guards to Pentheus' question about their mission to arrest Bacchus.

[5], [6] and [7] follow a summary description of the aftermath of Pentheus' death in his mother's hands (3.732-33); the scenic narrative is continued with the primary narrator's report of the sisters' metamorphosis.

The narrative context of [8] is rather difficult to describe in terms of duration. *Narrat Agenorides* (4.772) introduces a combination of indirect speech (4.772-86, Genette's **transposed discourse**) and summary (4.787-9, Genette's **narratized discourse**), before a scene starts with the directly quoted question that was put by someone among the frustrated audience. Despite a short summary that accounts for events simultaneous with Perseus' narration, the battle that follows is essentially narrated in the scenic mode.

[9a] and **[9b]** form part of a scene on Mt. Parnassus followed by a scene in Lydia.

[15] follows a summary narration of the Athenian embassy's arrival in Aegina. After a summary covering the night and what some other characters are doing the next morning scenic narrative is resumed with **[16]**.

[17a-e] and **[18]** are told within a scenic context that covers the time from (presumably) the evening until the next morning (9.93) in 430 lines (including the metanarratives).

[19] continues in the scenic mode of Hercules' apotheosis, which is not abandoned even after the metanarratives of Alcmene **[19]** and Iole **[20]**.

[21] is part of the scenic narrative of the last day in Orpheus' life; even though there is no indication of the time of the day from which the narrative starts, the sun is probably about to set when the Thracian women attack him dressed up like Maenads.

[23] and **[24]** are part of the largely scenic narrative of the day that Peleus visited Ceyx seeking asylum.

[25] is probably narrated the same day Alcyone was transformed, although there a certain ellipsis must be posited between the two events, and the immediately preceding line (11.750) is a summary of another verbal act.

[26a] is part of the summary narrative of the feast day of Pallas Athene while **[26b]** is essentially an appendix to **[26a]**, belonging to the same scenic section of narrative, which continues in the same mode after the rest of that night is summarily represented in half a verse (12.579 *nox est data cetera somno*).

After a summary of Aeneas' reception by king Anius of Delos a question by Anchises directly quoted gives the cue for **[27]**.

[28] also follows a summary about Scylla's former life as a woman but scenic narrative continues to provide the context for **[29]**.

[30] is a scenic interlude in the summary narrative of Aeneas' descent to the Underworld.

[31] is also a scene that interrupts an otherwise summary narrative, Aeneas' Italian journey, while part of Macareus' narration is summarized before his own metanarrative [32] is introduced.

[34] is part of a scenic interlude to the otherwise extremely summarized account of the war waged by the Trojans against the Latins.

[35] comes within a speech that constitutes the major part of the scenic section of 'Pomona and Vertumnus', which is preceded by a quite long summary.

[36] is the only scenic segment of the otherwise heavily summarised narrative of Numa's visit to Croto. And so is [37] within the context of Egeria's story, which becomes again scenic in the description of the nymph's metamorphosis.

To sum up, two major trends emerge from the evidence listed above: Metanarrative scenes either (a) belong to a wider scenic context or (b) disrupt the more or less summary overall rhythm. This is roughly what was described above as the classical objective of *variatio*. It could be further argued that this preference for mimetic metanarrative discourse (we have only noted a few examples of narrativised metanarrative, e.g. Perseus' just before [8] and Peleus' preceding Ceyx' [23]) brings oral narrative activity to the foreground as a source of metamorphic stories.

II.2.3 Frequency

Even though two events are never exactly the same (not even two repetitions of the same habitual event), narrators often compress narrative time, i.e. textual space, by giving the permanent elements of such repeated events. Thus singular presentation of singular events (**singulative narrative**), apparently the most recurrent narrative frequency, is often supplemented by **iterative narrative**, in order to avoid the peculiarly rugged effect that would probably result from a constant use of the former mode.

Just as in the modern classical novel, iteration in the *Met.* is the frequency usually employed to sketch the background to singulative presentation. Galatea's narrative [28], for instance, is presented as a singular event within the context of the nymphs' habit of getting together and telling each other *elusos iuvenum ... amores* (13.738 how they scorned young men's amorous desire), while Virbius' narrative [36] could be an example of iterative narrative itself. It is introduced with *quotiens* ...

dixit (15.492-3), which suggests that he told the widow the same story more than once. An iterative metanarrative is not unlikely in itself: Aeneas is reported to have told the story of his adventures until he reached Carthage again and again at Dido's request. Far from being bored by the repetition, the widowed queen "would hang on his lips as he told the story" (*Aen.*4.79). It is the specific words with which Virbius introduces himself to Egeria at the beginning of the actual narrative (15.497ff.) that could not be repeated every time. In such a case, i.e. when one singular instance (here the first) is narrated as an illustration of a repeated event, it would be more accurate to talk of **pseudo-iteration**, a device that was employed excessively by Proust in modern times.

What is absent from the *Met.* is the third Genettian category of narrative frequency, the **repetitive** sort. The obsessive telling several times of what happened once would be tedious in a poem that involves repetition of a basic story-line (e.g. amorous pursuit) and variation on a singly type of mythic subject-matter, namely metamorphosis.

II.3 Temporal Micro-Analysis

Now that all the major categories of temporal analysis have been introduced and our corpus of metanarratives has been examined with regard to its place and function within the overall temporal scheme of the poem, we can proceed with some remarks on their internal temporal structure in the order that has been outlined above.

II.3.1 Order
Events within individual stories are generally told in their proper order. This is what classical rhetoric, for example Cicero (*de orat.*2.329) and the author of the *Rhet. ad Her.* (1.15) recommended if the narrative is to be lucid (*perspicua* is Cicero's term). *Refer ordine carmen* ("Tell me your song in its proper order!"), Minerva bids the Muse brusquely at 5.335. The common explanation of the ablative *ordine*, i.e. 'in due order', considered "almost redundant" by Bömer, is rather superficial. The Ovidian parallel cited by the same commentator (7.520 *ordine nunc repetam, neu longa ambage morer vos*), from Aeacus' metanarrative **[15]** together with Servius' gloss on VERG.G.4.506 (*ordine: sine intermissione*) seem to suggest more something like "without pauses or digressions." This is

not far from the Homeric κατὰ κόσμον (*Od*.8.489), which J. B. Hainsworth interprets both in terms of order and exclusion of digressive ornamentation.[21]

If this is the true semantic scope of the phrase it is tempting to sense Ovidian humour in the fact that the Muse's song is full of digressions, i.e. episodes that do not contribute anything to the progress of the story, like the tale of the Sirens (5.551-563). Instead of finding them offensive, like Anderson who declares that "the Muse does not know how to produce an effective narrative; she cannot refrain from getting herself involved in secondary tales of metamorphosis"[22] we should probably appreciate them as yet another aspect of the quintessentially Ovidian tendency to undermine the principles that supposedly informed the old masters' narratives, even though their practice is more varied that we are led to think. Finally, a third invocation of *ordine referre*, this time by Achelous **[17e]** at 9.5, seems to extend the phrase's scope to include the avoidance of possible omissions, which could save the river-god's honour as a fighter but would destroy his credibility as a narrator.

There are, nevertheless, a few exceptions to this rule of chronological order. First, the analepsis in **[3]** about the narrator's metamorphosis. This comes as a surprise when "we might expect the crow to bring her recital to an end after she has drawn the moral of her story in accordance with that announced at the outset".[23] It is, however, compatible with the traditional garrulity of this bird that she should not end quickly. "A suspicion that the raven may not believe her," in other words her desire to authenticate her story (with another story!), may have something to do with her decision to continue.[24] But, to my mind at least, what the crow seems at pains to emphasize is that she did not act of her own accord; that since Minerva herself sought her out as her protégée, the crow considered it her duty to report the bad news.

Quintilian's principle of *utilitas* with regard to the arrangement of the events narrated (4.2.83) is also evident when analepsis is used as an

---

[21] For a census of interpretations see Ford 1992: 122 and 123 n.50.
[22] Anderson on 5.294-678.
[23] Keith 1992: 22.
[24] Keith 1992: 22.

expository device in **[7]**.[25] To a certain extent this anachrony is necessary because the story features two characters that need to be introduced. Hermaphroditus is presented first in proper chronological order, from his very birth to the moment he arrives at the place that is going to change his life. Assuming that nymphs are immortal and eternally young it would be hard and certainly unimportant to determine whether this homodiegetic analepsis is internal or not. The fact that Alcithoe picks up the thread of her story at the point where Salmacis is picking flowers, as she has just been said often to do, gives this brief analepsis a semblance of completeness despite its iterative manner of presentation.

The same method of transition appears in the very similar context of the presentation of Hylonome, a secondary character in Nestor's Lapithocentauromachy **[26]**. A short flashback about Cyllarus' relationship with this female Centaur and the ways she managed to keep him away from her rivals (12.404-415) is appended to the pause of Cyllarus' description. The return to the present of the primary story, i.e. the day of Pirithous' marriage with Hippodameia, is signalled by *et tum* (12.417) just as in the previous example by *et tunc* (4.315). This external analepsis also gives an impression of completeness: we finally return to the precise moment that Nestor suspended the Lapithocentauromachy at 12.393, when Cyllarus' death is introduced with a pathetic asyndeton and change of grammatical subject: *auctor in incerto est* (12.419).

By far the most frequent type of anachrony in the *Met.* is the presentation of the story's gist or even the revelation of its outcome at the very beginning. Whether it is this initial précis as proleptic or the subsequent narrative as analeptic it is a mere techincality This technique has been identified by de Jong as characteristic of Euripidean messenger-speeches and early (i.e. archaic and classical) Greek literature in general.[26] It is also shared by many Ovidian intradegetic narrators, as Peters remarked in his seminal dissertation on Ovid's narrative artistry.[27] Jupiter **[1]**, for instance, anticipates the outcome of the story in an effort to calm down his worried audience. The Muse **[9b]** also gives away the main event at the very beginning (5.300-1), satisfying Minerva's curiosity

---

[25] For further references to rhetorical manuals see Cousin's Budé edition ad loc.
[26] de Jong 1991: 61.
[27] Peters 1908: 88.

about the birds that have attracted her attention with their peculiar capacity to imitate the human voice: they were humans beaten in a contest and transformed, as a consequence, into birds. The rest of the metanarrative is apparently a more detailed description of the song contest and the final metamorphosis.

A third example of this technique is provided by **[13]**, where the lines 6. 317-8 again present the story in a nutshell: *Lyciae quoque fertilis agris / non impune deam veteres sprevere coloni* (Long ago, in the fertile land of Lycia, there were peasants who also showed contempt for this goddess and were punished for it.) Its narrative setting, the protagonists and their (re)actions are all included. The anonymous Lydian further complicates his narrative's order by introducing proleptically (with regard to the main story) his trip to Lycia. This is not only the place where the events of the primary story took place but also where the Lydian heard this legend from a local guide. As the narrator recalls how his steps were guided to the very spot of the miracle, the narratees (both intradiegetic and extradiegetic) are invited to travel back in time. First to the time of the third level narration from which the second level narrator derives his knowledge and authority, and second to the actual time of the miracle, which thus recedes even further into the past, just after Leto gave birth to the twin gods Apollo and Diana.

The fourth example comes from a metanarrative that is cast precisely as a messenger speech **[24]**. The important fact (13.349-50 *magnae ... cladis*) is disclosed as soon as Onetor the cow-herd enters Ceyx' palace at Phocis. Only once he has been given permission by his master does he go back in time, beginning his narrative 'at the beginning', when he brought the king's cattle to the sea-shore. The events then are recounted "very much as he experienced them at the time they took place," i.e. in the typical manner of Euripidean messenger-speeches.[28]

II.3.2 Duration / Speed
II.3.2.1 Summary
Summary is frequently used to introduce background information that is essential for the understanding of the main event that normally climaxes with a metamorphosis; the use of summary itself is an indirect

---

[28] De Jong 1991: 32, 34.

means of reminding the narratee that these are events of secondary importance. For instance, in **[1]** narrative proper starts with a summary of the events that led to Jupiter's visit to Lycaon's court (1.211-13). This is supplemented by a metanarrative comment on the impossibility of recounting all the instances of impiety and mischief that he came across on earth, which also serves as a kind of indirect narrative summary (1.214-15). It is not suggested here that the events at Lycaon's palace are not narrated summarily on the whole. Still, there is a considerable slow-down of the narrative tempo (exact words are reported, time is divided into day and night), until it nearly freezes in a pause when the results of Lycaon's transformation are described (1.237-39). This scheme of progressive retardation is found again in **[12]**, for example. After a sketch of her life until the day she lost her virginity, which provides her audience with the background necessary for the understanding of that day's significance, Arethusa proceeds to narrate in detail the circumstances that led to the central event, her pursuit, amorous and literal, by Alpheus.

This kind of constant and gradual dilation of narrative time is well illustrated by the way the introductory 'paragraph' of the last Orphic tale **[21g]** is structured: each period constitutes the explanation of the previous one. First we get a summary of what happens while time 'flies' by (10.520ff.). Then one of the events summarised (Venus falling in love) is further expanded by means of scenic narrative. On the whole, however, the story of Venus' courtship of Adonis has been related mainly in summary until the central episode is introduced by means of what is normally a transition technique from one story to another: *te quoque...*(10.542 cf. e.g.162 *Te quoque, Amyclide,...*).

An interesting variation of this technique is employed in battle narrative, which is illustrated by Nestor's Lapithocentauromachy **[26]**. The mêlée (12.245-301) is preceded by a description of mass attack (12.240-44). The latter provides a kind of general grid to be filled in with the details of the individuals' fortunes in the ensuing narrative. This is not an Ovidian invention but traditional Homeric practice. As Fenik has observed in his examination of the Iliadic material, such general descriptions regularly open the battle scenes (cf. *Il.*4.446, 8.60, 11.47, 13.125, 14.388, 15.263, 20.31); they also appear before new phases in a fight that is already under way: (*Il.*16.562, 17.262).[29] Once we realise that the man-to-man fight is not subsequent to the mass attack but rather a focused version of the same event, we can no longer find awkward or contradictory the presence of 'first' in both sections: *prima...pugna* (12.242) alongside *Primus Ophionides Amycus* (12.245). Even the latter is probably not an absolute first. As J. Latacz[30] has argued on the basis of Homeric battle-narrative, the typical πρῶτος does not (necessarily) signal the onset of the 'real' battle (as distinct from the beginning of the battle-narrative) but the start of the detailed battle-narrative. In other words, who is mentioned first depends on the memory and the poetic plan of the individual story-teller, just as much as who is mentioned at all.[31] This must also be true of its Latin equivalent (*primus*). What is obviously certain is that it does not necessarily imply that others followed his example, using the sacred offerings and candelabras as ammunition.

Summary is also a convenient expedient for sections of the narrative that are imposed by generic conventions but do not fit Ovidian emphasis on metamorphosis. For instance, it is used in **[10]** in order to present Ceres' trip from Sicily to Athens, where she teaches Triptolemus the art of agriculture. So far the praise of Ceres has been chiefly glorification of divine power in acts of vengeance while the giving of laws, agricultural fertility, and cultural order, the topics announced in the proem of Calliope's song (5.341-45), seem to have slipped from view.[32] Thanks to this summary appendix, Calliope remains true to the expectations raised by her proem. The latter are not only thematic but also generic: the *Homeric Hymn to Demeter*, which, as Hinds 1987 has convincingly argued, was one of Ovid's sources, also ends with another of Ceres' gifts to humanity, the Eleusinian mysteries.[33] What the Muse

---

[29] Fenik 1968: 79.
[30] Latacz 1977: 83. This does not mean that I am convinced by his particular arguments and especially by his supposition that were this the 'real' beginning of the fight, the narrator would continue the enumeration of the individual participants as second, third, and so on.
[31] As Nestor admits in 542ff.
[32] Cahoon 1996: 52; but see following n.
[33] This may be the reason why Ovid's Calliope has chosen to tell not about the mysteries but about agriculture (a motif absent from the Homeric Hymn), although the former may

has neglected in using this summary to conclude her hymn to Ceres is the causal relation between Kore's rape and Ceres' trip to Athens by air, while "Lyncus' envy and violence receive minimal preparation, motivation, and description."[34]

II.3.2.2 Scene

It is always useful to bear in mind that summary and scene are just the two ends of a whole spectrum of possible ratios between narrated time and textual space. Accordingly, the transition between these two poles can be effected through a gradual slow-down or acceleration. In Aeacus' tale **[15]**, for example, the summary turns into scenic narrative, as the narrator's merely emotional involvement in the story (7.538 *infelix...arator*, 582-3 *quid mihi tunc animi fuit? An, quod debuit esse,/ ut vitam odissem et cuperem pars esse meorum?*)[35] becomes active participation (7.596 *ipse ego*; 614, 621, 627 *dixi*; et passim in lines 630ff.).

What exactly each intradiegetic narrator chooses to report in greater detail (and therefore greater textual length) depends on his/her individual interests as well as those of the narratee. The Muse's narrative about Pyreneus' recent attempt to rape all nine of them **[9a]** includes enough direct speech and covers such a short period of time that despite the ellipsis between 5.284 and 285 (i.e. between the Muses' entrance in his home and the end of the rain) it does not give the impression of a summary. The Thracian warrior's death, however, is described in three lines characterised by unusual expressive abundance and a particular mixture of static (*iacit* 5.291) and dynamic elements (*cadit* 5.292, *tundit* 5.293). This description creates a discordant effect within the narrative: a warrior finds a 'heroic' death in the battlefield of lust, soaking the earth with his own blood instead of that of the pursued virgins.[36] Apparently, the Muse derives some kind of sadistic pleasure in recalling vividly the death of their persecutor, as if he were an enemy killed on the

---

be cryptically (as befits mysteries) alluded to with the phrase *sacros iugales*, if Kretschmer 1923: 53 is right that ἱερὸς ἄροτος formed part of the rites.

[34] Cahoon 1996: 60; for an implausible sexual interpretation of the tale see *ibid.* n.36

[35] I do not include *miseros...colonos* (552), *miseris* (572) as BÖMER quite convincingly argues that they simply mean "ill" cf. *tristes...morbi* (601).

[36] For a similar effect see Alden-Smith 1990.

battlefield.[37] This rhetorical strategy would certainly appeal to Minerva, the *diva armipotens*, the story's immediate narratee.[38]

Rhetorical strategy is also the decisive factor for the heavily detailed narration of two more 'deaths' in the final pentad of the *Met.* First, the miraculous 'death' of Periclymenus (*mira...mors* 12. 556) is recounted by Nestor **[26b]** in six lines –I am only counting from the moment that the hero in the shape of a bird is mortally wounded (12.567-72). Not only is this almost certainly a sign of the narrator's sympathy but also his main weapon in his effort to silence a Heracleid's concern for his father's fame: Hercules' arrows were capable of producing not only relief but also great pain. Second, Hippolytus-Virbius **[37]** dwells on his mutilation in horror-inspiring detail apparently in an effort to prevent Egeria from continuing her lament. In this case, however, τὸ τερατῶδες seems to be wittily undercut by the "fanciful enframing context" of the deceased himself telling the story to a bereaved nymph.[39] It is hard not to detect grim humour in the boastful tone of 15.530-31 (*num potes aut audes cladi conponere nostrae,/ nympha, tuam?*): it is as if Hippolytus has lingered on the bloody details of his gruesome death for the sake of establishing that no horror could surpass that of his *dies fatalis*, except, of course, the terror of the dark and steaming underworld.

Creating suspense is another possible motive for deceleration. Orpheus' narrative about Myrrha's incest with her father **[21f]** is a good illustration of this technique. Myrrha's way from her chamber to that of her father is meticulously recorded stage by stage (10.446-64), step by step as the narrator's eye follows her in the darkness (Myrrha's actions are marked in italics):

It was the time when all things are silent, and Bootes had guided his wagon, by means of its slanting pole, in between the Bears. *Myrrha set out* to perform her guilty deed. The golden moon fled from the sky, black clouds concealed the stars as they shrank from sight. Night was robbed of its starry fires, Icarus being the first to cover up his face, and Erigone, raised to heaven by her devoted love for her father. *Three times an unlucky*

---

[37] Cf. the military language of 5.285-6.
[38] Cf. the Muse's introductory remark: *O, nisi te* **virtus** *opera ad maiora tulisset* (269) and Cahoon 1996: 49. The use of military language is carried on in the next story, cf. *committit proelia* (307).
[39] Segal 1984: 314.

stumble checked Myrrha's steps, three times the funereal screech-owl gave its ominous warning, with fatal croaking, but still *she went on,* and the darkness and shadows of the night lessened her feeling of shame. With her left hand she clung to her nurse, *with the other she groped the way along a road she could not see. Now she reached the threshold of Cinyra's bedchamber, now she opened the door, and was led inside.* Her trembling knees refused to support her, the colour left her face, as the blood drained from her cheeks; her senses were reeling *as she went. The nearer she came to the scene of her crime,* the more horrified she was, repentant of her rash behaviour, and anxious to be able to go back while she was still unrecognized. As she hesitated, the old nurse took her by the hand, and *led her close up to the king's high couch.*

This is in stark contrast with the three words that sum up the nefarious act, which the narrator has postponed as long as possible: *devotaque corpora iunxit* (10.464). Four additional lines (10.465-68) do not provide any more details about the act itself; they are rather intended to highlight its obscenity and the paradox that father and daughter basically behave as they did in the opening scene of the *thalami certamen* (10.361-2), but that only now is their behaviour morally reprehensible.[40]

II.3.2.3 Ellipsis

If summary narration marks the relative lack of importance of certain events in a story, ellipsis is a convenient way of passing over mere trivia. In the previous section we noted the gap between 5.284 and 285; one assumes that the rain did not stop immediately upon the Muses' entrance in Pyreneus' house. From the very beginning it is their harassment that has been declared as the focus of the story, and once the setting and a good reason for the Muses' entrapment have been provided the narrator feels she ought to move on to the crucial moment.

Unlike the Homeric narrator who eschews ellipsis as if he abhorred temporal vacuum, the extradiegetic narrator of the *Met.* and his surrogates are not afraid to leave gaps.[41] In **[1]**, for example, the gods present at the council are spared the details of the destruction of Lycaon's impious *tecta/domus* (summarised in one and a half lines) while

---

[40] This is not the only parallel between the two scenes; *par est Myrrhae* (441) recalls *similem tibi* (364); see Sharrock 1991: 178.
[41] On 'Homer' see Richardson 1990: 20 and on 'Ovid' see Bernbeck 1967: 64f.

Jupiter's journey back to the safe tranquillity of Olympus is completely left out, just as it is left out in the similar story of Baucis and Philemon **[18]**.The lack would go completely unnoticed but for the introductory description of the journey to earth (1.212-13 and 8.626-27), however compressed this happens to be. Only the Muse **[9a]** avoids this sort of ellipsis: "By taking to our wings, we escaped his assault" (5.288).[42]

A more notable ellipsis is the lack of any reference to sexual intercourse in stories like that of Ganymede (10.155-61). Orpheus' [16a] emphasis lies rather on Jupiter's transformation (156-8) and Ganymede's life in heaven (160-1), while the actual *amor* is tersely narrated with typical phrases: *amore arsit* (155-6) and *abripit Iliaden* (160). But as Cicero remarked half a century before the composition of the *Met.*, *quis (...) de Ganymedi raptu dubitat, quid poetae uelint?* (*Tusc.*4.71). A similar sort of information gap is observed in Kleist's 'The Marquise of O-' where the most crucial moment in the story, the Marquise's rape by the Count F-, is elided in the text.[43]

3.2.4 Pause

Intradiegetic narrators in the *Met.* normally avoid long descriptive pauses, like the *Regia Solis* (2.1-18), the *domus Somni* (11.592-612) and the *domus Famae* (12.39-63).[44] Unlike the latter two, however, which incorporate blocks of iterative narrative, time really freezes when Nestor gives a thorough description of Cyllarus' beauty in 12.395-403 **[26a]**. It is notable that he follows an order that will be codified as the appropriate one for descriptions of living creatures by rhetoricians of the imperial period, such as Nicolaus the Sophist (*Rhet.Gr.*III 492.18-24): from up/front (face) to down/back (legs/back).

---

[42] The Muses are winged in Pind.*Isthm.*64-65 and Bacchyl.fr.20b3-4; see Pfeijffer 1994: 307.
[43] Rimmon-Kenan 1983: 56.
[44] Hamon 1993 and the special issue of *Yale French Studies* 61 (1981) remain the two major modern theoretical discussions of description *per se*. Here we are only incidentally interested in this literary phenomenon inasmuch as it constitutes an "effort to resist the constraining linearity of the text" (Hamon 1993: 5). On the relation between narration and description in Latin literature see Fowler 1991. Fusillo 1985: 327 recognizes the theoretically "extradiegetic" character of the simile as a stylistic figure and yet offers an analysis of the similes' "narrative integration" in the *Argonautica*.

Shorter descriptive pauses can be found in the section of the metanarrative that recounts the results of a character's metamorphosis. Jupiter **[1]**, for example, combines pure narrative (1.233-37) with static description (1.238-39 *canities eadem est, eadem violentia vultus,/ idem oculi lucent, eadem feritatis imago est*) in his account of Lycaon's transformation into a wolf. In other metanarratives it is the very last line that gives the impression that time freezes as the concluding tableau-vivant brings to a halt the action narrated: *quodque rogis superest, una requiescit in urna* (4.166); *vertitur ad solem mutataque servat amorem* (4.270); *pectore in adverso, quos fecit, sustinet angues* (5.803). The world of the *Met.* is certainly in constant change as a whole and in the long run, but its individual elements stop evolving after their metamorphosis. Metamorphosis appears to be the natural *telos* towards which every creature, including the poet himself, is moving, but it is itself irreversible and curiously promoting a new order of stability in a universe where nothing is completely obliterated. Sometimes, however, it is only the result of the metamorphosis that is describable, because the actual moment of transformation eludes the homodiegetic narrator Glaucus **[29]** (13.960-64) no less than the heterodiegetic narrator Anius **[27]** (13.671f.).[45]

Pause is commoner, though much shorter in the case of similes: similes in the *Met.*, whether in the primary narrative or in metanarrative, are normally shorter than three lines (e.g. 3.682, 685). The obvious explanation is that Ovid does not want to be distracted from the story.[46] But even three lines are occasionally enough to disrupt narrative continuity. For it is not only the length of a simile, and generally of a pause, that matters; its subject-matter may be so incongruous and surprising that will make the reader pause longer. The prime example of this technique is, of course, the notorious simile of the burst water-pipe that describes the issue of blood from Pyramus' wound **[5]**: [47]

cruor emicat alte,
non aliter, quam cum vitiato fistula plumbo
scinditur et tenui stridente foramine longas
eiaculatur aquas atque aera rumpit (4.121-4)

---

[45] Nagle 1988a: 82 considers Glaucus' statement as characteristic of a scrupulous narrator.
[46] Wilkinson 1955: 170-1.
[47] The most recent and complete discussion with all the bibliography is Schmitzer 1992.

Clearly, "the simile is designed, from the narrator's point of view, to shock and to indicate how rash Pyramus' suicide is," as C. Newlands has observed.[48] From the generic point of view too, this is the first disruption of the conventions of New Comedy/Romance, which have been closely followed so far.[49] Assuming that romantic tales, whether oral or written, circulated even before Chariton's *Callirhoe*, this comes as a shock to the reader (Ovid's narratee), who knows that lovers never die and expects a happy ending of 'catastrophe averted'.[50] Precisely because simile is an artificial dilation of a moment in narrative time or pause, it is tempting to seek in it a key to the story's interpretation as intended by the author (and his persona, the Minyeid). In the present case, N. Holzberg argues that by undermining the traditional comic/novelistic story-pattern, the narrator reveals how far from the everyday reality of contemporary city-life such a story is.[51]

The simile employed by Achelous in his final autobiographical tale **[17e]** is not only the longest one in a metanarrative, measuring four lines, but also illustrates another kind of shocking effect, which makes the pause seem longer than its actual textual time. Comparing the two combatants to bulls (9.46-9), the simile enhances the impression that Achelous and Hercules are parodically assimilated to Turnus and Aeneas respectively, alluding to the famous simile towards the end of the *Aeneid* (12.716-24). The parody was first observed by Galinsky. In particular, he found comically incongruous "not the use of Vergil's noble lines in a factually unsuitable context, but their degradation to a trivial low level and their use in the mouth of a shaggy, dull-witted river-deity."[52] The simile proves to be even more pointed, when Achelous in a final effort to break free from Hercules' grip transforms himself into a "real" bull

---

[48] Newlands 1986: 146.
[49] For this approach to the tale's analysis see mainly Holzberg 1988. For a recent codification and discussion of the novel's typical elements see Létoublon 1993.
[50] On the plausibility of the assumption made here see Konstan 1994: 186 and Létoublon 1993: 183-4. *Callirhoe* is generally held to be the earliest extant work of Greek prose fiction, composed some time between 100 B.C. and 100 A.D., see *CAGN* 17.
[51] Holzberg 1988: 276; similarly Schmitzer 1992: 529-30. For an alternative interpretation focused on the narrator's character see Newlands 1986: 146-7; but cf. Anderson on 4.122-24 (p.425), who cautions that "any sexual inferences drawn from the word [*eiaculatur*] must be regarded as anachronistic and heavily biased by modern emphases."
[52] Galinsky 1972: 98.

(9.80-81 *sic quoque devicto restabat tertia tauri/ forma trucis: tauro mutatus membra rebello*).

On the other hand, our poet often piles up variant similes for their own sake, while Homer reserved this device for particularly impressive effects.[53] This does not mean that the device is completely deprived of any emphatic expressiveness. For instance, the reddish colour on Hermaphroditus' cheeks is illustrated by means of three successive short similes (4.331-33): obviously this blush is not something only Salmacis but also the narrator and her audience found attractive.[54] Pairs of alternative similes are commoner: they are used by Arethusa in 5.626-9 **[12]**, by Nestor in 12.480-1 **[26]**.

Similes are used so sparingly that they are absent from the one narrative where they are required for generic reasons. I am referring to Onetor's 'tragic messenger-speech' **[24]** and Virbius' transcription of this sub-genre into the autodiegetic mode **[37]**. A feature of epic narrative which obtrudes into the messenger-speech of both Euripides (*Hipp.*1221) and Seneca (*Phaed.*1072-74) on Hippolytus' death, the simile is absent from the version of the *Met.*[55] Furthermore, perhaps because of their brevity, there are no similes that "go a step further and show the unusual ability to carry the story forward surreptitiously." [56] This type, rare even in Homer, actually transcends the limits of narrative pause, reminding us that narrative time is a mere illusion that largely depends on conventions.

II.3.3 Frequency

Unlike the 'Homeric narrator', who employs iterative summary especially in the mass slaughters in the Iliadic battle scenes, in order to convey the basic fact, "many were killed," intradiegetic narrators in the *Met.* reserve iterative frequency for the presentation of characters and background information. In such cases, iterative summary is combined with

---

[53] See Owen 1931: 105 and Edwards 1991: 40.
[54] For blushing in Latin litterature see Lateiner 1996: 236 n.19, where he announces a forthcoming lengthier treatment of the relevant material.
[55] See Coffey & Mayer on SEN.*Phaed.*, pp.175-6. Another epic feature present in both Euripides (*Hipp.*1199-200) and Seneca (*Phaed.*1057-8), but absent in the Ovidian version is the familiar *est locus* motif.
[56] Richardson 1990: 65

descriptive pauses. Mercury **[2]**, for example, expands a three-line pause (2.689-91) with seven lines of iterative summary (2.692-98). Thus the portrait of Syrinx is enlivened with action, and the episode of her fateful meeting with Pan is put in perspective. Likewise, the efforts of the other nymphs to persuade Salmacis **[7]** to change her life-style in a gesture of socialisation (4.305-15) are presented in the iterative mode (*saepe* + imperfect indicative) in a mini-scene consisting of direct speech. Pygmalion's **[16c]** behaviour towards his creation (10.254-69) is also presented iteratively (*saepe* 254, *modo...modo* 259).

Galatea's tale of her ill-starred love for a sixteen-year-old youth named Acis **[28]** provides the best illustration of the various introductory techniques. The nymph's opening words (13.750 *Acis erat*) strike a familiar note: "beginnings of this kind are no doubt as old as the art of narrative itself." The only difference from traditional oral tales is that the hero is named.[57] The five-line presentation of her sweetheart, in broadly static terms with the exception of the parenthetic confirmation of his fidelity (13.752 *nam me sibi iunxerat uni*), is followed by a succinct encapsulation of her misery: *hunc ego, me Cyclops nulla cum fine petebat* (13.755). The beneficial effect of love on the Cyclops' appearance and behaviour, the latter more emphatically highlighted by the counterfoil-description of lines 13.759-61, is also narrated in iterative summary with striking anaphora (13.764-69).

Iterative narration is normally marked by the use of the imperfect tense, sometimes in combination with such adverbs as *saepe* (e.g.1.428, 461, 481, 2.493), *non semel* (1.692) v.sim. Leuconoe's **[6]** use of achronous present is a unique exception to this rule. It occurs in her presentation of the Sun's everyday routine (4.213-16), which of course continued unchanged even at the time of narration. If this is adequate justification for the use of the present instead of the imperfect, it should not go unnoticed that it also makes the shift from iterative to singulative (4.218), still in the present tense, though now dramatic, almost completely imperceptible. A further way of achieving a seamless transition from the iterative to the singulative mode is twice exploited in metanarrative: on the critical day a nymph is made to do what she has just been reported to enjoy doing, picking flowers in the tale of Salmacis

---

[57] Kenney on APUL.*Met*.4.28.1 *Erant in quadam civitate rex et regina*.

(4.315 *saepe legit flores. et tunc quoque flores legebat*) and singing in the story of Canens (14.340-41 *ore suo volucresque vagas retinere solebat./ quae dum feminea modulatur carmina voce,...*)

A notable irregularity in the narrative representation of time has already observed by Perraud in the case of the first daughter of Minyas [5].[58] The initially stable situation is narrated in 4.69ff. in the iterative mode (*solebat, saepe*). This then gives way to the narration of a specific, singular occasion almost without notice. The variations of paragraphing in the editions produced by Anderson, Lafaye and Haupt-Ehwald –they seem to have left no further possibility– is symptomatic of this lack of clarity in boundaries. The only indication seems to be the shift from imperfect to perfect tense (*dixere, dedere*), which could well amount to nothing if *saepe* is still born in mind. Thus the words of the two lovers both create a total picture of their courtship and at the same time represent the last such "conversation",[59] the culmination and epitome of all the previous ones, they had on the eve of the day that put an end to their human existence (108 *una duos (...) nox perdet amantes*).[60] The anonymous Boeotian woman of the mythical age[61] blurs the borderline of singulative and iterative narrative, creating a **pseudo-iterative** narrative, which is not as modernist as one might be inclined to think *prima facie*.[62]

II.4 Conclusions

Time is such an important aspect of narrative technique, of narrativity itself, that it would be surprising if Ovid did not thematise it in at least one of the stories in the *Met*. The metanarrative that presents a particular

---

[58] Perraud 1983/4: 135.
[59] A further imprecision is detected in *dicebant* (73), which is resumed by *locuti* (78): is this a duet uttered in unison, as Perraud 1983/84 interprets it, or does *in vices* (72) suggest some kind of antiphonal performance? In any case, there is only one speech in the text, as in Longus 2.8.2-5.
[60] Cf. Perraud 1983/4: 136.
[61] Two generations before Nestor's birth (and therefore four before the Trojan War), since the latter is a grandson of Fersefone, Minyas' daughter according to Schol. ad *Od*.11.281.
[62] Genette 1980: 122, whose examples from *Quixote, Eugénie Grandet* and *Lucien Leuwen* also involve speech.

interest in this respect is a tale whose tragic outcome apparently is the result of bad timing: Pyramus and Thisbe **[5]**. First, Pyramus is late (4.105 *serius egressus*), as he himself admits in the self-deprecatory apostrophe to the veil of his beloved: *ego te, miseranda, peremi,/ nec prior huc veni* (4.110-11).[63] Then, as if by his rashness he were to counterbalance the effect of his previous delay, he takes his life immediately (4.120 *nec mora*).[64] Finally, despite her good intention (*ne fallat amantem* 4.128) Thisbe comes out of her hiding place just too late to prevent the young man's suicide. That the aspect of time is central to the story is also evident in the description of daybreak, the most elaborate in the *Met.*, which marks the important day for the couple and the beginning of *catastrophe* (4.81-2): *postera nocturnos Aurora removerat ignes,/ solque pruinosas radiis siccaverat herbas.* "Next day Aurora had put out night's starry fires and the sun's rays had dried the frosty grass."

This chapter, however, has examined time not as a concept inscribed in Ovidian metanarrative, but as an essential aspect of the poem's structure. First, we introduced the basic analytical categories of Genette's narratology, illustrating them with the results of our analysis of the metanarratives' place in the temporal structure of the diegesis, the story of the world as told by Ovid, the extradiegetic narrator. The principal points made in the discussion were the following:

- All analepses in the poem are internal with regard to its large temporal scale. With regard to their extent, the narratives of Macareus and Achaemenides **[31, 32]** come closest to completeness.

- One third of the metanarratives that occur in the *Met.* helps the reader/narratee fill gaps in his/her knowledge about the primary story, i.e. they are homodiegetic. To a large extent the point of contact is the intradiegetic narrator himself.

- Metanarrative is by definition a scene. Metanarrative scenes in the *Met.* either (a) belong to a wider scenic context or (b) disrupt the more or less summary overall rhythm. The overall effect is one of *variatio*.

---

[63] Rohrer 1980: 83 blames Thisbe, who "like so many Ovidian females made bold by her desire (IV.96) reaches the appointed spot too soon."
[64] Cf. 1.717, 3.46, 4.481 (diegetic narrative) and 4.344 (another Minyeis).

- Iteration in the *Met.* is the frequency usually employed to sketch the background to singulative presentation. Virbius' narrative [37] could be an example of iterative narrative itself, or rather of *pseudo-iteration*.
- Repetitive narration is absent from the *Met.*

The second section was dedicated to the presentation of the conclusions from the temporal analysis of the metanarratives themselves, in other words their internal temporal structure. The basic facts are the following:

- Events within individual stories are generally told in their proper order with a few exceptions like the analepsis in [3] or the use of analepsis as an expository device in [7].
- By far the most frequent kind of anachrony in the *Met.* is the presentation of the story's gist or even the revelation of its outcome at the very beginning.
- Summary is frequently used to introduce background information that is essential for the understanding of the main event; the use of summary itself is an indirect reminder that these are events of secondary importance.
- Summary is also a convenient expedient for sections of the narrative that are imposed by generic conventions but do not fit Ovidian emphasis on metamorphosis.
- What exactly each intradiegetic narrator chooses to report scenically depends on his/her individual interests as well as those of the narratee. Creating suspense is another possible motive for deceleration.
- Ellipsis is a convenient way of passing over mere trivia. Unlike the Homeric narrator who eschews ellipsis as if he abhorred temporal vacuum intradiegetic narrators in the *Met.* are not afraid to leave gaps.
- Intradiegetic narrators in the *Met.* normally avoid long descriptive pauses. Shorter descriptive pauses are frequently found in the section of the metanarrative that recounts the results of a character's metamorphosis.
- Pause is commoner, though much shorter in the case of similes: similes in the *Met.*, whether in the primary narrative or in metanarrative, are normally shorter than three lines. But even three lines are occasionally enough to disrupt narrative continuity.

- Intradiegetic narrators in the *Met.* reserve iterative frequency for the presentation of characters and background information in combination with descriptive pauses.
- Iterative narration is normally marked by the use of imperfect, sometimes in combination with such adverbs as *saepe*.
- Pseudo-iteration is only employed by the anonymous Minyeid narrator of **[5]**.

III Mode

III.1 Mode

In his recent critical discussion of narratology in the light of postmodern critical thought and literary practice, Andrew Gibson singles out "the change wrought in our views of narration as representation" as the most important achievement of narratology.[1] In its most important and interesting manifestations, narrative theory sought to analyse narratives as sets of signifying practices, to explore and describe them in terms of the codes by which they operated, to make us see narratives as forms of cultural production. This objective is founded on the axiom that language signifies without imitating and that narration, whether oral or written, does likewise. For, it is a linguistic activity, as Genette reminds us in the early pages of his chapter on *mode*. Gibson's criticism that "in its elaboration of a 'system of narrative', narratology relapsed into the very essentialism, representationalism and metaphysics it had sought to resist" cannot be denied.[2] I believe, however, that while "it is always clear that Genette conceives of the narrative system of Proust's *Recherche* as *supervening* upon a certain material that is taken to have some kind of prior existence, as in orthodox mimetic theory,"[3] it is equally clear that narration is understood as an act of semiotic representation, not direct imitation; only words can be imitated or rather copied.[4]

Distance and **Perspective** (or **Focalisation**) are the two modalities that pervade the organisation of narrative information. Genette's choice of terms was made on the basis of an analogy with pictorial art: the particular way a painting is viewed is essentially determined by the viewer's distance from it as well as his/her particular vantage point. *Mutatis mutandis* the presentation of narrative events varies according to the distance at which the narrator places the events (i.e. the signified) and the particular point of view he/she adopts. Just as viewing distance determines the amount of details one can see in a painting, distance is the factor that has to do with the amount of information that the

---

[1] Gibson 1996: 69.
[2] Gibson 1996: 75.
[3] Gibson 1996: 76.
[4] Genette 1972: 185-6.

narrator provides, creating an effect of directness or remoteness. Focalisation, on the other hand, is also relative to the amount of information disclosed, though this time with reference to the characters' knowledge and perception.

III.2 Distance

Genette's study of distance was mainly a piece of criticism aimed at the Platonic distinction between *diegesis* and *mimesis*, and in particular the valorisation of the latter by contemporary literary criticism and practice. The predominantly negative nature of his discussion in combination with the fact that some of the parameters contributing to distance overlap with the categories of time or the narrative voice have led to its neglect or complete rejection, e.g. by Mieke Bal.

Mimesis is but an illusion and we would do better to talk about different degrees of diegesis, argues Genette.[5] He even provides a mathematical formula that involves the two parameters that determine the degree of diegesis:

$$information + informant = C$$

C is a constant, which means that the amount of information and the informant's, i.e. the narrator's, perceptible presence, are in inverse ratio. In other words, **mimesis** (Genette falls back on the traditional term) or **dramatic narration** means maximum information combined with minimal presence of the narrator while **diegesis** (in the Platonic, not the Genettian sense of the term) is defined as minimum information accompanied by maximum perceptibility of the narrator.

It is obvious that the quantity of information is related to the speed (or duration) of narration, which has already been discussed in the second chapter.[6] Our conclusion there was that in Ovidian metanarrative summary predominates over scenic narration; the latter is reserved only for special effects, often the concluding metamorphosis. How does this compare with the degree of the narrator's presence? Genette is rather vague on this issue; he only makes an indirect reference with regard to Marcel Proust: the narrator is present as source, guarantor and

---

[5] Genette 1972: 186.
[6] See p.47-50 and 54-63 above.

organiser of the narrative, as analyst and commentator, as a stylist and particularly as producer of metaphors.[7] This definition is more or less coextensive with that of the narrator's functions, both narrative and extra-narrative, which will be dealt with in chapters 4 and 6 respectively.

There remains only one factor that conditions distance and does not overlap with other narratological categories of analysis: speech representation. The narrative of verbal actions is not uniform; it can assume various forms that cover the whole spectrum from mimesis to diegesis. Genette himself distinguishes three different "conditions of character discourse": (a) **narratized or narrated** discourse, (b) **transposed** discourse in indirect speech, and (c) directly **reported** discourse. This tripartite scheme has been further refined by McHale into a seven-grade scale from *diegetic summary*, *summary*, and *less 'purely' diegetic* through *indirect content paraphrase*, *indirect discourse* and *free indirect discourse*[8] to *direct discourse* and *free direct discourse*.[9] These categorisations are equally applicable to internal, non-enunciated discourse and to words that have "actually" been spoken. For, literary convention demands that thoughts and feelings are nothing but articulated discourse.

By definition, metadiegetic narrative involves direct discourse, whether written or oral. As a consequence, Perseus' account of his adventures, which is presented in indirect discourse (4.772-89) and the tale of Marsyas (6.385-400), which is told by an unidentified narrator in what appears to be free indirect discourse, have been left out of our corpus of material. It also follows that our study of mode with regard to metadiegetic narrative will have to be limited to the representation of speech within the metanarratives.

2.1 Narratized Discourse

"I shall not attempt to reproduce his words, now irrecoverable. I prefer truthfully to make a resume of the many things Ireneo told me. The indirect style is remote and weak; I know that I sacrifice the effectiveness

---

[7] Genette 1972: 188.
[8] According to the scholarly *communis opinio*, free indirect discourse is not documented before the seventeenth century and starts to be extensively used only after the middle of the nineteenth century; see Pavel 1992: 23.
[9] See McHale 1978.

of my narration; but let my readers imagine the nebulous sentences which clouded that night," admits self-consciously the narrator of Jorge Luís Borges' short-story "Funes el memorioso".[10] 'Narratized' is Genette's term for the discourse that is presented as a mere event by the narrator him/herself. This is evidently the most distant and reductive mode of speech representation, as not merely any formal characteristics of expression are effaced, but even the content is drastically reduced. The narrator is satisfied to simply indicate that a speech act has taken place. For example: *vulgusque precari / coeperat : irridet pia vota Lycaon* (1.220-1 "The people started praying, but Lycaon laughed at their pious prayers"); *interea medias fallunt sermonibus horas* (8.651 "In the meanwhile they chattered on to pass the hours without noticing the time").

The cases in which we are not given the slightest hint of the content of the speech act are very rare; even when the verb is not supplemented with an object of the vaguest sort (*loquiturque* [10.256] cf. *talia verba refert* [1.700], *haec mihi non vani... narravere senes* [8.721-22]), the verb or verbal periphrasis itself may convey a certain attitude or the illocutionary force of the speech-act: prayer (1.220, 2.574, 4.237, 8.682), blandishment (2.575, 4.70, 10.259, 10.416), exhortation (10.257, 10.467), complaint (4.251, 10.724), gratitude (14.306-7, 15.49-50) or lamentation (11.331; 14.744-45; 14.428-29) and much more (4.41 *sed vetuere patres* "but their parents forbade it," 4.84 *multa prius questi* "at first they lamented a lot," 10.417 *terret* "she threatened," 10.426-27 *multaque, ut excuteret diros, si posset, amores,/ addidit* "she proceeded to admonish the girl at length, to rid her, if she could, of a love so disastrous," 10.466 *virgineosque metus levat* "he soothed her girlish fears," 13.650 *Delius augurium dedit huic* "the Delian god gave this oracle," 14.714-15 *addit/ verba superba ferox* "she added arrogant words").

A step in the direction of the mimetic pole is the inclusion of an indirect indication of the content of the speech act performed by one of the characters. This is normally incorporated in the narrator's discourse. For example: *contigerat nostras infamia temporis aures* (1.211 "Scandalous rumours concerning the state of the times had reached my ears"), *acta deae refero* (2.562 "I told the goddess what had happened"), *vulgat adulterium diffamatumque parenti/ indicat* (4.236-38 "She spread the story of

---

[10] Borges 1998: 101.

Leucothoe's adultery and, by publishing it abroad, brought it to the notice of the girl's father"), *et nomine quemque vocando/ exhortatur equos* (5.402-3 "he encouraged the horses, calling each one by name"), *criminis extemplo ficti temerarius index / Procrin adit linguaque refert audita susurra* (7.824-35 "hastily this rush informer hurried to Procris with the tale of my supposed crime, and added what he had heard me whisper"), *et veniam dapibus nullisque paratibus orant* (8.682-83 "and they begged the gods' indulgence for a poor meal"). A similar case is that of the verb *vocare* supplemented with an accusative of the person addressed; although it is certainly possible that e.g. *comites voco* (3.604) actually reflects a cry "comites!" it is more probable that *comites* summarizes a number of individual names. The same applies to *deos hominesque voco* (2.578 "I call upon gods and humans").[11]

All these cases exhibit a minimal degree of character-speech representation in the narrative, emphasizing the distance that separates both narrator and narratee from the event, i.e. the character's speech-act itself. As Richardson observed about narratized discourse in Homeric diegesis, it is not the case that certain types of speech acts do not deserve full reproduction in the discourse, whether reported or transposed.[12] It is rather the narrative economy of the particular episode, in our case of the particular metanarrative, that dictates this mode of representation. We have noticed, for instance, that prayers are sometimes reported as mere events, i.e. narratized. Yet much more frequently (the ratio is 9 to 4, i.e. twice as frequently) the characters' prayers are reported verbatim by both heterodiegetic (4.383-86, 10.274-76, 483-87, 13.880-81, 15.39-40) and homodiegetic narrators (5.618-20, 7.615-18, 8.595-602, 10.640-41).[13] Even narrators on the third (Venus: 10.640-41) and fourth (Arethusa: 5.618-20) diegetic level are allowed the luxury of quoting prayers to (the former) and by (the latter) themselves.

III.2.2 Transposed Discourse

"In the *Iliad* we find 20 cases of embedded direct speech and about four

---

[11] The remaining instance of the verb is in the passive voice (14.294 *ad insidiosa vocatus*), with Ulixes as the understood subject, i.e. probable content of the speech act.
[12] Richardson 1990: 78.
[13] Narratized prayers are also present in the discourse of both kinds of narrator.

times as many cases of embedded indirect speech," observed De Jong.[14] This is not only the reverse of the practice followed by the primary Homeric narrator but also the opposite of the situation in Ovidian metanarrative in the *Met.*, where pure indirect speech appears only thirteen times, one tenth of the times that direct speech is employed (precisely 145 instances).[15]

No.	Lines	Passage
3	2.556	[*Pallas*] *et legem dederat, sua ne secreta viderent*
3	2.559-60	*timidas vocat una sorores/ Aglauros*
6	4.187-88	*atque aliquis de dis non tristibus optat/ sic fieri turpis*
13	6.329	*naiadum Faunine foret tamen ara rogabam*
21	10.392-3	*precatur,/ ut sibi committat, quidquid dolet:*
21	10.405-6	*quodcumque est, orat, ut ipsi/ indicet...*
21	10.441	*quam postquam adducere iussa est*
21	10.552	*quae causa, roganti:*
22	10.583	*ne quis iuvenum currat velocius, optat*
23	11.321-2	*quae se preferre Dianae/ sustinuit*
26	12.407	*et amare fatendo*
27	13.658-9	*alantque/ imperat Argolicam caelesti munere classem.*
30	14.137-8	*quot haberet corpora pulvis,/ tot mihi natale contingere vana rogavi;*

It is clear that indirect speech forms the exception to the rule of direct speech. But is it possible to determine the circumstances in which intradiegetic narrators are made to opt for the indirect representation of discourse? Indirect speech is used by the Homeric narrator primarily to render commands,[16] while thoughts and songs as well as commands are frequently recorded indirectly by means of content paraphrases rather than through the actual words spoken. De Jong did not distinguish between the two types of transposed discourse either, arguing that indirect speech is employed mainly (a) when the primary Homeric narrator wishes to summarise speeches, e.g. "when several speeches are

---

[14] De Jong 1987: 171.
[15] De Jong 1987: 115 and Richardson 1990:71.
[16] Richardson 1990: 72.

involved which can be supposed to have more or less the same content,"[17] or when the speaking characters and/or the speech's content are not deemed important enough to be quoted directly;[18] and (b) when the speech belongs to a time anterior to the beginning of the primary story of the *Iliad*. The latter, however, does not apply to Homeric intradiegetic narrators despite the overall greater frequency of indirect speech.

Ovidian scholars have not dealt with the issue extensively. The view underlying Bömer's commentary on the *Met.* is that important utterances in the poem are normally given in *oratio recta*. This rule seems to break down in the case of Perseus' account of his adventures at the court of Cepheus in Ethiopia. There *narrat Agenorides* (4.772) does not signal a change of narrative level. Instead, it introduces a combination of indirect speech (4.772-86) and summary (4.787-89), i.e. a clearly mediated form of Perseus' narration despite its distinct focalisation, suggested by the inconsistency about Atlas and the hero's characteristic preoccupation with the veracity of his account (*non falsa* 4.787, cf. *inveni, qui se vidisse referret* 4.797). Scholars have explained the use of indirect speech variously as Ovid's attempt to reduce the personal drama of the hero,[19] as humorous exposure of the conventionality of the hero's autobiographic narrative at a banquet where he is the guest of honour,[20] and most recently as an implied intertextual contrast with the banquet speakers Odysseus and Aeneas, and Ovid's nod to his implied audience's lack of interest in such a hackneyed topic as Perseus' conquest of Medusa.[21]

Far from being conventional and hackneyed, the Pierids' song (5.319-31) is the only case of speech hastily and distastefully summarised by an Ovidian intradiegetic narrator that has exercised the acumen of scholars. The standard interpretation since Leach's seminal paper is that the use of content paraphrase forms part of the Muses' strategy of belittlement

---

[17] De Jong 1987: 115.
[18] De Jong 1987: 116.
[19] Anderson on 4.772-75.
[20] Due 1974: 78.
[21] Wheeler 1999: 115.

and exposure of their competitors as incompetent artists.[22] This view is clearly congruent with De Jong's explanation of Agamemnon's recapitulation of Calchas' speech (*Il*.1.93-100) in indirect speech (1.109-13). She argues convincingly that the indirect form enables Agamemnon to show his ironic disbelief and disapproval of the seer's pronouncements, and leave out unpleasant details.[23] We should not, however, press this line of interpretation too hard, as it does not account for the sudden shift of the Muse's report into *oratio recta* (5.327-31). Given that the part of the Pierids' narrative directly reported involves metamorphosis and aetiology, the two major interests of the primary narrator and his presumed audience, it is tempting to combine this piece of evidence with the fact that only Perseus' account of the *causa* behind Medusa's *crinita draconibus ora* (4.771 "head which has snakes instead of hair") was deemed *digna relatu* (4.793 "worthy to be reported") in direct speech, and draw the conclusion that there is a supplementary reason for the narrator's preference of indirect speech for the rest: the content of the narrative does not conform with the implied author's overall plan for the poem.

The other twelve instances of transposed discourse in metanarratives involve commands, wishes, questions and statements in even proportions; half of them belong to two of them, the Crow's admonitory tale [3], which does not include a single line of direct speech, and Orpheus' song [21]. The obvious explanation for the use of indirect speech is that the utterances are important only as action, i.e. for their illocutionary force, not as words. An interesting case is the words ascribed to an unidentified divinity by Leuconoe [6] (4.187-88): they are a transposed and summarised version of Hermes' response to Apollo's question whether the former would mind being chained together with Aphrodite in Demodocus' song ἀμφ' Ἄρεος φιλότητος ἐυστεφάνου τ' Ἀφροδίτης (*Od*.8.266ff.): αἴ γὰρ τοῦτο γένοιτο (*Od*.8.339). One important difference between the present and the Odyssean context of Hermes' words is that the story of Mars and Venus merely provides the background to Leuconoe's main story about the Sun's amours, while as

---

[22] Leach 1974: 114 and Cahoon 1996: 50.
[23] De Jong 1987: 176 and 179.

is evident from the title-line quoted above Ares and Aphrodite are the sole theme of the Phaeacian bard.

III.2.3 Directly Reported Discourse

52 percent of the *Metamorphoses* is presented as direct speech of the characters.[24] This is slightly higher than the percentage of 'character-text' in the *Iliad*, which is reckoned at 45% by De Jong.[25] Unlike the primary narrator, intradiegetic narrators in the *Iliad* show a marked preference for what the ancient critical tradition called "pure narrative", only rarely incorporating *mimesis* (direct speech) in their discoure. In other words, they are more reluctant to relinquish their point of view.[26] This is also true of their counterparts in the *Metamorphoses*, where the average metadiegetic narrative contains only a few lines of quoted speech with the momentary shift of focalisation that this gesture implies. Yet, if one includes the third and fourth level narratives embedded in the longest second-level ones (the Muse's narrative **[9b]** and Orpheus' song **[21]** but also the anonymous' narrator's report of the Lycian guide's sacred tale **[13]**), the total lines of direct speech in metanarrative rises to about 1023 (precision is difficult to achieve because direct speech in Ovid does not always involve whole lines) or 28% of metanarrative text. This is a considerably lower figure than that of primary-narrator text occupied by *oratio recta*, but not out of proportion with the amount of direct discourse in third-level narrative (32%) —the only fourth-level narrative in the poem, that of Arethusa **[12]**, has a mere 6 percent (4 out of 67 lines).

The one-line speech is an obvious Ovidian mannerism, already recognised by Heinze in his pioneering work in the study of Ovid's narrative techniques.[27] On occasion, such short utterances may seem dramatically improbable. W. S. Anderson, for example, has objected to the nurse's reply to Myrrha's reluctant disclosure of her illicit love in *Met.*10.429-30 **[21f]**: *'vive' ait haec, 'potiere tuo' —et non ausa 'parente'/ dicere*

---

[24] The calculations are based on the figures provided by Wheeler 1999: 163 (graph). Our corpus of metanarratives forms 58.5 percent of the character-text in the poem, i.e. 30.5 percent of the whole poem.
[25] De Jong 1987: 149.
[26] Dickson 1995: 68, discussing the characteristic case of Nestor.
[27] Heinze 1919: 65.

conticuit promissaque numine firmat (" 'Go on living!' said she 'You shall have your...' and, not daring to utter the word 'father', she fell silent, and sealed her promises by calling upon the gods"). As Euripides perceived in *Hipp*.433ff., it takes more than the nurse's determination to persuade the woman to live and pursue her guilty passion. Ovid, however, is hurrying toward his climactic scene and relies on our sophistication to expand his brevity."

This tendency to brief utterances does not rule out the possibility of longer speeches: Iole's not particularly long (68 lines) narrative **[20]**, for instance, includes a long (21 lines) speech by her sister Dryope (9.371-391 *siqua fides miseris*...) delivered in the process of her transformation into a lotus-tree. Longer narratives, like those of Calliope **[11]** and Orpheus **[21]** quote characters and other narrators at length. The former **[11]** includes Venus' admonitory address to her son (5.365-79), Cyane's address to Dis (5.414-18), Arethusa's consolation *ad Cererem* (5.489-508), Ceres' plea to Jupiter (5.514-22) as well as his response (5.523-32) and in a final metadiegetic leap Arethusa's autobiographic *amores* (5.576-641) with its customarily short but hauntingly echoing cries of Alpheus (5.599, 600 *quo properas, Arethusa?[...] quo properas?* and 625 *io Arethusa, io Arethusa!*) and Arethusa's urgent prayer to Diana (5.618-20). This amounts to 130 lines of direct speech out of a total 321 lines (40.5 %) in Calliope's song.

Orpheus' *carmen* in Book 10 **[21]** quotes Apollo's lament for his beloved Hyacinthus (196-208), Venus' soliloquy (230-34), Pygmalion's timid prayer (274-6), Myrrha's internal (*secum*) monologue (320-5), her brief exchange with her father on the subject of the ideal husband (364-66), the epigram that was meant to be her last words (380 *care vale Cinyra causamque intellege mortis*), the nurse's imploring speech (395-401) and her subsequent conversation with the *puella* (408-10; 411-13; 422; 429), three further brief words of the nurse with the father and the daughter (441, 442-43, 463-64), and finally Myrrha's prayer (484-87); but the longest speech in Orpheus' song is Venus' aetiological narrative of Atalanta and Hippomenes (560-707), which follows a short conversation (Venus 543-52 —Adonis 552 *quae causa?* —Venus 553-56). Out of 592 lines of hexameter song 269, slightly less than half (45%), are dedicated to direct speech.

As we have already noted in the theoretical introduction to the chapter, thoughts and feelings may be reported as if they were actually articulated. In the *Metamorphoses* even direct speech is used to represent mental discourse.[28] In 1.222-23 **[1]** (*mox ait 'experiar, deus hic, discrimine aperto,/ an sit mortalis; nec erit dubitabile verum.'* "And then he said: 'I shall find out, by an clear test, whether he be god or mortal: there will be no doubt about the truth.'") direct speech seems to be used to represent what despite the introductory *ait* looks more like that character's (i.e. Lycaon's) intimate thoughts. His plan is meant to be secret (*necopina ... morte* 1.224) but fails, as nothing eludes Jupiter's (i.e. the narrator's) omniscience.[29] Within Orpheus' song **[21]**, the omniscient goddess of love **[22]** makes Adonis (and the audiences of the first and second-level narratives) privy to the innermost thoughts of the maiden. These are presented in a monologue, in which Atalanta addresses Hippomenes in her imagination (10.611-35 *'quis deus hunc formosis' inquit 'iniquus/ perdere vult ... cubilia vellem...'/ dixerat*). For despite the repeated verbs of speaking (*inquit* 611, *dixerat* 636) and the second-person pronouns and verb-forms, which alternate with the third-person, it does not seem probable that this brilliant piece of amazing mastery and knowledge of female psychology (Wilamowitz *apud* Bömer on 10.609-35) was actually uttered. That thoughts can be presented in direct speech introduced with a verb of speaking rather than of thinking is shown by another section of the same metadiegetic narrative: *'sed cur certaminis huius/ intemptata mihi fortuna relinquitur?' inquit,/ audentes deus ipse iuvat.'* (10.584-86 " 'Why should not I, too, try my fortune in this race?' he said. 'The gods help those who show themselves bold'."). The resumptive phrase *dum talia secum/ exigit Hippomenes* (10.586-87 "Such were the questions that Hippomenes asked himself") makes clear that the speech is an exteriorised internal monolgue.

---

[28] Free indirect discourse, a common means of rendering thought in modern third-person narration is not used in the *Met* (see n.1 above), unless line 10.289 from Orpheus' song (*corpus erat: saliunt temptatae pollice venae* "It was indeed a human body! The vains throbbed as he pressed them with his thumb") could be taken as an example of FID, especially within the context of mental action set by line 10.287.
[29] See Anderson 1989: 96.

Dramatic dialogue is not commonly associated with hexameter narrative. Yet early Greek epic is not lacking in "great conversation scenes, such as that at the court of Alcinous (e.g. *Od.*11.353ff.), or in the palace of Odysseus (e.g. *Od.*17.369ff.), or as in the assembly in *Iliad* 2, in which Achilles and Agamemnon, Calchas and Nestor converse, (...) and Achilles himself speaks no fewer than eight times; or lengthier duologues as in *Odyssey* 1, where there are four exchanges between Athena and Telemachus").[30] The third book of the *Argonautica* also features long conversations between Hera, Athena and Aphrodite (lines 10-110 with eleven speeches organised mainly in pairs), between Medea and Chalciope (674-738 involving three pairs of speeches), and between Medea and Jason (974-1144 with three paired speeches plus a speech by Jason).[31] In the *Aeneid*, however, "the most common kind of interchange is between two speakers and takes the form of only one utterance and one response"[32]

Ovidian metanarrative is not particularly rich in conversationally organised speeches. Only Acoetes' **[4]** narrative style deviates not only from the Ovidian norm, but also from the practice followed in Homeric hymns. The latter is relevant since one of the major subtexts of this metanarrative is the Seventh *Homeric Hymn to Dionysos* –the other is Euripides' *Bacchae*. The former is not lacking in direct discourse: all the main characters, the prudent helmsman (17-24), the taunting captain (26-31) as well as benign Dionysos (55-57) are granted a speech; but only the first two form a dialogic pair. In the *Met.*, speeches never exceed four lines en bloc and are organised in quasi distichomythic, i.e. truly dramatic, exchange only once (3.632-37). Bacchus wakes up and tries to find out what is going on:

'quid facitis? Quis clamor?' ait 'qua, dicite, nautae,
huc ope perveni? Quo me deferre paratis?'
'pone metum' Proreus 'et quos contingere portus
ede velis' dixit: 'terra sistere petita.'
'Naxon' ait Liber 'cursus advertite vestros!
illa mihi domus est, vobis erit hospita tellus.'

---

[30] Heinze 1993: 315.
[31] Examples derived from Heinze 1990: 320-21.
[32] Heinze 1990: 315.

"What is going on here? What means all this shouting?" he asked. "Tell me, sailors, how came I to this place? Where do you mean to take me?" "Fear not!" Proreus said, "Tell us what harbour you want to reach, and you will be set down in the land of your choice." "Direct your course towards Naxos," said Liber. "There lies my home, that land will give you hospitality." (translation by M. M. Innes, adapted)

Earlier, however, Acoetes' speech, half of which is addressed to his fellow-sailors and half offered as a prayer to the unknown divinity, provokes a dismissive response from Dictys in half a line (3.611-14):

et sensi et dixi sociis: 'quod numen in isto
corpore sit, dubito, sed corpore numen in isto est.
quiquis es, o faveas nostrisque laboribus adsis.
his quoque das veniam.' 'pro nobis mitte precari'
Dictys ait.

When I realized this, I said to my companions: "What god is inside this body, I cannot tell, but a god there is. Whoever you are, be gracious and assist our labours. Grant pardon, too, to these men." "Stop praying on our behalf!" said Dictys. (translation by M. M. Innes, adapted)

Later, too, when Acoetes tries to take the situation in his hands, three directly reported speeches are organised responsorially and supplemented by narratized discourse (3.641-4, 646-48):

'quid facis, o demens? Quis te furor' inquit, 'Acoete?'
pro se quisque timet 'laevam pete!' maxima nutu
pars mihi significat, pars, quid velit, aure susurrat.
obstipui 'capiat' que 'aliquis moderamina!' dixi (...)
increpor a cunctis, totumque inmurmurat agmen;
e quibus Aethalion 'te scilicet omnis in uno
nostra salus posita est' ait

"You fool, what are you doing? What madness has possessed you, Acoetes?" he said. And scared for themselves, each one cried: "Make for the left!" Most of them indicated by a nod, but some whispered in my ear what they meant to do. I was horrified. "Someone else take the rudder!" I cried (...) They all cursed me, my whole crew muttered angrily. Then one of them, Aethalion said: "I suppose you think the safety of us all depends on you alone." (translation by M. M. Innes, adapted)

The pervasive presence of directly quoted speech in Acoetes' metanarrative is perhaps best appreciated within its intertextual framework. As I. Gildenhard emphasised in his paper for the First Craven Seminar (2-5 July 1997), the stranger's apology interrupts "what appeared to be Ovid's intertextual adaptation of Euripides' *Bacchae*" with his own version of the *Homeric Hymn to Dionysos*.[33] The transition is effected smoothly as the first twenty-four lines of the metanarrative flesh out the biographical indications provided in the Euripidean tragedy (*Bacch*.461-64) while the latter part sheds light on the vague answer to Pentheus question about the origin of his priesthood (*Bacch*.470): ὁρῶν ὁρῶντα, καὶ δίδωσιν ὄργια. Acoetes' story is one of call and divine epiphany, "born out of a situation of actual need" like most classcial Greek autobiographic discourse, as G. W. Most has recently shown.[34] This double generic subtext may account for the infiltration of the dramatic practice of narration through dialogue into hexameter verse. Besides it is natural for a Dionysiac acolyte to adopt a narrative style characteristic of the Dionysiac literary genre, i.e. drama, in order to present a Dionysiac story to a character drawn from Euripides' *Bacchae*.

Ovid's use of direct discourse in metanarrative is quite sophisticated. The story of Pyramus and Thisbe **[5]**, narrated by an anonymous Minyeid, includes a directly reported speech that is attributed to both ill-starred lovers (4.73-77):

'invide' dicebant 'paries, quid amantibus obstas?
quantum erat, ut sineres toto nos corpore iungi,
aut, hoc si nimium est, vel ad oscula danda pateres?
nec sumus ingrati: tibi nos debere fatemur,
quod datus est verbis ad amicas transitus aures.'

"Jealous wall," they said "why are you standing in the way of lovers? How much would it be to let us touch each other with our whole body, or if that is too much, that you should at least open wide enough for us to kiss? Not that we are ungrateful: we admit that it is thanks to you that we have any way at all by which our words can reach our true love's ears." (adapted from M. M. Innes' translation)

The wall, the material embodiment of their parents' objection to this relationship, is made to play the role of the door in the imagined space of Roman elegy. The difference is that the *exclusus amator* is here doubled. This metamorphosis of the *paraklausithyron* is presented as an iterative scene. Yet it is unrealistic to suppose that the two lovers repeated each

---

[33] Quoted in A. Barchiesi's handout for the same seminar from I. Gildenhard-A. Zissos, *Epic Inflections* (working draft 1996).
[34] Most 1989: 127.

time the exact words quoted. Because of the duplication of the figure of the *exclusus amator* it is also unclear who actually uttered these words. Are we to assume that this is a duet performed in unison, as Perraud 1983/84 maintains? Or does *in vices* (72 "in turn") suggest some kind of antiphonal performance? In any case, there is only one speech in the text, as in Longus' romance (2.8.2-5), a genre with which 'Pyramus and Thisbe' has many structural features in common, as Niklas Holzberg has shown.[35]

A similar phenomenon of pseudo-direct discourse occurs in the story told by the third daughter of Minyas **[7]**.[36] Again, the context is iterative in terms of narrative frequency, which clashes with the directly quoted advice of the nymphs to Salmacis (4.305-7): *saepe suas illi fama est dixisse sorores:/ 'Salmaci, vel iaculum vel pictas sume pharetras / et tua cum duris venatibus otia misce!'* ("Often, so runs the story, her sisters would say to her: 'Salmacis, get yourself a javelin, or a gaily painted quiver, and vary your hours of leisure with hard hunting'.").

But Salmacis would not listen to her sisters. Her denial is described by the narrator with words that echo almost verbatim the nymphs' advice. This kind of repetition appears to be a universal of oral (heroic) poetry. By using the same words as closely as possible, story-tellers imply that the order or suggestion is executed exactly as it had been formulated; some poets, however, delight in this device for its own sake "as an almost ritualistic procedure which imparts an additional dignity to a point by repeating it."[37] It is precisely the use of this "curious expedient to summarize several speeches," i.e. pseudo-direct sppech, that enables the Minyeid to have the echo-effect of the repetition.

Another type of echo, this time intertextual (as opposed to the Minyeid's intratextual), is observed in the Muse's **[9b]** account of the Pierids' challenge to the Muses of Helicon (5.308f.): *'desinite indoctum vana dulcedine vulgus / fallere.'* The Pierids are presented accusing the Muses of

---

[35] See Holzberg 1988. To his observations we could add the principle of equal love (see Konstan 1994: esp.7 and ch.4, and Létoublon 1993: 118) and the parents' prohibition as a starting-point for the development of the intrigue (see Létoublon 1993: 86 and cf. Konstan 1994: 144).

[36] The name 'pseudo-direct speech' was introduced by Richardson 1990: 79.

[37] Bowra 1952: 256-58 and De Jong 1987: 208ff.

deceiving the ignorant masses (*indoctum volgus*) with sweet lies (*vana dulcedine*), evoking (and implicitly invoking) words the latter had addressed to the *indoctum volgus* of the shepherds in Hes. *Th*.27: ἴδμεν ψεύδεα πολλὰ λέγειν ἐτύμοισιν ὁμοῖα. Irrespective of how the Hesiodic passage is to be understood –P. Pucci seems to be right that it is a "strong indictment of the powerlessness and ignorance of men before the poetic *logos*," the daughters of Pieros are thus made to quote in support of their argument their interlocutors' words in an older poem like Mars' quoting of Jupiter's words in Ennius' *Annales* in 14.814.[38]

Another aspect of the sophistication with which Ovid's intradiegetic surrogates employ direct speech is precisely its limited use. The story told by Aeacus in Book 7 **[15]** is permeated by father-son relationships. Aeacus is the offspring of Jupiter's illicit affair with the nymph Aegina. It is because of this and Aeacus' filial *pietas* to his mother, expressed in renaming his insular kingdom after her, that the plague is sent by Juno. It is precisely his descent from Jupiter that the king invokes in his prayers for an end to his misfortunes (7.615-18 *'Iuppiter o!' dixi 'si te non falsa loquuntur / dicta sub amplexus Aeginae Asopidos isse / nec te, magne **pater**, nostri pudet esse parentem, / aut mihi redde meos, aut me quoque conde sepulcro.'*). Again he addresses Jupiter as his father when he asks for a miracle, for Aeginetans that would equal the number of ants he has just seen passing by (7.627-28 *'totidem, **pater** optime, dixi / 'tu mihi da cives et inania moenia supple.'*) When finally his literal dream of ant-men has come true, it is his son Telamon that tells him the good news (7.648-49 *'speque fideque, **pater**,' dixit 'maiora videbis./ egredere!'*). Through this inspired and limited use of direct speech only between fathers and sons –a fourth directly quoted speech (7.620-21 *'accipio, sintque ista, precor, felicia mentis / signa tuae' dixi; 'quod das mihi, pigneror omen.'*) is also addressed by Aeacus to Jupiter but lacks an invocation, perhaps because in a sense it forms a unity with the prayer (7.615-18)– Aeacus has presented his rule as founded on and

---

[38] Pucci 1977: 12. In support of Pucci's interpretation cf. Apollo's statement in the *Homeric Hymn to Hermes* 541-42: "One man I will harm, another I will help, shifting about the many tribes of miserable mortals"; see Pratt 1993: 109.

benefiting from his descent from *Iuppiter optimus magnus*, and himself as a caring father to his people, Jupiter's counterpart on earth.[39]

Another way in which direct speech becomes a significant device of speech representation is its reservation for a single speaker in a certain narrative. The anonymous Lycian guide's story about the local farmers' misbehaviour towards Niobe **[14]** applies this strategy: the verbal acts of the *rustica turba* are narratized (6.348 *rustica turba vetat*) or summarized (6.361-62 *hi tamen orantem perstant prohibere minasque, ni procul abscedat, convicia insuper addunt.*) while the goddess' words are given in direct discourse (6.349-59 *'quid prohibetis aquis?'* and 6.369 *'aeternum stagno' dixit 'vivatis in isto!'*). Indeed, the second speech attributed to the persecuted divinity is also typical of a category of utterances that are normally quoted directly: the angry god's order for transformation. In metanarrative this occurs again in 11.323 (*'fatis'que 'placebimus' inquit*) and 15.543-44 (*'qui' que 'fuisti/ Hippolytus' dixit, 'nunc idem Virbius esto!'*). Action is also preceded by a short utterance in the case of Arachne's punishment by Minerva, narrated by the extradiegetic narrator at the beginning of Book 6: *'vive quidem, pende tamen, inproba' dixit, / 'lexque eadem poenae, ne sis secura futuri, / dicta tuo generi serisque nepotibus esto!'* (6.136-38). The word is not always enough to effect metamorphosis on its own though: Minerva resorts to the juice of a magic herb (6.139ff.) and Circe employs *carmina* in combination with a magic ritual that involves the use of a magic wand (14.386-87) in **[33]**. The latter is the only case in metanarrative where the actual words are not reported on such an occasion –perhaps because of their arcane power and number (*tria* 14.387).

Directly reported speech is also commonly used to punctuate combat narrative. "Both unwarranted boasting (...) and a reply to it are familiar ingredients of the fighting," as Fenik observed in his study of the Homeric battle-scene.[40] In his recently published study of 'flyting' in heroic epic, Ward Parks reconstructed a pattern of single-combat scenes, like the one in Achelous' final story on his struggle with Hercules for

---

[39] For a similar strategy on the diegetic level (Book 1) linking Jupiter with Augustus see Feeney 1991: 199-200 and Wheeler 1999: 173f.
[40] Fenik 1968: 32.

Deianira's hand **[17e]**.[41] Having met at Oeneus' house and declared their intention to marry his daughter (Parks' **engagement**), "the heroes engage in an adversarial verbal exchange (Parks' **flyting**) that has two qualitatively distinguishable yet mutually interpenetrating aspects: (a) **eris**, i.e. the heroes contend for *kleos* or glory [14ff. *ille Iovem socerum dare se famamque laborum,/ et superata suae referebat iussa novercae;/ contra ego 'turpe deum mortali cedere' dixi (...) 'dominum me cernis aquarum'*] and (b) **contract**, i.e. they agree on a course of action from at least a range of possibilities, at least one of which entails a trial of arms or some other form of manly display. The two major alternatives are set out at 9.29-30: *'melior mihi dextera lingua!/ dummodo pugnando superem, tu vince loquendo' congrediturque ferox*. The only part of the narrative sequence identified by Parks that is missing here is the **ritual conclusion**, the retrospective speech and symbolic action by which the heroes terminate their contest. But this should not surprise us since the narrative represents the point of view of the defeated.

Tauntingly ironic is also the predominant tone of the directly reported utterances in Nestor's "aggressively epic narrative" in Book 12 **[26]**. *'non inpune feres, teli modo copia detur!'*(12.265) "You will suffer for this, if I can but lay hold on a weapon," shouted Exadius before piercing his opponent's eyes with a set of stag's antlers. When Charaxus kills one of his own side, Rhoetus cannot contain his exultation and before renewing his assault on his foe: *'sic, conprecor,' inquit/ 'cetera sit fortis castrorum turba tuorum!'* (12.285-86) "May the others in your camp display their bravery with like result!" A few moments later Evagrus protests against Rhoetus' cruel attack on young Corythus, shouting "What glory is there in routing a boy?" (*'puero quae gloria fuso/ parta tibi est?'* 12.292-93). But Rhoetus' flaming brand proves more effective a weapon than Evagrus' tongue, which is silenced at once. Even a word of reassurance and encouragement to bravery can be tainted with irony. To Nessus, who was afraid of being wounded, Astylos said: "Don't run away: you will be kept safe, to be a target for Hercules' bow!" (*'ne fuge! ad Herculeos' inquit 'servaberis arcus.'* 12.309). Phorbas hurled his javelin at Aphidas, crying "You will drink your wine diluted with the waters of the Styx" (*'miscenda' que dixit / 'cum Styge vina bibes'* 12.321-22). Aphidas falls dead

---

[41] Parks 1990.

without answering his foe's sardonic remark, which nicely summarizes the theme of merriment turned into disaster because he had already "sunk deep in unending slumber". It has already become clear that unlike Homeric battle-narrative, which often includes speeches of both combatants, Nestor prefers a drastically limited version with one speaker per confrontation.[42]

This rhetoric of macho aggressiveness culminates in Latreus' words that filled the air with virile tension before he charged at Caeneus with his Macedonian *sarisa* (12.470-76), highlighting the main issue raised by the story: can a woman become a man, or to put it differently, is gender something acquired or is it genetically determined once and for all, i.e. identical with biological sex? (12.470-76 *'et te, Caeni, feram? ... bella relinque viris!'*). This first speech is followed up with two lines of angry determination after Latreus' failure at his first attempt (12.484-85 *'haud tamen effugies! Medio iugulaberis ense,/ quandoquidem mucro est hebes'*). Caeneus' speech is even shorter but he has the last word and gives the last blow (12.490-91 *'nunc age' ait Caeneus, 'nostro tua corpora ferro/ temptemus!'*). The amazement that struck Latreus at Caeneus' impenetrability is quickly spread and multiplied among the Centaurs. In response, Monychus comes up with a speech that contains the necessary ingredients for a *paraenesis* in the battlefield, mainly indignant questions (501-3) and a call to action: *'heu dedecus ingens!' / Monychus exclamat, 'populus superamur ab uno/ ... pro vulnere pondus.'* (12.498-509). The last speech in this long metanarrative is an epitaph for the transexual super-male hero Caeneus put in the mouth of the seer Mopsus: 12.530-35 *'o salve' dixit, 'Lapitheae gloria gentis, ...noxque removit.'*

III.3 Focalisation

One of the major achievements of modern narrative theory, and of G. Genette in particular, is the distinction drawn between the agent of narration and the filter that determines the amount of information presented. Since it is almost impossible to speak without betraying a personal point of view, a narrator is capable of both speaking and

---

[42] For Homeric practice, which clearly follows no fixed pattern, see Fenik 1968: 32 and 101.

filtering, which facilitates the confusion between the two activities. But it is also conceivable that a narrator tells what another person sees, has seen or will see. This possibility makes theoretically necessary the distinction between the two activities. Only on this basis "can the interrelations between them be studied with precision," the objective of every theory.[43]

Far from leading to an easy consensus, focalisation's crucial position in narratology has produced a variety of typologies and criteria of categorisation. By and large, however, they revolve around the basic polarity (a vestige of narratology's structuralist lineage) of external versus internal focalisation. "External focalisation occurs where the focalisation is from an orientation outside the story (what this seems to mean is that the orientation is not associable with that of any character within the text)."[44] "Internal focalisation," on the other hand, "occurs inside the represented events" (**diegesis**) "and almost always involves a character-focalizer, though some unpersonified position or stance could be adopted."[45] A practical way of testing whether the focalisation of a certain narrative segment is internal or external would be its rewriting in the first person. As R. Barthes suggests, if this does not entail any changes besides that in grammatical person then the segment is internally focalised. Another important parameter, which is often neglected, is whether focalisation remains **fixed** throughout a narrative, as in Henry James' novel *What Maisie Knew*[46] or varies between two or more positions (**variable**). A special type of variable focalisation occurs when the same event is presented more than once with a different focalisation (**multiple**).[47]

Focalisation is a powerful aspect of narrative technique because it can have a crucial impact on the way the narrative world is perceived by the actual readers. A character whose focalisation is adopted has a special claim not only on readers' attention but also on their sympathy. For, as Bal observes, "the reader watches with the character's eyes and will, in

---

[43] Rimmon-Kenan 1983: 72.
[44] Toolan 1988: 69.
[45] Toolan 1988: 69.
[46] See Bal 1997: 146.
[47] Barthes 1977: 40.

principle, be inclined to accept the vision presented by that character" as true and and ethically superior.[48] But only when the focalisation is external does the reader tend to forget that any focalisation is by definition subjective and give up all resistance to the supposedly 'objective' vision of the extradiegetic focalizer.[49] In fact, the focalizer's bias is not absent but remains implicit.[50]

Anyone has has read Genette's work on narratology will have already discerned several deviations from his rather static conception and subsequent typology of focalisation. First of all, his paradigm is tripartite, including what he calls **zero focalisation**, obviously on the analogy of the primitive structuralist notion of 'zero-degree of narration'. This term was invented as an alternative for the famous divine omniscience which offers the reader a vision that does not coincide with any single character's but also has more depth than the *stricto sensu* **external or "behaviouristic" focalisation**, which is limited to the visible surface of the characters and their actions and excludes access to their thoughts and feelings. Genette himself admits that only long sections of narrative can be described in this way, which almost coincides with variable focalisation.[51] But the term itself involves a logical contradiction in terms and should rather be avoided.[52]

A way out is offered by Toolan's distinction of two types of **focalized**, i.e. object of focalisation: focalized from outside and focalized from within.[53] This would be symmetrical to the distinction between external and internal focalizers but also presupposes the Balian scheme of focalisation as "the relationship between the 'vision', the agent [focalizor/-er], and that which is seen [focalized object]."[54] But this is completely alien to Genette's thought: "To my mind, there is neither focalizing nor focalized person: *focalized* can only apply to the narrative

---

[48] Bal 1997: 146.
[49] O'Neill 1994: 96.
[50] Bal 1997: 149.
[51] Genette 1983: 49.
[52] For a concise critique see Τζούμα 1991: 109-10 n.67.
[53] Toolan 1988: 70-71.
[54] Bal 1997: 146.

itself, and *focalizer* could only apply to the person who *focalizes the narrative*, that is the narrator, if it applies to anyone at all."[55]

III.3.1 Zero Focalisation

The gods of Greek myth "do not enjoy absolute ubiquity any more than any one of them possesses omniscience or omnipotence." Jean-Pierre Vernant[56] may be right in absolute theoretical terms. Yet, as the same scholar observes in a footnote from the same essay, "Zeus's eye is always open, his vigilance is faultless. Nevertheless, when Zeus is asleep, Typhon takes advantage of the occasion to try to steal his thunderbolt. The attempt goes badly for Typhon; before he is able to lay a hand on the royal weapon, Zeus's eyes have already struck him with lightning."[57] Furthermore, according to *Il.* 2.485, words uttered by the Iliadic narrator himself and addressed to the Muses: ὑμεῖς γὰρ θεαί ἐστε, πάρεστέ τε, ἴστε τε πάντα. The Muses know everything and are present everywhere, men can only repeat hearsay.

Both Jupiter and the Muses appear as narrators in the *Met.* The former is honoured with the privilege of being the first intradiegetic narrative voice in the poem, when he reveals to the divine council Lycaon's plot against him **[1]**. Although he is himself in involved in the story as the victim who avenges himself, Jupiter's focalisation is appropriately omniscient (i.e. zero). His account is focussed on his own actions until he comes to Lycaon's reaction to his visit. Then direct speech (1.222-23) is used to present what despite the introductory *ait* looks more like Lycaon's intimate thoughts: "I shall find out, by an infallible test, whether he be god or mortal; there will be no doubt about the truth." The precise nature of the test is revealed by Jupiter in pure narrative and involves the very essence of divine existence: the absence of death. His plan is meant to be secret (*necopina. ... morte* 1.224) but fails, as nothing eludes Jupiter's omniscience, his "sharp mind" that prevented Typhoeus from usurping his power in Hesiod (*Th.*838 ὀξὺ νόησε), and

---

[55] Genette 1983: 48.
[56] Vernant 1991: 46.
[57] Vernant 1991: 46 n.29; he refers here to the version of the myth in Epimenides fr. 8; see further West on Hes.*Th.* 820-80 (p. 380).

the Trojans from being completely routed by Diomedes and Nestor in the *Iliad* (8.132 ὀξὺ νόησε).

Ovid is the only source of the murder plan. Its chronology in Jupiter's narrative is obviously inverted for rhetorical effect. As Haarberg remarked,[58] "Lycaon's plan is, one should think, (1) to serve the god the flesh of the hostage at dinner, and then (2) to kill him during the night." He also mentions Giulia Piccaluga's view that "Jupiter would simply pass away if he ate human flesh; in other words that the meal would entail the killing."[59] However, one objection that could be raised against her neat solution is that the mannered introduction of the second part of the plan with *nec contentus eo est* (1.226), which elsewhere in the poem (1.274, 2.638, 5.593, 7.738 and 13.249) is normally used of a further development. It would make more sense, then, to consider stages (1) and (2) as distinct. The first is merely another manifestation of Lycaon's cruel character and it could lead only indirectly to a revelation of Jupiter's divinity, i.e. his power to know a man's secret plans and punish sacrilege. The second, on the other hand, is the main test of his visitor's divinity.[60]

Jupiter's omniscience as a character vitiates the danger of Lycaon's assassination plan.[61] The same applies to the Muses when they were confronted with Pyreneus' plot to entrap and rape them in his lodgings, a tale one of the sisters tells Minerva in Book 5 **[9a]**. Indeed, this is one of the main reasons that the story "seems bizarre, surreal, and paranoid, without apparent rationale or motivation, unless, perhaps, she [i.e. the Muse] is striving for additional solidarity with Minerva (a virgin goddess) by demonizing the male intruder," as L. Cahoon put it from a feminist perspective.[62] Calliope's song **[11]** is also that of an omniscient narrator, indeed the omniscient narrator *par excellence*: the leading Muse shows clear and secure knowledge of the characters' thoughts and feelings (e.g. 5. 357-58, 425-26) and is able to quote their very words (5.365-79, 489-508, 514-22 and 523-32).

---

[58] Haarberg 1983: 112-13.
[59] Haarberg 1983: 113 n.6.
[60] This view is also essentially different from Halm-Tisserant 1993: 150 f., who maintains that anthropophagy could result in Jupiter's death.
[61] Anderson 1989: 96.
[62] Cahoon 1996: 49.

Orpheus **[21]** presents himself as son of the Muse (10.148) and Apollo (10.167). This genealogy obviously invests him with the authority to narrate stories which he has neither witnessed nor learned from anyone.[63] For instance he is able to present Pygmalion's behaviour towards his creation not only in its external manifestations (e.g. *admovet, dat, loquitur*) but also in its psychological depth (*putat, xredit, metuit*). However, as we have already seen, omniscience does not exclude the occasional adoption of an internal focalisation. The crime of the Cerastae, for example, is presented from a stranger's perspective (*advena* 10.236). This strategy creates a twin paradox. First, what appears to be an expression of ritual piety, a sacrifice to *Jupiter Hospes* (10.224), turns out to be a hideous violation of the laws of hospitality (10.228 *hospes erat caesus*). Second, any stranger, like the generic focalizer, may fall victim to appearances. A further advantage of this mode of presentation is that it prevents the readers' eyes from contamination by the *nefas* of a description of the crime; rather like the hypothetical stranger we see only the *corpus delicti*.

III.3.2 Internal Focalisation
A further example of variable internal focalisation being adopted by an "omniscient" human heterodiegetic narrator will provide the bridge to this new section. It comes from Alcithoe's narrative about Hermaphroditus **[7]**. After a long journey Hermaphroditus is found in Caria, where he discovers a *locus amoenus* (4.297-301), which the narrator explicitly focalizes through him: *videt hic* (297). One might think that the negative *non illic* (298) mars this illusion; but this apophatic colon may indeed express what Hermaphroditus himself expected to see on the basis of his traveller's experience and actually did not. Just as the lake defied Hermaphroditus' expectations, so the nymph defies the audience's notion of a nymph: *sed nec ... nec ... nec ... sola ... non ...* (4.302-4). Of course, all this may still be claimed to represent the hero's perceptive focalisation, although not explicitly this time. But he could not possibly know about the efforts of the other nymphs to persuade Salmacis to change her life-style (4.305-15).

---

[63] Coleman 1971: 467.

Both *scilicet ut ... inobservatus* (4.341) and *tum vero placuit* (4.346) suggest that at least the perceptual focalisation of this section is that of Salmacis staring at Hermaphroditus from behind some bushes as he undresses and dives into the lake. This use of internal focalisation may imply negative criticisms of the nymph's voyeurism, while at the same time it offers the audience, both the female narratees of the Minyeid and the mixed (?) audience of the extradiegetic narrator Ovid, an entrance into the world of sexual fantasy. Although the "gaze", a pervasive characteristic of Alcithoe's narrative,[64] is considered characteristic of the "masculine discourse of desire",[65] Stehle notes that Sappho, one of the rare female voices that survive from antiquity, often describes a woman gazing (fr. 22, 23, 31.7-10, 96 and 122 Voigt).[66]

But even a homodiegetic narrator, in other words one that tells a story in which (s)he features as an acting character or passive witness, may not be limited to the narrator's internal perspective. For the time that has passed since the events happened as well as the events' very outcome naturally add to the narrator's knowledge. Her perspective is no longer the same as when she lived or witnessed the events. Acoetes **[4]** is characteristic in this respect. His parenthetical affirmation of knowledge from hindsight in 3.630 (*Bacchus enim fuerat*) gains particular significance in the mouth of someone presented as a pious follower of Bacchus' *numen*. Piety may appear "total naiveté", since "so far, he has in no way proved that the boy is divine";[67] but it is only natural that Acoetes would assert his faith in Bacchus' divinity on every possible occasion even if this entails the imposition of his *ex eventu* focalisation on the predominant internal focalisation by himself as he was then. Also redolent of Acoetes' piety is the hypothetical comparison at 3.650-51 (*tamquam modo denique fraudem / senserit*), which prevents him from believing that a god could ignore the secret intentions of his kidnappers.

The majority of intradiegetic narrators, however, leave gaps in the narrative, avoiding the divine perspective of omniscience. For instance, Lelex **[18]** gives no reason for Jupiter's incognito visit to earth. Perhaps

---

[64] Nugent 1990: 172.
[65] Nugent 1990: 177.
[66] Stehle 1996: 219.
[67] Anderson on 3.629-31.

we ought to understand that the god has the same motive as when he did the same in Book 1, that is to verify the rumours about scandalous human behaviour. The epic world at large seems to believe in such visits: in *Odyssey* 17.485-87 one of the suitors admits that

καί τοι θεοὶ ξείνοισιν ἐοικότες ἀλλοδαποῖσι,
παντοῖοι τελέθοντες, ἐπιστροφῶσι πόληας,
ἀνθρώπων ὕβριν τε καὶ εὐνομίην ἐφορῶντες.

Alternatively the lack of motivation could reflect the limited understanding of divine activity by a human narrator. Something similar occurs when Nestor **[26]** concedes divine intervention in favour of Theseus: *Theseus ... recessit / Pallados admonitu: credi sic ipse volebat* (12.359-60). Of course, there are plenty of reasons why the advice would be ascribed to Pallas: her connection with fighting, wisdom and Athens is important in this respect as well as the Iliadic precedent of 1.194ff., where Athena advises Achilles to retreat. But this self-conscious comment also contributes to Nestor's maintaining the illusion of internal focalisation. He also pretends ignorance of the slayer's identity in the case of Cyllarus' death (*auctor in incerto est* 12.419). The precise words of his companion's lamentation elude him, too (*dictis, quae clamor ad aures / arcuit ire meas* 12.426-27). Alongside these negative indications of the perceptive and cognitive limitations of his focalisation, Nestor has added a few positive ones: twice he introduces a new item in the catalogue of deaths by inscribing himself as the focalizer of the narration: *vidi ego* (12.327) and *ante oculos stat et ille meos* (12.429).

A striking feature of Achelous' account of his fight with Hercules **[17c]** is the repeated allusion to the possibility that he might not have given a full and truthful account of the events (9.53 *certum est mihi vera fateri*, 55-56 *siqua fides neque ficta mihi nunc gloria voce / quaeritur*) or to the difficulty in knowing what really happened (9.37-38 *modo crura micantia captat, / aut captare putes*, 56 *inmposito pressus mihi monte videbar*). Lines 9.37-38, in particular, were criticized by Solodow for the "unmotivated and gratuitous" introduction of a distinction between appearance and reality, especially since "it is made by Achelous himself, who was in a position to know."[68] But as lines 9.55-56 suggest, it is precisely Achelous' personal involvement with the events that make him suspect that his

---

[68] Solodow 1988: 68

vision may have been blurred and so his version of the story may be liable to inaccuracies and self-flattering exaggerations.

The story of Dryope's metamorphosis [20] is told as it was witnessed by the narrator Iole herself. This is emphasized again and again (9.344 *namque aderam: vidi*, 359 *spectatrix aderam*). By contrast, for the story of Lotis, recounted briefly just before Dryope's transformation in lines 9.346-48 in order not only to explain action but also to retard it, Iole refers to the authority of *tardi agrestes* (9.346). Ceyx [23] also clearly inscribes himself as the focalizer of Daedalion's metamorphosis: *mihi currere visus* (11.336). As Murphy observed (*ad loc.*), the presence of the spectator makes the metamorphosis appear "natural and almost imperceptible." Nonetheless, the actual moment of metamorphosis sometimes eludes homodiegetic narrators like Glaucus [29]: *hactenus acta tibi possum memoranda referre,/ hactenus et memini; nec mens mea cetera sensit* (13.956-57 "So much can I tell you of the wonderful things that were done, so much do I remember: but of the rest my mind knew nothing") and Anius [27]: *nec qua ratione figuram / perdiderint, potui scire aut nunc dicere possum* (13.671-72 "How they lost their human shape I could not discover, nor can I tell you now"). It is only the final outcome that they are able to describe (13.960-64 and 673-74). However, the process of metamorphosis does not always entail a loss of consciousness. A rare description of the process of one's own metamorphosis is offered by Arethusa (5.632-36) and, including even its reversal, by Macareus (14.279-84 and 302-5).

Glaucus' *hactenus memini* (13.957) signals a gap in his account of the perceived sequence of events that constitute his story, an irremediable gap caused by the traumatic experience of his transformation. It is this blank space in his memory that makes the focalisation of his narrative internal, bound to his character. Arethusa's parenthetical *memini* (5.585) is a positive marker of the same idea: that memory is the necessary condition for narratives that have a claim to truth. Her affirmation is almost certainly to be heard with a sigh, signalling "an attempt to recover by recollection a past which is lost forever, irretrievably gone," as Jacobson remarks on another description of a setting with a "dreamlike pastoral quality," representing another eutopia destroyed by the harsh reality of *amor*.[69] The intense fear she felt that day may have affected her perception of her running away from Alpheus (5.615 *nisi si timor illa videbat*) but has not incapacitated her memory.

If it is true that, as Sappho put it in *Ep*.15, *meminerunt omnia amantes* (lovers remember everything), it is also true that *memoria minuitur* with old age (CIC.*Sen*.55). Nestor **[26]**, a particularly self-conscious narrator,[70] testifies to this in the introduction to his long-winded story about Caeneus, the impenetrable superman(12.182-84): *quamvis obstet mihi tarda vetustas / multaque me fugiant primis spectata sub annis,/ plura tamen memini, nec quae magis haereat, ulla / pectore res nostro est inter bellique domique.* ("Though the long years, slowly passing, hamper my memory, and many things I saw in my early days escape me now, yet I remember more than I have forgotten.").

Memory not only wanes naturally with age; its content is also determined by the narrator's will to remember. Forgetfulness is sometimes more beneficial than eternal remembrance. This is the point that Nestor tries to make in his reply to Tlepolemus' complaint for the omission of his famous father's deeds in the battle with the Centaurs: "Why do you force me to remember unhappy things? To tear open wounds that time has healed, and speak of my hatred for your father, and of the wrongs he did me?"

The principle of selection is all the more important when one tries to start a narrative, to name the move that signalled the onset of a battle, to name the warrior that dared to strike first. Even when "it is easy to mark the beginning," as the self-conscious narrator of Ian McEwan's *Enduring Love* thinks, we soon realize that we "could suggest a few other moments," as the same narrator observes in the next chapter.[71] For "when we talk about the beginning, we refer to an artificial term and what makes one..."[72] It is within this theoretical frame that we should approach Nestor's apparently contradictory statements about the

---

[69] Jacobson 1974: 187.
[70] Twice in the first section on Caenis' sex-change he emphasizes that he is merely reporting hearsay (12.197 *ita fama ferebat*, 200 *eadem hoc quoque fama ferebat*), unlike the next section on Lapithocentauromachy, which he relates as an eye-witness.
[71] McEwan 1997: 1.
[72] McEwan 1997: 17.

beginning of the battle: *prima pocula pugna/ missa volant fragilesque cadi curvique lebetes* ("As the battle began, goblets were hurled and went flying through the air, along with fragile jugs and curved basins" 12.242-43) and *Primus Ophionides Amycus penetralia donis/ haud timuit spoliare suis et primus ab aede/ lampadibus densum rapuit funale coruscis* (12.245-47 "Amycus, son of Ophion, was the first who dared to rob the inner shrine of its offerings: he gave the lead by snatching from the sanctuary a branched candlestick, thickly hung with flaring lamps"). As J. Latacz suggested about the typical πρῶτος in Homeric battle-narrative, *primus Ophionides Amycus* does not necessarily signal the onset of the 'real' battle (as distinct from the beginning of the battle-narrative) but the start of the detailed narrative, the moment that Nestor's mind has marked as pregnant with what was going to happen. *Prima ... pugna*, on the other hand, belongs to the description of a mass-attack that frequently precedes detailed battle-narratives.[73]

Even though it is the warrior society of the λαός that "sets the ethical standards of our *Iliad* in terms of the bonds that unite the **phíloi** 'friends', who are the members of the **laós**,"[74] the masses certainly belong to the fringes of the epic world. Perhaps reacting to this reality, Vergil made Achaemenides present the adventure in Polyphemus' cave focalized internally through Ulysses' companions as a group. Except for an initial reference to Ulixes as the person who conceived the plan of escape from Polyphemus' cave, Achaemenides presentes the action as a collective achievement: *nos ... precati ... fundimur ... terebramus ... ulciscimur* (VERG.*Aen*.3.633, 635, 638). Ovid has not copied the Vergilian model in this respect in Achaemenides' metanarrative **[31]**. The same intertextual movement from collective to single-character internal focalisation is observed in the case of Virbius' narrative: while Euripides' messenger emphasized the efforts of the attendants (to whom he also belonged) to keep up with the maddened steeds "since Ovid's Hippolytus is his own messenger, as it were," the emphasis is clearly and appropriately put on the narrator's personal efforts to avert

---

[73] Latacz 1977: 83. Cf. the entrance of the *turba* (5.2) that precedes the detailed narrative that opens with *primus* ... Phineus (5.8) in the other major battle-narrative in the *Met.*
[74] Nagy 1979: 83.

catastrophe.[75] Internal focalisation through a group rather than an individual resurfaces partly in the narrative of Circe's maid **[33]**. Ovid makes her relate not only the events concerning the *dux* (14.321 *rex*) but also what happened to the *comites* (14.397ff.).

An important and clear indicator of focalisation is the use of deixis. It has been argued by Solodow, for instance, that Ovid violates the illusion of internal narration/focalisation in Orpheus' narrative about Myrrha on the grounds that *nostro orbi* (10.305) and *huic terrae* (10.306) can only refer to Italy.[76] But, as Solodow himself admits, the triple signifier for Thrace (10. 305-6 *gentibus Ismariis et nostro gratulor orbi, / gratulor huic terrae*) is "an abundance that Ovid is certainly capable of." Furthermore, sexual promiscuity is one thing and perversion of nature is another; it is therefore irrelevant that Thrace "was notorious for its libidinousness, not its sexual restraint." Finally, the echo of VERG.G.2.139, part of Vergil's famous praise of Italy, does not constitute sufficient evidence on its own that Ovid's words also refer to Italy not Thrace.

III.4 Voice Usurpation

The debate over the precise reference of Orpheus' topography opens our eyes to the possibility that there may be occasional lapses in the focalisation of the intradiegetic narrators. Indeed there are a few such instances, all involving similes. Nobody would be surprised by cultural anachronisms in similes used by the extradiegetic narrator. For this figure is the locus *par excellence* where the narrator's present is made manifest, in order to illuminate from a different, perhaps more familiar angle visual, auditory or psychological aspects of the events narrated. However, the simile of the burst water-pipe that describes the issue of blood from Pyramus' wound (4.122-24) is a striking cultural anachronism because it is put in the mouth of a woman from mythical Boeotia. The simile of the Scythian arrow (10.558) used by Venus to illustrate Atalanta's speed is explicitly focalized by Hippomenes (10.589 *Aonio visa est iuveni*). In other words, it appears to illustrate an event as it

---

[75] Segal 1984: 316 (Euripides) and 320 (Ovid).
[76] Solodow 1988: 40, following Haupt-Ehwald and Fränkel.

was experienced by one of the characters (de Jong's *assimilated simile*).[77] Yet, there does not seem any particular reason why a young man from Boeotia should think of the girl's speed in terms of Scythian archery. By contrast, Ovid's Roman audience (the primary narratee), as Anderson suggests, would probably be reminded of the fearsome Parthian archery. But it is the simile of the scarlet awning drawn over gleaming marble halls that glaringly betrays the focalisation of the extradiegetic narrator, as nothing comparable existed in the mythical times of Venus and Adonis; this blatant anachronism was already noticed by Peters.[78]

This phenomenon, labelled by Félix Martínez-Bonati "usurpation of voice", is not uncommon in Cervantes's works. "In the discourse of a character, concepts and points of view emerge that are foreign to the character, thus rupturing the consistency and verisimilitude of the figure and its speech. (...) The voices of Don Quixote and Sancho are often possessed by the lucidity of the narrator, whose thought and style creep into the characters' autonomy. Cervantes occasionally indicates the intentionality of these games of mental transfusion, as when Don Quixote observes to Sancho that one of his utterances does not properly belong to him. 'That question and answer are not your own, Sancho: you have taken them from somebody else.' And to Sancho's reply he insists, 'You have said more, Sancho, than you possibly know' (II.22). What makes our heads spin here is that, at the same time that Don Quixote is indicating that Sancho's voice has been taken over by an alien spirit, it is the critical-humoristic spirit of the author-reader that is speaking through Don Quixote's own voice. This doubling underlines the inverisimilitude of these deliberate transgressions." [79]

---

[77] De Jong 1987: 126ff.
[78] Peters 1908: 79.
[79] Martínez-Bonati 1992: 89-90. *Don Quixote* is among "the most important polyphonic novels", all of which "are inheritors of the Menippean, carnivalesque structure" that pervades even Ovid's *Metamorphoses*, according to Kristeva 1980: ch.3, esp. 79 and 82 [first published in her Σημειωτική, Paris 1969, pp. 143-73]. For further examples of anachronism in the *Met.* see Solodow 1980: 75-89.

III.5 Conclusions

This chapter has explored the two modalities that pervade the organisation of the events that constitute a story and their presentation in the narrative text: distance and perspective (or focalisation). The only parameter of the former that does not overlap with other narratological categories of analysis is speech representation. By definition, metadiegetic narrative involves direct discourse, whether written or oral. Our study of distance was, therefore, limited to the representation of speech within the metanarratives.

Although narratized discourse is not at all rare, there are hardly any instances in which we are not given the slightest indication of the content of the speech act. Even when the verb is not supplemented with an object of the vaguest sort, it may convey a certain attitude or the illocutionary force of the speech-act by itself. A step in the direction of the mimetic pole of discourse representation is the inclusion of an indirect allusion to the content of the speech act performed by one of the characters and incorporated in the narrator's discourse. Our analysis of the relevant data has shown that there are no certain types of speech acts that do not deserve full reproduction in the discourse, whether reported or transposed. What determines the mode of representation is the narrative economy of the particular metanarrative.

Pure indirect speech appears only thirteen times, one tenth of the times that direct speech is employed. Indirect speech seems to be preferred when the utterances are important only as action, i.e. for their illocutionary force, not as words, or when the content of the narrative does not conform with the implied author's overall plan for the poem.

The average metadiegetic narrative contains only a few lines of quoted speech with the momentary shift of focalisation that this gesture involves. Yet, if one includes the third and fourth level narratives embedded in the longest second-level ones (the Muse's narrative **[9b]** and Orpheus' song **[21]** but also the anonymous' narrator's report of the Lycian guide's sacred tale **[13]**), the total lines of direct speech in metanarrative rises to 28 percent of metanarrative text. This is a considerably lower figure than that of primary-narrator text occupied by *oratio recta* but not out of proportion with the amount of direct discourse in third-level narrative (32%) The one-line speech is an obvious Ovidian mannerism. Yet this tendency for brief utterances does not rule out longer speeches. In particular, directly reported speech is commonly used to punctuate combat narrative. Thoughts and feelings may be reported as if they were actually articulated, even in *oratio recta*. Ovidian metanarrative is not particularly rich in conversationally organised speeches with the exception of Acoetes' narrative **[4]** and the story of Myrrha **[21f]**. The dramatic hypotext or generic framework of these tales may account for the infiltration of dialogue into epic.

Ovid's use of direct discourse in metanarrative is quite sophisticated. Pseudo-direct discourse is used twice by the Minyeids **[5-7]** in iterative contexts in terms of narrative frequency. The use of this "curious expedient to summarize several speeches," creates an echo-effect. The intertextual echo in the Muse's **[9b]** account of the Pierids' challenge to the Muses of Helicon (5.308f.) also adds an extra layer of significance to the use of direct discourse. The same is achieved through its limited use, e.g. its reservation for a single speaker in a certain narrative.

The omniscient perspective is by and large reserved for divine narrators, like Jupiter **[1]** and the Muses **[9, 10]** or artistic narrators, like Orpheus **[21]**. Yet even a common homodiegetic narrator, in other words one who tells a story in which (s)he features as an acting character or passive witness, may not be limited to the narrator's internal perspective. For not only the time that has passed since the events happened but also the events' very outcome naturally add to the narrator's knowledge. The majority of intradiegetic narrators, however, leave gaps in the narrative, avoiding the divine perspective of omniscience. These gaps are caused by both the limitations of human perception and the games that memory plays with stories. Human memory wanes naturally with age, creating problems for elderly narrators like Nestor **[26]**. Forgetfulness is sometimes judged more beneficial by the narrator him/herself. Collective internal focalisation is partly used in the narrative of Circe's maid **[33]**. Finally there are a few instances of "usurpation of voice", all involving similes focalized by the extradiegetic narrator.

IV Voice

IV.1 Voice: A Complex Category

Genette's narratology is ultimately a narratology of voice.[1] Voice is the secure foundation that assures the coherence of narrative geometry itself. Questions of voice must be distinguished from questions of focalisation, but both can and must be combined for a proper description of the narrative situation.[2] Besides, voice is not merely about answering the question "who speaks?" as Gibson implies in his critique of Genette's apparent phonocentrism, as it were.[3] Voice includes all traces of the circumstances of narration which have been left in the narrative discourse, i.e. the narrative text which it is supposed to have produced: both narrator(s) and narratee(s) as well as the spatio-temporal parameters of narration and the relation of the narrative situation under consideration with the other ones which comprise the overall narrative.[4]

The categories that Genette uses for the analysis of voice are the following:

1) **Time of narrating**, i.e. the temporal position of the narrative instance relative to the story told on that occasion.

2) **Narrative level**, i.e. the level at which a narrative act is situated with regard to what is assumed to be the primary diegesis.

3) **Person**, i.e. the form of the narrator's presence in the narrative. Genette does not discuss explicitly and extensively his choice of the term 'voice' as comprehensive metaphor for the analysis of the narrating instance, and not merely the narrator, as Ulf Olsson mistakenly writes.[5] Yet, in his introduction to the *essai de méthode* he explained that the terms *temps* (time/tense), *mode* and *voix* (voice) were borrowed from the grammar of the verb, conceding that their narratological sense was not strictly homologous to grammatical usage.[6]

---

[1] Gibson 1996: 144.
[2] Genette 1972: 205 and 1983: 77-89; cf. also Bal 1997: 19 "This is, emphatically, not to say that the narrator should not be analysed in relation to the focalizing agent."
[3] Gibson 1996: 145.
[4] Genette 1972: 227.
[5] Olsson 1996: 84.
[6] Genette 1972: 76.

Admittedly, voice is the category whose narratological meaning is farthest removed from its use in traditional grammatical descriptions of the verb. Reductive descriptions of the former like that used by Gibson (i.e. "who speaks?") in combination with everyday usage of the word, in the sense of the physical ability to produce speech sounds or even of someone's opinion on a particular topic, has further complicated the issue. Thus even narratologists like Richard Aczel have found problematic the application of the term to (silent) written texts despite "its more technical delimitation as a textual function or effect."[7] For someone of postmodern convictions like Gibson, this is yet another manifestation of the privileged status of voice (as opposed to writing) in western metaphysics, a thesis emphatically put forward by Jacques Derrida.[8] His conclusion is naturally that "we do not actually encounter a narrative voice in narrative. We encounter an equivalent of voice that we have created for ourselves as a simulacrum and insisted on identifying with voice."[9]

IV.2 Can The Written Text Speak?

In the case of ancient literature the relation between oral voice and written text is further complicated by the fact that the reception of texts remained largely aural even in Ovid's time.[10] As our author predicts in the poem's concluding lines: *quaque patet domitis Romana potentia terris,/ ore legar populi* (15.877-78 "And wherever Roman power extends over conquered lands, I will be read by the lips of people"). Nowhere in the poem does Ovid represent himself as a writer or his poem as a written text. Only here "does he allude to the fact that he will be read in the future, implying the transformation of his song into text."[11] On the contrary, as Wheeler has emphatically remarked, the extradiegetic

---

[7] Aczel 1998: 467.
[8] Derrida 1976 and 1981. For a balanced presentation of Derrida's argumentation see Τερζάκης 2000: ch.6. Gibson 1996 indeed cites Derrida in p.145.
[9] Gibson 1996: 146.
[10] On the practice of *recitatio* see e.g. Salles 1992: ch.V; more generally see Valette-Cagnac 1997.
[11] Wheeler 1999: 65. Callimachus also dropped his overall phonocentrism when referring to the preservation of his work *qua* material book (fr.7.13-14); see Lowrie 1997: 60 and Fowler 1994: 251 who sees it as an instance of "romantic irony".

narrator of the poem presents the narrating instance as though it were an oral performance.[12]

In this sense, Ovid follows the example of Vergil and Horace in representing himself as a *vates*.[13] The persona of the epic's proem (1.1-4) and *sphragis* (15.871-79) is definitely vatic: *si quid habent veri vatum praesagia* (15.879 "If there is any truth in vatic prophecies"). The authority of the poet is complemented by that of the gods: *di coeptis* (...) / *adspirate meis* (1.2-3 "gods ... look favourably on my attempts"). Towards the end of the poem he invokes the Muses in particular: *Pandite nunc, Musae, praesentia numina vatum –scitis enim, nec vos fallit spatiosa vetustas–* (15.622-23 "O Muses, ever present to assist a poet, now unfold –for you know the story, nor can long intervening years distort your memory"). Alessandro Barchiesi has repeatedly pointed out that the Muses are strangely invoked as witnesses of unfailing memory whenever the subject-matter is officially documented recent history: the temple of Aesculapius was founded on the first of January, 293 B.C. and was dedicated in 291.[14] The concept of the poet-seer had been developed by the previous generation of Augustan poets (Vergil and Horace) as an encapsulation of their experiment of putting "Alexandrian technique in the service of national, civic poetry."[15] It has been argued that Ovid did not really understand this ideologically charged usage of *vates*.[16] It is perhaps more accurate to say that the Ovidian narrator of the *Met.* is consciously playing with this concept –"it may be exaggerated to speak of an actual doctrine (after all, the use of *vates* remains very limited)."[17]

---

[12] Wheeler 1999: 40.
[13] On Horace's adoption of phonocentrism as a way of inscribing his *Odes* into the performance tradition of the Greek *lyrici vates* (*C.*1.1.35) and of aligning his poetic production with the valorisation of the present, lived moment throughout his oeuvre, see Lowrie 1997: 57.
[14] Barchiesi 1997a: 187-91. His views on the matter appeared earlier in Barchiesi 1991: 5-6 and Barchiesi 1997b: 138.
[15] Newman 1967: 12. For a revisionist view see O'Hara 1990: ch.5 insists on the ambiguity of the term and argues that the Augustan poets, and Vergil in particular, exploited the old associations of the *vates* with deception and illusion. Perkins 2000 argues for an ironic use of the term in Ovid's *Amores* in an analysis based on Newman's theory.
[16] Newman 1967: 112.
[17] The quotation is from Knecht 1968. See also Ahern 1990, Casa 1995, and Jocelyn 1995.

IV.3 *Vox* vs. *Littera*

The world of mythological epic is largely ignorant of writing as a form of communication. The only definite reference to it in Homer is *Il.*6.168-9, the σήματα λυγρά inscribed on the folded tables given to Bellerophon by Proitos in Argos.[18] On the whole, the intradiegetic narrators of the *Met.* are represented as oral performers. Yet, writing is not completely absent. The metamorphosed Io ingeniously identifies herself to her father by pawing on earth the two letters of her name: *littera pro verbis, quam pes in pulvere duxit,/ corporis indicium mutati triste peregit* (1.649-50 "Instead of words, she traced letters in the dust with her foot, and thus conveyed the sad news of her changed body"). Later in the poem and its universal chronology, Philomela also resorts to writing when deprived of speech: *purpereasque* **notas** *filis intexuit albis,/ indicium sceleris* (6.577-78 "and she wove purple letters on white threads as evidence of the crime").[19] Book 9 contains the tale of Byblis, which in terms of absolute chronology is analeptic. The time of its action is fixed by means of a reference to Minos, whom we have seen active already in Book 7. Silenced by shame at the incestuous passion for her brother, Byblis writes him a love-letter: *si pudor ora tenebit,/* **littera** *celatos arcana fatebitur ignes* (9.515-16 "if modesty keeps my lips shut, a secret letter will reveal my hidden love").[20] Another lover who commits his feelings to tablets is Iphis, the hero of Vertumnus' tale of spurned love included in his admonition to Pomona **[35]**: *saepe ferenda dedit blandis sua verba tabellis* (14.707 "often he gave [Anaxarete's attendants] letters with flattering words to carry [to their mistress]").

---

[18] For 'writing' in the *Odyssey* see Saussy 1996.
[19] Steiner 1994: 37 comments on the ambiguity of the term *nota*, which serves as a synonym of *signum* ("sign") but also refers to the written letters of the alphabet (CIC. *Tusc.*1.25.62 and Hor.*c.*4.8.13) and the cryptic symbols used to keep the message's content secret (SVET.*Caes.*56).
[20] Paratore 1970: 308-9 suggested that the episode of Byblis as a whole is a summary representation of the world of the *Heroides* and their major motifs. 'Canace to Macareus' (*Ep.*11) is the most closely comparable, inasmuch as it also concerns incest between brother and sister. In terms of time-perspective Byblis' *epistula* is similar to another of the *Heroides*, Phaedra (*Ep.*4), who also writes before the critical moment, i.e. when she finds herself betrayed. Jacobson 1974: 146 offers interesting hypotheses on this crucial difference of Phaedra from most of the *Heroides*.

Besides letters the poem records three *carmina* inscribed on stone:[21] (i) the epitaph set up by the nymphs of Hesperia for Phaethon (2.327-28); (ii) the dedication of gifts to Isis by another Iphis (9.794); and (iii) the epitaph of Aeneas' nurse Caieta (14.443-44). To this we may add the botanical inscription of the woeful letters AI AI on the hyacinth's petals: *ipse suos gemitus foliis inscribit et AI AI / flos habet inscriptum,* **funestaque littera** *ducta est* (10.215-16 "he himself inscribed his own grief upon the petals, and the hyacinth bears the mournful letters AI AI marked upon it").[22] Last but not least, indeed the ultimate example of writing in the *Metamorphoses*, as Wheeler has called it, is the monumental record of fate.[23] In the final episode of the poem, echoing a scene in the first book of the *Aeneid* (1.257-96), Jupiter reassures Venus, referring to the dictates of fate which are kept in the archive of universal records (15.810 *rerum tabularia*): *invenies illic incisa adamante perenni / fata tui generis* (15.813-14 "you will find there the fate of your descendant engraved in everlasting adamant").

The closest we get to the extradiegetic narrator's ambiguous position between oral performance and written text is the figure of Apollo in Orpheus' tale about the god's ill-starred love for Hyacinthus. Janan, to whom we owe a very perceptive reading of the tale, observes that "Apollo composes and oral *and* a written text by inscribing his mourning cries on the hyacinth's petals." [24]

IV.4 Time Of Narrating

All 37 metanarratives in the *Met.* involve subsequent narration. See further chapter 2 and Table 3 in section 7 below.

---

[21] Philomela's embroidered letter is also described as *carmen miserabile* ("sorrowful song" 6.582).
[22] For an illuminating reading of this flower-text with postmodernist emphasis on its nature of absent-presence see Janan 1988: 121-23.
[23] Wheeler 1999: 55; to this book I owe the whole collection of evidence for writing in the *Met.*
[24] Janan 1988: 121.

IV.5 Narrative Level

Every narrative has an extradiegetic narrator who produces it; any character within this primary narrative who also produces a narrative is an intradiegetic narrator. The boundaries of metadiegesis are almost always clearly defined by means of attributive discourse. These phrases which accompany direct discourse in general, attributing it to a particular character, may seem insignificant. But given that they belong to a wider system of signification (narrative), they must be significant themselves. This is argued with numerous examples from modern novels by Prince 1978.[25]

In the *Iliad* the predominant mode of the speaker's denotation is his/her name or patronymic, often accompanied by an epithet. Irene de Jong convincingly explained this norm as a consequence of the formulaic character of Homeric attributive discourse in combination with the highly formulaic nature of phrases made up of a proper name and an epithet.[26] Ovid is not writing within an oral-formulaic tradition. Character-narrators in the *Met.* are frequently referred to by name: *Iuppiter, cornix, Leuconoe, Alcithoe, Musa, Arethusa, Aeacus, Lelex, Alcmene, Iole, Anius, Galatea, Sibylla, Achaemenides, Macareus* (40.5% of the narrators). Yet, their names are only mentioned once, either at the beginning (*Iuppiter, cornix, Leuconoe, Alcithoe, Aeacus, Lelex, Alcmene, Anius, Achaemenides* or 60% of the instances) or at the end (*Musa, Arethusa, Iole, Galatea, Sibylla, Macareus* or 40%). An alternative way of identifying the narrator is by means of a periphrasis. This can refer either to the character's parentage (*Daneius heros* of Perseus, *Lucifero genitus* of Ceyx, and *Theseius heros* of Hippolytos) or the place with which (s)he is associated (*Calydonius amnis* of Achelous, *Threicius vates* of Orpheus). Only twice a Greek (or Greek-style) patronymic is used: *Oenides* of Diomedes, and *Neleius* of Nestor, who is also identified with the Greek toponymic *Pylius*.

Sometimes an intradiegetic narrator is identified indirectly: *deus* (Mercury), *hospes* (Perseus), *una sororum* (a Muse), *dea* (a Muse), *e nobis maxima* (Calliope), *heros* (Cephalus), *amnis* (Achelous –twice), *nurus* (Iole), *agrestis* (Onetor), *senior* (Nestor), *nereis* (Galatea), *vates* (the Sibyl), *formas*

---

[25] Prince 1978: 305.
[26] De Jong 1987: 197.

deus aptus in omnes (Vertumnus). De Jong has shown that in the *Iliad* such indirect references are almost without exception significant: they stress the capacity in which the speaker is speaking.[27] In the *Met.* a similar tendency is observed, though perhaps not so obviously or intensely as in the *Iliad*. For example, Perseus tells the story of his adventure as part of the hospitality ritual, which lends significance to his description as *hospes*. *E nobis maxima* not only reaffirms the Muses' respect for hierarchy but also implies that her song was bound to win the competition. Immediately after his introduction as *senior*, Nestor will make a reference to his advanced age and its detrimental effect on his memory.

Perhaps most interesting is the Sibyl's designation as *vates*. Her narrative is not proleptic, i.e. prophetic, and the term's use could be interpreted as the extradiegetic narrator's confirmation of what the Sibyl is about to say regarding her status. Besides, she is not the only person in the poem to be called *vates*. Teiresias (3.348, 511, 527), the Theban Sphinx (7.761), Amphiaraus (9.407), Orpheus (10.12, 82, 89, 143; 11.2, 8, 19, 27, 38, 68), Helenus (13.720) and Telemus (13.774) are also described as seers/poets. What makes the Sibyl special is the similarity of the end she predicts for herself with that tentatively prophesied by Ovid for himself at the poem's sphragis, in which he indirectly includes himself in the class of *vates* (15.879). Both will continue to exist after death as mere voices. "The fates will leave me my voice, and by my voice I shall be known," (14.153 *voce tamen noscar, vocem mihi fata relinquent*) claims the Sibyl, while Ovid in the passage quoted above affirms that he will be on the lips of everyone who can read Latin and has a copy of his work. The similarity of the two 'voices' becomes all the more striking if we bear in mind that in Ovid's time the Sibyl's voice was also lent by her readers. The Sibylline Oracles were written and kept by the *quindecemviri*, who would consult the books and make recommendations accordingly when their advice was asked.[28]

Four times the pronoun *ille* replaces the name of the intradiegetic narrator: 3.582 (Acoetes), 10.708 (Venus), 11.290 (Ceyx), 11.352 (Onetor). Much more frequently the verb introducing the metanarrative lacks grammatical subject (23 times or 31.5% of the instances listed in

---

[27] De Jong 1987: 198.
[28] Liebeschuetz 1979: 7.

the Table). This ellipsis occurs slightly more frequently in the concluding than in the introductory phrase (13: 10 times). Normally one of the two phrases includes a reference either direct or indirect to the character's identity. There are only three exceptions: the anonymous Pierid **[10]**, Glaucus **[29]**, and Circe's anonymous handmaid **[33]**.

In the *Iliad* the extradiegetic narrator sometimes prefaces the actual introductory formula with a description of the speaker. With the exception of Thersites, these descriptions draw attention to two important aspects of rhetorical ability: eloquence and good sense. In other words, they serve to recommend the speaker to the extradiegetic narratee.[29] In the *Metamorphoses* there are no such descriptions. The intradiegetic narrators are either very well known mythological characters (e.g. gods) or are presented through action (e.g. the Crow, the Minyeides, the Pierides). Even in the introductory phrases themselves information about the speaker's character are extremely rare: the Crow **[3]** is loquacious, Lelex **[18]** mature in mind and in years, and the anonymous Crotonian **[36]** who tells the story of the city's foundation is presented as well-versed in history. At least in the latter two cases, de Jong's observation that the extradiegetic narrator's introduction aims at authenticating the intradiegetic narrator's story seems to be valid.

The narratee (see further Chapter Seven) is rarely mentioned in attributive discourse (9% of the instances): *Cephenum medio* ... / *agmine* **[8]**, *deae* **[9b]**, *quam* **[20]**, *silvas animosque ferarum* / ... *et saxa* **[21]**, *quibus* **[23]**, *Crataeide natam* **[28]**, *mihi* **[33]**. To these we should add two descriptions of the narrative situation where narrator(s) and narratee(s) are mentioned as a group. Aeacus' narrative **[15]** is concluded with a phrase summarizing the narrative activities during the first day of the Athenian embassy's visit at his court in Aegina: "They whiled away the long day with this and other such tales." A similar phrase follows Anius' narrative **[27]**: "With these and other tales besides, the company whiled away the time as they feasted." In both cases the narrative situation involves an exchange of tales, only one of which we are allowed to hear/read.

---

[29] De Jong 1987: 199, who does not distinguish between narrative and non-narrative speeches.

By contrast, the verb of speaking is naturally a vital component of attributive discourse. A simple verb is usually sufficient, especially when the scene of the narrative event has already been drawn in some detail. *Inquit* (x5), *referre, dicenti, orsa* (x3), *dixerat* (x3), *dixit* (x6), *dictis, ait* (x7), *commemorat, adfata est* (x2), *loquebatur, narravit, rettulit* (x3), *locutus, fatur* (x2), *memorabat, adloquitur, coepit, incipit, refert* (x2), *monuit, profatur, narrat, referente, resecuta est, loqui, dicentem, memorante, narrata, edidit* (x2) are used to describe the narrator's locutionary act.[30] Nonetheless, even the verb of speaking can be omitted both in the introductory and the capping phrase: *tum senior* **[26a]**, *tristis ad haec Pylius* **[26b]**, and *hac Arethusa tenus* **[12]**, *hactenus Oenides* **[34]** respectively. It can also be replaced by a verb denoting falling silent: *desierat* **[5, 18]**, *tacuit* **[17ab]**, *finierat* **[32]**. On special occasions, a weightier periphrasis is used: Jupiter shatters the silence with his speech **[1]**, the Pierid moved her singing mouth **[10]**, Calliope matched her song to the chords struck **[11]**, while Orpheus used his voice to sing **[21]**.

Besides identifying the narrator, the narratee and denoting the verbal act, attributive discourse sometimes contains additional information. De Jong has perceptively distinguished between information that is available to the characters and information which reaches only the extradiegetic narratee.[31] The use of musical accompaniment, indicated in the periphrases mentioned in the previous paragraph, obviously belongs to the former class. Calliope and Orpheus strike a few chords to find the right intonation. Hair is also involved in a self-conscious gesture of narrative beginning, which attracts the audience's and the narrator's attention. Calliope **[11]** binds her hair with ivy (5.338), Arethusa **[12]** dries it with her hands (5.575), of course, while Achelous **[17]** garlands his unkempt hair with reeds (9.3), before explaining how he lost his one horn. The postures adopted by the narrators may also be indicated: Achelous raised himself on his elbow, a movement fitting the context of a symposium **[17cd]**.

Last but not least, the extradiegetic narrator gives us palpable indications of the character-narrators' emotional involvement in their

---

[30] The term derives from the so-called *speech act theory*, introduced by Austin 1962; see Levinson 1983: 226-83. For further bibliography see Simpson 1993: 157 n.1.
[31] De Jong 1987: 204.

stories: Aeacus **[15]** groaned and there was sadness in his voice, as he began to tell Cephalus about the plague that befell his island some time ago; Cephalus' **[16]** eyes are flooded with tears when he reluctantly reveals the sorrows his extraordinary spear has brought him; Alcmene **[19**; cf. also *dolentem* in the introductory phrase to **20]** is moved to deep sighs by her own story about the fate of a handmaid that saved her (and Hercules') life when she could not be released from birth pangs; and the Sibyl **[30]** prefaces the story about her foolish youth with deep sighs. Sadness is not the only shade of tone indicated in attributive discourse: Acoetes **[4]** responds to Pentheus' inquiry without fear, while Nestor's speech to Tlepolemus **[26b]** is delivered with a sorrowful yet sweet voice.

By contrast, the extradiegetic narrator ('Ovid') does not give information of the second category identified by de Jong, i.e. information only available to the extradiegetic narratee/reader, such as indications as to how the latter is to understand the metanarrative or how to evaluate it. Only a second-degree narrator, the anonymous Muse who relates to Minerva the story of the Pierids' punishment **[11]** recommends her sister's song as "learned"; she "prejudice[s] the case, to prepare for the verdict of the nymph-judges."[32] Apparently, the extradiegetic narrator would agree with the characterization, since he has earlier attributed the same epithet to all nine sisters (5.255). It is also used in the last book of the poem to describe Pythagoras' precepts (15.74).[33]

What is frequently mentioned at the beginning of a long, formal narrative is silence. Paradoxically, silence is required for the narrative performance as a sign of the audience's focused attention, but is marred by the narrative event. Alcithoe **[7]** does not embark on her arcane tale of Salmacis and Hermaphroditus until her sisters have fallen silent: *poscitur Alcithoe, postquam siluere sorores* (4.274 "When the sisters were quiet, Alcithoe was asked for the next tale"). Leuconoe **[6]** imposed silence

---

[32] Anderson on 5.662-64.
[33] Cf. Hutchinson 1988: 282: *Doctus*, one may note, does not really mean "learned" as a term of praise, more "skilled": it is not limited to Hellenistic poets or poets who could be thought in any sense erudite. *Contra* Anderson on 5.253-55: as exemplary singers, the Muses have the ideal asset of contemporary Roman poets: they are erudite in the Alexandrian tradition.

with the beginning of her narration: *et orsa est / dicere Leuconoe; vocem tenuere sorores* (4.168 "Leuconoe began to speak; her sisters kept quiet"). Jupiter **[1]** shatters the silence he has himself imposed on the assembled Gods with words and gestures (1.205 *voce manuque*).

Table 1: Attributive Discourse

No.	Lines	Attributive Discourse
1	1.208	*Iuppiter hoc iterum sermone silentia rupit*
2	1.689	*Tum deus ... inquit*
2	1.700	*restabat verba referre*
3	2.548-50	*cornix / auditaque viae causa ... / inquit*
3	2.596	*Talia dicenti ...*
4	3.582	*ille metu vacuus ... dixit*
5	4.54	*talibus orsa modis lana sua fila sequente*
5	4.167	*Desierat*
6	4.167-8	*et orsa est / dicere Leuconoe*
6	4.271	*Dixerat*
7	4.274-6	*poscitur Alcithoe .../ quae radio stantis percurrens stamina telae/ ... dixit ...*
7	4.389	*Finis erat dictis*
8	4.793	*hospes ait*
8	5.1-2	*Dumque ea Cephenum medio Danaeius heros / agmine commemorat*
9a	5.268	*quam sic adfata est una sororum*
9a	5.294	*Musa loquebatur*
9b	5.300	*miranti sic orsa deae dea*
9b	5.337	*Musa refert*
10	5.327	*dixit*
10	5.332	*hactenus ad citharam vocalia moverat ora*
11	5.340	*atque haec percussis subiungit carmina nervis*
11	5.662	*Finierat doctos e nobis maxima cantus*
12	5.576	*fluminis Elei veteres narravit amores*
12	5.642	*Hac Arethusa tenus*
13	6.316-7	*a facto propiore priora renarrant./ e quibus unus ait*
13	6.382-3	*sic ubi nescio quis Lycia de gente virorum / rettulit exitium*
14	6.330	*talia rettulit hospes*
15	7.517	*Aeacus ingemuit tristique ita voce locutus*

15	7.661-2	*Talibus atque aliis longum sermonibus illi / implevere diem*
16	7.688-9	*tactusque dolore / coniugis amissae lacrimis ita fatur obortis*[34]
16	7.863	*haec lacrimans heros memorabat*
17ab	8.577	*amnis ad haec ... inquit*
17ab	8.611	*Amnis ab his tacuit*
18	8.617-8	*ante omnes Lelex animo maturus et aevo / sic ait*
18	8.725	*Desierat*
17cd	8.727-8	*innixus cubito Calydonius amnis / talibus adloquitur*
17e	9.3-4	*sic Calydonius amnis / coepit inornatos redimitus harundine crines*
17e	9.89	*dixerat*
19	9.280-1	*sic / incipit Alcmene*
19	9.324-5	*Dixit et admonitu veteris commota ministrae / ingemuit*
20	9.325	*quam sic nurus est adfata dolentem*
20	9.394	*Dumque refert Iole factum mirabile*
21	10.147	*hoc vocem carmine movit*
21	11.1-2	*Carmine dum tali silvas animosque ferarum / Threicius vates et saxa sequentia ducit*
22	10.559	*sic ait ac mediis interserit oscula verbis*
22	10.708	*illa quidem monuit*
23	11.290	*quibus ille profatur*
23	11.346-7	*Quae dum Lucifero genitus miracula narrat / de consorte suo*
24	11.352	*ille refert*
24	11.379	*dixerat agrestis*
25	11.751	*proximus, aut idem, si fors tulit ... dixit*
26a	12.182	*Tum senior*
26a	12.536-7	*Haec inter Lapithas et semihomines Centauros / proelia ... Pylio referente*
26b	12.542	*tristis ad haec Pylius*
26b	12.577	*Haec postquam dulci Neleius edidit ore*
27	13.643-4	*Huic Anius niveis circumdata tempora vittis / concutiens*

---

[34] The most recent and satisfactory treatment of the problems posed by these lines is Tarrant 1995, who concludes that no form of 7.687 is believably original and proposes e.g. *at silet ipse diu Cephalus tactusque dolore / coniugis amissae lacrimis ita fatur obortis.*

		et tristis ait
27	13.675-6	*Talibus atque aliis postquam convivia dictis / inplerunt*
28	13.749	*Nereis his contra resecuta Crataeide natam est*
28	13.898	*Desierat Galatea loqui*
29	13.916-8	*innitens, quae stabat proxima, moli / .../... inquit*
29	13.966	*talia dicentem*
30	14.129-30	*Respicit hunc vates et suspiratibus haustis / ... dixit*
30	14.154	*Talia convexum per iter memorante Sibylla*
31	14.165-7	*iam non hirsutus amictu, / iam suus et spinis conserto tegmine nullis / fatur Achaemenides*
32	14.323	*inquit*
32	14.441	*Finierat Macareus*
33	14.318	*ait*
33	14.435	*Talia multa mihi longum narrata per annum*
34	14.512	*Hactenus Oenides*
35	14.663	*ait*
35	14.765-6	*haec ubi nequiquam formas deus aptus in omnes / edidit*
36	15.10-11	*sic e senioribus unus / rettulit indigenis veteris non inscius aevi*
36	15.58-9	*talia constabat certa primordia fama / esse loci positaeque Italis in finibus urbis*
37	15.492	*quotiens flenti Theseius heros / ... dixit*

Attributive discourse also normally includes demonstratives, like *talis*, *sic*, and *hic*. Their distribution is presented in Table 2 (the numbers refer to metanarratives). *Sic* appears to be most frequent in introductory phrases and *talis* in capping phrases. It is also obvious that demonstratives are not an essential component of attributive discourse as it was in Homer.[35] Sometimes Ovid prefers to summarize the story's content either without a demonstrative (*fluminis Elei veteres ... amores* **[12]**, *factum mirabile* **[20]**, *miracula ... de consorte suo* **[23]**) or in combination with a one (*sic ... exitium* **[13]**, *haec ... proelia* **[26a]**, *talia ... certa primordia ... loci positaeque Italis in finibus urbis* **[36]**).

---

[35] De Jong 1987: 205, 207.

Table 2: Position of Attributive Discourse

	Introduction	Conclusion	Total
Talis	5, 14, 17cd	3, 15, 21, 27, 29, 30, 33, 36	3+8
Hic	11, 21, 28	16, 17ab, 26a, 26b	3+4
Is		8	0+1
Sic	9a, 9b, 18, 17e, 19, 20, 36	13	7+1
Ita	16		1

There are, nonetheless, a couple of cases in which expectations of a change of level are first raised and then, apparently, frustrated. First, the story of Marsyas (6.382-400) is introduced as if told by an anonymous Lycian (*satyri reminiscitur alter* 6.383) but *inquit*, instead of marking the start of a third-person narrative, introduces the agonised cry of flayed Marsyas: '*quid me detrahis?*' (6.385). The capping formula is too vague to affirm any conclusion about the narrator: *talibus extemplo redit ad praesentia dictis / vulgus* (6.401-2). The second case is far more intriguing. A traditional device of authentication, the invocation of the Muses is "famously and conspicuously absent" from diegetic narrative until 15.622-25.[36] In Homeric poetry the invocation of the Muse at the very onset of the recorded performance creates unresolved ambiguities about the narrator's identity. "If the Muse, in conferring ἀοιδή upon the singer, gives the completed song as performed rather than a skill, then what we would loosely call the singer's knowledge of facts must consist in the song itself as provided by the Muse," argues G. B. Walsh.[37] The most recent study of the Homeric narrator, on the other hand, maintains that "the invocations to the Muses are directed neither to the level of the story [Walsh's "knowledge of facts"] nor to that of the discourse [Walsh's "the song as performed"] but to the sphere that oversees the construction of the narrative discourse out of the fabric of the story [Genette's "narration/narrating"].[38] The link between story and discourse is the narrator himself. Accordingly, Richardson sees the invocation of the Muse as essentially a self-referential gesture, which is

---

[36] Myers 1994: 163.
[37] Walsh 1984: 10.
[38] Richardson 1990: 182. See also de Jong 1987: 52.

meant to direct the audience's attention to his own act of creation, narration. This means that it is 'Homer' and not the 'Muse' who is the Homeric narrator. Likewise, 'Ovid' should be understood as the narrator of the stories that follow the invocation in Book 15.[39] This view seems to be corroborated by the first-person conclusion of the Book (861 ff.), where the 'I' is to be identified with a mortal anticipating his life beyond death.

IV.6 Meta-Metadiegetic Narrative

Just as the extradiegetic narrator gives way to character-narrators, so the narratives of the latter (first-level metadiegetic narratives) may incorporate narrative acts of their own characters (second-level metadiegetic narratives) to a theoretically infinite degree. In the *Met.*, the highest level of metadiegesis is represented by Arethusa's autobiographical story **[12]** told by Calliope **[11]** in the hymn to Ceres performed as the Muses' entry for the singing competition against the Pierids (second-level metanarrative), recounted to Minerva by an unidentified Muse **[9b]**.[40] There are another three second-level metadiegetic narratives: (a) the Lycian guide's story about the Lycian farmers' transformation into frogs **[14]**, reported by an unidentified Lydian **[13]**,[41] (b) Venus' tale about the transformation of Atalanta and Hippomenes into lions **[22]**, inserted by Orpheus **[21]** in the tale of the goddess' love-affair with Adonis, and (c) the story of Picus and Canens **[33]** told to Macareus by an unidentified servant of Circe and later reported to Achaemenides and the Trojans by Macareus **[32]**.

Three out of four second-level metanarratives are reported by the narratees of the second-level narrative situation (the Muse, the anonymous Lydian, and Macareus); only one **[22]** is told by someone who was an actual witness with some active involvement in the second-level metanarrative. In particular, the anonymous Lydian's second-level metanarrative **[13]** merely sets the scene for the Lycian guide's third-level metanarrative **[14]**; the former is not even resumed once the latter

---

[39] For a similar view see Holleman 1969: 52.
[40] Nagle 1988b: 108.
[41] Frécaut 1984: 540.

is over. Obviously, neither Ovid nor the anonymous Lydian can take the responsibility for this *res obscura* (...) *ignobilitate virorum* (6.319 "The story is not well-known, for the men it concerns were of humble birth"); they would rather ascribe it to someone else, a nameless stranger, who is however endowed with the authority of the local person. Finally, it is perhaps significant that both 'professional' intradiegetic narrators of the poem, the Muse/Calliope and Orpheus attribute a tale to one of their song's characters. Orpheus, in particular, resembles even further Ovid inasmuch as he modulates for a while to a voice doubly different from his own: both female and divine (Venus). Ovid, however, does not use the voice of the goddess of erotic desire to speak more overtly about sex. *Temerat sacraria probro* (10.695 "He defiled the sanctuary with his sacrilegious act") is all she considers appropriate to say.

IV.7 Relation to Story

In terms of participation in the narrative reality presented (what Genette calls *diegesis*), a narrator may either play a greater or lesser role as a character in his/her own narrative (*homodiegetic*) or may be entirely absent from it (*heterodiegetic*).[42] The choice between a narrator who tells about others and a narrator who tells about him/herself entails a difference in the narrative rhetoric of truth. A homodiegetic narrator usually proclaims that (s)he recounts true facts about him/herself. (S)he pretends to be relating his/her true autobiography, even if the story is blatantly implausible, fantastic, absurd, metaphysical. The rhetoric of a heterodiegetic narrator, on the other hand, may also be used to present a story about others as true, but sometimes points to the presence of invention.

One of the major advantages of changing narrative level is that it gives the opportunity to view the story from a more personal, involved and empathetic angle. The extradiegetic narrator 'Ovid' appears as homodiegetic narrator in the proem's narrative, which is apparently simultaneous with the act of narrating the *Metamorphoses*, and the predictive (prior) narrative of his catasterism in the conclusion to Book

---

[42] Bal 1997: 22 uses the terms *character-bound narrator (CN)* and *external narrator (EN)* respectively.

15. Yet, on the whole, he is not and could not be involved either as a witness to or as an active participant in the poem's action. In other words, he is rather a heterodiegetic narrator for the greater part of his narrative.[43] By contrast, more often than not (59,5%), intradiegetic narrators in the *Metamorphoses* relate events in which they are themselves involved in one way or another. Homodiegetic narrators include Jupiter [1], the Crow [3], Acoetes [4], the Muse [9], Arethusa [12], Aeacus [15], Cephalus [16], Achelous [17], Alcmene [19], Iole [20], Venus [22], Ceyx [23], Onetor [24], Nestor [26], Anius [27], Galatea [28], Glaucus [29], the Sibyl [30], Achaemenides [31], Macareus [32], Diomedes [34], and Virbius [37].[44] Their narratives constitute therefore specimens of a kind of discourse for which the ancients themselves had no name but which in the modern era is commonly called autobiographical.[45]

A stimulating discussion of the Greek autobiographical discourse in literature was published by G. W. Most in 1989. He maintained that "all the genuine autobiographies that remain in pre-Hellenistic Greek literature (...) include complaints about misfortunes or mistreatment (however much self-praise they may also contain), all are produced in a situation of need organically linked with that misfortune or mistreatment."[46] By contrast, "explicit and detailed autobiography without defensiveness or complaint is thoroughly at home in Latin literature."[47] In support of his argument, he quotes TAC.*Agr*.1.3: *ac plerique suam ipsi vitam narrare fiduciam potius morum quam adrogantiam arbitrati sunt, nec id Rutilio et Scauro citra fidem aut obtrectationi fuit.* (Indeed, many men even counted it not presumption, but self-respect, to narrate their

---

[43] Myers 1994: 72.
[44] Achelous [17] is heterodiegetic when he tells the stories of Proteus and Mnestra (8.728-878).
[45] A good bibliography on this relatively under-researched subject is to be found in *DNP* 1 s.v. Autobiographie, to which the important article Hendrickson 1933 should be added.
[46] Most 1989: 124; by "genuine autobiographies" he means "extended first-person narrative[s] told to strangers" (p. 122), an evidently defective definition unless 'first-person' is taken in an arbitrarily limited sense. On the problem of defining autobiography see Lejeune 1975: 13-46, first published as an article with the same title in *Poétique* 4 (1973) 137-62, and Πασχαλίδης 1993: ch.1 Here we are not interested in the autobiographical genre (if there is such a thing) but in autobiographical discourse, a vocal mode.
[47] Most 1989: 125.

own lives. Rutilius and Scaurus could do so without being disbelieved or provoking a sneer.)

Even though, on the whole, Most shows a sound knowledge of his material, his portrayal of Roman autobiography betrays a superficial consideration of the primary evidence, however scanty this may be. To refer only to the two cases mentioned by Tacitus, which also happen to be the earliest Roman specimens of autobiography, the circumstances of their production (viz. retirement in exile) suggest that they also were an "apologetic literature", meant to establish the authors' view of recent history and remind the public of their valuable contribution to Rome's interests.[48] In the case of Scaurus, moreover, we have evidence that he tried to attenuate the effect of self-glorification (Cicero refers to Scaurus' memoirs as *Scauri laudes*!) by praising others as well.[49] Ovid himself would write an autobiographical letter from exile, which was placed at the end of Book IV of the *Tristia*, sealing as it were the book. It is emphatically a review of the poet's life from the perspective of his exile.[50]

Personal-experience (homodiegetic) narration is naturally an emotionally charged event. Aeacus **[15]** groaned, and there was sadness in his voice (7.518), as he told Cephalus about the plague that befell his island some time ago. Cephalus' **[16]** eyes are flooded with tears when he reluctantly reveals the sorrows his extraordinary spear has brought him (7.689). But this is not a mere pose assumed at the beginning; both men's narratives are full of little touches of emotional involvement with the story, even though a considerable number of years separates the narrated from the narrative event. Not unexpectedly, such "easy" emotion is attributed not only to narrators of advanced age, but also to narrators of feminine sex. Words and tears flow together as Iole **[20]** relates to Alcmene her sister's transformation into a lotus-tree (9.394-96). Before serving as Iole's narratee, Alcmene **[19]** has been a narrator herself. Her narrative is described as *questus aniles* (9.276) and moves her to deep sighs after its completion: *dixit et admonitu veteris commota ministrae / ingemuit* (9.324-25).

---

[48] Pais 1918: 71. Cf. also Ogilvie and Richmond on TAC. *Agr*.1.3. **Rutilio**.
[49] See Hendrickson 1933: 173.
[50] Fredericks 1979: 142.

Only divine or divinely inspired singers, i.e. Calliope **[11]** and Orpheus **[21]** are represented as heterodiegetic narrators, alongside the local old men, who are the immediate or ultimate source for the stories of the Lycian farmers' metamorphosis into frogs **[14]** (told by an anonymous Lydian **[13]**), Baucis and Philemon **[18]** (told by Lelex), and the foundation of Croton **[36]**. This clear-cut distinction seems to reflect Ovid's concern with narrative authority. He has taken great care in choosing the person to whose mouth he entrusts each of the stories. Being a heterodiegetic narrator does not entail neutrality in the presentation of the story. Divine narrators in the *Met.* do promote their own self-interests just as their counterparts do in the *Fasti*, as Harries 1989 has shown.[51] Unlike those, however, they do not rely on suppressing information, but rather on positively presenting their story in a way that advocates their interests.

IV.8 Function and Motivation

As Peradotto acutely observes, it is crucial to distinguish between the function and the motivation of a metanarrative. The former, what Genette has classified, is the purpose it serves in advancing the narrative towards its conclusion (of course, this applies more closely in narratives that conform to the Aristotelian model, i.e. narratives with a teleological perspective). Motivation, on the other hand, refers to ways, often conventional, in which a metanarrative dissimulates its function(s). Genette distinguishes three main type of relationships that can connect the metadiegetic narrative to the narrative into which it is inserted. First, the events of the metadiegesis and those of the diegesis may be causally related. This means that the metanarrative has an *explanatory* function. In other words, the metanarrative answers, explicitly or not, a question of the type "What events have led to the present situation?" Thus the curiosity of the intradiegetic narratee, which often motivates this kind of metanarrative, is actually a pretext for satisfying the curiosity of the extradiegetic narratee/reader.[52] Second, the relationship between metanarrative and the narrative into which it is inserted can be purely

---

[51] See also Newlands 1995: 68ff.
[52] Genette 1972: 242.

thematic. In this case, no spatial or temporal continuity is implied between the two narrative levels. The thematic relationship can be one of either analogy or contrast. When it is perceived as such by the narrator and/or the narratee, the metanarrative functions as an *exemplum*.[53] Third, a metanarrative may be completely unrelated to the narrative into which it is inserted in any explicit way. In this case, the function of the metanarrative lies in the very act of its narration.[54] From the first type to the third, the importance of the narrating situation grows while the relationship between the two levels of narrative becomes more and more abstract.

William Nelles has recently proposed a different approach to the analysis of a metanarrative's function.[55] Building freely on the terminology that Roland Barthes developed for *S/Z*, he distinguished three basic functional codes that may be implemented by the structures of narrative embedding: the hermeneutic, the proairetic, and the formal code.[56] Inserting a narrative within another one creates the sense of an enigma (*hermeneutic code*): how is this new story related to the story we have followed so far, if at all? In this sense, "the invocation of the hermeneutic code, the code of interpretation, would seem to be an inherent function of all embedding."[57] Second, every metanarrative foregrounds the *proairetic code* of action –in this case, the act of narrating itself. The mirroring of the communication paradigm (narrator-narrative-narratee or emitter-discourse-recipient) marks out the three major components of the communicational act as loci of potential significance. In particular, it invites the reader to determine (a) the relation between the two stories: analogy, contrast, irrelevance or identity; (b) the implications for the extradiegetic narrator's motivation and credibility; and (c) our relation to the intradiegetic narratee's reaction to and interpretation of the metanarrative. The third code activated by the change in narrative level is the *formal* one: boundaries within the text require us to examine those around the text more closely. "The characteristic interpretative consequences of such formal analysis cluster

---

[53] Genette 1972: 242-3.
[54] Genette 1972: 243.
[55] Nelles 1997: 140 ff.
[56] Bartes 1970.
[57] Nelles 1997: 140.

around such properties as unity/fragmentation, closure/openness, and symmetry/asymmetry."[58] Nelles' model appears to have a greater scope than Genette's. In fact, Genette's distinctions only cover Nelles' proairetic code with particular reference to the relation between the two stories (2a). But, since the hermeneutic function (1) is common to all metanarratives, it has limited usefulness for a description of individual metanarratives such as the one attempted in this dissertation. The implications of the narratee's doubling (3a) will be discussed in a separate chapter. Thus, the only elements of Nelles' model that could be discussed here as a supplement to Genette's classification would be the relation between the extradiegetic and intradiegetic narrators (2b), and the formal code, although some basic ground has been covered above in the section on changing narrative level.

But before we consider the relation of intradiegetic narratives to diegesis we have to face the problem of what constitutes the diegesis in the *Metamorphoses*, a poem without a central character (unlike the *Odyssey*) or character-bound theme (unlike the *Iliad*), a poem in which the emphasis "is on the individual scenes and their richly varied narration rather than on a grand design."[59] Still, in the proem it is suggested that the material will be presented in chronological order from the first origins of the universe through to Ovid's own time. The poem does conform to an overall chronological sequence, however loosely. "First there is the creation, then the fall of man, thereafter the flood, followed by the repopulation of the earth. The myths of Hercules and the Argonauts precede the fall of Troy, which is followed by the adventures of the Greek and Trojan leaders. The stories of Romulus, Numa, and Caesar's deification come at the end of the poem."[60]

Further complications arise from three frequent characteristics of metanarrative in the poem. First, sometimes one metanarrative follows almost immediately after another. This makes even more difficult to figure out the story on the diegetic level and consequently its relation with that told by the intradiegetic narrator. The tales of the Minyeides **[5-7]**, for instance, do not explain any element of the story on the

---

[58] Nelles 1997: 147.
[59] Galinsky 1975: 86.
[60] Galinsky 1975: 85.

diegetic level (the sisters' resistance to Bacchic ritual and their subsequent punishment). Besides metamorphosis, there is no thematic link between the two levels either: the tales are about love stories set primarily in exotic, oriental locales (Babylon, Persia, Asia Minor). In fact, it is rather ironic that Pyramus and Thisbe **[5]**, for instance, "a story of lovers who are impatient with the obstacles to their desires and leave the safe limits for [*sic*] house and city for the risks of the nocturnal meeting in an unfamiliar place outside the walls of the town," should be told by someone "deliberately distancing [herself] from the intoxicating energies of Dionysiac participation."[61] Finally, the only formal parallelism can be traced between the extradiegetic hymn to Bacchus (4.11ff.) and Leuconoe's parodic hymn to the Sun, although they belong to different sub-genres: the former is a 'cultic' hymn in the second person while the latter is a 'rhapsodic' hymn in the third person.[62]

The second factor has also been observed by de Jong in her examination of Iliadic external analepses told by characters: they "are told for a variety of reasons, always in subservience to the rhetorical purpose of the speech as a whole."[63] For example, as Haarberg has remarked about the story of Lycaon **[1]**, "as an element of the narrative it serves both as Jupiter's private motivation for being indignant, staging his wrath, and as his best argument," in order to gain the consent of the divine assembly to proceed with the extermination of men (1.190-91). Narrative is sometimes used in speeches as *exemplum*, e.g. **[3]**, **[22]**. Since all cautionary tales in the poem fail, these metanarratives serve as a kind of mirror, projecting the future in store for the characters that do not

---

[61] Segal 1985: 387. The unhappy ending, however, is completely in line with the narrator's morality. More generally, as Newlands 1986: 146 observes, the Minyeides' "stories, which all concern unhappy love or tragic relations between the sexes, reflect their pessimism about love and their suspicion of the emotions associated with Bacchus that break beyond the bounds of civilized behaviour." From a different perspective, focusing more intensely on Leuconoe's tales **[6]**, Janan 1994 argues that the daughters of Minyas do not resist desire so much as pose the question of a gendered desire. In her view, "the Eastern sites featured in their tales reflect the sisters' own Orchomenos as a conceptual abstraction, The City: a set of boundaries culturally imposed on bodies, speech, and thought, as well as on territory" (Janan 1994: 428). This view, which applies best in the case of **[5]**, is not further developed in the rest of her essay.
[62] See my forthcoming article in *Platon*.
[63] De Jong 1987: 161.

heed the intradiegetic narrator's advice.[64] At times, e.g. in the case of Acoetes' testimony **[4]**, the rhetorical purpose may not be explicit. Yet, it is quite clear that the thematic parallelism between the Lydian sailors' disbelief and Pentheus' rejection of Bacchus' divinity is meant by Acoetes as a warning about the imminent punishment that awaits the Theban king.[65]

Last but not least, most of the metadiegetic narratives involve some sort of transformation. This means that in a sense they are all essentially related to the diegesis in terms of theme. That metamorphosis is the structuring theme of the poem is announced in the proem: *in nova...mutatas...formas / corpora* (1.1-2). Consequently, when we seek a thematic relation we normally take metamorphosis for granted and look for something particular to the immediate context and the metanarrative inserted. Besides, "metamorphosis often, far from being the center or the climax, is incidental to the main line of the story." [66]

Thematic relations between diegesis and metadiegesis have been competently examined by scholars like A. Bartenbach and M. Boillat. Their aim was mainly to find links and unity in the apparent chaos of the *Metamorphoses*. Solodow, however, has questioned the significance of thematic links between individual stories in the poem. "Similarities between stories may invite the reader to see in them the examination of some human problem from varying perspectives; but on closer look he discovers little substance behind the similarity. (...) Like the forced narrative links [i.e. transitions], they remind us that the world does not conveniently arrange itself thematically."[67] Of course, this is a generalisation that does not concern our particular object of inquiry, i.e. the thematic relation between metanarrative and the narrative into which this is inserted. So, it may not be surprising to observe that the thematic parallelism between the story of Pan and Syrinx **[2]** and the diegetic

---

[64] Nagle 1988c: 43 tentatively suggests that they fail "for the same reason that unwanted suitors' tales fail, namely the audience knows the end and the motive, and so there is no suspense about the 'point'." NB that the cautionary tale of Meleager in *Iliad* 9 has the same fate. For the mirroring effect see Davis 1969: 20.

[65] Rosati 1983: 103. For a different interpretation of the narrative's rhetorical purpose, based on the plausible, yet unnecessary, assumption that Acoetes is a persona of Bacchus himself, see Solodow 1988: 34.

[66] Solodow 1988: 26.

[67] Solodow 1988: 28-9.

story of Jupiter and Io is not exactly pointless: unlike Jupiter, the rustic divinity is unable to enjoy the object of his desire.[68] This affects the character of the metamorphosis in the two stories: Io's new form as a cow is a punishment while Syrinx' transformation into reed is a means of saving her virginity. Perhaps there is no conclusion, no moral to be drawn from the parallelism and the theme's variations; but these are not arid antitheses, "rhetorical in the narrowest sense" either.[69]

Table 3: Relation of Metadiegesis to Diegesis

No.	Place (Narrating: Narrated)	Time (Narrated)	Relation
1	Olympus: Arcadia	not long ago (antediluvian)	causal: to justify Jupiter's decision to destroy the universe
2	Argos: Arcadia	unknown	thematic: Pan and Syrinx is parallel to Jupiter and Io
3	Thessaly: Athens, Phocis, Lesbos	long time ago	thematic: the Crow presents her story as an exemplum
4	Thebes: Lydia, Aegean sea	after Jupiter's love affair with Semele	thematic?
5	Boeotia: Babylon	after Ninus' death	
6	Boeotia: Olympus, Persia	unknown (after Sun's love affair with Clymene, mother of Phaethon)	

---

[68] The thematic link is reinforced by linguistic similarities: the transition to the focal part of the narrative (*redeuntem colle Lycaeo / Pan videt hanc* 1.698-99) is effected in the way used by the extradiegetic narrator in the story of Io (*viderat a patrio redeuntem Iuppiter illam / flumine* 1.589-90).
[69] Solodow 1988: 28.

7	Boeotia: Asia Minor	Phaethon) unknown	
8	Ethiopia: temple of Minerva (unknown location)	unknown	
9a	Helicon: Phocis	unknown	
9b	Helicon: Parnassus	not long ago (*nuper* 5.300)	
10	Helicon: Olympus to Egypt	ante-diluvian	
11	Helicon: Sicily, Olympus, the Underworld, Eleusis	ante-diluvian	
12	Sicily: Peloponnese, Sicily	unknown, ante-deluvian	thematic: analogy
13	Lydia: Lycia	not long ago	thematic: analogy
14	Lycia: Lycia	unknown (before Python and Daphne!)	
15	Aegina: Aegina	not long ago (earlier in the narrator's lifetime)	causal
16	Aegina; Athens, Olympus, Thebes	not long ago (earlier in the narrator's lifetime)	causal?
17ab	Acarnania: Acarnania	unknown	
18	Acarnania: Phrygia	unknown	thematic: analogy
17cd	Acarnania: sea, Thessaly, Scythia	unknown	thematic: analogy
17e	Acarnania: Acarnania	unknown	
19	unknown:	not long ago (in the	thematic: analogy

20	unknown: Oechalia	not long ago (in the narrator's lifetime)	thematic: analogy
21	Thrace: Olympus, Phrygia, Sparta, Cyprus	unspecified	thematic: analogy
22	Cyprus: Boeotia	unspecified	thematic: *exemplum*
23	Trachis: Trachis	not long ago (in the narrator's lifetime)	
24	Trachis: Trachis	minutes ago	
25	Trachis: Troy	in Priam's reign (not long ago)	thematic: analogy
26	Troy: Thessaly	in the narrator's lifetime (not very long ago)	thematic: analogy
27	Delos: Delos	in the narrator's lifetime, during the Trojan war	
28	Sicily: Sicily	not long ago	thematic: contrast
29	Sicily: Euboea, Sicily	not long ago	
30	Cumae (Italy): Cumae	seven hundred years ago	
31	Italy: Sicily	not long ago	
32	Italy: Italy	not long ago	
33	Italy: Italy	unknown	
34	Italy: Italy	not long ago (in the narrator's lifetime)	
35	Italy: Cyprus	unknown	
36	Croto: Argos, Croto	long ago (after Hercules' deification)	
37	Italy: Troezen, the Underworld, Italy	unknown (in the narrator's earlier mortal life)	

Motivation for changing narrative level, on the other hand, is often provided by means of a question. It may be a simple and concrete inquiry for information as in the case of king Numa visiting Croton **[36]** or it "may evince a sympathetic concern, as when Peleus and his companions ask Ceyx **[23]** why he suddenly begins to weep: *moveat tantos quae causa dolores, / Peleusque comitesque rogant* (11.289-90). Or, again, a question may express an avid curiosity to hear a story narrated, as when Achilles eagerly asks Nestor **[26]** to tell the story of Caeneus (12.176-81) and when Achaemenides **[30]** and Macareus **[31]** swap adventures (14.158ff.)."[70] Galatea's sighs and tears excite Scylla's appetite, who urges her to continue and tell her the whole story of her unhappy affair with Acis **[28]**. The motivation for Lelex' narrative **[18]** is the challenge to the power of the gods stated by Pirithous (8.611-15). Accordingly, his goal in telling this story is to convince his audience of the gods' power to perform metamorphosis.

The dinner-party is a popular setting for questioning as far back as Alcinous' banquet in *Odyssey* 9-12 and as recently as Dido's reception of Aeneas and his companions in *Aeneid* 1-3.[71] For, as Sandy observes, "the fulness of good food and good wine and good stories are often associated, as if to say that the ideally satisfied audience are stuffed with tasty words."[72] Myers 1994, who tries to distinguish between the elegiac and epic material in the poem, suggests that although Callimachus' elegiac *Aetia* are the single most importance influence for Ovid's presentation of intradiegetic narratives, considers Nestor's long story about the battle of the Lapiths and Centaurs **[26]**, related at Achilles' request during the feast with which the Greek warriors besieging Troy celebrate Achilles' defeat of Cygnus, as an acknowledgement of the heroic-epic tradition of the motif.[73] Earlier, in Book 4, Perseus is involved in an exchange of narratives within the context of a nuptial banquet. The hero asks about the region and is in turn invited to relate his adventures in capturing Medusa's head (4.770-71). But *narrat Agenorides* (4.772) does not mark a change of narrative level. Ovid

---

[70] Myers 1994: 72. See also **[9b]**, **[15]**, and **[16]**.
[71] See Sandy 1970: 471 and Myers 1994: 75 for further examples and secondary literature.
[72] Sandy 1970: 26.
[73] Myers 1994: 75.

Genette's *transposed speech*) and summary in catalogue form (4.787-89, Genette's *narrated speech*). Due suggested that the use of indirect speech is meant to reveal the conventionality of the hero's autobiographical narrative at a banquet, and thus make fun of this epic convention.[74]

The elaborate reception of Theseus and his companions, Pirithous and Lelex in Achelous' grotto naturally includes some conversation. This all-male symposium is in more than one sense the counterpart of the all-female domestic celebration of Minerva by the Minyeids in Book 3. Not only is it an exchange among a group of peers of stories concerned (in one way or another) with love, but also the same question of divine power crops up and is fervently debated.[75] Theseus, presumably as the guest of honour, asks the first question: *quis ... ille locus?* (8.574-5 "What is that place?"). That this is the right sort of subject for a conversation during a hospitality-dinner is suggested, for instance, by the story the narrator is told by a local in *Fasti* 4.691 while being entertained as a guest or by Numa's first question during his reception in Croton (15.9f.), which provides motivation for the old man's local foundation story **[36]**. When upon hearing Achelous' stories of metamorphosis **[17ab]** Pirithous expresses his doubt about the limits of divine power (8.611-17), he offends his host like the nymphs did in the story just told by Achelous. Unlike them Pirithous is not punished with metamorphosis: apparently a certain looseness of behaviour was condoned at *convivia* and did not involve a breech of *decorum*.[76]

---

[74] Due 1974: 78. It is interesting to not that a ten-book *Perseis* attribute to Musaeus is the only multi-book poem of the Hellenistic age with the characteristic title of an epic, according to Cameron 1995: 283. Denis Feeney and Philip Hardie (*per litteras*) suggested an alternative reason for the avoidance of direct speech: Medusa is not to be looked at directly and therefore her decapitation is not to be directly narrated by either the extradiegetic narrator (his narrative begins after the event has taken place) or Perseus. To put it another way, the extradiegetic narratee/reader of the poem looks at Medusa's decapitation in the mirror of Perseus' indirect speech. However sophisticated this explanation may be, it ignores the mediated nature of all narrative and the fact that Perseus would be holding up the mirror for us (as he held it up for himself according to 4.783) even if his narrative had been in *oratio recta*: the focalisation would be his own either way.

[75] On the symposium in general see Sáez 1991. On *erotica* as a symposiastic theme see Jouanno 1996, esp. 160-4 and Bowie 1993, while on the symposium as an occasion for exchange of mythic narratives see Jouanno 1996: 166f.

[76] See D'Arms 1990: 314.

apparently a certain looseness of behaviour was condoned at *convivia* and did not involve a breech of *decorum*.[76]

Other situations that call for story-telling in the *Met.* are not so relaxed. They include the interrogation of someone arrested by the authorities **[4]**, refuting someone's *makarismos* **[9a]**,[77] competing for the best song **[10-11]**, reporting a catastrophe to the authorities **[24]**, explaining why someone is unable to help **[34]** and trying to console someone by suggesting that others have suffered worse **[37]**. But more often than not stories are told for pleasure. To its use as a means of relaxation and entertainment after the completion of a heroic task like hunting **[17, 18, 22]** or fighting **[26]** discussed above, we should add its use by women to while away the tedium of menial tasks, like spinning and weaving wool **[5-7]**, and the long hours spent at home, explaining the rationale of a wish **[19]**, or competing for the most moving story **[20]**, or on a forced holiday on a remote island **[33]**. Perhaps the ultimate illustration of narrative for narrative's sake is Orpheus' song **[21]**. In contrast to the epic tradition of Demodocus' songs in *Odyssey* 8 and Iopas' song in *Aeneid* 1, professional performance in the *Metamorphoses* is dissociated from hospitality. Instead it is presented as a consequence of the poet's need for self-expression, his *animus*, as Ovid puts it in the first line of the proem, and is addressed to the *animus* of his audience (11.1). It is probably because they are inserted in a poem which refuses to demonstrate its utility that storytelling is so frequently presented as an end in itself. This is particularly significant within the context of the literature by the previous generations of Augustan writers, who aimed at producing works that would influence their readers' beliefs and way of living.[78]

A consequence of storytelling for its own sake is, of course, that, in contrast to Homeric practice, analeptic metadiegetic narrative is not normally presented in "a casual, allusive and elliptical way." With few exceptions the speaking character does not presuppose the stories to be known to his addressee(s).[79] Intradiegetic narrators who include brief references to stories other than their main one include the Crow **[3]** and

---

[76] See D'Arms 1990: 314.
[77] See Palla 1983: 171-85.
[78] Barchiesi 1997: 125-6.
[79] De Jong 1987: 160-61.

Lesbian girl who slept with her father and became an owl (2.591 *res est notissima*), while the latter refers to the rape of his wife's sister Orithyia as a story that may have spread out of Athens to nearby Aegina: *si forte magis pervenit ad aures, Orithyia tuas, raptae soror Orithyiae* (7.694-95 "You are more likely to have heard of Orithyia, the princess who was snatched away; if you have, Procris was Orithyia's sister"). The world of the *Metamorphoses* is definitely one in which stories are appreciated and circulated.

IV.9 Conclusions

This was the first chapter dedicated to the study of the Genettean category of voice, which involves every aspect of the narrating instance that has left its traces in the narrative text. In this chapter we discussed the traces of the narrator in its abstract structuralist conception as the narrative agent. Although Genette clearly used 'voice' on the analogy of its grammatical sense, the word has unavoidable connotations of orality. Following the example of Vergil and Horace, Ovid presents the extradiegetic narrator as an oral singer (*vates*). Yet, writing is not unknown to the diegetic world of the poem, and even the extradiegetic narrator thinks of himself as being read throughout the Latin-speaking world in the concluding prophecy of his own assumption to heavens. The only written text presented in the poem that could be called a narrative is Byblis' letter to her brother (9.530-63); it is closer to the elegiac narrative of Ovid's earlier *Heroides*.

All 37 metanarratives of the poem are supposed to have been performed after the events recounted had taken place (*subsequent narration*). On the whole, metanarrative is clearly signalled by means of phrases that attribute it to a particular character-narrator (*attributive discourse*). Intradiegetic narrators in the *Met.* are usually introduced with their name either at the beginning (60%) or at the end (40%). The character's name is occasionally replaced by a periphrastic or generic designation of his/her identity. The latter, in particular, can be significant, denoting the capacity in which the character is telling the story. Normally this is all the information the reader is offered about the narrator; colourful details about the narrator's character are rare. The narratee is rarely mentioned in attributive discourse (9%). The verb of narrator; colourful details about the narrator's character are rare. The narratee is rarely mentioned in attributive discourse (9%). The verb of speaking, however, is essential. Additional information concerns the use of musical instruments, details about the narrator's hair-do, and indications of his/her emotional involvement in the story. By contrast, there is hardly any information on the narrative's intended meaning and value. Silence is also frequently mentioned in relation with the beginning of a narrative. Demonstratives also are frequent elements of attributive discourse in the *Metamorphoses*.

V Towards a Pragmatics of Narrative Voice

V.1 Feminist Narratology: Moving Forward Or Backward?

As recently as 1989, Robyn Warhol was expressing concern at the absence of a feminist narratology. Narrative theory has been gender-blind, androcentric (Mezei) or androgynist (Showalter).[1] This was symptomatic of its general disregard for the social properties and political implications of narrative. On the other hand, with a few exceptions, feminist criticism did not ordinarily consider the technical aspects of narration. This was also symptomatic of feminists' suspicious attitude towards formalist poetics: it seemed "naively empiricist, masking ideology as objective truth, sacrificing significance for precision, incapable of producing distinctions that are textually meaningful."[2] Thus, the emergence of a feminist narratology has been claimed to represent an important, new resistance to narratological structuralism. Andrew Gibson, nonetheless, fears its effect has also been bi-directional:[3]

> "Feminist narratology has constituted a necessary and crucial intervention in a narrative technology whose models and methods have been almost exclusively masculine in their sources and orientation, and whose ideology has been profoundly patriarchal. But even as it has appeared to resist narratological tradition and displace some of its emphases, the feminist critique has also given a powerful new boost to narratological geometrics and thematics. It has therefore been reimplicated in the very metaphysics that, on another level, it has successfully called in question."

His suggestion for a way to break this vicious circle is the feminist narratologist's recourse to deconstruction. This "deconstructive turn" was brilliantly elaborated, for instance, in Alice Jardine 1985 and recently –in a rather different context– in the work of Drucilla Cornell.[4]

By contrast, the leading feminist narratologists Robyn Warhol and Susan Lanser have more or less explicitly posited a move beyond Jardine's kind of feminism as a move back to the systematic study of discursive conventions. According to Warhol, "what makes narratology so useful is that it can take gender studies a step further into a tangible,

---

[1] Mezei 1996: 11 and Showalter 1986, reported by Gibson 1996: 119.
[2] Lanser 1992: 4-5.
[3] Gibson 1996: 120.
[4] Cornell 1991 and 1992. Both Jardine and Cornell are missing from the bibliographies of Mezei 1996.

arguable position on particular texts: instead of simply talking in generalities about 'women's styles', it can genuinely point to the features that constitute those styles in narrative."[5] Departing from an all-inclusive view of narratology as the study of narrative structures and strategies, Warhol investigated the structure of direct address in Victorian novels by women writers as an example of contextualized female discourse that evidences striking gender differences in narrative expression. Lanser also appreciates the safety for investigation guaranteed by the precision and abstraction of narratological systems that more impressionistic theories of difference between men's and women's writing do not provide.[6]

From Gibson's postmodernist point of view, however, this kind of feminist narratology represents a regressive development, instituting "a thematics of gender as determining and structuring difference, both in the relations between different kinds of text and internally, within specific texts themselves."[7] For example, "even as Warhol historicises in distinguishing between 'engaging interventions' (female) and 'distancing interventions' (male) in the Victorian novel, she also perpetuates a binary mode of thought as though it were somehow outside history and had not itself been at the very least inflected by gender relations."[8] The essays in the section on 'Gender, Difference and Narration' in Fehn, Hoesterey and Tatar's *Neverending Stories* are also liable to the same criticism:[9] the contributing feminist narratologists repeatedly adopt models from a discipline "that has never ceased to be masculine in all its predispostions."[10] This is a typical example of what Jardine calls "the essential virility of metaphysics, even when practised by women." [11]

---

[5] Warhol 1989: 14.
[6] Lanser 1986: 346.
[7] Gibson 1996: 121.
[8] Gibson 1996: 122.
[9] Ingeborg Hoerstery, "Introduction," in Fehn 1992.
[10] Gibson 1996: 123.
[11] Jardine 1985: 188. It is no coincidence that Jardine's name is missing from that volume's Index.

V.2 Feminist Narratology: The Story

A year after Jardine's *Gynesis* was published, Lanser 1986 opened the debate on feminist narratology, i.e. the intersection between feminism and narratology. As she admits in the second paragraph of the paper, her effort was not the first; it was preceded by Bal 1983, Brewer 1984, and her own *The Narrative Act*. But Lanser 1981 was limited to discussion of point of view from a feminist perspective, while Brewer's article merely offered a brief critique of narratology for reducing "textual effects by cutting them off from their discursive contexts, practices, and purposes. By seeking exclusively after a narrative syntax, such analysis decisively excludes the ideological, philosophical, and historical determinations of the narrative. When narratology does attempt to account for the contextual, it does so in terms of narrative conventions and codes. Yet their capacity to account for social, historical or contextual differences always remains limited by the original formalist closure within which such codes and conventions are defined."[12] Bal's article, on the other hand, is a narratological critique of two papers which "deal with the (hu)man fantasy, apparently vivid in male-dominated cultures, [arguing] that linguistic and semiotic competence has something to do with the sexes."[13] For her, this is an opportunity to stress "the fruitfulness of a dialogue between the study of specific literatures and theory —which is not, as some people fear, a unilateral 'commercial' relation in which hermeneutics or practical critics borrow tools from theory;"[14] it is not an occasion for celebrating the marriage of feminism and narratology. Lanser 1986 was its true manifesto, throwing down the gauntlet to traditional narratology and feminism alike.

Her point of departure was the obvious observation that virtually no work in the field of narratology had taken gender into account, either in designating a canon or in formulating questions and hypotheses, and her belief that "until women's writing, questions of gender, and feminist points of view are considered, it will be impossible even to know the deficiencies of narratology."[15] She admitted, however, that one of the crucial differences between feminism and narratology, and therefore a

---

[12] Brewer 1984: 1143.
[13] Bal 1983: 117.
[14] Bal 1983: 118.
[15] Lanser 1986: 343-44.

major obstacle in their co-operation is their view of narrative as semiosis (narratology) versus mimesis (feminism). For the purposes of a dissertation on a male author, the canon is not a real issue: Ovid may have been marginalized and excluded from the canon of the genuinely classical authors like Homer, Sophocles, Cicero and Vergil, as Cahoon deplores, but he is a male author whose work has survived almost complete, and is once more widely read, translated and studied.[16] Our focus then in examining the developments in feminist narratology will be its contribution to the evaluation and modification of the structuralist theoretical models.

Diengott 1988 and Prince 1995 have presented the most important arguments for opposing the project of feminist narratology. Diengott's critique is based on her belief that "narratology's apparent disregard for 'the role of gender in the construction of narrative theory' is not an androcentric oversight but is fundamental to its aims and methodology."[17] She thinks that the whole point of the various narratological models is that they are focused on the most general and abstract concepts for the purposes of describing the system. So just like time, which Lanser provisionally considered less likely to be affected by consideration of gender, they are indifferent to gender.[18] She admits, however, that gender can be of great significance in interpretation, i.e. the study of a single work's meaning, though not in a work of descriptive poetics (the scholarly activity involving an exhaustive study of the literary aspects of certain specific works of literature, according to the definition she quotes in.[19]

Prince 1995 is less dismissive, probably because he considers narratology to be a discipline in flux, which "keeps changing on as its boundaries are (re)drawn."[20] In particular, in his view, narratological models should ultimately include what he calls a pragmatic component.[21] He is also aware of the fact that despite narratology's proclaimed interest only in the *differentiae specificae* of narrative (an argument used by Diengott

---

[16] Cahoon 1990: 199-200.
[17] Diengott 1988: 42 quoting Lanser 1986: 343.
[18] Lanser 1986: 344.
[19] Diengott 1988: 45 and 43 (definition).
[20] Prince 1995: 75.
[21] Prince 1995: 79.

to counter Lanser's suggestion that "a theory that would define and describe *tone* in narrative" is necessary), one of the major narratological concepts, focalization, does not describe an exclusive characteristic of narrative.[22] Considering various criteria that would determine whether in principle gender should be taken into account, Prince suggests that it could prove productive alongside race, class, religion, age, ethnicity, sexual preference. His conclusion does not coincide exactly with Lanser's, though. Even though Prince accepts that "narratology can and must be cognizant of context," he is unwilling to endorse "the kind of 'expansive' narrative poetics that Lanser, for instance, calls for."[23] In other words, without yielding to the interpretive temptation (the narratologist's goal is not to determine the meaning of particular texts) and without renouncing the ideal of a description of narrative and its possibilities, narratology should strive for more attention to the concrete.

Susan Lanser responded to both articles with articles that appeared in the same issue of *Style* and *Narrative* respectively.[24] Naturally, her critique of Prince 1995 was far less blunt than that of Diengott 1988, since the latter embraced an open conception of narratology, which would allow for engendering of the discipline, at least in principle.[25] For, as Lanser herself observes, "just at the point which the essay might have explored the productivity of sex/gender (...) Prince shifts the discussion to general questions of context from which 'gender' has disappeared."[26] Still, Lanser moves on to make a positive contribution to "the engendering of narratology," to quote from the paper's title. She maintains that the presence or absence of sex/gender markedness should be included as a category of narrative voice. She adds that while in heterodiegetic narratives the narrator's sex is normally unmarked, it is an explicit element of most homodiegetic, and virtually all autodiegetic, narratives of length. She might have added that intradiegetic narrators are also normally marked in terms of sex/gender. It is remarkable that this time Lanser proposed a neat binary opposition of structuralist appearance,

---

[22] Diengott 1985: 48.
[23] Prince 1995: 82.
[24] Lanser 1988 and 1995.
[25] Lanser 1995: 85.
[26] Lanser 1995: 86.

tried to fit it within the already existing structuralist narratological model, and, above all, illustrated her argument with a novel, i.e. a straightforward narrative, whereas in her earlier essay she used a text of doubtful narrative character to discuss what she calls voice and propose the notion of public and private narrative levels as particularly relevant to the study of women's texts [narratologically speaking, narratives attributed to women, whether written by men or women]. To justify the importance of this distinction she cites Dale Spender's thesis that "there is no contradiction in patriarchal order while women write for women and therefore remain within the limits of the private sphere; the contradiction arises only when women write for men."[27]

In an essay published in 1990 Marianne Cave summarized the Lanser-Diengott debate. She sided with Lanser and employed Bakhtin's notion of chronotope to read Kate Chopin's *The Awakening* and Virginia Woolf's *To the Lighthouse*. Bakhtin's theories were developed from and for the study of the novel, a predominantly narrative literary genre, but they are not *stricto sensu* narratological. Indeed, Cave drew attention to them because of their concern with ideology: "Within current feminist criticism, then, there is a new movement to read narratives dialogically, to illuminate the embedded narrative structure which resists any simple thematic signification which threatens to limit the text to one class and race and ignores **ideological tension**."[28] The collection of essays edited by Kathy Mezei on British women writers, which appeared in 1996, including contributions from both pioneers of "feminist narratology", Robyn Warhol and Susan S. Lanser, represented the various feminist approaches to narratology (i.e. the study of narrative texts, rather than narrative theory itself) and established this new brand of literary criticism.

Lanser's essay is, in fact, an elaborated version of her response to Prince 1995 minus the polemic, in which she proposes to "argue that the categories of sex/gender/sexuality interact with other narratological elements from narrative person to paralipsis to realibility."[29] My personal

---

[27] Spender 1980: 192 quoted by Lanser 1986: 352.
[28] Cave 1990: 118 quoted by Kathy Mezei in her introduction to Mezei 1996: 9 [my emphasis].
[29] Lanser 1996: 251.

allegiances lie with the narratological purism of Diengott, Prince, and Culler, who as early as 1984 called for caution:[30]

> "The argument [of those who insist on assigning gender to narrators] would be ... that since every person has a sex, and narrators are people, every narrator must have a sex, and to omit discussion of the sex of narrators is to miss important aspects of novels. This argument is plausible only, it seems to me, because we have come to take for granted that we explain textual details by adducing narrators and explain narrators by adducing the qualities of real people.... The theory of fiction needs to be alert to the inadequacies of this orientation, which strives to convert everything in language to a mark of human personalities."

And yet, for the sake of experimentation and open-mindedness I have attempted to explore the relevance of these categories in the *Metamorphoses*, including two of the less trivial categories suggested by Prince 1995, class and age.

V.3 Female Narrators

V.3.1 The Literary Background

"The extensive 'oral composition' by Greek women is unrecognized in the written literary record. We hear about work songs in Homer: those of women at the loom (*Od.* 5.61; 10.221)."[31] It is almost certain, however, that in a predominantly oral society like the Greek and the Roman during the Republic, women story-tellers contributed a great deal to preserving and handing down the cultural tradition by word of mouth.

To make things worse, according to B. K. Gold, the authors of the master narratives of antiquity (e.g. Homer, Sophocles, Cicero, Vergil) have naturalized and normalized all of our most fundamental concepts (the good, the true, the natural) according to a particular masculine and aristocratic ideology, and they have created and subsequently reinforced all of the stereotypes of women that Jardine finds in the 20th century texts she discusses (passivity, treachery, powerlessness, fluidity).[32] She

---

[30] Culler 1984: 5. For a recent effort to escape the dilemma of choosing between a narratology of the individualised narrator and a narratology of "non-narrator" see Ryan 1999: 131-41.
[31] Thomas 1989: 105.
[32] Gold 1985: 84 with reference to Jardine 1985.

argues, however, that in certain authors (e.g. Propertius and other elegiac poets of the 1st century BC) we can see a "space" in the textual fabric, where there is an uneasiness in the representation of gender, where the language seems to have more potentiality to be interpreted from many different perspectives, where the marginalized characters seem to be trying to "speak".

There is, however, a potential pitfall in the study of male-authored texts from a feminist perspective (*gynesis*). Referring to Spivak's "Displacement and the Discourse of Woman," B. K. Gold wonders whether we can ask a male writer, who is embedded in a patriarchal hegemonic discourse and who is in total control of his subjects, to provide us with concepts and strategies that do not appropriate or displace the figure of woman.[33] And yet, several feminist readings against the text have appeared since the early 1980s, including Gold's paper on Propertius, which uncover a multiplicity of voices and attitudes in authors like Catullus, Propertius, Horace and Ovid. Two important papers for the author of the *Metamorphoses* are Nugent 1990 and Richlin 1992.

V.3.2 Ovidian Female Narrators: Numbers And Narratees
Given that Ovid started and established his literary career as a composer of erotic elegy in the line of Catullus and Propertius, it is perhaps not so surprising that he should be among the authors whose texts contain "breakages" through which those muted by the patriarchal culture are pushing. As Judith P. Hallett observed,[34] Propertius assigned more attention and attributed more dynamic, independent, and vocal activity to the female characters he portrayed than do comparable literary efforts of the Augustan period (Horace is the author uppermost in her mind). And all this against a cultural background that praised the woman who DOMVM SERVAVIT LANAM FECIT (she kept up the household and made wool).[35]

Indeed, what is impressive and innovative in the *Metamorphoses* within the context of ancient epic tradition is the narrative time, i.e. space,

---

[33] Spivak 1983: 170 in Gold 1985: 87.
[34] Hallett 1993: 63.
[35] Hallett 1973: 241 quoting *ILS* 8403 (late 2nd century BC). On wool-making in Rome see Wyke 1987: 174 n.17.

allotted to women. Out of 37 intradiegetic narrators 14 (i.e. 38%) are female (see **Table 1** below). No poem in hexameters before the *Metamorphoses* had privileged female narrative discourse to such an extent. In the *Odyssey* Helen told Menelaos, Telemachos and Peisistratos a tale from the Trojan saga (4.235-264) while in Apollonius' *Argonautica* Aegle told the Argonauts about Herakles' most recent exploit (4.1432-49). Moving to Rome, the *Aeneid* scores higher with four female narrators: Venus (1.340-68), Andromache (3.325-36), the Cumaean Sibyl (6.83-97), and Diana (11.535-84).[36] Of course, as Doherty reminds us, the prominence and sheer number of female narrators "do not guarantee that female perspectives will dominate the poem, or even provide an equal counterpoise to the male focalization" of the extradiegetic narrator 'Homer' (and the Muse).[37] In studying the female narrators in the *Metamorphoses*, following Doherty, we should address the question: Do female narrators "conform to the norms of female chastity and solidarity with males of the same class"? [38]

Table 1: Female Narrators

Character	Human	Female Audience	Homodiegetic	Erotic tale
The Crow [3] (was female as human)	-	-	+ and (Nyctimene)	+
Minyad [5]	+	+	-	+
Leuconoe [6]	+	+	-	+
Alcithoe [7]	+	+	-	+
Muse A [9a]	-	+	+	+
Muse B [9b]	-			
Pierides [10]	+	+	-	-
Calliope [11]	-	+	-	+
Arethusa [12]	-	+	+	+
Alcmene [19]	+	+	+	-
Iole [20]	+	+	+	-

---

[36] Diana's narrative has been studied by Suerbaum 1990 in comparison with Venus' tale of Hippomenes and Atalanta [22].
[37] Doherty 1995: 176.
[38] Doherty 1995: 127.

Venus [22]	-	-	+	+
Galatea [28]	-	+	+	+
Sibyl [30]	+	-	+	+
Circe's maid [33]	-	-	-	+

The female narrators in **Table 1** are first categorized according to "an equally potent (in symbolic terms) hierarchical opposition, that between divine and human."[39] Seven out of fourteen female narrators (i.e. 50%) are non-human: goddesses, nymphs or even (in one case) a bird.[40] As Doherty reminds us, "divine females were thought of as exercising powers and privileges far beyond the reach of human women."[41] This means that Helen (a figure of quasi-divine status), Aegle (a nymph) and half the female narrators of the *Aeneid* (Venus and Diana) represent a special category of females who are not subject to the limitations of male-controlled silence and modesty applying to mortal women. It is also significant that even human female narrators in the poem are mostly women of exceptional status, as often is the case with mythical characters.[42] The Minyads were the daughters of Minyas, king of Orchomenos. Alcmene and Iole are also royal offspring and the Sibyl is a priestess of Apollo.

A second thing that leaps to the eye in **Table 1** is the fact that most female narrators in the *Metamorphoses* address female narratees. In this respect Ovid breaks away from epic tradition. In the *Aeneid* it is the proem's *vir* (Aeneas) who is the privileged audience of Venus, Andromache and the Sibyl. This leaves only Diana, the virgin goddess, with a female audience: Opis, who is presented as one among the sacred virgin companions of the goddess (11.533 *unam ex virginibus sociis sacraque caterva*). But even the few female narrators that address a male audience

---

[39] Stehle 1996: 202.
[40] The crow is the only bird-narrator in the *Met.*, a poem full of stories about humans turned into birds. There is also the learned model of Callimachus' *Hecale* (fr.69-74 Hollis) or the popular stories about birds speaking with a human voice (cf. *Fast.*1.441ff.). For the relationship of [3] to Callimachus' epyllion see Keith 1992: 9-20 and Barigazzi 1991: 104; the latter also refers to A.R.3.927-38 and Nonn.*D*.3.97ff. as Callimachean imitations.
[41] Doherty 1995: 127.
[42] Arist.*Po*.1453a11-12 with reference to men.

in the *Met.* (the Sibyl→Aeneas, Venus→Adonis, and Circe's maid→ Macareus) do not break away from their circumscribed private space, addressing the community, men *en masse*. This is not an absolute disadvantage though, since storytelling among women can give ample opportunity for mutual corroboration. As Luce Irigaray observes in her classic *This Sex Which is Not One*, "there may be a speaking-among-women that is still a speaking (as) man but that may also be the place where a speaking (as) woman may dare to express itself. It is certain that with women-among-themselves (...) in these places of women-among-themselves, something of speaking (as) woman is heard."[43]

The exchange of narratives between females in the *Metamorphoses* sometimes has an agonistic character.[44] The daughters of Pieros are on a Panhellenic tour (5.306), which turns out to be so successful that they decide to challenge the Muses. Entering competitions must have been a habit of itinerant male singers, like Homer and Hesiod in the *Certamen* and the *Vita Hesiodea*.[45] Indeed, the 'Musomachia' of Book 5 has been compared with the *Certamen* by Bilinsky 1959: Homer, like the Pierids, sings of war, and is defeated by Hesiod, who, like Calliope, sings of peaceful farming. The jury for this contest between groups of female artists is also female: it is made up of local nymphs. But even Alcmene and Iole, two women among themselves in a place of women-among-themselves, their home, seem to "compete" for the right to be moved to tears.[46]

So far we have established that female narrators are a significant quantity in the *Met.* They are, however, of predominantly exceptional status and at the same time normally address their narratives to other women in the private space of the home. These two key parameters seem to reinforce these women's solidarity with the androcentric aristocratic ideology, which prevails in Greek myth. The fact that twice they appear to engage in competition, also characteristic of male values, also points in the same direction.

---

[43] Irigaray 1985: 135.
[44] For competition among women cf. *Odyssey* 6.92 (washing clothes).
[45] For evidence about itinerant singers see Hardie 1983: 18f. For poetic contests in archaic Greek poetry see Ford 1992: 94 (with further bibliography in n.5).
[46] This narrative situation was probably derived from the bucolic poem *Megara* attributed to Moschos. See Breitenstein 1966: 57.

V.3.3 Ovidian Female Narrators: Thematics

Another salient feature of female narrative in the *Metamorphoses* is its preoccupation with love (see **Table 2** below). Pyramus and Thisbe **[5]**, Venus and Mars, Leucothoe-Sol-Clytie **[6]**, as well as Salmacis and Hermaphroditus **[7]**, the four tales of the three daughters of Minyas are all essentially love stories set in the exotic East and of a high escapist value.

V.3.3.1 Love in the Tales of the Minyeides

Pyramus and Thisbe **[5]** reflects the conventions of the so-called Greek romance but frustrates the readers' expectation for a happy conclusion (i.e. reunion in this life). By undermining the traditional comic/novelistic story-pattern, the narrator reveals how far from the everyday reality of contemporary city-life such a story is.[47] The two lovers lose their lives in their effort to escape the parental prohibition against their marriage. However, they end up entrusting their *post mortem* union to their parents. Leucothoe **[6]** is represented as a good domesticated virgin (4.219-21), who passively consents to male desire (4.232-34). She is cruelly punished by her father for defiling her virtue, i.e. his honour. Finally, Salmacis **[7]**, despite her narcissistic female obsession with mirrors, essentially reproduces the male gaze and desire.[48] Even though Alcithoe chooses to tell a tale about the rape of a male and his apparent castration, topics potentially disruptive of androcentric discourse, she manages to recuperate "the virility ostensibly lost or diminished" "by the insertion of a masculine discourse of desire," "by the maintenance of a masculine subjectivity, even by the potency of Hermaphroditus' curse." [49]

Love is then the theme that links the tales of the three sisters: "each derogates uncontrolled desire to a greater degree. Among mortals, love leads only to death; among the gods, to humiliation and disgrace (…). The tales culminate in Alcithoe's tale of Salmacis and Hermaphroditus, an eerie, disturbing affair that ultimately suggests love is a perversion of nature."[50] So, not only are these female narrators literally surrounded by the walls of the household and defined by their relation to the male head

---

[47] See Holzberg 1988: 276 and Schmitzer 1992: 529-30.
[48] See Nugent 1990: 172 on gaze and the masculine discourse of desire.
[49] Nugent 1990: 160 and 177.
[50] Ginsberg 1983: 69.

of the house, their father Minyas, but they also support the patriarchal order and androcentric viewpoint through their tales. Not only do they reject by their words and actions the vices regularly attributed to Woman since Hesiod, aligning themselves with a particular masculine construction of the feminine ideal, they also tell stories in which the expression of female desire is ruthlessly punished.[51]

V.3.3.2 Rape
With the exception of 'Pyramus and Thisbe' [5], 'Hippomenes and Atalanta' [22] and the love-triangles of the tales told by Galatea [28] and Circe's maid [33], all other erotic tales involve rape, attempted or perpetrated (Table 2).

Table 2: Erotic Tales by Female Narrators

Narrator	Rape	Successful	Autodiegetic
The Crow [2]	+	-	+
	(Coronis)		
Minyad [5]	-	-	-
Leuconoe [6]	+	+	-
	(Leucothoe)		
Alcithoe [7]	+	+	-
Muse [9a]	+	-	+
Calliope [11]	+	+	-
	(Proserpina)		
Arethusa [12]	+	+	+
Venus [22]	-	-	-
Galatea [28]	-	-	+
Sibyl [30]	+	-	+
Circe's maid [33]	-	-	-

This amounts to 64% of erotic stories told by female narrators in the poem. Only half of these rapes, however, could be described as successful, i.e. concluded with intercourse in some sense. This percentage includes two marginal cases: (a) Arethusa and Alpheus, who

---

[51] Janan 1994: 430 and Nugent 1990:161.

mingle in liquid form, and (b) Salmacis and Hermaphroditus: although it is not clear whether they manage to get any further than hugging intimately, violence and lack of consent are strongly suggested by the triple simile in 4.362-67.[52] Indeed, the tale of Arethusa is the only one out of four rape stories related by the victim herself (*autodiegetic*) that belongs to the 'successful' category.

Early studies of rape in the *Metamorphoses* merely observed that "the majority of (...) heterosexual relationships (...), particularly when one party is divine, suggest violence, a chase, ultimate rape," a fact which confronted the reader with "the world of the primitive hunting instincts of man" and defloration as "an elemental act with potentially violent repercussions, a mystery akin to the ferocity of nature herself."[53] Alternatively, they emphasized the lighter, witty aspects of Ovidian rape narrative, e.g. Stirrup 1977. Leo Curran's detailed exploration of the rape stories, first published in 1978, anticipated by some years the work of later feminist critics. He concluded that by the time he wrote the *Metamorphoses*, Ovid was beginning to see that rape is "less an act of sexual passion than of aggression and that erotic gratification is secondary to the rapist's desire to dominate physically, to humiliate, and to degrade."[54]

His view of rape is indeed identical with that put forward by the feminist critique of sexual violence during the 1970s. Feminists argued then that violence "is fundamental to the functioning of patriarchy, and rape, or the threat of rape, operates as a means of limiting women's freedom."[55] In the words of Susan Brownmiller, author of the first major study of rape from a feminist point of view, rape "is nothing more or less than a conscious process of intimidation by which *all men* keep *all women* in a state of fear." [56]

---

[52] Even the ivy-simile, traditional in erotic contexts (see R. Hunter on Eubulus fr.104.5), implies that Salmacis' embrace can prove harmful for the boy; see PLIN.*Nat.*16.151, 243, 17.234 and HOR.*Epod.*15.5, where the noxious quality of the ivy is introduced almost openly by *artius* and *lentis* (Babcock 1966: 408).
[53] Parry 1964: 273, 277-8.
[54] Curran 1984: 283.
[55] Allwood 1998: 107.
[56] Brownmiller 1975: 5.

Her argument was based, amongst else, on ethnological research of primitive peoples, which suggests that rape is used "as an expression of manhood, as an indication of the property concept of women, and as a mechanism of social control to keep women in line."[57] This representation of male violence as a means of social control of women, and of the attacker as an agent of the patriarchal system has persisted in the 1980s. Fréderique Vinteuil, for instance, argued that[58] "The rapist who prevents women from going out late (...), from going for a walk on their own, who makes them live in constant fear, does more for the moral order than the Pope and more for the domination of women than all the socio-biology texts on women's natural inferiority put together."

Feminists also challenged the belief that women enjoyed being raped (shared by the *praeceptor* of Ovid's *Ars Amatoria* 1.673ff.), and that they unconsciously "ask for it". This subconscious desire to be raped, feminists insisted, is a male fantasy.[59] Brownmiller even went so far as to claim that the Freudian analysts' belief that rape is a frequent female fantasy is false, because it implies belief in an inherent wish for rape on the part of all women.[60] She argued that this is only part of the female victim psychology (the mass ideology of the conquered), which arose as a mirror-image of the male ideology of rape (the mass ideology of the conqueror).[61] The fact that in our case it is a male author/narrator who represents women as "fantasizing" about rape could be used as an argument to corroborate Brownmiller's thesis. Yet, the fact that in the majority of these "fantasies" the female survives with her chastity intact (not to mention that in one case the female –Salmacis– is the aggressor) arguably fits better with the notion of a genuinely feminine fantasy of "controlled" rape.[62]

---

[57] Brownmiller 1975: 319.
[58] Vinteuil 1985: 10.
[59] Allwood 1998: 102.
[60] Brownmiller 1975: 358.
[61] Brownmiller 1975: 360.
[62] See Gordon 1997: 282. According to Nugent 1990 and Richlin 1992, Ovid treats Salmacis' behaviour as a threatening usurpation of male privilege for which punishment is swiftly exacted. For a modern woman's fantasy of seducing a young adolescent see Friday 1994: 183.

Ovid's previous poetry also included several rape narratives. One that has been scrutinized by several critics in an effort to get to Ovid's 'real' attitude to the matter of sexual violence is the Rape of the Sabines. Brownmiller, who was not a classicist and was writing in the militant atmosphere of the 70s, accused Ovid, "the Roman celebrant of love," of "setting a flippant attitude toward rape in war that has persisted for two thousand years." For, apostrophizing Romulus, the instigator of the rape of the Sabine women, he exclaims in *Ars* 1.132: *haec mihi si dederis commoda, miles ero.* Ten years later, however, in 1985 Julie Hemker argued that by means of ironic references to Livy's 'canonical' account and an eight-line description (*Ars* 1.117-24) of the victimized women's response, Ovid undercut his narrator's praise of the Sabine incident. Ovid, she argued, exposed "the tragedy inherent in any philosophy which espouses domination as a means of gratifying one's own desires." [63] Her argument is vitiated not only by her indirect description of rape as a crime of lust, which ignores the feminist critique of rape sketched above, but also by neglect of line 1.126 *et potuit multas ipse decere timor.* This line suggests an alternative reason for the eight-line description of the victimized women's fearful response: it is a turn-on for the male reader, as the women's fear contributed considerably to the rapists' excitement. Or as Richlin put it "their fears are cute (...) and the whole thing is a joke." [64]

Ovid told the same story again in the *Fasti* (3.169-70; 229-34). Gary Miles has recently argued that this version "clearly challenges the prevailing ideology.[65] It does not imagine an alternative way of ordering society (...) women are still conceived as weak and essentially passive. But (...) it strips away any pretense that the abduction and rape of the women was anything other than an act of violence." Yet, he contradicts himself on the issue of the Sabine women's self-expression. In p. 201 of his book he maintains that "the women are voiceless, (almost) entirely passive, never more than vehicles for children," while in p. 217 Ovid is made to give voice "to the women's own desperation in the brief speech attributed to Hersilia [*Fast.*3.207-12]."

---

[63] Hemker 1985: 46.
[64] Richlin 1992: 168.
[65] Miles 1995: 216.

In her ground-breaking essay, building on contemporary theories of pornography, Amy Richlin explained the voluptuous appeal of female victimization scenarios by identifying them as vehicles for supplying Roman audiences (male and/or female) with a vicarious taste of sadistic and/or masochistic pleasure, provided that the psychoanalytic model of fantasy, in which the subject is said to oscillate among the terms of the fantasy, is diachronically applicable.[66] Richlin's arguments for considering the *Metamorphoses* as pornography are rather summarily presented in a single paragraph and are derived from

(a) Angela Carter's analysis of Sade, especially of the scenarios of *Justine* (i.e. a single pornographic work of a single early-modern pornographer), with their episodic structure, the elision of the act of rape (this is only true of the earlier version of *Justine*) and the physical cruelty; and

(b) Susan Griffin's study of pornography and silence, which concludes that the pornographer "gives woman a voice only to silence her." This certainly applies to Philomela, Lara and Lucretia, as Richlin tentatively suggests. But loss of speech is a conspicuous part of Ovidian metamorphosis in general, not just in the case of (would-be) rape victims.[67]

Richlin's thesis opposes and rejects Curran's earlier argument that "Ovid is not writing pornography but a kind of epic and does not have a lickerish interest in clinical and anatomical details." Their views coincide regarding the deleterious effects of rape or threat of rape on women: "rape does worse than undermine a woman's identity; it can rob of her humanity," according to Curran, who does not seem to take into account that many of the victims of (divine) male aggression are nymphs, not common humans (see **Table 3**).[68]

---

[66] Richlin 1992: 173-78.
[67] Richlin 1992: 173. On metamorphosis and silence see Luce 1993. She observes that "in the forty stories reflecting some aspect of the silence/speech motif, women outnumber men" and it is mostly women's stories of silencing that "are especially memorable and told at considerable length: Echo, Daphne, Io, Callisto, Niobe, Arachne, Procne, and Philomela." Even from this selection it is evident that rape is not always involved.
[68] Same observation apropos of Callisto (a human virgin though) in Luce 1993: 317. "Dehumanization" is a word used in pornographic theory to evoke the objectification of women, see Gubar 1987: 713.

Table 3: Rape-stories by Female Narrators

Narrator of Rape	Human Aggressor	Human Victim
The Crow [3]	- (Neptune)	+ (Coronis)
Leucone [6]	- (Sol)	+ (Leucothoe)
Alcithoe [7]	- (Salmacis)	+ (Hermaphroditus)
Muse [9a]	+ (Pyreneus)	- (Muse)
Calliope [11]	- (Dis)	- (Proserpina)
Arethusa [12]	- (Alpheus)	- (Arethusa)
Sibyl [30]	- (Apollo)	+ (Sibyl)

But, unlike Richlin, he considers this Ovidian emphasis on the intellectual and emotional experience of the suffering woman as a manifestation of a sympathetic imagination. He even sees this attitude as a positive development away from Ovid's earlier works, in which a woman's obsession with premarital virginity was ridiculed as uncouth *rusticitas*. Apparently, he ignores Arethusa's self-deprecation in 5.583-84:

Quaque aliae gaudere solent, ego **rustica** *dote*
Corporis erubui crimenque placere putavi.

"In my simplicity, I blushed for those attractive looks on which other girls pride themselves, and thought it wicked to please men's eyes."

Before expressing any personal views on the subject of rape in the *Metamorphoses* in general and female metanarrative in particular, it would be useful to examine another aspect of these myths, which is usually neglected these days. Sophia Kaempf-Dimitriadou produced in 1979 a study of divine amours in the Attic art of the 5th c. BC,[69] in which she examined these stories with reference to the hierarchical opposition of immortal divinity vs. mortal humanity rather than that of male vs. female, precisely because the victim's gender does not make any difference to the manner of representation, a question which will come up again in our discussion of Orpheus' *Carmen*. She argued that the fear, frustration and embitterment of the mortal beloved, which forces the divinity to resort to force and violence, is used by the artists as a means of representing

---

[69] Curran 1984: 264 objects to the use of such euphemisms as "amours" or "loves" by classical scholars to describe the sexual exploitation of women by gods, ignoring the fact that the word *amores* is used in the classical texts themselves, e.g. Calliope's description of Arethusa's rape as *flumini Elei ... amores* (5.576), and Leuconoe's description of Leucothoe's rape as *Solis ... amores* (4.170).

human powerlessness, the frailty of human nature, which cannot live up to the challenge of intercourse with divinity.

It is, further, often ignored these days that these rape myths are also stories of initiation into what it means to be a sexually mature (wo)man. "The rape motif recalls the reality of marriage customs, of the fact that the first sexual encounter for a young woman may well have seemed like a rape," as Kathleen Wall reminds us.[70] The pattern of initiation by rape is indeed "found in a number of male-centered, misogynistically inclined cultures."[71] That rape was represented in Roman Comedy as a catalytic event in the development of adolescent males into manhood was recently argued by Sharon L. James.[72] This observation does not prevent her, however, from arguing that "in *Hecyra* and *Eunuchus* Terence breaks with the traditions of rape in Roman Comedy and presents rape in the worst possible light, showing it as a violent act that injures its victims physically as well as seriously threatening their features."[73] And this despite the fact that rape was so common a plot device in Roman Comedy that it cannot have offended the sensibilities of viewers [male and female?], who would have rested easy in their certainty that it would lead to citizen marriage.

It is precisely the fact that they do **not** lead to marriage that offends some modern readers in the case of Ovidian rapes. Pamela Gordon, for example, finds it offensive that "male rapists in Ovid usually enjoy their prey and move on to a new victim." [74] But even from our small selection of rape stories told by female narrators, it is evident that this is not absolutely true. Dis **[11]** and Alpheus **[12]** for instance, never appear again as sexual aggressors in the poem, while Pyreneus **[9a]** falls dead, chasing the winged Muses. It is true that Neptune **[3]**, Sol **[6]** and Apollo **[30]** attack at least another female in the poem. Neptune successfully raped Caenis according to Nestor's sources in 12.197. Sol fathered Phaethon from Clymene according to the extradiegetic narrator in 1.762ff. as well as Leuconoe in 4.204, who adds Rhodos and Circe's mother to the catalogue of Sol's lovers. Finally, Apollo is the first god to

---

[70] Wall 1988: 19-20.
[71] Lincoln 1979: 228
[72] James 1998.
[73] James 1998: 31-32.
[74] Gordon 1997: 287.

attempt rape in the poem: *Primus amor Phoebi Daphne Peneia* (1.452).[75] Among his later victims one could mention Chione, whom the god rapes *en travestie*: *Phoebus anum simulat praeruptaque gaudia sumit* (11.310). We should not forget, however, that these three males are also powerful gods, who cannot get married to mortal females, just like free-born Romans may not marry their slaves. They can only get married to females of the same status, like Dis and Proserpina, who are described as husband and wife by Arethusa (*pollens matrona tyranni* 5.508), Jupiter (*nobis gener ille* 5.526) and Calliope (*cum coniuge* 5.567). Alpheus and Arethusa, on the other hand, are not actually designated as a married couple in the poem, but they were often so represented in art.[76]

The attacked females also have to choose between two options. They can either (a) escape by changing their mode of existence or (b) succumb to male desire and get punished by male authority. Metamorphosis, the first option, has been variously interpreted by modern readers as an evasion of serious moral issues on the part of the narrator[77] or as a metaphor. The latter approach is illustrated by Leo Curran's remark that one way of reading the story of Daphne's transformation into a tree in order to avoid rape "is to conclude that a woman who is unwilling to accept what is the potential threat faced by every woman might as well be a tree." [78] Punishment, on the other side, is the lot of Leucothoe **[6]**, the virgin who *quamvis inopino territa visu / victa nitore dei posita vim passa querella est* (4.232-33). Despite Janan's deconstructionist effort to emphasize "the sentence's logical dissonance," Bömer's smooth solution is fairly evident, in my view, and far from "agonized":[79] "Leucothoe, though frightened by the unexpected sight, was overcome by the god's magnificence, and succumbed to his virile force without a murmur" (adapted from Mary M. Innes).

In this section we examined rape as an important element in the erotic stories told by female narrators in the poem not only because of its frequency but also because in modern feminists' view, it represents a

---

[75] It is interesting that he is later presented by the extradiegetic narrator to desire *conubia Daphnes* (1.490 to marry Daphne)!
[76] See *RE* 1.1635, 39ff.
[77] See e.g. Segal 1994: 277.
[78] Curran 1984: 274.
[79] Janan 1994: 441.

major act of male domination and female objectification. Discussion of the actants' identity in rape-narratives corroborated the view that lust is only secondary to aggression and the desire for physical domination as a power-statement. The representation of women as narrators of rape-stories in a male-authored poem addressed to a presumably mixed audience has been variously interpreted. Two basic strands have emerged: (a) we are dealing with a mirror-image of the male ideology of rape, which is founded on the belief that women, however unconsciously, "ask for it" or even enjoy being forced to have sex (classical feminism of the 1970s) and (b) rape scenarios offer male and female narrators and narratees as well as the author's mixed audience ample and varied opportunities for a vicarious taste of sadistic and/or masochistic pleasure (gender studies' view of pornography). Although a narratological study does not have to adopt either interpretation, the former view, which is earlier chronologically, seems preferable for the reasons presented above. Our discussion has also emphasized an aspect of rape which has been neglected: its relation to marriage.

V.3.4 Female Narrators And Patriarchal Order
Despite her *post factum* protestations that '*ille vim tulit invitae*' (4.238-39 "he forced me to have sex with him against my will") Leucothoe is buried alive by her father. Still, the female narrator criticizes Leucothoe's father as *ferox inmansuetusque* (4.237 "ferocious and savage") and *crudus* (4.240 "cruel"). This could be an indication that Leuconoe as a narrator does not conform to the norms of female chastity and solidarity with males of the same class, even though in diegesis she is represented as a devout follower of Minerva, "chaste avatar of reason and feminine domestic industry, 'supporter of the male in all things' [Aesch.*Eu*.737]".[80] Exploring further this contradiction and realigning all the tales told by the Minyads along the axis of a "feminine" desire, M. Janan has argued that Leuconoe and her sisters do not care about the public meaning their stories should have; instead they re-appropriate storytelling for private pleasure. In other words, although these women do not challenge patriarchal order in their narratives, they rejoice in their femininity,

---

[80] Janan 1994: 130. See also above p.137. Cf. SVET.*Aug*.64.2 on knitting as enforced occupation for the females of Augustus' household.

seeking pleasure in ways other than those prescribed by the community, which currently seems to be under the spell of Bacchus (4.4-32).

The Muses are another interesting case with regard to the question of the female narrators' attitude towards the patriarchal order.[81] According to Hesiod's *Theogony*, their true mission is to proclaim the praises of the glorious existence and the powerful manifestation of the Olympian divinities: "They celebrate first in their song the august family of gods" (44); "Second they sing of Zeus, **father** of gods and men" (47), "how far the highest of the gods he is, and the greatest in power" (49). The Muse persists as the "emblem of the feminine power in its transformed, harmonized state, subordinated to the Olympian patriarchy and allied to the masculine ends of glorifying a form of the Father" into the fifth century.[82] This was the function awarded to the Muses by Horace in the fourth Roman Ode (*Descende caelo*). Augustus is represented as reposing safe in the cave of the Muses (3.4.37-40):

> *vos Caesarem altum, militia simul*
> *fessas cohortes abdidit oppidis,*
> *finire quaerentem labores*
> *Pierio recreatis in antro.*

In verses 25-36 we find intertwined the themes of safety under the protection of the Muses and safety under the rule of Caesar, in whom strength is hopefully joined to *consilium*.[83] The poem seems to have a special affinity with the Ovidian *Musomachia*, since it includes an orthodox version of the Gigantomachy, which is held up by the Ovidian Muses as the only true story against the heresy of the Pierides.[84]

In the light of all this mainly extratextual evidence, it would seem unlikely that Calliope's **[11]** entry for the competition could represent a challenge to patriarchal (and Augustan) order. Her choice of subject, a

---

[81] Zeitlin 1996: 7 points out that 'patriarchal' is a problematic term, which has been rendered reductive through overuse. Rich 1986: 57 offers an wide-ranging definition: "Patriarchy is the power of the fathers: a familial-social, ideological, political system in which men —by force, direct pressure, or through ritual, tradition, law, and language, customs, etiquette, education, and the division of labor, determine what part women shall or shall not play, and in which the female is everywhere subsumed under the male."
[82] See Segal 1986: 177 and 178n.26.
[83] Hornsby 1962/3: 104.
[84] This is also a favourite subject for the Muses' song, according to the Hesiodic *Theogony* 43-46.

hymn to Ceres, a female divinity, is the first surprise. The next one is that the plot of the hymn's narrative section is put in motion by the imperialist desire of another goddess, Venus. This is a striking innovation of Calliope's version of the *Raptus Proserpinae*.[85] And yet, Jupiter has the final word on the matter (5.564-65):

At medius fratrisque sui maestaeque sororis
Iuppiter ex aequo volventem dividit annum.

"Jupiter, however, intervening between his brother and his sorrowing sister, divided the circling year in equal parts."

Helene P. Foley has recently argued that already in the *Homeric Hymn to Demeter*, the maternal politics of the goddess represent a genuine challenge to the patriarchal politics of Zeus. The Father attempts to impose on Persephone a form of marriage which in modern times would be recognized as "patriarchal and virilocal exogamy (a marriage between members of two different social groups arranged by the father of the bride in which the bride resides with her husband)."[86] But the goddesses finally refuse to be more than partially bound within the confines of the original marital arrangements, which disrupted an idyllic mother/daughter relationship.[87] What is even more important is that Demeter's wrath and rebellion, far from being regarded as dangerous and disruptive of the divine order, is represented as eventually creative and positive, resulting in the institution of the mysteries and a new relation of humankind with death.

Venus is also made to present reality as a situation in which the supreme male divinity (Jupiter), as well as his partner in world-dominion (Neptune), are at the mercy of a lesser divinity (5.369-70):

Tu superos ipsumque Iovem, tu numina ponti
Victa domas impsumque, regit qui numina ponti.

"You have conquered the divinities of the upper air, including Jupiter himself, and hold them in subjection; yes, and the gods of the sea, also, not excepting their overlord." This is reminiscent of the introductory section of the *Homeric Hymn to Aphrodite* (V), a hymn which, in Ann Bergren's view, attempts "to resolve the tension between a cosmos

---

[85] Johnson 1996; 16n.3 lists some indications that Venus and Amor may have been associated with the tale before Ovid, but does not consider them conclusive evidence.
[86] Foley 1994: 105.
[87] Foley 1994: 107 and 110.

controlled by Aphrodite and a cosmos controlled by Zeus into a stable hierarchy in which the immortal male "tames" the principle of sexuality as an immortal female."[88] This tension is also manifested in Aphrodite's silence about Zeus' compulsion during the entire affair, apart from her single and indirect allusion to κρατερή ἀνάγκη.[89] In Calliope's song Venus' effort to establish and extend her own repressive authority of compulsory (hetero-)sexuality is soon forgotten, as if her revolutionary act was in fact serving Zeus' plans for his daughter.

Alcmene **[19]**, a rape-victim of Zeus (9.288-89), and Iole **[20]**, a rape-victim of Hercules (9.140), do not exchange their own stories of sexual violence. Instead, they focus on two other aspects of the female existence: birth and child-care. These are equally political questions, "not simply questions of the history of midwifery and obstetrics," as Adrienne Rich observes.[90] "Patriarchy has told the woman in labor that her suffering was purposive —was *the* purpose of her existence; that the new life she was bringing forth (especially if male) was of value and that her own value depended on bringing it forth."[91]

Hercules' birth is clearly represented as the key event in Alcmene's existence. Now that her son has been translated to the heavens, the old woman's only consolation is to tell again and again the stories of his labours (9.277). The story of Hera's intervention in Heracles' birth first appears in *Iliad* 19.119. In his speech of reconciliation with Achilles, Agamemnon tells the story of Ate's victory over Zeus, in order to prove her irresistible power. The Mycenean patriarch, of course, is not interested in the details of Alcmene's labour or the way her pains were finally relieved; he focuses on the threat that Hera's tricks pose for the patriarchal order. Ovid's Alcmene admits that in her frenzy she heaped abuse on Jupiter for his ingratitude (9.302-3). But she was *demens* (9.302) and her complaints were *vana* (9.303), as she acknowledges from hindsight.

In the antiphonal narrative by Iole, Dryope undergoes metamorphosis a year after giving birth, leaving behind an orphan boy. In a gesture untypical of Ovidian intradiegetic narrators, Iole dedicates almost one-

---

[88] Bergren 1989: 7.
[89] Parry 1986: 257.
[90] Rich 1986: 128.
[91] Rich 1986: 159.

third of her narrative time (21 out of 68 lines) to Dryope's last words. The central part of her speech is taken up by detailed instructions about the child's upbringing, a particularly female preoccupation: "Give him to a nurse, and let him often drink his milk and play beneath my boughs. When he can talk, let him greet his mother, and sadly say: 'My mother is hidden inside this tree-trunk.' Let him beware of pools, and not pick flowers from trees, but believe that all fruitful shrubs are the bodies of goddesses!" (9.376-81).

Galatea's story **[28]** of her love triangle with Acis and Polyphemus gives us a further opportunity to explore female narrative in comparison with male versions of the same story. As Nagle has observed (1988a: 80 n.9), "Ovid has restricted the reader's knowledge of the preliminaries to what Galatea sees fit to report, and naturally in her account she is completely innocent, a stylization by Ovid, according to Dörrie, of the way that women tell one another about their experiences with men."[92] The fact, however, that in both the male Theocritean/Polyphemean and the female Ovidian/Galatean version of the story there is no sign of Galatea's flirting with Polyphemus before rejecting him in favour of Acis weakens the validity of Nagle's observation on the relation between gender and the narrator's reliability.[93]

In this section we examined the attitude towards patriarchy reflected in female metanarratives, starting from stories of rape, the subject of the previous section, and moving to tales about other aspects of female life, like child-bearing. Far from attempting to undermine patriarchal order, female narrators in the *Met.* only seek pleasure through telling each other stories that foreground the female experience. Even narrators like the Muses who are traditionally considered as spokespersons of the patriarchal order focus on female divinities who threaten the Olympian patriarchy. In the end, however, these potentially destructive female activities turn out to have been promoting Jupiter's plans. If a conclusion should be drawn from the above discussion of textual evidence it would probably be something similar to Froma Zeitlin's view of Attic tragedy: the stories of female intradiegetic narrators in the *Metamorphoses* generally

---

[92] The reference is to Dörrie 1969.
[93] Besides, she only mentions such male versions as PROP.3.2.7 and Poempeian wall-painting.

reassert male structures of authority at closure, but before that they have managed to open up the masculine view of the universe, through energizing the narrative resources of the female.[94]

V.3.5 Ovide En Travestie?

In a book published in 1986, Taylor discussed the use of a female persona as a "literary masquerade" through which certain classic male authors have expressed vulnerabilities and emotions that the culture denies to men.[95] Jacobs suggested professional "drag", female impersonation by male homosexuals, as "a useful, if somewhat anachronistic analogue to this narrative practice."[96] Without reference to these works, Richlin has emphasized the transvestism of Roman pantomime as an essential aspect of the cultural milieu of Ovid and his readers.[97] In the light of this evidence, she suggested that Ovid empathized with his rape victims "as a great pantomimus might; but not with any but a delicious pity for them, a very temporary taking on of their experience, their bodies."[98] This temporary experience of the woman's form is shared by Ovid with such great divinities as Jupiter (with Callisto in 2.425ff), Sol (with Leucothoe in 4.219ff.) and Apollo (with Chione in 11.310), but also with an intradiegetic narrator, the rustic Italian god Vertumnus. According to Richlin, they are all rapists that first dress as a woman, "so that the phallus can be a surprise and teach its lesson about gender again."[99] Sarah Lindheim, on the other hand, has recently argued that through the story of Vertumnus "Ovid questions the illusion that gender and identity can meaningfully exist in a vacuum."[100]

---

[94] Zeitlin 1996: 364.
[95] Taylon 1981: ch.1.
[96] Jacobs 1986: 207.
[97] Richlin 1992: 173ff.
[98] Richlin 1992: 176.
[99] Richlin 1992: 176.
[100] Lindheim 1998: 27.

V.4 Sexuality

"Orpheus' own sexuality, and his own notions of others' sexuality, is more complex than what we find in Metamorphoses 1. So it is not surprising to find him telling tales of unapproved sexuality." This is Ahl's explanation for the content of Orpheus' song dating from the 1980s.[101] By the late 1990s, however, classicists have started doubting, if not downright denying, that the Romans had a self-conscious idea of their sexuality. As a consequence, our late twentieth-century views of sexuality are bound to distort the meaning of Roman works of art (both visual and literary) with sexual subjects.[102] For example, acts that we would term "homosexual" remained unidentified in Roman culture, because the sex of the partner whom a man chose to penetrate was unimportant.[103] Of course, this means that the modern reader/viewer adopts the viewpoint of the penetrator, i.e. normally an adult elite male. In the following discussion neither of these views will be taken as an axiom. Instead our aim will be to see whether the only narrator in the *Metamophoses* whose sexual behaviour is foregrounded is affected by this in fulfilling his narrative function.

The first pentad of the *Met.* concluded with Calliope's *Hymn to Ceres*.[104] Likewise, the greatest part of Book 10 is taken up by the song of another intradiegetic narrator, Orpheus, who claims to be the son of the Muse (10.148) and Apollo (10.167). The performance reported by Ovid takes place three years after Orpheus' failed attempt to reclaim Eurydice from the Underworld. By then he has decided to avoid sex with women, and focus his erotic desire on adolescent males (*mares citraque iuventam* 10.84). As Segal observes in his study dedicated to the figure of Orpheus in literature, "his rejection of homosexual love and procreation cannot be traced back further than the Hellenistic period."[105] In surviving literature Orpheus is represented as lover of boys in Phanocles' influential Ἔρωτες ἢ Καλοί.[106] Although the Hellenistic poet did not

---

[101] Ahl 1985: 214.
[102] Clarke 1998: 8-9.
[103] Clarke 1998: 85.
[104] On the poem's pentadic structure see Holzberg 1998.
[105] Segal 1989: 9.
[106] I.e. *Amores* (the title chosen by Ovid for his own collection of amatory elegy). Barchiesi 1989: 64-73 exhaustively explores the relevance of Phanocles' poem and in p.67

exactly use homosexuality in order "to explain the reason for Orpheus' death," as Segal put it, he clearly associated these two elements of the mythical poet's biography.[107]

W. S. Anderson was probably the first to pursue the link between Orhpeus' pederasty and his song in an essay published in 1982.[108] This was spoiled, however, by the false assumption that Ovid's *carmen* is a camouflaged argument in favour of pederasty.[109] Founded on this premise, he proved that "Orpheus' advocacy of pederasty" was "self-contradictory",[110] and therefore Ovid's Orpheus is "a weirdly incompetent" poet.[111] In his book on Orpheus Segal did not refute either Anderson's premise or his presentation of the case; he only objected that had Ovid wished us to see Orpheus as "emotionally and poetically incompetent" he would have provided us with a more explicit indication of such a failing, "especially as we are dealing with myth's most celebrated singer."[112] But this is an argument from probability with limited persuasive force.

It is, of course, possible that Orpheus' account of *pueros ... / dilectos superis* (10.152-53 boys whom the gods have loved) is part of an effort to justify his own sexual behaviour after Eurydice's death. This was allegedly the Cretans' aim in creating the myth of Ganymede, according to Plato's *Laws* 1.636d: "And we all charge the Cretans that they made up the story of Ganymede; they were convinced, we say, that their legislation came from Zeus, so they went on to tell this story against him that they might, if you please, be following his example when they indulged in this pleasure."[113] The tales about *inconcessis puellas / ignibus attonitas* (10.153-54 girls seized with unlawful passion) may then be

---

tentatively argues that it is possible that Ovid even echoes Phanocles fr.1.10 Powell οὐδὲ πόθους ἤνεσε θηλυτέρων, distorting its meaning from "desire for women" into "women's lust." Alfonsi 1953 and Marcovich 1979 remain the most interesting studies of Phanocles' elegy, the latter esp. concerning its literary influence.
[107] Segal 1989: 57. The style of the poem, reminiscent of Hesiodic catalogue poetry, and its fragmentary survival do not allow absolute certainty on this matter, but it seems that his death is an appendage to the entry "Orpheus' love for Kalais."
[108] Anderson 1982: 25-50.
[109] Anderson 1982: 44.
[110] Anderson 1982: 45.
[111] Anderson 1982: 46.
[112] Segal 1989: 89.
[113] The same attitude is expressed in Call.*ep*. 6 Pf., 3-4 (= *A.P.* 12.230).

regarded as a manifestation of "violent misogyny", another argument in Orpheus' advocacy of pederasty.[114]

Nevertheless, such a manifesto would be pointless in a performance addressed to an audience made up of plants, animals and birds (10.143-44). The song is introduced as representative of the *leviore lyra* (10.152 "lighter lyre") type. It is not heroic epic, no Gigantomachy (10.150), nor is it didactic; it is light erotic poetry. That an *ab Iove* beginning was not misplaced in such a poem is evident from the passage whose echo is heard most clearly here: Vergil's third *Eclogue* (line 60: *ab Iove principium Musae*).[115]

Another argument adduced by Anderson in order to prove his theory of Orpheus as a failed advocate of homosexuality is derived from Ovid's own lack of interest in pederasty. Admittedly, Ovid himself, or at least his persona in the *Ars Amatoria* (1.522, 3.438), took a rather negative stance regarding male homosexuality, though not on moral grounds. "The reason why Ovid prefers a heterosexual relationship is his wish that both partners should derive equal satisfaction from the intercourse (*Ars* 2.648f.)."[116] Apparently, he was ignorant of the fact that "in terms of male homosexual activity in particular, it is, of course, equally possible to seek sexual satisfaction by being penetrated, or by nonpenetrative sexual activity," as Walters informs us.[117] We should, however, bear in mind that "every variety [of homosexuality] was reduced [by the Romans] to one supposedly typical model: the relationship of an adult with an adolescent who derived no pleasure from it."[118]

This is indeed the way Orpheus presents Jupiter's relationship with Ganymede.[119] It is probably no coincidence that this is the only 'happy' pederastic affair in Orpheus' song. Not only because it involves Jupiter, the supreme deity, as the singer himself proclaims in the proem (10.148 *cedunt Iovis omnia regno*); it is also the only one which fits the pattern that

---

[114] Anderson 1982: 44.
[115] *Contra* Galinsky 1975: 185, who believes that such an introduction was at home in serious epic.
[116] Lilja 1983: 84.
[117] Walters 1997: 33. As Clarke 1998: 84 observes, "we look in vain for records of the feelings of the receptive partner of these phallic acts, whether male or female, of equal or lesser status."
[118] Veyne 1985: 33.
[119] For a view of the myth as the perfect homoerotic fantasy see Shapiro 1992: 58ff.

least offended Roman morality.[120] By contrast, Apollo's passion for Hyacinthus is portrayed in the familiar terms of amatory *obsequium* (10.170-73). This means that the roles are the reverse of Roman practice: the god is the servant and the boy the master. And this is certainly important in the cultural context of a society that constructed sexual relationships in terms of domination and subordination, of superiority and inferiority, as Catherine Edwards reminds us.[121]

So far, so good. For after the story of Hyacinthus, in a contrived, Ovidian manner Orpheus introduces a few tales from Cyprus. Two of these tales (the Cerastae and Pygmalion) do not seem to be related to the poem's main themes, as announced in the proem by Orpheus. But even the other two (Propoetides and Myrrha) which can be described as "girls seized with unlawful passion" pose a problem to the reader: given that *pace* Gordon Williams,[122] it seems unlikely that all homosexual practices were penalized by Roman legislation, much less that they were conventionally regarded as disgraceful, why should stories about pederastic affairs be lumped together with incest and 'agalmatophilia'? Is it because of the "violent misogyny" of Orpheus, the "stereotyped shrill advocate" of male homosexuality, as Anderson would have us believe?

Catullus and Tibullus wrote poems about their own homosexual loves. And yet it would be considered perverse to read the poems addressed to their female lovers as misogynist. Ovid "himself is not indifferent to the fascination of *pueri*. In the first book of the *Amores* [1.1.20] (...) he declares that inspiration for his verses can come either from a *puer* or a *puella* with long and well-kept hair."[123] As for incest, this is not its first appearance in the *Metamorphoses*. The Crow's warning tale to the Raven alluded to the allegedly notorious case of Nyctimene who seduced her father, before becoming Minerva's favourite bird (2.589-93). Far more extensive is the tale of Byblis' passion for her brother Caunus, which is narrated by Ovid *in propria persona* in Book 9. It must be conceded that Orpheus' narrative is more prurient, and that unlike Ovid's Byblis, Orpheus' Myrrha (like Nictymene) does succeed in seducing the object of her illicit desire. Still, I find it difficult to accept

---

[120] MacMullen 1982: 491. See more recently Williams 1995 and 1999.
[121] Edwards 1993: 70.
[122] Williams 1962: 39-40, who adduces CIC.*Tusc*.4.70-1, NEP.*praef*.2-5 and SAL.*Cat*.13.
[123] Cantarella 1992: 137-38.

that it is Orpheus' sexuality that motivates or justifies his choice of myths.

So, is there an alternative explanation? Galinsky's approach seems more satisfying in terms of interpretative value. In his 1975 book he argued that although none of the stories is exactly homologous to Orpheus' situation, they reflect various facets of it.[124] "The stories of Ganymede and Hyacinthus provide links to Orpheus' own homosexual love after the loss of Eurydice. *Hyacinthus* and *Adonis* focus attention on Orpheus' loss of his beloved and on his incurable grief." This argument was taken up by Jörg Döring, who adds to the list of analogies that between Orpheus and Pygmalion: they both try to give life to the lifeless (Eurydice, the ivory statue) and renounce real women.[125] As for Myrrha, the point of contact is the recourse to a quasi-legal discourse, in order to discuss the issue of love and sexual desire.[126] So, in all the major stories, there appears to be an implicit point of reference to the narrator's personal story of loss, recovery, and punishment for immoderate love. Far from diverting attention from Eurydice's loss, the stories narrated by Orpheus transform his own sorrow, enriching it with a variety of overtones.

V.5. Age

As a tribute to M. I. Finley's seminal paper, let us begin with the obvious question:[127] Who are the elderly narrators?

Table 4: Narrators Explicitly Designated as Elderly

Cephalus [17]	*et veteris retinens etiamnum pignora formae* (7.497)
	cui grandior aetas (7.655)
Lelex [19]	*ante omnesque Lelex animo maturus et aevo* (8.617)
Alcmene [20]	*questus ubi ponat aniles* (9.276)
the anonymous old man of Book 11 [26]	*aliquis senior* (11.749)
Nestor [27]	*o facunde senex* (12.178)

---

[124] Galinsky 1975: 90.
[125] Döring 1996: 53.
[126] Döring 1996: 54.
[127] Finley 1981. On old age in the *Met.* see now my article in *Mnemosyne* 61 (2003) 48-60.

	tum senior: 'quamvis obstet mihi tarda vetustas' (12.182)
Sibyl **[31]**	*nam iam mihi saecula septem / acta vides* (14.144-45)
the anonymous old man of Book 15 **[37]**	*e senioribus unus* (15.10)

In other words, seven out of 38 intradiegetic narrators (18.4%) are explicitly designated as persons of advanced age, five men and two women. To these, however, we should probably add five more: (a) the proverbially long-lived Crow **[3]**[128] (b) the anonymous Lycian guide **[14]**, who addressed the narrator as *'o iuvenis'*, implying that he no longer belonged to the same age group; (c) Aeacus **[16]**, assuming that he is coeval with Celphalus; (d) Anius **[28]**, who is presented as belonging to the same generation as Anchises (13.642-43); and (e) Vertumnus **[36]** disguised as an old woman (14.654-56).

For the old, the past is long but the future is short. They live through their memories since they have little to hope for. They take pleasure in reminiscing and this is the reason why they are so loquacious.[129] In oral societies their rich memories are valued and often earn them high social standing and privileges.[130] Old people are the vehicles of communal memory, their individual memories being a particular viewpoint, actualisation and manifestation of communal memory.[131] Ovid thought it pointless to supply the elderly narrators with names, when they were not otherwise known from myth and their stories were not personal but parts of communal memory, like local aretalogies **[14]**,[132] aetiological tales **[26]** and foundation myths **[37]**. These stories are generally short (51, 45, and 46 lines respectively).

---

[128] Hes. fr. 304 M-W: "nine generations lives the sqawking crow of human youth" (trans. D. Russell) and see Esler 1989: 172 with n.1 and 177].

[129] Aristot.*Rhet*.B13 (1390a6 ff.). *Senectus est natura loquacior*, observed Cicero in the treatise *De Senectute* (55) despite the fact that *memoria minuitur* (21).

[130] Beauvoir 1980: 76.

[131] Halbwachs 1950: 33 and 1992: 40.

[132] i.e. stories of a religious nature related by a local story-teller, concerning what happened to real individuals of no great prominence. See most recently Beck 1996: 137-38 and Scobie 1979: 243; also Longo 1969, Smith 1971 and Reitzenstein 1906.

The anonymous Lycian's narrative **[14]** about the transformation of local farmers into frogs is strongly biased against the impious farmers. "They leapt around in pure malice, their foul tongues kept bickering, they had no sense of shame at all and, even under the water, they still tried to be abusive" (6.365ff.). The same indignation against the impious motivates the narrative of another old man, Lelex **[19]**: 'Baucis and Philemon' is a tale of piety rewarded, involving a poor, aged couple. Nestor, "as concpicuous a gerontocrat as is to be found among the Achaeans," is represented in *Odyssey* 3 as particularly pious: Telemachus finds him engaged in sacrifice.[133] Neither Aristotle nor Cicero, however, thought that there was a particular link between piety and age. Indeed, several of the characteristics attributed by the former to the elderly would be more akin to an impious person: they are malign (κακοήθεις *Rh.*13, 1389b20) and suspicious (καχύποπτοι, ἄπιστοι *Rh.*13, 1389b22); only their sense of pity could be associated with piety, but this is not exclusive to them, as Aristotle explicitly observes (*Rh.*13, 1390a18). So, perhaps the piety of these two elderly narrators is to be explained by other factors. The anonymous Lycian is a local guide, i.e. someone who benefits from impressing his clients and instilling in them a sense of awe at the places they are visiting.[134] And "Lelex has imbibed the teaching of his mentor, the *righteous* Pittheus." [135]

Most named elderly narrators tell personal reminiscences from their youth –except Aeacus **[15]**, Lelex **[18]**, Anius **[27]**, and Vertumnus in drag **[35]**. This seems to mean different things for old women and men. For the Crow **[3]** (who used to be the princess Coronis), for Alcmene **[19]**, and the Sibyl **[30]**, youth is the age of being sexually attractive and productive. For Cephalus **[16]** and Nestor **[26]**, on the other hand, youth means being able to take part in such manly activities as hunting and fighting.

Among the Romans, old women were also the story-tellers *par excellence*, even though we hardly know anything about their tales in the nursery. The famous tale of 'Amor and Psyche', for instance, in Apuleius' *Metamorphoses* is told by an old woman (4.27). Cicero

---

[133] The quotation is from Falkner 1989:30.
[134] And Ovid remembers the scene from *Od.*19.35-42 involving Telemachus and his father.
[135] Hollis on 8.617 (my emphasis).

disapprovingly speaks of *anilis superstitio* and contrasts reasonable arguments with *aniles fabellas*.[136] On the whole, Alcmene **[20]** is cast by Ovid as a typical *anus*. Soft-hearted (9.324-27, 396) and garrulous (9.277-78), she is sitting at her charge's side and telling stories about her son, in this particular instance his birth.[137] It is perhaps not without some relief that she looks back on those days when she had to fight against Juno's jealousy. Yet, it is difficult to tell whether her story would fit Cicero's idea of an old woman's tale: she certainly fears Juno instead of loving her, but her fear is far from *inanis*.[138]

The Sibyl **[31]** almost regrets having turned down Apollo's offer of eternal youth in exchange for her virginity, even though *praecorrumpere* (14.134) suggests that she still disapproves of the god's scheming, just as much as of her own juvenile foolishness to ask him only for length of days (14.138 *vana*). Even at seven hundred years of age she seems just as vain as when Apollo fell in love with her: what hurts her most is that in the years to come she will no longer be desirable (14.149-51): *nec amata videbor / nec placuisse deo: Phoebus quoque forsitan ipse / vel non cognoscet cel dilexisse negabit* "No one will think that I was ever loved, or that I pleased a god, and perhaps even Phoebus himself will fail to recognize me, or else deny that he ever had any affection for me."[139]

Old men enjoy telling stories (11.748-9), particularly when this gives them an opportunity for self-glorification, as Cicero again perceptively noted in the *De Senectute* (31): *videtisne ut apud Homerum saepissime Nestor de virtutibus suis praedicet?* "Don't you see how frequently in Homer Nestor relates his feats of prowess?"[140] Such is the case of Aeacus **[16]**, the king of Aegina, who tells the story of how he saved his island from a pestilence with the help of his father Jupiter. It is, therefore, impossible not to read ironically Lelex' **[19]** concluding comment on the source of his story about Baucis and Philemon: *haec mihi non vani (neque erat, cur fallere vellent) / narravere seni* (8.721-22) "This tale was told to me by

---

[136] Bremmer 1987: 201.
[137] For the stereotype of the old woman in Latin literature see Rosivach 1994.
[138] Cf. Cicero's definition of *superstitio* in N.D.1.117: *in qua inest timor inanis deorum* (when gods are feared).
[139] For the stereotype of the wrinkly old woman who still has an interest in having sex see Rosivach 1994: 111 and Richlin 1983: 112.
[140] Cf. also CIC.*Sen*.82: *more senum glorier*.

truthful old men, who had nothing to gain by deceiving me." [141] Nestor unashamedly admits in his narration of the battle against the Centaurs at 12.182ff. that old men can occasionally be unreliable. He awards himself a complete *aristeia* (12.439-51), reserving it for just before the culmination of his narrative with Caeneus' *aristeia* (12.459-93) and surpasses not only Peleus but even the invulnerable Caeneus in number of victims (seven vs. six), by slaughtering seven Centaurs, even though he is wounded. Furthermore, under the pressure of Tlepolemus' angry intervention, Nestor is compelled to admit that oblivion can also be a psychological mechanism of self-protection against traumatic experiences, like losing all one's brothers (12.542-44).

The Crow introduces her tale with a paradoxical statement that faithfulness can prove disastrous for the person who shows it. Lelex also states at the very beginning the view that his story will attempt to support; he will reaffirm his piety at the very end of his narrative (8.723-24). A *sententia* opens Anius' **[28]** narrative too: *tanta homines rerum inconstantia versat* (13.646). The same technique, firmly established by rhetorical theory at least since Aristotle,[142] is used by the extradiegetic narrator to introduce a story (3.135ff.; 7.453ff.).[143] In the case of these elderly narrators, however, it appears to be particularly appropriate (Ar.*Rh*. B 21/1395a2ff.):

ἁρμόττει δὲ γνωμολογεῖν ἡλικίᾳ μὲν πρεσβυτέρων,[144] περὶ δὲ τούτων ὧν ἔμπειρός τίς ἐστιν, ὥστε τὸ μὲν μὴ τηλικοῦτον ὄντα γνωμολογεῖν ἀπρεπὲς ὥσπερ καὶ τὸ μυθολογεῖν, περὶ δὲ ὧν ἄπειρος, ἠλίθιον καὶ ἀπαίδευτον.

---

[141] As Gamel 1984: 129 observes, they were locals who obviously wanted to impress the foreigner Lelex with their narrative. The Nikandrian parallel adduced by Griffin 1991: 67 is no parallel at all, since Kragaleus is not a narrator in Ant.Lib.4.

[142] Ar.*Rh*. B 21 (1394b8f.) ἀποδείξεως μὲν οὖν δεόμεναι εἰσὶν ὅσαι [sc. γνῶμαι] παράδοξόν τι λέγουσιν ἢ ἀμφισβητούμενον and cf. ib. B 20 (1894a9f.) δεῖ δὲ χρῆσθαι παραδείγμασι οὐκ ἔχοντα μὲν ἐνθυμήματα ὡς ἀποδείξεσιν (ἡ γὰρ πίστις διὰ τούτων) and ib. A 9 (1368a29f.) τὰ δὲ παραδείγματα τοῖς συμβουλευτικοῖς [sc. ἐπιτηδειότατα] (ἐκ γὰρ τῶν προγεγονότων τὰ μέλλοντα καταμαντευόμενοι κρίνομεν).

[143] Cf. also 9.454 (*Byblis in exemplo est, ut ament concessa puellae*). For the Homeric use of *exempla* see the bibliography in de Jong 1987: 160; add Slatkin 1991: 61ff. For Propertius see Lechi 1979. For Ovid's amatory poetry see Weber 1983.

[144] Nestor is the embodiment of this idea in archaic Greek epic, see Hainsworth on *Il*.11.656-803. At Aristotle offers a psychological interpretation of senile loquacity: ἀναμιμνησκόμενοι γὰρ ἥδονται. The crow demonstrates yet another symptom of old age according to Aristotle (ibid.): καὶ μᾶλλον ζῶσι κατὰ λογισμὸν ἢ κατὰ τὸ ἔθος· ὁ μὲν λογισμὸς τοῦ **συμφέροντος** (cf. *non utile carpis* 549) τὸ δὲ ἦθος τῆς ἀρετῆς ἐστιν.

V.6 Class

Class will be the last factor which will be considered for its possible influence on the intradiegetic narrators' choices of story-type and particularities of narrative strategy and technique. It is a commonplace in classical literary studies that all our extant literary texts view social relations from the viewpoint of the elite. This means that the diminished subjectivity allowed to the slaves and the lower classes remained largely unspoken. Nothing comparable to the rich tradition of American slave narratives and oral stories of ex-slaves survives from antiquity.[145] Illiteracy has nothing to do with this, as many slaves were employed as teachers, and indeed many important figures in the Roman literary scene were slaves or freedmen. It is more probable, as Fitzgerald suggested, that the reason for the dearth of slave narratives is the fact that "slavery was too much an unquestioned part of the way things were for the experience of the slave to be conceived as an object of interest."[146] Homer gave speech to the underprivileged, but they will have to wait until the late 5th century to find a prominent place in Euripides' plays.[147]

Eumaios in the *Odyssey* (15.403-84) is one of the few labourers of ancient literature who are presented as narrators.[148] His narrative is all the more interesting since it is an autobiographical one, thus closely related to the question of whether slavery is natural, an inborn lack of virtue (the quality characteristic of the freeborn).[149] The matter is even more complicated by the story of Eumaios' nurse, enfolded in his account of his life (*Od.*15.415-81). As William G. Thalmann concludes his recent study of the issue, "the nurse might be taken as illustrating the truth of Eumaios' statement that Zeus takes away half a person's virtue when the day of slavery comes (17.322-23) if he did not himself exemplify the persistence of the qualities associated with high birth in

---

[145] Fitzgerald 2000: 2. He considers the animal fable as a possible exception in ch.5; see also Hopkins 1993 on the *Life of Aesop*.
[146] Fitzgerald 2000: 2.
[147] On the latter see Neuberger-Bonath 1970: 80-81.
[148] "Nothing indicates (...) that there was a strict separation of slave labour from free labour." (Bradley 1994: 65).
[149] This view underlies most ancient literature and found its theoretical expression in Aristotle's *Politics* 1; see Schlaifer 1936 and Thalmann 1998: 28-45.

reduced circumstances. With the figure of the 'good' slave, the representation of slavery becomes inescapably contradictory."[150]

Sustained narrative in Athenian drama is normally ascribed to the messenger. Something that is not often mentioned in relation with tragic messenger-speeches is the frequent representation of *angeloi* as persons of lowly status.[151] In Sophocles' *Oedipus Tyrannos* the messenger is addressed by Jocasta as πρόσπολος (945). In Euripides' *Medea* he is presented by Medea as Jason's ὀπαδός (1119), in *Hippolytus* as the young man's ὀπαδός (1151), and a similar status is implied for the messenger in *Andromache* (1085). In the same tragedian's *Supplices* he introduces himself as Capaneus' λάτρις (639), in *Electra* (which also features a farmer as the heroine's husband!) as Orestes' πρόσπολος (766), while in *Iphigeneia in Tauris* the first messenger is presented by the chorus as a βουφορβός (237). But it is in *Ion* (also a play which features a servant as one of the main characters, Ion himself) that we come across a *nuntius* who is explicitly called a slave (ὦ ξύνδουλε 1109), while in *Orestes* the first messenger presents himself as πένητα (870) and the second one is addressed by the chorus as Ἑλένης πρόσπολ', Ἰδαῖον κάρα (1380). For Euripides a man's value lies not in his social rank but in his company and conduct (*El*.384-8 τῇ δ' ὁμιλίᾳ βροτῶν ... καὶ τοῖς ἤθεσιν). It is not surprising then that so many persons of lowly origin are presented on stage as reliable narrators, even though they are not telling their personal stories, which would make them full subjects.

Besides Onetor [25], Ceyx' herdsman who reports to Peleus and his court the story about the wolf of Trachis, intradiegetic narrators that are presented as persons of low social status include Acoetes [4], the fisherman who became Bacchus' apostle, and the anonymous maid of Circe [34], who tells about her mistress' erotic triangle with Picus and Canens. Perhaps we should also assume that all the anonymous narrators [13, 14, 25, and 36] are of low social standing. Their identity is obscure probably because they are *viri ignobiles*, like the Lycian farmers of the story told by the first of them [13]. Yet, the comment made by the anonymous narrator of 'Aeacus and Hesperia' [25] that despite being

---

[150] Thalmann 1998: 99.
[151] De Jong 1991: 67 refers to their occupation as an explanation for their witnessing the events reported.

born in a pastoral landscape, the hero's heart was not boorish, nor was it proof against love (11.767-68), betrays his own urbane, courtly identity.[152]

The narrative of Acoetes **[4]** is the only one of these that is strictly autodiegetic. The narrator has now become "a follower and attendant of the rites" (*comitem famulumque sacrorum* 3.574) of Bacchus, but he began his life as a humble fisherman, the son of a fisherman.[153] Following a cue from the Stranger of Euripides' *Bacchae* (461 οὐ κόμπος οὐδείς),[154] Acoetes offers a version of the *Homeric Hymn to Dionysos* (VII). His story is also very much akin to the autobiographical story of calling. In Christian narrative discourse the archetypal example(s) of this theme is St. Paul's triple narration of the episode on the road to Damascus.[155] Even the narrative situation is similar to that of Paul's second account (*Acts* 26.1): they are both performances in the context of a trial judged by a king. In this respect both narratives illustrate what G. W. Most (1989: 127) considers as exclusively characteristic of classical Greek autobiographic discourse: they are "born out of a situation of actual need."

Onetor **[25]**, on the other hand, is a cowherd who works for Peleus (*armenti custos* 11.348). His job is similar to that of Eumaios in the *Odyssey* but his narrative is cast in the mould of the tragic messenger-speech, i.e. a homodiegetic witness narrative. His role is announced by himself at the beginning of his speech: *nuntius* (11.349). His story is particularly reminiscent of the messenger-speech of the ox-herd in Euripides' *Iphigeneia in Tauris*. Both of them have brought their cattle *ad litora curva* (11.352 cf. *I.T.*254-55) when a *monstrum* emerges from the sea "flecked with blood and foam" (11.367 cf. *I.T.* 308) and attacks the cattle (11.370ff. cf. *I.T.* 296ff.). Onetor's narrative closes with an urgent appeal

---

[152] Cf. Ovid in *Am*.3.10.17f: *nec tamen est, quamvis agros amet illa feraces,/ rustica nec viduum pectus amoris habet*; of course, Ovidian elegy is the genre most closely linked with urban society and the "rhetoric of the city" (Rosati 1983: 83).
[153] Fishing is considered unheroic in archaic Greek epic; see R. Janko on *Il*.16.407-8.
[154] Against most modern editors of Euripides' play, I accept the reading of the manuscripts, following J. Roux (see his note *ad loc.*).
[155] See Courcelle 1957: 29. That what Paul experienced was a calling rather than a conversion was first demonstrated by Stendhal 1976: 7-23.

for quick action, as if the speaker has not been wasting time by giving such a long-winded account of the situation on the coast of Trachis.[156]

Taking the hint from Vergil (*Aen.*7.189 *Picus equum domitor*), Ovid makes Macareus [32] put in the mouth of Circe's maidservant [35] a tale of love, envy and metamorphosis, starring Picus, Canens and her mistress, mighty Circe. Although the maid herself did not take part in the action (i.e. she is a heterodiegetic narrator), she is able to quote the very words of both her mistress (14.355-57, 372-76, and 383-85) and Picus (14.378-81). We are probably meant to assume that she has been told the story by Circe herself, although her sympathy seems to be shared between the innocent victim (14.362 *inscius*, 364 *spemque sequens vanam*) and her mistress (14.377 *ille ferox ipsamque precesque relinquit*).[157] The tale, which is probably an Ovidian invention,[158] has a clear aetiological frame. Not only Macareus' questions **quare** *sacra coletur in aede,/* **cur** *hanc ferret avem* (316-7) but also the imperatives of the maid's reply (318-9 *accipe...disce...tu dictis adice mentem*) point in this direction.[159] The tale itself contains etymological (i.e. aetiological) comments on the names of Canens (14.337-38 *sed rarior arte canendi, / unde Canens dicta est*) and Picus (14.396 *nec quiquam Pico nisi nomina restant*).[160]

Aetiological is also the character of the stories told by two other anonymous narrators: the Lycian guide [14] and the old Crotonian [36]. The former's story explains why the altar he and the Lydian man have encountered is dedicated to Latona. K. S. Myers has analysed the net of

---

[156] This does not seem to be a common feature of the Euripidean messenger-speech; only the first ἄγγελος of the *I.A.* concludes his ῥῆσις with 'orders' (435-38).

[157] Bömer, without offering any explanation, asserts that *ferox* here does not have its usual negative meaning; as for his two parallels (5.35, 15.515), neither is in an amatory context. If he is right, the narrator admires Picus' heroic behaviour. It is interesting that Picus is actually transformed into a bird which **duro fera** *robora rostro / figit* (391-2).

[158] See Myers 1994: 108.

[159] See Bömer *ad loc.*

[160] I am not, however, convinced by the evidence adduced by Myers 1994: 106 with regard to the frame's particularly Callimachean colouring. The statues of the Graces on Paros (*Aet.*1 fr.7.11-12) are only discussed *en passant*, while where there is a sustained narrative and the identity of the narrator is clear from the surviving evidence,[160] it is often the represented divinity (*Aet.*inc.libr.fr.114.4-17; *Iamb.*7 fr.197, 9.fr.199) or the poet himself (*Aet.*3.fr.84 and 4.fr.100) that reveals the *aetion*, not some local informer, as in the present occasion. As for the parallels collected from the *Fasti*, 1.133ff. and 4.219-20 do not in fact discuss "the attributes of **certain** [my emphasis] cult statues," while 3.437-44, 5.129-42 and 6.569-624 are narrated by 'Ovid'.

allusions to previous aetiological, i.e. learned poetry, especially Propertius 4.9.[161] She further suggested that it would "be a typical mark of Ovid's humor to attribute to this rustic narrator such a complexly allusive tale, and then to highlight the aetiological models for the story by embedding it in a narrative framework typical of these poems."[162] The old Crotonian **[36]** satisfies king Numa's curiosity about the origins of the city of Croton (15.9-11). The foundation of a city was "an archetypal theme of Greek poetry, which was revived as a suitable subject for poetry by the Alexandrians."[163] This is not the only foundation story in the *Metamorphoses* (Miletus in 9.447-49, Caunus in 9.633-34, and Thebes in 3.1-130, though Rome's foundation is conspicuously absent), but none of these is framed as an aetiological narrative as clearly as this one.[164]

To sum up, we have two narrators with clear Euripidean lineage, which is not surprising in view of the tragedian's interest in characters of low social status, and a few who are presented as reliable informants about local *aetia*, a favourite theme of Callimachus, who could be said to have been a follower of Euripides in spite of his famous abhorrence for everything vulgar (epigram 29 Pf.). His description of Hecale's material poverty in the poem of the same title (fr.26ff. Hollis), full of "picturesque and recherché elements," suggests that he relished the flavour of this low and sordid subject.[165] His epigrams also show an interest in labourers like Astakides the goatherd (epigram 22 Pf.), Mikylos (epigram 26 Pf.), Simon the prostitute (epigram 38 Pf.), and Aiskhre the Phrygian nurse (epigram 49 Pf.). This intertextual dimension has naturally led to metapoetic readings of these narratives. J. J. Clauss in his 1989 article, for instance, suggested that Latona's attempt to drink from a public pool looks like an inversion of the customary Callimachean exclusive taste for private springs. And the Ovidian version of the Euripidean messenger-speech (Onetor **[25]**) could be seen as a demonstration of the tensions inherent in this narrative form, especially between the amount of circumstantial detail and the urgency of the situation.

---

[161] Myers 1994: 86-90.
[162] Myers 1994: 88.
[163] Knox 1986: 67.
[164] Myers 1994: 81. On Thebes see Hardie 1990.
[165] Hutchinson 1988: 57.

But such considerations would take us away from our main focus, the issue of the narrators' class. Perhaps, we should conclude that, as in the case of women narrators, the very presence of underprivileged intradiegetic narrators in the poem is a gesture of recognition of their existence and contribution to the tradition, oral and written, which culminates in this narrative of all narratives. It is, however, significant that only one of these narratives is related to these people's everyday lives, while the real emphasis is on the unusual emergence of the monster. If "even today workers and women are marginalised if not invisible in most written narratives, highbrow and lowbrow," it is no surprise that it should be so in the context of early imperial Rome.[166]

V.7 Conclusions

In the light of new developments in narrative theory, in particular its opening up to feminist, ideological, and other contextual perspectives, we have experimented with their potential for a more accurate and detailed description of the narrative voices in the *Metamorphoses*. It is important to emphasize the experimental character of our discussion and, consequently, the tentative nature of these conclusions because of the great variety of approaches to the feminist, ideological, etc. analysis of narrative. In terms of numbers, female narrators are a significant quantity. There are also intradiegetic narrators who are markedly old, socially low-standing and sexually deviant. Some of these categories were represented in earlier epic, but what is remarkable is their number and co-presence in a single work. Yet, a parameter of the narrator's identity is not enough on its own to change a work's ideological perspective.

To put it in narratological terms, the variety of intradiegetic narrators does not entail a multiplicity of voices, in the sense of distinct ideological positions. We have seen that female narrators, for example, are mainly individuals of exceptional status, divine or royal. They also normally address their stories to other women in the private, female space of the home. These additional elements of the narrative situation seem to reinforce the women's solidarity among themselves, but also align them with the androcentric aristocratic ideology, typical of epic. Even among

---

[166] Toolan 1988: 246.

themselves, women engage in competition, which is also characteristic of aristocratic male values. Something similar happens with the only male narrator who is represented as currently limiting his sexual orientation to young males. His audience is one made up of animals, trees, and lifeless matter, who, presumably (and there is no indication to the opposite) cannot understand a word of his morally pernicious stories of pederasty, incest and other vices.

A striking feature of female narrative discourse in the *Met.*, though not exclusive to it, is the domination of love in its thematics. An important aspect of the representation of heterosexual love in the poem is the issue of rape, attempted or perpetrated, which is frequently an element of the erotic story told by female narrators. The rape motif probably recalls the reality of marriage customs in an androcentric, misogynistic culture, like that of Rome, where the first sexual encounter for a young woman may well have seemed like a rape. Rape was indeed a common plot device in Roman Comedy. But viewers of comedy were less shocked because they could safely assume that the wrong would be undone by marriage. By contrast, in the *Met.*, male rapists usually enjoy their prey and move on to a new victim. Although marriage is not excluded as a conclusion, the victims of rape may be transformed (the poem's overarching theme) or be punished by patriarchy for succumbing, however unwillingly, to male desire. Depending on the ethical view to metamorphosis and the representation of the erotic in literature that we adopt, we may see rape-stories told by female narrators as a denunciation of male domination and female objectification, which ultimately reinforces patriarchy and androcentrism because they adopt the male ideology of rape. Or, perhaps, they offer ample and varied opportunities for a vicarious taste of sadomasochistic pleasure for those who can dispense with ethics completely and enjoy the porn. Narratology is not required or entitled to decide such an issue of narrative ethics but merely map the possibilities. The same applies to the question of Ovid's "transvestism" in employing female intradiegetic narrators.

Orpheus is the only narrator who explicitly prefers the love of young men. The aim of our discussion was to determine the relation between his sexuality and his narrative strategy. He has been presented as a failed advocate of homosexuality. But if we take into account the narrative situation, i.e. his audience (birds, beasts and trees) and the time of narrating (after his ultimate failure to lead Eurydice back to life), the picture becomes more complex. Orpheus' song becomes an effort of artistic re-enactment of Orpheus' own sufferings out of love for his wife.

Aged narrators are frequently anonymous, probably because they represent communal memory. These stories are rather short and are generally about *aetia*, e.g. foundation or local cult myths. Most named elderly narrators, on the other hand, relate at great length their personal reminiscences from the time of their youth. For men this means stories of hunting and fighting, while for women youth is the time they were sexually attractive. Two secondary characteristics of aged narrators are self-glorification and sententiousness.

Most narrators in the *Met.* are mythological characters who enjoyed a privileged social or cosmic status. There are, however, three named narrators of low social standing, to whom all four anonymous intradiegetic narrators in the poem should be added. Their stories are often aetiological and some of them have a clear literary lineage, which goes back to Euripides and Callimachus, two poets with a marked interest in non-elite characters. As in the case of women narrators, the presence of non-elite narrators is a gesture of recognition of their contribution to the long tradition of oral narrative, which culminates in Ovid's *summa narrativa*.

VI Extra-narrative functions of the narrators

VI.1 Extra-Narrative Functions of the Narrator

A narrative text like the *Metamorphoses* incorporates types of discourse other than narrative. Since these are also perceived as proceeding from the same source as narration itself, the narrator, the hypostasized narrative voice can be said to perform extra-narrative functions. Genette designates four functions of the narrator (*directing, communicative, testimonial,* and *ideological* or *interpretative*) besides the main function of telling a story.[1] Although only the latter is absolutely indispensable, none of the others can be completely avoided. Their performance is instead a question of relative importance.

The more frequently and obtrusively they are performed the more perceptible the narrator becomes, not only hypostasized but also characterized. This notion of perceptibility or overtness of the narrator was particularly developed in the American strand of narratology, whose major exponents are S. Chatman and S. Rimmon-Kenan.[2] These two narratologists combine inspiration from Booth with an influence in part deriving from Genette and in part from thematic narratology. Chatman, in particular, has elaborated a fourfold typology of different types of commentary: interpretation, judgement, generalization, all three involving commentary on the story, and commentary on the discourse.[3]

Given that commentaries constitute engrafted specimens of a non-narrative type of discourse, which could be called explanatory and argumentative,[4] they are usually considered to affect narrativity negatively. In other words, "the more commentaries in relation to narration, the lower the degree of narrativity."[5] By narrativity I mean "what in a text underlines its possibly narrative nature, what emphasizes the presence and semiotic role of narrative structures in a textual economy." This should be distinguished from the so-called "reportability" of a narrative, i.e. what makes a narrative worth telling

---

[1] Genette 1972: 261ff.
[2] Chatman 1978 and Rimmon-Kenan 1983.
[3] Chatman 1983: 219-253.
[4] See Adam 1997.
[5] Florin 1996: 17. I am greatly indebted to this essay for its systematic presentation of the various developments in narratological theory on voice.

(*dignum relatu*), interesting, appealing, for which the only criterion explicitly established in the *Metamorphoses* is the aetiological interest of a story (4.791-93).[6] On the other hand, the narrativity of a text depends, among other things, on the extent to which it "involves a hierarchical organization as opposed to a mere temporal concatenation of events," and such a structure is often supported by commentary and evaluative statements.[7]

VI.2 Directing Function of the Intradiegetic Narrators

This involves any kind of metanarrative comments on the narrative text itself, i.e. remarks on the text's articulations, connections, and interrelations. Metadiegetic narratives in the *Met.* are generally short and do not normally involve more than one story. It would be surprising if the intradiegetic narrators commented frequently on their text's organisation. Another particularity of their texts which affects the quantity and formulation of such comments is their oral nature (see section IV.3 above). Oral narrators are not generally thought to be sophisticated enough for self-conscious commentary, nor is it easy to point out the interrelations between different parts of a narrative that only exists momentarily. In the following **Table 1** have listed all passages in the 37 metadiegetic narratives that refer to what the narrators propose to include or leave out.

Table 1: Directing Function

No	Lines	Passage
1	1.210	*quod tamen admissum, quae sit vindicta docebo*
1	1.214-5	*longa mora est quantum noxae sit ubique repertum,/ enumerare*
3	2.551	*quid fuerim quid simque, vide meritumque require*
6	4.170	*Solis referemus amores*
7	4.276-84	*'Vulgatos taceo' dixit 'pastoris amores / Daphnidis Idaei, quem numphe paelicis ira / contulit in saxum: tantus dolor*

---

[6] This aspect of the poem's structure and discourse has long been recognised. Its most interesting recent treatment is found in Myers 1994
[7] Prince 1996: esp. 103.

> *urit amantes;/ nec loquor, ut quondam naturae iure novato / ambiguus fuerit modo vir, modo femina Sithon;/ te quoque, nunc adamas, quondam fidissime parvo, / Celmi, Iovi largosque satos Curetas ab imbri/ et Crocon in parvos versum sum Smilace flores/ praetereo dulcique animos novitate tenebo.*

11	5.462-3	*Quas dea per terras et quas erraverit undas,/ dicere longa mora est.*
15	7.518-20	*Flebile principium melior fortuna secuta est:/ hanc utinam possem vobis memorare sine illo! / ordine nunc repetam, neu longe ambage morer vos.*
16	7.796-7	*Gaudia principium nostri sunt, Phoce, doloris:/ illa prius referam*
17e	9.5	*referam tamen ordine*
26	12.245	*primus Ophionides Amycus*
34	14.473	*neve morer referens tristes ex ordine casus*

A recurring element in three of these comments (1.214-15, 5.462-3, 14.473) is the invocation of *mora* (waste of time) as an excuse for cutting a long tale short. As he explicitly announced at the beginning of his narrative, Jupiter **[1]** intends to focus on Lycaon's punishment and therefore thinks it is a waste of time to mention all the examples of human malice he came across during his visit on earth. Calliope **[11]** admits that she will not attempt to catalogue the numerous places Ceres visited in her search for her daughter, a task the narrator of the *Fasti* does not find tiresome, daunting or boring (4.467-80 and 563-72). Finally, Diomedes **[34]**, understanding the urgency of the Latins' situation, considers it a waste of time to tell about the fates of the other Greek heroes after they left Troy, their *nostoi*; instead he proposes to focus on his own. This concern about *mora* is also shared by Ulixes (13.205f.) and the extradiegetic narrator (5.2-7-8). This does not prevent 'Ovid' from name-dropping on the occasion of Medea's voyage by air, not to mention other types of catalogue in the poem. Arethusa **[12]** also gives a two-line catalogue (5.607-8) of her wanderings while hunted by

Alpheus.[8] Avoidance of *mora* is not a permanent rule of narrative organisation.

Diomedes' comment (14.473) also makes reference to another principle of narrative organisation: *ex ordine*. Aeacus **[15]** and Achelous **[17e]** also refer to it. Its exact meaning is far from clear. Commenting on Minerva's use of the term in her injunction to the Muse to quote Calliope's song instead of summarizing it (5.335 *refer ordine carmen*), Bömer explains it literally as meaning "in due order" and considers it almost redundant. Servius' gloss on VERG.G.4.506 *ordine: sine intermissione* seems to suggest more something like "without pauses or digressions." This is not far from the Homeric principle of telling a story κατὰ κόσμον, which Brian Hainsworth interprets both in terms of order and exclusion of digressive ornamentation.[9] Indeed, Aeacus' phrase (7.520) seems to suggest that *ordine referre* lies between the two extremes of an extremely detailed account that gives the impression of a labyrinth (*ambage*) and a dry summary which lacks the charm of a proper narrative. In Pentheus' view, Acoetes' narrative **[4]** represents the former type of excess. Although it is certainly one of the longest metanarratives (110) by a non-professional story-teller and includes many named characters, whose words are often quoted, it is not longer than Aeacus' narrative.[10] Whether a narrative is told *(ex) ordine* or not seems to be a subjective judgment. When applied by the narrator him/herself it is probably a way of reassuring the audience that they will neither be exhausted or bored, nor cheated with an abbreviated version devoid of colourful details.

Sometimes intradiegetic narrators introduce the topic of their stories in a formal way. Jupiter **[1]**, for instance, uses a term (*docebo* 1.210) which is often used by or about orators delivering formal speeches in court, in the senate or the army, setting a tone appropriate to the context of a

---

[8] For a narrator's concern with *mora* see also *Fast*.1.492, 2.248, 3.407f., and 3.768. Heinze 1919: 9 finds Calliope's comment less subjectively coloured than the corresponding one in *Fast*.4.573.

[9] Hainsworth on *Od*.8.489. For a census of interpretations see Ford 1992: 122 and 123n.50.

[10] The length of the metanarratives can be found in the last column of Appendix A in Wheeler 1999: 207-10. Other metanarratives of comparable length are those of the first Minyeid **[5]**, Lelex **[18]**, Venus **[22]**, Galatea **[28]**, Macareus **[32]**, and Circe's maid **[33]**.

Divine Assembly.[11] Leuconoe's description of her theme with the phrase *Solis referemus amores* (4.170), with the god's name placed before the verb denoting the performer's task, not only alludes to hymnic tradition but also to a type of narrative frequently encountered in the *Met.*: *primus amor Phoebi* (1.452) is the phrase used by the extradiegetic narrator to introduce the story of Daphne's pursuit by Apollo, and *fluminis Elei veteres narravit amores* (5.576) is the introductory verse employed by Calliope [11] before quoting Arethusa's metanarrative [12]. To these phrases we should probably add Orpheus' formal proem, in which he asks the Muse for an *ab Iove* song (10.148). Indeed, Orpheus' song is one of the few metanarratives, where we would expect the narrator to have a considerable directing role: it is a professional narrative that includes a series of stories. Yet, only the second one (Hyacinthus) is introduced with a connective, which combined with apostrophe, suggests the narrator's presence: *Te quoque, Amyclide,...* (10.162). The third (Cerastae) is introduced with an apostrophe to the narratee, while the rest are in chronological/genealogical order.

In the previous paragraph we referred to the extradiegetic narrator's use of *primus* in order to introduce a story, viz. that of Daphne. It is also employed by Nestor [26] in the context of a battle-narrative. Joachim Latacz must be right when he argues that the typical πρῶτος, the Greek equivalent of *primus*, does not (necessarily) signal the onset of the 'real' battle (as distinct from the starting point of the battle-narrative) but rather the start of the detailed battle-narrative.[12] This view is corroborated by the use of the same adjective a few lines earlier (12.242 *prima ... pugna*) in an introductory description of a mass-scene (the Centaurs' attack). If this is true it follows that who is mentioned first depends on memory and the narrative strategy of the individual storyteller, just as much as who is mentioned at all.

---

[11] See *TLL* V.1, 1709, 76ff. Cf. also QVINT.*Inst.*9.4.134 *narratio ... docere et infigere animis res semper cupit*. It should be noted, however, that the word also occurs in less formal contexts, most notably in VERG.*Aen.*3.717 *Sic pater Aeneas intentis omnibus unus / fata renarrabat diuum cursusqusque docebat*, 8.346 (sc. *Rex Euandrus*) *testaturque locum et letum docet hospitis Argi*, and 12.111 (sc. *Aeneas*) *tum socios maestisque metum solatur Iuli / fata docens*.
[12] Latacz 1977: 83. This does not mean that I find his argumentation convincing, in particular his supposition that should this be the 'real' beginning of the fight, the narrator would continue the enumeration of the individual participants.

In his proem Orpheus **[21]** mentions an *ab Iove* beginning for his song, which he would rather not use, i.e. his triumph over the Giants (10.150-51). Likewise, Alcithoe **[7]** rejects several stories, before eventually choosing the one she will tell her other sisters and domestic female slaves. Her narrative starts with a *Priamel/praeteritio*, a beginning typical of Greek choral lyric.[13] The reason why none of the tales mentioned is deemed worth telling is encapsulated in the very first word Alcithoe utters (*vulgatos* 4.276). This implies that it is novelty of subject-matter that she aspires to, but not necessarily (or even probably) originality of treatment. In this respect the Minyeid resembles archaic Greek bards.[14] Phemius in *Odyssey* 1.351-2 declares that men would rather listen to the song that happens to be the newest:

τὴν γὰρ ἀοιδὴν μᾶλλον ἐπικλείουσ' ἄνθρωποι,
ἥ τις ἀκουόντεσσι νεωτάτη ἀμφιπέληται.

Although novelty may have Callimachean associations,[15] it must be pointed out that even Cicero, a self-avowed anti-Callimachean, can claim that *animos hominum ad me dicendi novitate converteram* (*Brut.*321).[16] Novelty (καινότης) also was a term of praise in the critical vocabulary of ancient scholiasts, e.g. *Ad* Arat.117-18: καὶ τὸ καινότερον ἔχει τι ἄμεινον. For, as Schol. *ad* Dem.4.58 explains, τοιοῦτοι γὰρ οἱ ἄνθρωποι ἀεὶ τῶν καινοτέρων ὀρέγονται.[17]

Only Aeacus **[15]** and Cephalus **[16]** make comments on their narratives' internal structure. The former announces a movement from misfortune into happiness, the latter the reverse. Of course, the period of Cephalus' happy marriage to Procris has been preceded by several ordeals (his abduction by Eos and her desertion of their home after the unfair test of her loyalty by her husband in disguise). Yet, these descriptions fit the portions of narrative text they introduce. It is interesting to note that both types of story would be described by Aristotle as tragic. In fact, Cephalus' transition ἐξ εὐτυχίας εἰς δυστυχίαν coincides with Aristotle's best type of tragic myth. What is their tragic

---

[13] Race 1982: 8 and 21.
[14] See Thalmann 1984: 125.
[15] See e.g. Anderson on 4.276-78.
[16] Nisbet-Hubbard on HOR.*Carm.*1.26.10 (*novis*) offer a useful collection of material from Greek and Latin poetry.
[17] See also Detienne 1986: 86.

error (ἁμαρτία)? In Cephalus' case it must be the *error nominis* (7.857) admitted by the narrator himself, i.e. his careless invocation of *aura* in words with potential double-meaning. Aeacus, on the other hand, has unintentionally offended Juno, by renaming the island after his mother, Aegina (7.474), who was the goddess' rival (*paelex* 7.524). Finally, both comments also betray something of the narrator's emotional attitude towards his story, which will be further examined under the category of *testimonial function* below.

VI.3 Communicative Function of the Intradiegetic Narrators
The communicative function is performed whenever the narrator seeks to establish and maintain a contact with his/her audience (*narratee*). Most of the intradiegetic narrators in the *Met.* try to involve their audience in the narrative, by addressing them directly or indirectly in all the various ways examined in Chapter 7.

VI.4 Testimonial Function Of The Intradiegetic Narrators
The testimonial function refers to whatever indicates the emotional, moral or intellectual attitude of the narrator towards the story (s)he tells. By intellectual attitude, in particular, Genette seems to mean any means of indicating the sources from which the story is derived and the narrator's comments on the degree of precision his memories can attain. In **Table 2** appear all the relevant passages categorised according to the type of "testimony" they offer.

Table 2: Testimonial Function

No.	Lines	Passage	Type
3	2.570	*(nota loquor)*	intellectual
3	2.591	*quae per totam res est notissima Lesbon*	intellectual
6	4.189	*haec fuit in toto notissima fabula caelo*	intellectual
12	5.585	*(memini)*	intellectual
13	6.318-9	*res obscura quidem ... mira tamen*	intellectual
13	6.320-1	*vidi praesens stagnumque locumque / prodigio notum*	intellectual
15	7.549	*mira loquar*	intellectual

16	7.790	*(mirum)*	intellectual
16	7.813	*(recordor enim)*	intellectual
16	7.827	*ut mihi narratur*	intellectual
18	8.622	*ipse locum vidi*	intellectual
18	8.721-3	*haec mihi non vani (neque erat, cur fallere vellent) / narravere senes*	intellectual
17e	9.4-5	*Triste petis munus. Quis enim sua proelia victus / commemorare velit?*	emotional
17e	9.53	*(certum est mihi vera fateri)*	intellectual
17e	9.55-6	*siqua fides neque ficta mihi nunc gloria voce / quaeritur*	intellectual
19	9.290-1	*quin nunc quoque frigidus artus,/ dum loquor, horror habet, parsque est miminisse doloris*	emotional
19	9.316	*fama est*	intellectual
20	9.327-8	*mira sororis / fata meae*	intellectual
20	9.344	*(namque aderam)*	intellectual
20	9.346	*ut referunt tardi nunc denique agrestes*	intellectual
20	9.359-60	*spectatrix aderam ... quantumque valebam*	intellectual
21	10.300ff.	*dira canam...*	moral
22	10.561-2	*non fabula rumor / ille fuit*	intellectual
25	11.763	*fertur*	intellectual
26	12.182ff.	*quamvis obstet mihi tarda vetustas / multaque me fugiant primis spectata sub annis, / plura tamen memini*	intellectual
26	12.197	*(ita fama ferebat)*	intellectual
26	12.200	*(eadem hoc quoque fama ferebat)*	intellectual
26	12.264	*constabat*	intellectual
26	12.327	*vidi ego*	intellectual
26	12.360	*credi sic ipse volebat*	intellectual
26	12.444	*signa vides, apparet adhuc vetus inde cicatrix*	intellectual
26	12.453	*memini et...*	intellectual
26	12.461	*vulnera non memini, numerumque nomenque notavi*	intellectual
26	12.522	*exitus in dubio est*	intellectual
26	12.523	*...ferebant*	intellectual

26	12.532	*credita res auctore suo est*	intellectual
26	12.545	*maiora fide*	intellectual
26	12.556	*mira Periclymeni mors est*	intellectual
27	13.671-3	*nec qua ratione figurae / perdiderint, potui scire aut nunc dicere possum. / summa mali nota est*	intellectual
28	13.788	*auditaque verba notavi*	intellectual
28	13.870	*(nam cuncta videbam)*	intellectual
29	13.935	*res similis fictae: sed quid mihi fingere prodest?*	Intellectual
29	13.956-7	*hactenus acta tibi possum memoranda referre/ hactenus et memini; nec mens mea cetera sensit.*	Intellectual
32	14.310-1	*quod clam mihi rettulit mea / quattuor e famulis ad talia sacra paratis*	intellectual
33	14.334	*dicitur*	intellectual
33	14.406	*(dictu mirabile)*	intellectual
35	14.696	*referam tota notissima Cypro / facta*	intellectual
36	15.14	*fertur*	intellectual

It is evident from a quick glance at the last column of the above table that the majority of comments concern the narrative's sources and consequently the narrator's authority. One notable exception from this general tendency to establish one's credentials is Jupiter **[1]**. It is, of course, natural that the supreme deity should be omniscient and his every word true. But precisely the fact that his narrative is used as a rhetorical argument in support of his plan to destroy the world has made modern readers suspicious of his story's *non sequiturs*. For example, although he visited the earth in human form (1.213), presumably *incognito*, he expected everyone to believe that he was a god upon arriving at Lycaeus' residence (1.220-1). It is further unclear what exactly Lycaon's secret murder plan (1.224) was. Haarberg, for instance, thinks that the plan's chronology is inverted while Piccaluga argued that serving the god human flesh *is* the way to kill him.[18] It is such considerations

---

[18] Haarberg 1983: 112-13 (Piccaluga's interpretation is mentioned in 113 n.6).

that have led modern critics like Anderson, to suggest that Jupiter's paradigm of theodicy is flawed ("failed").[19]

The Crow [3], on the other hand, cannot rely on the assumption that she knows everything. Instead, twice during her narration she alludes to her stories' belonging to the reservoir of common knowledge. These comments have been variously interpreted: the first as an index of the crow's self-importance or as a learned poet's 'footnote' to his literary source (VERG.G.1.388-9) and his literary allegiances (Call.fr.612 Pf.);[20] the second has been explained as an "ironical mask" for the narrator's bias against the owl.[21] Her inimical attitude is undeniable and is expressed more overtly through her ascription of the responsibility for the incestuous sex to her rival rather than her father, a possibility enacted in Hyginus' version (204). At the same time this comment functions as the crow's excuse for offering an extremely synoptic version of a sordid story of incest. A similar comment is made by Vertumnus [35] on the story of Iphis and Anaxarete: it is famous in Cyprus, where it took place. Comments of the type "famous in [place]" obviously serve as indications of setting and provenance of the local myth.

Leuconoe's [6] version of the formula (her story was notorious in the heavens!) will look less bizarre if we bear in mind Ovid's description of *caelum* in Book 1 as a chic neighbourhood, the Olympian version of the Palatine hill. The story of Ares and Aphrodite is certainly not new to hexameter poetry; it features as the middle song of Demodokos, the *aoidos* of Skheria, in *Odyssey* 8.266-369. It is a curious coincidence that the same comment was made in the previous appearances of the story in Ovid's poetry, a reference in *Amores* 1.9 (*notior in caelo fabula nulla fuit*, line 40) and a narrative in the Second Book of the *Ars Amatoria* (*fabula narratur toto notissima caelo*, line 561). Yet, Baldo's suggestion that this is "a deliberate auto-citation, well judged for its effect on the reader, aiming to evoke the eroto-didactic and elegiac content of the previous version" seems less convincing and appealing than Steiner's interpretation, which is more concerned with the story's place in the Minyad's narrative

---

[19] Anderson 1989. Although I agree that Jupiter's reliability as a narrator, and consequently his justice, is suspect for the reasons presented above, I cannot fully endorse Anderson's argumentation in this article.
[20] Haupt-Ehwald *ad loc.* and Keith 1992: 29-31 respectively.
[21] Anderson on 2.591-95.

discourse. He argued that Alcithoe's comment is meant to justify her decision to present the story as an appetizing preamble to the rarities she is about to share with her sisters and female domestics.[22] What is common in all these instances is that the narrator can offer no evidence to prove the veracity of her account. They can only appeal to the audience as her witness, as Demosthenes suggests in 40.53f.[23]

Early in her narrative Arethusa **[12]** asserts parenthetically that she still remembers (*memini*) in detail the circumstances of her pursuit by Alpheus: she was tired on her way back from the woods of Stymphalia (5.585). Bömer notes that the word *memini* belongs to the register of elegiac poetry and occurs mainly but not exclusively in amatory contexts.[24] On the "intellectual" level it is clear that Arethusa is trying to persuade Ceres about the veracity of her account, including such realistic details as the place which she had just visited. Yet, is not clear what kind of emotional overtones her admission of having precise memories of that day is supposed to carry. Perhaps it is "an attempt to recover by recollection a past which is lost forever, irretrievably gone," a blissful past which was destroyed by the reality of *amor*, as Jacobson observes with reference to another description of a setting with a "dreamlike quality" in the *Heroides*.[25] An alternative interpretation could be that the narrator has not yet recovered from that day's traumatic experience. This is rather unlikely, since there are no traces in the narrative text of a particularly negative attitude to the incident from hindsight. She dwells on the *timor* she felt that day, which she almost blames for her illusionary perception of the *fuga*.[26] However, she describes her persecutor's motive as *amor* (5.634) and their union after they have both transformed into water with the verb *miscere* (5.638), which is an obvious Graecism without negative quotations.

---

[22] Baldo 1986: 127 Steiner 1958: 227n.17 followed by Due 1974: 127 and Castellani 1980: 48.
[23] For an explanation of the psychological basis of this practice see Ar. *Rhet*.1408a32-6; see further Carey & Reid on Dem.39.2. Cf. also *Od*.4.200 μέλλεις δὲ σὺ ἴδμεναι.
[24] Pichon 1902: 198 includes in his catalogue the cognate *memor*, notice especially usage (3) *aliquotiens quoque qui iniuriam ab amante acceptam mente sua revolvit* PROP. *3,12,20*. (Cf. also TIB.1.3.26 with Putnam's note).
[25] Jacobson 1974: 187.
[26] Bömer on 615.

Recordor, a verb with similar meaning is also inserted parenthetically in Cephalus' **[16]** narrative of a scene with elegiac/amatory overtones, viz. his invocation of *aura*. *Memini* is used by Nestor **[26]** in a context which could not be further removed from the pastoral scenes evoked by Arethusa and Cephalus: it introduces an incident of the battle against the Centaurs, viz. the deadly blow with which Nessus killed Cymelus. A few lines later, however, the same narrator admits that he cannot remember (*non memini* 12.461) the blows dealt by Caeneus in his *aristeia* (12.459-93). Presumably these particular details are not included in the *plura* that Nestor claims to remember despite his old age in his introductory disclaimer. As such details add to the glory of a hero's *aristeia* Nestor is probably trying to undermine Caeneus' achievement in a battle in which he took part himself, killing the same number of Centaurs as the Thessalian transsexual hero. That battle narratives can be affected by the narrator's participation is also admitted by Achelous **[17e]**. In the account of his fight with Hercules there are repeated allusions to the possibility that he might not be telling the whole truth: *certum est mihi vera fateri* (9.53 "for I am resolved to tell the truth"); *siqua fides neque ficta mihi nunc gloria voce / quaeritur* (55-56 "Believe me, I am not just trying to enhance my glory with my words").

Orpheus' narrative of Myrrha's incestuous affair with her father **[21f]** is preceded by quite a long disclaimer (10.300-315), in which the themes of *fides* and *natura* are prominent. The passage opens with a parody of the ritual formula (*procul hinc*) "employed by Romans to warn away the *profani*, who might disturb the purity of a religious rite and so make it unacceptable to the gods."[27] Orpheus, the mythical founder of a mystic religion, assumes the posture of a priest about to reveal the mysteries of human sexuality, warning away the pure in heart. Underlying the whole set-up is a belief in the power of stories to incite imitation, which is widespread in ancient erotic literature. For example, in the preface to Longus' novel the narrator promises that his story "will cure the sick, comfort the distressed, stir the memory of those who have loved, and educate those who haven't ... As for me —may the god Love let me write

---

[27] Anderson on 10.300-3.

about others' passions but keep my own self-control."[28] The subject-matter may be dire, but Orpheus' enchanting poetry is hard to resist. *Mulcebunt* (10.302) not only "suggests the sensuous appeal of Ovid's [i.e. Orpheus'] verse" (Anderson *ad loc.*), but also echoes archaic Greek ideas about the art of poetry. "For most audiences in the *Odyssey*, the pleasure song gives seems by definition to consist in the listener's unconsciousness of himself and his present situation" (*thelxis*).[29] This is exactly what Orpheus recommends to his audience, to let themselves enjoy his art without engaging in active judgement. If there is truth, this is to be found in the 'order' (*kosmos*) of the poetic discourse. Truthfulness is only "an impression produced by the singer's fluency in making and remaking the story for each performance."[30] It is within this metapoetic framework that we should interpret the alternative instruction to believe the punishment if we are prepared to believe the crime (10.303). Parts of the story may seem hard to accept as truthful but the ordered whole, the system of signs, which is always more than the sum of its constituent parts, has a truth all of its own.

In a gesture of self-consciousness Glaucus **[29]** admits that his story seems like fiction (13.935 *res similis fictae*) but hastens to add that he has no reason to make up a story like this (19.935 *sed quid mihi fingere prodest?*). That somebody must have a reason to tell a false story is also the premise of Lelex' **[18]** parenthetical comment about the old people who were his source for the story of Baucis and Philemon. It is also implicit in the Pierides' accusation of the Muses for telling sweet lies: *desinite indoctum vana dulcedine vulgus / fallere* (5.308 "Stop deceiving uneducated people with your sweet lies"). A false story is called *fabula* (10.561). When the narrator is reporting something (s)he has not witnessed (s)he refers to it as a rumour (*fama*).[31] For example, both Caenis' rape and Neptune's promise to materialize one wish of Caenis are reported as mere hearsay,

---

[28] For the idea of sentimental education as initiation to mysteries, cf. e.g. Ach. Tat. 1.2 (the extradiegetic narrator speaking to Kleitophon): "You have the look, I know it well, of one who has progressed far in his initiation into Love's mysteries."
[29] Walsh 1984: 14.
[30] Walsh 1984: 16.
[31] Cf. also *fertur* and *ferebant* as signals of the narrator's reservations about an event's veracity. At the same time, as Bömer (on 15.435-6) remarks, such expressions give the event reported an aura of antiquity ("den Schein besonderer Altertümlichkeit"). On the personified *Fama* in the poem see most recently Hardie 1999: 97-100.

unlike the next section on Lapithocentauromachy, which Nestor [26] relates as an eye-witness: *ita fama ferebat* (12.197 "thus the story spread"); *eadem hoc quoque fama ferebat* (12.200 "thus the same story spread too").

Nestor, the most conspicuous embodiment of advanced age and command of persuasive speech in Homeric epic, is a very self-conscious narrator. Even as an eye-witness, his narrative cannot aspire to Olympian omniscience. His narration is introduced with a discussion of the importance of good memory for any kind of story, including those told from first-hand knowledge (12.182-84). Nestor proves to be a self-conscious narrator once more, when he concedes reluctantly that Theseus' retreat was advised by Pallas: *credi sic ipse volebat* (12.360 "–or so he himself would have us believe"). There is more than one good reason why the advice would be ascribed to Pallas: her connection with fighting, wisdom, and Athens is important in this respect as well as the Iliadic precedent of 1.194ff., where the goddess advises Nestor's main addressee in the present narrative instance, Achilles. Yet, perhaps because this is an obvious explanation, Nestor is critical of his source, apparently Theseus himself.

Being a homodiegetic narrator, Nestor [26] is justified in admitting or pretending ignorance about this or that detail of his narrative, as he does with regard to the identity of Cyllarus' killer: *auctor in incerto est* (12.419 "the killer is unknown"). He abdicates omniscience once more about the last words of Hylonome to Cyllarus: *dictis, quae clamor ad aures / arcuit ire meas* (12.427-8 "words which the uproar prevented me from hearing"). Nestor's narrative ends with Caeneus' metamorphosis, introduced with a testimonial comment: *exitus in dubio est* (12.522 "What happened in the end is uncertain"). Nobody, including the eye-witnesses, can know what happened to the impenetrable hero. It is only a matter of conjecture, a question of vatic vision and authority: *credita res auctore suo* (12.532 "We believed what he said, because he said it"). Others say that his body was forced down to the Underworld (possibly Pindar's version in *Thren*.VI=fr.128 Snell), while Mopsus asserts that he was transformed into a bird. Livy's history (4.10) contains a notorious case of *credita res auctore suo*, which is connected with Augustus himself: Cossus' consulship. The *auctor* there is double: Caesar as "the founder of the temple itself" (*ipsius templi auctorem*) and Cossus as "the person responsible for the battle" (*auctor pugnae*) which led to the dedication of the *spolia opima*. Livy has heard from the former *auctor* that the latter presented himself as consul, and not as tribune, in the inscription he added to the linen breastplate dedicated as part of the spoils.[32]

Nestor [26] is obviously at pains to establish his narrative authority. He frequently reminds his audience that he reports the events mostly as an eye-witness: 12.327 (I saw), 12.429 (he also stands before my eyes).[33] While performing a testimonial function these phrases are also useful for the introduction of a new item in the chain of slayings that is Nestor's account of the Lapithocentauromachy. His efforts to prove his credibility are climaxed during the account of his own *aristeia*. He appeals to Achilles' father (who conveniently cannot be consulted on the spot), but the real trump card is the scar a wound has left him.[34] *Cicatrices ostendere* was not only a means of proof used in trials but also a republican custom for consular candidates.[35] Far from being embarrassed by the public exposition of his aged body, Nestor breaks out in a four-line embittered contrast of his youthful vigour with his present *aetas deterior*.

Several of the passages listed in **Table 2** describe the event narrated as a marvel (*mirum*). The anonymous Lydian [13], Aeacus [15], Cephalus [16], and Nestor [26], and Circe's maid [33] use this word to describe their reaction to metamorphosis and other phenomena that defy natural order, like beasts not eating dead men or trees springing up fully grown. Unlike Homeric θαῦμα, *mirum* does not seem to describe the visual perception of a divinely created event;[36] it is characteristic that instead of

---

[32] For a recent discussion and bibliography see Miles 1995: 40-47, who concludes that Livy has succeeded in acknowledging Augustus' personal authority generously and uncompromisingly while at the same time undermining it by suggesting that the difference evidence upon which Augustus and the other authorities based their respective conclusions is equally unimpeachable.

[33] Cf. also *spectata* (12.183) and *spectatorem* (12.187), both referring to Nestor.

[34] Cf. Dippel 1990: 54.

[35] Loraux 1995: 88 with n.1 (p. 283). See also Leigh 1995, who does not mention the present passage even though he refers to 13.262ff., where Ulysses cruelly exploits Ajax' legendary invulnerability. Unlike Loraux, Leigh would consider the valorisation of wounds as common to Greek and Roman cultures rather than specific to the latter. In the recent French novel/film *Un héros très discret*, Albert Dehousse is forced to reveal that he is a fake Resistance hero when people start asking him about his supposed *cicatrice* (Deniau 1989: 221 and 239).

[36] Fisher 1995: 12.

the Homeric ϑαῦμα ἰδέσϑαι we have the phrase *dictu mirabile* (a marvel to tell).[37] "As a miracle is an event, it has to be witnessed or experienced by someone and described or recorded as an event extraordinary enough to cause wonder (*mirus*=wonderful, *miraculum*=object of wonder)."[38] In Ovidian metanarrative telling is more important than witnessing; experiences are worthwhile when they can be narrated. On the other hand, events like the emergence of the Aeginetan ant-men, which fit better our notion of miracle, i.e. "an event of an extraordinary kind, brought about by a god and of religious significance," are not described as *mirum*.[39]

To sum up, this section concerned the narrators' testimonial function, i.e. all comments about the story's authenticity or its emotional impact on themselves. Most of the 37 intradiegetic narrators of the poem perform this function. Probably because their stories are about metamorphosis, which is considered *mirum*, most of these comments concern the narrative's sources and consequently the narrator's authority. Some present the stories as belonging to the reservoir of common knowledge. These comments have been variously interpreted, e.g. as a learned poet's (i.e. the historical Ovid's) 'footnote' to his literary source and his literary allegiances. Whether this is true or not, it is significant that such comments are made when the narrator can offer no other evidence to prove the veracity of his/her account; (s)he can only appeal to the audience as his/her witness. Homodiegetic narrators frequently pepper their stories with reminders that they rely on their memories (e.g. *memini, recordor*). But they are careful to signal the failing of their memories too (*non memini*): age and personal involvement are presented as factors that erode memory. Another topic of testimonial comments is the story's truthfulness, as truth often surpasses belief or looks like lies. Lies are thought to be told in order to achieve a certain aim, whereas truth comes naturally. Finally, narrators keep critical distance from events that they have not witnessed themselves and sometimes even signal their own wonder (*mirum*) that the events they narrate are actually true, at least as true as they are themselves.

---

[37] On the Homeric phrase see Fisher 1995: 7.
[38] Fisher 1995: 3.
[39] Swinburne 1970: 1.

VI.5 Ideological Function of the Narrator

The concept of ideology has been crucial to critical social thinking. Whether one accepts the term itself as well as the exact meaning which is ascribed to it, are important issues, because they imply significant epistemological and methodological choices. For instance, Michel Foucault has expressed very strong reservations with regard to the concept's use and usefulness.[40] Despite its semantic polyvalence ideology is a word that is inscribed in the way modern subjects define their identity and a concept that still preoccupies social scientists throughout the world. It seems, therefore, more logical to keep the term but try to be more precise about its meaning and usage.[41]

Genette's description of the narrator's ideological function contains two important elements. First, the function's vector is all the interventions, whether direct or indirect, concerning the story, the events narrated and their agents. Second, these interventions are presented as an authorised commentary on the narrative action. In other words, Genette refers to a broad, inclusive concept of ideology as "a body of ideas characteristic of a particular social group or class" or an "action-oriented set of beliefs".[42] There is clearly nothing inherently negative in this conception of ideology, no hint at falseness, distortion or illusion, no implicit juxtaposition with science, truth or self-consciousness.[43] This more or less coherent and systematic set of beliefs is offered as a rational explanation and justification of action, which serves to legitimate the dominant power of the narrator, his/her authority. Legitimation is achieved by means of six basic strategies, interacting with each other in complex ways: the *promotion* of beliefs and values congenial to the dominant power, the *naturalisation* and *universalization* of such beliefs, the *denigration* of ideas which might challenge it, the *exclusion* of rival forms of thought and the *obfuscation* of social reality in ways convenient to itself.[44]

---

[40] See Foucault 1977: 60.
[41] See Λίποβατς-Δεμερτζής 1998: 26-27.
[42] See Eagleton 1991: 1-2 definitions (*b*) and (*l*).
[43] Λίποβατς-Δεμερτζής 1998: 25.
[44] Eagleton 1991: 5.

For instance, through judgement of characters, "the narrator is doing something more complex than telling us what the people in the story are like; he tells us in such a way as to display his own authority for their characterizations, and also invites our complicity by assuming that we share the values he announces."[45] This observation comes from Roger Fowler's discussion of the Barthesian category of the *cultural* or *referential code*, introduced in *S/Z*.[46] Both linguistic forms associated with the referential code, generic sentences of claimed universal application and similes, could certainly be described as commentary, direct and indirect respectively, on the narrative action. In other words, there is a considerable overlap between the two analytical categories.

The reason I have referred to this alternative post-structuralist approach to narrative theory is to raise a question of terminology. What is a more accurate description of the material covered by these nearly coextensive concepts: ideology or culture?[47] Their confusion and interchangeable usage is not an unusual phenomenon in social and political theory.[48] Admittedly, both terms are rather vague and have been used with so many different meanings that they have arguably lost their usefulness.[49] It seemed, therefore, preferable to keep to Genette's terminology (*ideological function*), however imperfect this may be, since this is the model generally followed in this dissertation.

VI.5.1 Ideological Function in Ancient (Epic) Narrative before Ovid
One of the few narratological analyses of ancient literature that has paid attention to the ideological function of the narrator is Richardson 1990. In his description he combines Genette's model with Chatman's refinements. It is on the latter that he has founded his treatment of 'commentary' (Ch. 6) and 'self-consciousness' (Ch. 7) in Homeric epic. I quote his own concluding summaries:

> "The Homeric narrator's explanatory interruptions are almost all very brief statements of a fact or a circumstance of which we have not been informed earlier, an omission resulting from the narrator's practice not to mention them before they are of any consequence; or they are simply a means of expressing a

---

[45] Fowler 1981: 101.
[46] Barthes 1970.
[47] See Geertz 1973: 193-233.
[48] See e.g. Hargreaves 1982 and Abercrombie 1978.
[49] On 'culture' see e.g. Geertz 1966: 3.

fact concurrent with the present moment. Homer chooses to let the story itself do the explaining." (p. 148)
"The narrator's attitude toward the story and the exigencies of oral delivery lead to a far greater concentration of explanatory interpretations [i.e. interpretations of fact] than we find in modern narrative. Interpretations on other levels [i.e. psychology, symbolism, morality and ultimate significance], on the other hand, are conspicuously absent. (...) Analysis on these [other] levels is the bailiwick of some of the more pensive characters and of the readers." (p.158)
"Judgments and personal feelings are only seldom spoken by the narrator *in propria persona*; they are, rather, expressed by the characters themselves as well as by the structure, the themes, and the subject matter." (p. 166)

Four years earlier Elizabeth Block had published a paper on "Narrative Judgment and Audience Response in Homer and Vergil," which put Homeric practice in a wider perspective not only temporally (comparing him with Vergil) but also theoretically (combining narratology with the so-called reader-response criticism).[50] She agrees with Richardson that "the [Homeric] narrator avoids the kinds of judgments that describe transitory or alterable states."[51] Furthermore, "this positive slant is accompanied by a dearth of negative, derogatory, or condemnatory words in the Homeric narrator's vocabulary."[52] "Vergil's practice is similar to the Homeric model at the level of the judgmental epithet." This picture is, however, "constantly and subtly undermined, or challenged" in three ways: "first, when he does use negative or judgmental words, the narrator frequently assigns them in ways that clash with the Roman perspective of the poem. (...) Second, the narrator makes use of a wider range of words than the Homeric narrator."[53] By far the most important factor of modification is, however, Vergil's "use of apostrophe and aphorism, coupled with the interplay between epithet and rhetoric."[54]

R. O. A. M. Lyne's extension of the "Two Voices" approach[55] in his celebrated *Further Voices in Vergil's Aeneid* could not have taken into account that article, since it was published only one year later.[56] Having

---

[50] Block 1986.
[51] Block 1986: 157.
[52] Block 1986: 158.
[53] Block 1986: 159.
[54] Block 1986: 160.
[55] See Parry 1963.
[56] Lyne 1987.

declared that the Vergilian narrator's voice in the *Aeneid* "is consonant: substantially epic,"[57] he proceeds "to identify the precise point at which further voices actually impinge," including "for consideration passages in which *some scholars believe* [my emphasis] that not just a further voice but a *personal Vergilian voice* [the author's emphasis] is evident."[58] The narratological framework adopted in this dissertation makes irrelevant scholarly preoccupation with the genuine author's 'voice' in the text; our focus of interest is limited to the narrator, the voice audible in the text, the voice that is the combined result of a network of functions both properly narrative and extra-narrative. This means that a question such as "On what authority, in what voice, are Dido and Nisus to be 'unfortunate' [*infelix*] and 'pitiable' [*misera*]?" can only have one answer: the narrator's.[59] That Lyne uses the term 'voice' in a non-narratological sense is made evident in n. 38 of Chapter 6: "The topic I am touching upon here could be called ambiguity in *point of view*."[60] Even in that case, however, for a narratologist there are two options (the narrator's and/or a character's point of view), neither of which involves the author's 'personal voice'.[61]

Finally, Lyne turns to "actual 'interventions' in the text (...): apostrophe, exclamation, and the like;" in other words, to manifestations of the narrator's ideological function, as defined by Genette and Chatman. The passages discussed had already been assembled by R. Heinze in his pioneering study of *Virgil's Epic Technique* under the heading "Subjectivity".[62] The latter is also concerned with Homeric excuses for deviations "from strict 'objectivity'."[63] In this sense, his approach is not essentially different from Lyne's, more than eighty years later. As Lyne admits he disagrees with his forerunner's interpretation, not his analytical categories and general line of approach to the material.[64] Another difference is Lyne's concern with the

---

[57] Lyne 1987: 226.
[58] Lyne 1987: 227.
[59] Lyne 1987: 230.
[60] Lyne 1987: 231.
[61] Cf. e.g. Lyne 1987: 233 "and impossible not to wonder whether this abruptly discordant participle does not issue from a further voice, from a personal voice."
[62] Heinze 1993: 295-6.
[63] Heinze 1993: 297. in n.42 (p.233)
[64] Lyne 1987: 233 n.42.

ideological implications of these further voices audible to those prepared to listen: "the *Aeneid* probes, questions, and occasionally subverts the simple Augustanism that it may appear to project."[65]

Gordon Williams, on the other hand, is rather negatively disposed towards the idea of the *Aeneid* having an ideology. "It is easy to sense that many complex ideas are there expressed, but indirectly and in such a way that they bear no clear relevance to Augustan ideology. (...) In short, there are many ideas in the *Aeneid* and no ideology."[66] In an earlier chapter, nonetheless, he admitted that Vergil's comments on the action (e.g. the dead warriors' epitaphs) express "a sense of values in concrete images: hatred of war, a modest life of hard work combining fishing and agriculture, and a contentment that sought neither influence nor possessions," i.e. values that "played a part, too, in Augustan ideology."[67] In other cases, however, he discerns in the Vergilian narrator's intrusions (e.g. at 9.446) "a timeless point of view that will be valid as long as Latin continues to be understood – that is, as long as Rome itself lasts."[68] In the following section we will take a closer look at contemporary conceptions of 'Augustan ideology', a value-laden discourse available to, and to a certain degree unavoidably used by, everybody living under the Augustan regime.

VI.5.2 'Augustanism': the (dominant) ideology

Since the late 1980s a lot of emphasis has been put on "the protean character of the principate."[69] Augustan ideology is hard to pin down because "what appears in retrospect as a subtle program resulted in fact from the interplay of the image that the emperor himself projected and the honors bestowed on him more or less spontaneously, a process that evolved naturally over long periods of time." This is one of the most important arguments in Paul Zanker's extremely influential *The Power of*

---

[65] Lyne 1987: 217.
[66] Williams 1983: 234.
[67] Williams 1983: 198.
[68] Williams 1983: 231. *Aen.* 9.446-49 is regarded by Philip Hardie (*ad loc.*) as "the most emphatic authorial intervention in the epic and the only explicit reference to the power of his own poetry."
[69] Phillips 1983, repeated and elaborated magnificently by Feeney 1992: 1ff.

Images in the Age of Augustus.[70] Difficulties are also created by two major characteristics of the Augustan pictorial vocabulary: (a) "its broad spectrum of associations and the general applicability of the individual symbols," and (b) "a corresponding lack of specificity in any one particular case."[71] Even at a basic level of consistency, the *Prinzipatsideologie* was not free of internal contradictions.[72] As Denis Feeney reminds us, "magnificent splendour and praiseworthy *paupertas* are *both* Augustan."[73] As for the sources, "even the assertion that the *Res Gestae* necessarily contains valid statements of Augustan intent does not hold." For, as C. R. Phillips observes, "while autobiographical data can be important, it does not always possess a privileged claim."[74]

It seems then that official Augustan art did not project a coherent message,[75] not only because of its ambiguous vocabulary but also because of its "lack of narrative" and its "intellectualized symbolism."[76] Yet Zanker admits that the Augustan age was fanatically preoccupied "with law and order"[77] and the fusion of "past and future in a single image."[78] And while the greatest part of Augustan poetry was published while the princeps' power was not yet consolidated and the new order was still in the process of emerging,[79] Ovid's *Metamorphoses* came out unofficially after the New Golden Age was proclaimed in the year 17 BC.[80] The moral renewal which seemed to Vergil and Horace the only way for a new future, no longer represented for Ovid an inner request.[81] "Despite all the ambiguities of the *Aeneid*," perhaps themselves

---

[70] Zanker 1988: 3.
[71] Zanker 1988: 177.
[72] Kloft 1984: 325.
[73] Feeney 1992: 2.
[74] Phillips 1983: 783. The latest edition of the *Res Gestae* with extensive introduction and good bibliography is Guizzi 1999. On the issue of the date he is agnostic, though the work must have begun after 28 BC
[75] Zanker 1988: 76.
[76] Zanker 1988: 253.
[77] Zanker 1988: 181. Wallace-Hadrill 1989: 159 agrees that "in Augustanism there must always be order."
[78] Zanker 1988: 205.
[79] Kienast 1999: 276.
[80] If we can trust Ovid's voice in *Tr.*1.7.30 that the poem lacks the *ultima lima* it is unlikely that an authorised copy was published.
[81] Kienast 1999: 300.

reflecting the ambiguities of the emerging *novus ordo*, Vergil could "still hope for an all-embracing world-order and for one who will realize it..."[82] Ovid, on the other hand, advocated perpetual *metamorphosis*, i.e. "disorder in the face of a regime that wanted order in everything and at all costs."[83] "As men become animals or plants, as gods become animals or men, any unitary moral perspective dissolves." [84]

The lack of clarity in and considerable ambiguity of the so-called Augustan ideology is perhaps caused by its heavy reliance on myth as a legitimating device.[85] The new official mythology consisted of relatively few figures. There were no new elements but at its heart lay a combination of two mythical cycles, the Trojan legend and the story of Romulus.[86] Mythical figures were used in pictorial art in order "to convey a message in terms of set slogans."[87] This explains why "the figures are simply arranged beside one another in axial symmetry" while narrative "became wholly subsidiary."[88] Mythological subjects were "restricted to just a few individual scenes" adjusted to Augustus' needs. Annoying myths like the adulterous affair between Venus and Mars, the divine ancestors of the Romans, were skirted. Contrary to the official line, Ovid emphasised the erotic aspects of such sacrosanct figures of the official mythology as Venus, Mars, Jupiter and Apollo, and at the same highlighted the narrative aspect of myth.[89]

VI.6 Ideological Function of the Intradiegetic Narrators

However hazardous and ambiguous it may be to talk of a literary work's ideology, meaning its particular "framework of belief" or "world

---

[82] Segal 1969: 87. On the moral ambiguities in the *Aeneid* see Williams 1983: ch.8.
[83] Phillips 1983: 815. See also Segal 1969a: 265.
[84] Segal 1969: 266.
[85] Λιποβατς-Δεμερτζής 1998: 55 and Zanker 1988: 193.
[86] Zanker 1988: 195.
[87] Zanker 1988: 201.
[88] Zanker 1988: 201 and 206.
[89] Zanker 1988: 209, Kienast 1999: 301. Whether this was, oppositional to, subversive, or ultimately consolidating of Augustus' ideological position is not easy to judge (see Kennedy 1992: 46). But even if "Ovid's challenge to Augustus may reinscribe the emperor's power (in the sense that co-option tends to overcome subversion), (...) in responding to the poet the emperor alters his power and himself: Augustus was not the same man or emperor that was before banishing Ovid" (Johnson 1997: 373-4 n.12).

picture," it is still a useful term to describe the ways literature is related to extra-literary reality, through evoking the discourse of various social realities and ideological schemes.[90] Of course, as M. Bal observes, "it would be naïve to suppose that only argumentative parts of the text communicate ideology."[91] They do, nonetheless, offer explicit information on the taken-for-granted assumptions, beliefs and value-systems of the story. In the following discussion of the ideological function three distinct categories of ideological commentary on narrative action will be discussed: (a) judgement, i.e. any kind of evaluation of mythical characters and their actions, (b) explanation, i.e. any comment that supplies information that was withheld so far and is introduced in order to clarify action, and (c) generalisations, i.e. statements of universal truths, which are illustrated by action. All three categories normally involve values and ideas that are supposed to be shared by narrator and narratee. Our aim in the following discussion is to identify these values and ideas and compare them and their presentation with whatever evidence there is about their place in Augustan discourse.

VI.6.1 Judgement
The most obvious and overt means of evaluating the action and its agents is the use of qualitative adjectives or adverbs. These "narratorial intrusions" are one of the narrative techniques that may seem to distance the style of intradiegetic narrator from that of traditional epic narrative. This suspicion is all the stronger when the immediate hypotext of a certain metanarrative is an archaic Greek hexameter poem, as in the case of Acoetes [4], whose story derives mainly from the Seventh Homeric Hymn.[92] Yet, the latter is not completely devoid of such premonitory comments. Right at the beginning of the action the hymnic narrator declares that the pirates were led by bad fate (8 τοὺς δ' ἦγε κακὸς μόρος). Likewise, the steersman (i.e. Acoetes in the Ovidian version) is said to be of modest disposition (49 κυβερνήτην ... σαόφρονα θυμὸν ἔχοντα). This similarity is not surprising, since Acoetes and the performer of the

---

[90] See Τζοῦμα 1991: 20 n.15, and 146; instead of "ideological" she suggests the use of "evaluative".
[91] Bal 1997: 34.
[92] Anderson on 3.664-65.

Homeric Hymn are devout followers of Semele's son. By careful placement of judgmental adjectives near the beginning, the narrator may anticipate later developments in the story. Jupiter **[1]**, for example, discloses that Lycaon's palace is *inhospita* (1.218) at the moment of his entrance. Such an anticipation is particularly apposite in the mouth of a god, who thus affirms his divine foreknowledge.

Intradiegetic narrators comment disapprovingly on the characters' lack of hospitable feelings (*inhospita tecta tyranni* 1.218, *nec inhospita tecta Crotonis* 15.15)[93], haughty recklessness (*furit audacissimus ... Lycabas* 3.623, *audax* 5.451)[94], impiety (*inpia turba* 3.629, *manus inpia* 8.761, *inpia* 14.237);[95] treacherousness (*fallaces* 3.638, *fallaci* 5.279), ruthless cruelty (*ferox inmansuetusque* 4.237, *crudus* 4.240, *dirus* 5.274,[96] *ferox* 5.277, *crudelis* 5.542, *inmanis* 8.584,[97] *fati crudelis* 9.359)[98], madness (*amens* 4.351, *vecors* 5.291)[99], heinous criminality (*scelerato* 5.293, *sceleratus* 8.754, 792, *foedo* 10.319), stupidity (*stolidarum turba sororum* "the band of stupid sisters" 5.305),

---

[93] R. D. Williams on VERG.*Aen*.5.627 "**inhospita**: a poetic word which is first found in Horace [*Ep*.1.14.9] and Virgil [also *Aen*.4.41]."
[94] Nisbet-Hubbard on HOR.*Carm*.1.3.25 "**audax**: *audacia* (τόλμα) is an impious self-assertion." The adjective is often used as the opposite of *pius*, see Opelt 1965: 55. No negative judgment is implied e.g. at HOR.*Carm*.1.12.21 *proeliis audax* (of the goddess Pallas). R.D.Williams on VERG.*Aen*.8.110: "Servius is right when he says that the implication of *audax* in Virgil's use is *uirtus sine fortuna*, 'ill-starred galantry' (or, as he puts it on ix. 3, *fortis sine felicitate*)." P. Hardie on VERG.*Aen*.9.625: "In the *Aen*. the word *audax* is particularly associated with Turnus and his followers."
[95] Williams 1983: 117: "*pietas* (...) – that devotion to the gods which later Romans thought responsible for their universal military success throughout the world." For *pietas* as the outstanding Roman quality see VERG.*Aen*.12.838-40. The word is often used by Vergil with special reference to civil war (*Ecl*.1.70, *G*. 1.468, 511, *Aen*. 1.294). On the whole, *pietas* is a favourite term of Ovid (Anderson on 8.477). Three times Ovid presents the moral paradox of an act that is pious and impious at the same time (*Met*.7.339, 8.477 and 9.408).
[96] Nisbet-Hubbard on HOR.*Carm*.2.13: the adjective suits deadly diseases and destructive emotions. Hardie on VERG.*Aen*.9.621: *dirus* in Virgil usually retains a religious overtone.
[97] Austin on VERG.*Aen*.1.616: very strong. Id. On VERG.*Aen*.2.150: *Immanis* is a favourite Virgilian word, and its shades of meaning are like those in 'monstrous' –size, savagery, uncouthness, sometimes just strangeness of some kind. The adjective is applied to a river already in VERG.*Aen*.3.702 and a river-god at ibid.8.330. See also Fordyce on VERG.*Aen*.7.305 and Harrison on VERG.*Aen*.10.318.
[98] *ferocia* can be a "positive and Roman military virtue (cf. Livy 9. 6. 13 'Romanam virtutem fercoiamque')," as S. J. Harrison observes on VERG.*Aen*.10.609-10.
[99] *Amens* is a word rarely used by Ovid *de furore amoris*, e.g. *Ars* 2.691, where the *praeceptor amoris* declares that this is the way he wants his lover to be: mad with love.

naïveté (*simplex* 5.535), imprudence (*inprudens actusque cupidine lusus* 10.183),[100] maliciousness (*saltu maligno* "leaping about maliciously" 6.365), baseness (*indignis* "people who did not deserve such consideration" 6.367) and use of foul language (*turpes ... / linguas* 6.374-5, *duri puer oris* 5.451)[101].

Not even a single one of the above adjectives appears in Augustus' *Res Gestae*, even though most of them do not belong exclusively to poetic diction, as Livian usage shows. Only one, *audax*, belonged "in the late Republican period to the current phraseology of political backbiting."[102] Apparently it was used "no less than *improbi* or *mali* (...) as a typological description of those who were conceived as the direct opposite of *boni*." Although the derogatory sense of *audax* "preponderates in the extant evidence from the very beginning," and "is an abusive term of long standing and wide application outside the sphere of politics," the notion of "*audacia* by itself can be applied both for appreciation and for reproach."[103] Accordingly, "Caesar's *audacia* is somewhat complicated by the fact that he was admittedly a bold general whose boldness must have often been praised or regretted, as the case may be."[104] Indeed, in Cicero's view expressed in a letter to Atticus (7.13.1) in January 49, it was his *audacia* that really caused the civil wars not the citizens' discord.

The same ambiguity of praise and blame is also inherent in other adjectives used in judgements, such as *inmanis* (cf. *Tr.*2.335 *immania Caesaris acta*), *ferox* (it can be a virtue for a warrior, see *OLD* s.v.2) and *simplex*, which is a virtue of archaic language (LIV.40.47.3 *sermo antiquae simplicitatis*) and religious people (LIV.24.10.6 *religiosi* not *pii*). Civil war associations were also attached to another adjective listed above, *impius*, especially by Vergil (*Ecl.*1.70, *Georg.*1.511, 468, and *Aen.*1.294 and 6.613).

---

[100] Carelessness is a characteristic associated with youth, cf. 3.425 (Narcissus), 10.130 (Cyparissus), VERG.*Aen.*9.386 (Nisus) and LIV.31.14.7.
[101] *turpis* is the opposite of *pulcher* (HOR.*Ep.*1.2.3) and *honestus* (HOR.*Ars* 213), synonymous with *indignus* (LIV.39.5.2) but less strong than *nefas* (LIV.5.51.2). It belongs to the vocabulary of moral philosophy (HOR.*Ep.*1.2.3) and one thing that is typically *turpis* in the life of a warrior is *fuga* (LIV.2.59.2, 4.43.2, 4.46.6, 31.41.14, 37.43.3, and PROP.4.2.54).
[102] Wirszubski 1961: 12 and 13.
[103] Wirszubski 1961: 15 with n.21.
[104] Wirszubski 1961: 17.

Pietas was, of course, central to the Augustan programme of cultural renewal.[105] "The revived *pietas* toward the gods found its expression in Augustus' extensive rebuilding of over eighty temples and shrines that had fallen into disrepair, as had the *res publica* in general."[106] Another Roman sense of *pietas*, filial affection, is used by the extradiegetic narrator of the *Metamorphoses* "as a criterion in evaluating the behaviour of persons," as von Albrecht reminds us.[107] Yet, three times (7.339, 8.477 and 9.408) he celebrates the paradox of pious impiety.

The problematic nature and the limits of *pietas* are also at stake in Orpheus' **[21f]** tale of incestuous love (Myrrha). When asked by her father what sort of husband she would prefer Myrrha answers: "a man like you" (*similem tibi* 10.364). Unaware of the incestuous *double-entendre* he answers: *esto tam pia semper*. The adjective is picked up by the narrator, who adds that *pietatis nomine dicto / demisit uultus sceleris sibi conscia uirgo* (10.366-367 "At the word 'devoted', the girl hung her head, conscious of her guilt"). Incest, one of the most wide-spread taboos of human culture, was considered in classical Greek culture as one of the "unwritten laws" established by the gods (Xen.*Mem*.4.4.19-20), and, naturally, it could be presented as a barbaric vice (E.*Andr*.174-5). Having said that, its presence in Greek myth, and consequently in literature, is overwhelming while Athenian law imposed a certain kind of it on female heirs (ἐπίκληρος κόρη). This has led scholars like O. Rank to suspect that "despite express prohibitions and strict punishments" incest was not as rare as one would think.[108]

Interestingly, Myrrha is trying to convince herself (and the reader?) that incest is only natural: *humana malignas / cura dedit leges, et, quod natura remittit, / invida iura negant* (10.329-31 "Human interference has imposed spiteful laws, so that jealous regulations forbid what nature itself allows.") Yet the narrator's (i.e. Orpheus') negative judgment is evident in his admiration for her resistance to "the horrible desire" (*foedoque repugnat amori* 10.319). The heroine's thoughts are presented as "frenzied prayers" (10.370 *furiosa vota*), her desire is *nefas* ("a horror" 10.404) to the narrator, a *scelus* ("a crime" 10.413) in Myrrha's view and *diros ... amores*

---

[105] See Zanker 1988: 102-35.
[106] Galinsky 1996: 88.
[107] Albrecht 1999: 180.
[108] Rank 1992: 347.

("a disastrous desire" 10.426) to the nurse's mind. This clear rejection of her desire does not preclude some sympathy on the part of the narrator. This breaks out when Myrrha is in mental turmoil, just before gratifying her desire: *infelix ... virgo* (10.443 "poor girl!").

Pietas can prevent someone from being cruel and reckless, as Hypermestra writes to Lynceus in *Heroides* 14.49 (*timor et pietas crudelibus obstitit ausis*). The Persian king **[6]** is, however, *ferox inmansuetusque* (4.237): he buried his pregnant daughter alive. *Crudelitas* is *inhumana* (LIV.21.4.9, 24.5.6), i.e. incompatible with Augustan *humanitas*,[109] but also characteristic of despotic behaviour (LIV.1.4.3, 25.28.7, 29.17.20, 31.30.1, 32.19.7, 32.21.21, 33.44.8), associated with impiety (LIV.1.53.8). The first impious king (*tyrannus*) in the poem, Lycaon **[1]**, is not called *crudelis* but *inhospitus* (1.218) by Jupiter. *Tyrannus* itself probably has no intrinsically negative connotations in Ovid, as Bömer observes. Yet, it is interesting to note that in Plato's *Republic* (8, 565d-566a) the myth is read politically as an allegory for the metamorphosis of the democratic leader into a tyrant.[110] Calliope **[11]**, on the other hand, does not hesitate to call Demeter's daughter, the *regina Erebi* (5.543), *crudelis* (5.542). Although, being queen of the *crudeles umbrae* (VERG.*Aen*.1.547) is a good enough reason for her to be cruel too, Cahoon may also be right to regard this, from a feminist point of view, as the effect of the hardening experience of her rape and subsequent captivity in the kingdom of death, a prefiguration of the moral metamorphosis of Procne and Philomela in Book 6.[111]

As Crabbe observes, "there is humour in Achelous' **[17]** pretensions to powers comparable to those of Diana. His inflated grandiloquence with its exaggerated word repetition, and the emotional identification of god and river in the first person, whilst evoking the earlier third person account of his own flood waters contrasts heavily with it."[112] Nonetheless, a problem is created by his use of the adjective *inmanis*, in order to describe his outraged self at the moment of exacting vengeance: *pariterque animis inmanis et undis* (8.584 "with heart and flood equally ruthless"). For, as Bömer remarks the word often has a negative

---

[109] Galinsky 1996: 266 with n.108.
[110] See Detienne 1989: 157f.
[111] Cahoon 1996: 57.
[112] Crabbe 1981: 2290.

semantic load, and indeed *TLL* classifies the present instance under the heading *praevalet notio saevitiae, crudelitatis (de moribus sim.) vel diritatis, atrocitatis sim. (de aspectu)*.[113] Admittedly, wrath is a typical motive of divine action in epic and the *Met.* in particular. In fact, as 1.166 (*ingentes animo et dignas Iove concipit iras* "his heart swelled with dreadful wrath, worthy of Jupiter") suggests, the greater the deity the greater the anger to be expected. It seems, therefore, that there is hardly anything reprehensible in the river-god's behaviour, especially as it has been sufficiently justified by human misbehavior, at least from the god's perspective.

Besides words concerning piety (*impius* but also *sceleratus, inmanis*), cruelty (*ferox,* crudelis, *malignus*) and recklessness, another category of negative judgement is truth, or rather its perversion. The impious Tyrrhenian sailors **[4]** that abducted Bacchus are called *fallaces* (3.638), while Pyreneus **[9]** is said to have shown false and deceitful piety when he venerated the Muses (5.279 *fallaci ... vultu*). However, the word's use by the extradiegetic narrator (e.g. 3.1. *deus posita fallacis imagine tauri* "when the god laid aside the false appearance of a bull") does not suggest that it automatically implies negative criticism. Besides, truth and falsehood sometimes are a matter of viewpoint: the Pierides' criticism of the Muses **[10]** on the grounds of veracity (5.308 *vana dulcedine* "sweet lies") rebounds on themselves: *falsoque in honore Gigantas / ponit* (5.319-20 "falsely assigning honour to the giants").[114]

The anonymous narrator of Aesacus and Hesperia **[25]** makes a comment that betrays his urbane, courtly identity. Aesacus was born in the pastoral landscape of Ida's shady mountainside, where he spent most of his life. "Yet his was no boorish heart, nor was it proof against love" (11.767-68 *non agreste tamen nec inexpugnabile amori / pectus habens*). As Bömer observes, the narrator shares the same values and prejudices as Ovid's persona in *Amores* 3.10.17f.: *nec tamen est, quamvis agros amet illa feraces, / rustica nec viduum pectus amoris habet* ("Even though she loves the fertile fields, she is not boorish nor is her heart empty of love"). And "erotic elegy, above all Ovidian elegy, is the genre most closely linked

---

[113] Bömer on 9.247. *TLL* VII 439, 50. See also Opelt 1965: 254.
[114] On this phrase Davis 1969: 70 founded a whole theory that the Pierids' *encomium* was a failure because "praise, like blame, must appear to be accurately assigned, if the eulogy is to be persuasive. (...) [but] we *know* who won the Gigantomachy" [i.e. the Olympians].

with urban society and the rhetoric of the city," as Rosati aptly put it.[115] The Sibyl **[30]**, on the other hand would have profited from urbane awareness of love-matters. Now that the *felicior aetas* ("the happier age" 14.142) is past it seems that she rather regrets having turned down Apollo's offer, even though *praecorrumpere* (14.134) suggests that she still disapproves of the god's scheming just as much as her own juvenile foolishness (14.138 *vana*).

Iole's account of her half-sister's transformation into a lotus-tree **[19]** is teeming with sympathetic comments about her ignorance (9.336 *fatorum nescia* "unaware of her destiny"; 349 *nescierat hoc soror* "My sister had known nothing of this") and misery (9.368 *misero de corpore* "her wretched body"). Naturally, the victim's husband and father are also *miserrimus* (9.363). Such tragedy can only be explained as the result of a cruel fate (9.336 *fatorum*, 359 *fati crudelis*). The binding laws of fate do not, however, exculpate completely careless youth like Hyacinthus (*inprudens actusque cupidine lusus* 10.183 "carelessly and in his eagerness for game").[116] The comment in 4.256-57 (*quamvis amor excusare dolorem, / indiciumque dolor poterat*), that Clytie **[6]** could be forgiven for her indignation, since it was due to love, and indignation might have excused her tale-bearing, clearly suggests that Leuconoe sympathizes with the female character rather than with the male divinity. For, the same excuse could be evoked in favour of the Sun, as his behaviour was also motivated by love and anger.

A rather more problematic comment is made by the Minyeid who tells the story of Pyramus and Thisbe **[5]**. The *paraklausithyron* (or more accurately *paraklausitoikhon*) of the two lovers is summed up in line 4.78: *talia nequiquam diversa sede locuti*. *Nequiquam* is a common word in the *Met*. It occurs both in metadiegetic (2.566, 577, 4.78, 5.438, 8.827) and diegetic narrative (5.33, 9.564, 10.3), adding an ominous note to the context. Bömer merely notes or rather quotes from Axelson that the word is common only in epic as far as poetry is concerned.[117] In the *Met*. there are, to be sure, straightforward instances like 5.33 or 12.559, where "in

---

[115] Rosati 1983: 83.
[116] *Inprudentia* is characteristic of youth in both the *Aeneid* (9.386 of Nisus) and the *Metamorphoses* (3.425 of Narcissus and 10.130 of Cyparissus), cf. also LIV.31.14.7 *iuvenes ... imprudentes*. For Aeneas' *imprudentia* in the *Aeneid* see Bowra 1933/4: 367.
[117] Bömer on 5.32-3.

vain" is easily intelligible as a comment on the unsuccessful result of someone's effort. But how should it be understood at 2.577, where *nequiquam* apparently qualifies a medio-passive (*lassor*)?[118]

In the present instance, the word seems to comment not only on the act of talking to the deaf wall (had Ovid used such an adjective things would be much clearer) but also on the content of their words, their wish to embrace and kiss each other (and whatever else is implied by *toto nos corpore iungi*), thus foreshadowing the story's unhappy end; it has the same function in 9.564 and 10.3.[119] An alternative interpretation for our passage may be that *nequiquam* qualifies not the participle *locuti* but the phrase *dixere "vale"* (they are both going to die soon) and *dedere oscula* (the vanity of the action is made explicit by the narrator with *non pervenientia contra*).[120] Finally, it was suggested to me by S. J. Harrison that *nequiquam* primarily qualifies the adjective *diversa*: the fact that they were not in the same room did not prevent them from talking to each other. Nevertheless, in view of the comic/elegiac motif which underlies the passage I still think the strongest meaning is the one mentioned first.[121]

Besides adjectives and straightforwardly critical nouns like *nefas* (8.764), *summa mali* (13.637), and *populator* (13.655) intradiegetic narrators in the *Met.* employ on occasion slightly more indirect expressions of judgement. For instance, Calliope **[11]** says that Ascalaphus, whose revelation of Proserpina's thoughtlessly picking and eating the prohibited fruit from Dis' garden cost him his human form, "may be thought to have earned his punishment" (5.552 *commeruisse potest*). Erysichthon's **[17d]** image of the *contemptor deum* is reinforced not only by means of the simile of the sacrificial victim (8.763-4) but also by several Virgilian echoes which hint that Erysichthon is another Mezentius, in the *Aeneid* the archetype of the god-spurning mortal.[122]

---

[118] Melville has put "in vain" in parenthesis as an exclamation, a postponed comment on the Crow's (before she became a crow) effort to escape.

[119] In the latter passage, Orpheus indeed responds to the call of Hymenaeus but not in the appropriate way, as the narrator goes on to make clear in 4f.; thus it is not his summons that are in vain, strictly speaking, but the chain of actions they trigger off.

[120] For the one-word direct speech on the diegetic level cf. 10.62; its frequency in the *Met.* is noted by Heinze 1919: 65.

[121] For the motif see Perraud 1983/4: 136. For the position of *nequiquam* in the sentence cf. 5.348-9.

[122] See Hollis on 738-878 (p.132) and Solodow 1988: 160.

The pathetic apostrophe in 360 (*quem non blanda deae potuissent verna monere?* "Who could have resisted the persuasive words of the goddess?") stigmatizes clearly the farmers' behaviour as rude lack of sensitivity and common sense.

Simile is a figure that may involve implicit commentary on the action. "For all its humorous exaggeration," the simile of the burst water-pipe that describes the issue of blood from Pyramus' wound in the Minyeid's story **[5]** "increases the contrast between the urban setting in which the lover has spent his life and the marginal wild place outside the walls," as Segal observes.[123] The reddish colour on Hermaphroditus' cheeks is further illustrated by Alcithoe **[7]** with three successive short similes.[124] The first and more extended simile seems at first sight somewhat unsuitable in implicitly comparing Hermaphroditus with a predator and Salmacis with its victim, although the admiration implicit in the periphrasis *regia ales* (362) apparently echoes the admiration for the boy's beauty and the unbending attitude he has shown towards the nymph. The ivy-simile is also traditional in erotic contexts[125] and implies that Salmacis' embrace could prove harmful for the boy.[126] In Ceyx' narrative about Chione **[23]** judgement is only indirectly conveyed through the use of two conventional similes: (a) the traditional sea-rock simile, to illustrate his brother's response to his consolatory words (11. 330 *haud aliter quam cautes murmura ponti* "as much as reefs heed the murmuring of the sea"), and (b) the traditional bullock-attacked-by-hornets simile, to illustrate the poor father's demented reaction to his daughter's cremation (11.334-36 *similisque iuvenco / spicula crabronum pressa cervice gerenti, qua via nulla ruit* "like a bullock whose neck, rubbed tender by the plough, is tormented by stinging hornets").

---

[123] Segal 1985: 391. For this contrast as a major theme of the entire story see Segal 1985: 389-90.
[124] For blushing in Latin literature, see Lateiner 1996: 236 n.19, where he announces a forthcoming longer analysis of the relevant material.
[125] See Hunter on Eubulus fr.104.5
[126] Cf. PLIN.*Nat.*16.151, 243, 17.234 and HOR.*Epod.*15.5, where the noxious quality of the ivy is introduced almost openly by *artius* and *lentis* (Babcock 1966: 408). Notice that the adjective attributed to the trees (*truncos*, which can also mean "torsos"), i.e. *longos*, "'tall and slender' (...) is not infrequently, and especially in conversational Latin, used with reference to people; rarely of trees" (Skutsch on ENN.*Ann.*223). For *longitudo* as an aspect of beauty see CATUL.86.1.

In this section we discussed the most obvious means of evaluation at the intradiegetic narrators' disposition: qualitative adjectives and adverbs (*judgement*). There are various aspects of human behaviour that are judged negatively, including impiety, cruelty, and ignorance. None of the exact words used seems to have been politically charged only in Augustan discourse. *Audax*, which was a catchword already in the late Republican period, *inmanis*, *ferox*, and *simplex* are words with potential ambiguity, as they can be used both for praise and blame. Another word which was particularly charged in the period of civil wars that preceded the Augustan regime, is *impius*. *Pietas*, a key-concept of Augustan discourse itself, is problematized in the tale of Myrrha **[21f]**. Mendacity is also another target for negative criticism, although the very concept is contested by the gods' assumption of false appearances to satisfy their lust or to save themselves, an idea hotly contested between the Pierids and the Muses. Not even cruelty, which is incompatible with Augustan *humanitas*, is unequivocally criticized by intradiegetic narrators; Achelous **[17]** can boast of his being *inmanis*. Rusticity and ignorance also attract judgement, which can be sympathetic rather than critical. The only adverb that may be a vector of judgement is *nequiquam* (4.78), while nouns include *nefas*, *summa mal*, and *populator*. Evaluation is also effected indirectly through allusions to previous literature and similes.

VI.6.2 Explanation

"An explanation requires the knowledge of a certain fact of which the narrator is only now apprising us; on occasion the fact might already be known to some (a generalisation, a name, a piece of traditional lore), but more often the narrator is supplying us with new information, whether out of the past or from the present scene."[127] An obvious form explanation may assume is that of parenthesis, "a regular feature of the Alexandrian poetic style."[128] This feature of Ovidian style was studied extensively, though mainly from a formal point of view, by Michael von Albrecht.[129] Parenthesis is recognized as a means of interpretation and illumination of the action from various angles.[130] A complete list of

---

[127] Richardson 1990: 141.
[128] F. Williams on Call.*H*.2.44; See also Albrecht 1964: 105 n.82.
[129] Albrecht 1964.
[130] Albrecht 1964: 23.

parentheses in the 37 metanarratives of the *Met.* is provided in **Table 2** of the next chapter, where it the figure is examined as a sign of interaction between the narrator and the narratee. Here we will present only two parentheses with content that deviates from the norm of explanation, as defined above.

Acoetes' **[4]** parenthetical affirmation (*Bacchus enim fuerat* 3.630 "For he was Bacchus!") supplies his audience with knowledge from hindsight, knowledge only Acoetes the narrator (as opposed to Acoetes the character of the tale) can have.[131] This statement gains particular significance and seems appropriate in the mouth of someone represented both by himself and the extradiegetic narrator as a pious follower of Bacchus' *numen*. For example, the hypothetical comparison at 3.650-51 (*tamquam modo denique fraudem / senserit* "as if he had only just perceived their treachery") is also redolent of Acoetes' piety. Obviously, the narrator cannot believe that an omniscient divinity could ignore the secret intentions of his kidnappers. Such piety may give the impression of "total naïveté" since, so far, Acoetes "has in no way proved that the boy was divine."[132] But an audience that shared the narrator's piety (i.e. not Acoetes' narratee, Pentheus) would understand that such insight is the result of the god's grace bestowed upon the good at heart and simple in mind like Acoetes.

Sometimes a parenthetic explanation adds nothing that the narrator had not yet disclosed or implied. In Ceyx' narrative about Chione **[23]** the only explanation offered is a parenthesis affirming that Chione gave birth to twins (11.316). At the end of the same tale an explanation is provided for the name and characteristic behaviour of the bird into which the character is transformed: Aesacus continues in the form of a bird to seek his death under water (11.795 *aequor amat, nomenque manet, quia mergitur illo* "He loves the waters of the sea, and has the name of diver, because he dives down into them."). Forbes Irving maintains that the *aition* which derives *mergus* from *mergor* only makes sense in Latin, and thus must be Ovid's invention.[133] But Myers seems to be right in

---

[131] Albrecht 1964: 58.
[132] Anderson on 3.629-31.
[133] Forbes Irving 1990: 224.

observing that the Greek name of the bird (κολυμβίς) has the same etymology from κολυμβάω ('to plunge headlong').[134]

But most explanations do not supply new facts but comment on the motives of the action narrated. A recurring theme in the interpretative comments of the Minyads **[5-7]** is *amor*.[135] It was love that made Thisbe bold enough to walk in the darkness in order to meet Pyramus, affirms the Minyad **[5]** at 4.96.[136] There is, however, a tinge of irony in the fact that Thisbe's audacity immediately collapses before a new and unexpected threat: Thisbe flees *timido pede* (100) at the sight of a lioness and does not return to the agreed meeting-place until she has got rid of her fear (*metu nondum posito* 4.128).[137] In the same vein, Pyramus' vision (sharpened by love) helps him discover the blood-stained scarf of Thisbe, yet deceives him as to her actual fate. The parenthetical comment made in Alcithoe's narrative about Salmacis and Hermaphroditus **[7]** also concerns love: *nescit enim quid amor* (4.330 "for he does not know what love is").[138] Its apparent aim is to explain Hermaphroditus' reaction to Salmacis' advances, i.e. to explain an action on the literal level –the only kind of interpretation offered by the Homeric narrator, according to Richardson.[139]

This frequency of *amor* in the Minyads' interpretations cannot be an accident. The stories they tell are essentially love-stories: the first is about *Pyramus et Thisbe* (4.55), whose love grew as time went by (4.60); the second sister announces her theme as *Solis amores* (4.170) –Alcithoe

---

[134] Myers 1994: 37.
[135] Albrecht 1964: 130.
[136] For the thought cf.*Am*.1.6.60 *illa* [= *nox*] *pudore vacat, Liber Amorque metu*. For the opposite thought see *Ep*.1.12 *res est solliciti plena timoris amor*. Medea (*Ep*.12.61) is made to say that *ipsum timor auget amorem*. In the inset tale of Atalanta and Hippomenes **[22]**, Venus the narrator acknowledges that the power of beauty can defeat fear: *tanta potentia formae est* (10.573). One can only agree with Anderson that the emphasis on the bride's beauty and the silencing of any other motive (wealth or political advantages to be gained) are in accordance with the epic norms of wooing; but we should take into account the fact that it is Venus who narrates and what else could she possibly be thinking of as a motive for marriage but beauty and desire?
[137] Anderson on 4.93-96.
[138] For the use of *enim* with the negatively expressed (*nescit*) interpretative comments, see 2.301, 62-22, 677-79, 766-67 and 4.43 on the diegetic level. The *rudis ignoto tactus amore puer* is the intended readership of Ovid's *Amores* (2.1.6).
[139] Richardson 1990: 148.

first refers to *amor* in the parenthesis of 4.330, though Salmacis' desire has already been manifest in *optavit habere* (4.315) and *voluptas* (4.327). Parentheses give the narrators the opportunity to make their theme resonate throughout their narrative without really interrupting the flow of their narration.[140] At the same time these comments provide the necessary justification for the action narrated and illuminate the characters' psychology, as e.g. at 4.234 *neque enim moderatus in illa Solis amor fuerat* ("for her love for the Sun knew no limits").[141]

And, naturally, who could know love in greater depth than Venus herself, the third level narrator of Atalanta and Hippomenes **[22]**? Whether ironic or sympathetic (it is difficult to be certain about the tone of this comment), the narrator asserts her superior position vis-à-vis Atalanta.[142] Atalanta's soliloquy (10.611-35) is followed by an epigrammatic comment by the goddess of love (10.636-37):

utque rudis primosque cupidine tacta,
quid facit, ignorans amat et sentit amorem.

"Inexperienced as she was, touched by the first stirring of passion, she did not know what she was doing, but loved without realizing that she was in love."

Finally, the story of Acis, Galatea and Polyphemus **[28]** is presented as a manifestation of the powerful control of Venus over everyone, including those who have no respect for the Olympians: *pro quanta potentia regni / est, Venus alma, tui! Nempe ille inmitis ... magni cum dis contemptor Olympi,/ quid sit amor, sensit* (13.758-61 "O gentle Venus, how powerful is your sway! For that savage creature ... one who despised great Olympus and the gods as well –even he understood what love means!"). Acknowledging the limitations of *fata* (13.885 *quod fieri solum per fata licebat* "the one thing that the fates allowed"), like Artemis in Euripides' *Hippolytus* (1328-30), Galatea goes on to narrate in detail how she transformed her beloved into a stream, a miracle no less (13.893 *miraque res*).

---

[140] Albrecht 1964: 68ff.
[141] Albrecht 1964: 114 with reference to VERG.*Aen.* 1.643-4 *neque enim patrius consistere mentem / passus amor*, for further parenthetical comments introduced with *neque enim* in the *Aeneid* see Austin on *Aen.*1.198.
[142] Cf. Winkler 1990: 116, who finds Longus description of Chloe's (another innocent girl in love) feelings "sympathetic (and always slightly ironic)."

We have thus touched upon another interpretative motif that is common in metadiegetic narrative: *fata*. Calliope's **[11]** initial explanation of the whole sequence of events that led to Ascalaphus' transformation is expressed in terms of fate: *non ita fata sinunt* (5.534 "fate did not allow this course of events").[143] The only explanation offered by the narrator himself in 'Cephalus and Procris' **[16]** invokes destiny: *sic me mea fata trahebant* (7.816 "for so my fate led me on").[144] This fatalism fits neatly with the general context of the tale which resounds with echoes from Athenian tragedy.[145] It also corresponds to Procris' reported words: *se fati dixit iniqui* (7.828 "she said her fate was cruel"). This is the closest Ovid comes "to a dimension of truly tragic suffering," according to Segal, who also argues that in this case the *fata* invoked are not "an instance of that apparently immoral violence of the world of the Metamorphoses" but the protagonist's character itself.[146] Hyacinthus **[21b]** is snatched away from his divine lover Apollo by *fata*. This is the explanation for the story's tragic end offered by the narrator, Apollo's son by the Muse, in the introduction to the narrative: *tristia si spatium ponendi fata dedissent* (10.164 "had cruel destiny allowed the god time to set him there" [i.e. in Heaven]) and confirmed by Apollo, "who cannot lie" (10.209) in his lamentation, reported in direct discourse: *quod quoniam fatali lege tenemur* (10.203 "since I am bound by the laws of fate").

Fata is a major theme in the canonical Augustan epic, the *Aeneid*. "Virgil retrieved this distinctive feature –the supremacy of divinely ordained Fate– from the Latin epic tradition but, in making it relative to his new semantic system, gave it an *ultimate* supremacy. This process prevents a truly dramatic form from being established in the poem and from shaping the poem's deep content."[147] It is evident from the above comments that in Ovidian metanarrative, at least, fate is just as *ineluctabile* as it was in the *Aeneid* (8.334). It is "no benign providence (...) but a power which is deaf to prayer and that holds a man in a grip of

---

[143] The phrase is used by the extradiegetic narrator in 11.408 and 13.624.
[144] Cf. SEN.*Ep.*107.11 (translating the Stoic Cleanthes) *ducunt volentem fata, nolentem trahunt*.
[145] Cf. especially Cephalus' entreaty at the end to be forgiven (e.g. Eur.*Alc.*202f., 250, 275, and *Hipp.* 1456).
[146] Segal 1978: 204 and 201-2.
[147] Conte 1986: 161.

inevitability from which no struggling can avail him to escape."[148] Cephalus, Procis and Hyacinthus come into conflict as individuals with their own personal destinies. Cephalus, in particular, has experienced the instability of human happiness. In his own words, *felix dicebar eramque;/ non ita dis visum est* (7.698-99 "Men called me happy and indeed I was; but the gods wished otherwise"). This comment bears echoes of the Vergilian *dis aliter visum est* (*Aen*.2.428 "but gods were of a different mind"), a comment made by Aeneas as an intradiegetic narrator and "comes from Virgil's private world of thought, to move each reader in his own private way: it may show resignation, it may be accusing."[149]

At the same time, the two vatic voices embedded in Ovid's *carmen*, Calliope **[11]** and Orpheus **[21]**, seem to have a wider vision of fate as a force that acts on a wholly suprapersonal plane, though without the Vergilian finality of Augustan Rome's glory, which ultimately derives from the Latin epic norm, as described by Conte.[150] In the latter Apollo is prevented by the *fatalis lex* from immortalizing his lover Hyacinthus, while in the former Demeter by the *Parcarum foedus* to enjoy the presence of her daughter throughout the year. Yet, another intradiegetic narrator, Lelex **[18]** puts forward "a typically Roman aspect of Ovid's attitude to the gods," their limitless power, as the view that his story will attempt to support: *inmensa est finemque potentia caeli / non habet et, quiquid superi voluere, peractum est* (8.618-9 "The power of heaven is measureless, and knows no bounds; whatever the gods wish is at once achieved").

We have seen that love is frequently used as an explanation for narrative developments in metanarratives. Yet, a few special cases of love need further clarification with reference to other events. Orpheus **[21e]** explains Pygmalion's abhorrence for women as the result of his indignation at the plethora of vices which is common to women by nature (10.244-45). This is obviously a deduction from the behaviour of the Propoetides **[21d]** but could also point to a variant version of

---

[148] Camps 1969: 45.
[149] Austin *ad loc*. The passage is not discussed in Lyne 1987. Albrecht 1964: 139 attempts a fine distinction between the picture of uncertainty of human expectation sketched by the comment in Vergil and the cruder (?) opposition between former happiness and eventual misfortune in Ovid, but I am not sure this is valid.
[150] Conte 1986: 161.

woman's creation along the lines of Hesiod's myth of Pandora (*Op.*76-77) permeated by Orpheus' misogynist attitude, as Sharrock argued in a brilliant article back in 1991.[151] The Thracian bard concludes his song with the story of Venus' affair with Adonis **[21g]**. In Leuconoe's narrative of the goddess' affair with Mars **[6a]** there was nothing about its origins. Orpheus, however, feels compelled to offer an explanation for the curious fact that Venus is in love with a mortal man: she fell prey to the fiery emotion accidentally inspired by her careless son (10.525-26 *namque pharetratus dum dat puer oscula matri,/ inscius exstanti destrinxit harundine pectus* "while her son, armed with a quiver, was kissing her, he unwittingly grazed her breast with an arrow which was projecting from the sheath"). That Venus would not otherwise become involved in such a mismatch is an assumption corroborated by the plot of the *Homeric Hymn to Aphrodite*. Lines 45-53 of that text attribute Venus's sweet desire for Anchises to Zeus' plan to make her fall in the same trap that she normally sets for the rest of the gods, including the Father himself. Of course, in Homeric theology Aphrodite is not the mother of Eros, and the omnipotent Zeus can also inspire love.

To sum up, explanations are not rare in the 37 metanarratives of the *Met.* Introducing information that the narrator has withheld so far, but is needed for the motivation of narrative developments, they are sometimes presented as parentheses. This way the flow of narrative is only momentarily interrupted. Two motives that recur in explanations are love and fate. Neither is without political implications. In a regime that has collapsed the division between private and public, e.g. with the introduction of the marital legislation, even statements about love can have political implications. This does not mean that these comments are not justified by such intratextual factors as the narrator's gender (female) and the stories' theme (love). Fate, which in the canonical Augustan epic, the *Aeneid*, mainly referred to Rome's destiny in the intradiegetic narrators' explanations becomes a cause of separation from loved ones and consequently of deeply personal suffering without a wider historical perspective.

---

[151] Sharrock 1991: 173-76; I do not, however, feel obliged to endorse all her suggestions, especially the verbal links with the Hesiodic text.

VI.6.3 Generalisation

Generalisations are the narrator's comments which are "not restricted to a specific character, event or situation but extend the significance of the particular case in a way which purportedly applies to a group, a society or humanity at large."[152] These statements may be perceived as pertaining to the world outside diegesis, i.e. the real world. Such comments serve what Aristotle considered as the *differentia specifica* of poetry (i.e. literature) with regard to history, its universality, and are the only kind that cannot be replaced by other indirect, less explicit devices.[153]

In his study of the Homeric narrator Richardson concluded that he "is not a philosophizing one; he prefers to let his characters make the general statements about the ways of the world."[154] His generalisations concern the nature of gods and their gifts, the nature of the mules, while the longest (3 lines) 'universal truth' in his own voice affirms that the mind of Zeus is stronger than that of men: he gives or removes success as he chooses. On the contrary, "in the Latin epic, an event –in itself empirical and arbitrary– becomes the motivated (justified) sign of a sense that is easily expressible as a general maxim."[155] More than any other single rhetorical device in Latin oratory and literature, the *sententia* became the supreme expression of Rome during its imperial period. Its importance in Roman rhetoric, literature, and public life during the early Principate indicates that it was intimately connected with the Principate's unique social code. In the rhetorical culture of imperial Rome "the ability to categorize, typologize, and formulate generalizations on human behaviour with concision and force was highly valued and admired, and could translate directly into power."[156]

Ovid was considered by his contemporaries a *bonus declamator*. According to Seneca's testimony (*Con*.2.2.8), he admired so much Porcius Latro, one of his teachers, that he transferred many of his *sententiae* to his own verses. Ovid really likes to introduce *sententiae*, either serious (e.g.1.414, 2.846) or amusing (2.436) in his stories. Cestius

---

[152] Rimmon-Kenan 1983: 99
[153] Booth 1961: 197.
[154] Richardson 1990: 145.
[155] Conte 1986: 146.
[156] Sinclair 1995: 3.

(SEN.*Con*.3.7.1) claimed that Ovid flooded the world not only with books on the art of love but also with *sententiae* (*hoc saeculum non amatoriis artibus tantum, sed sententiis implevit*). Although the Latin has a wider spectrum of meaning than 'generalisation', these testimonies and opinions are indicative of his rhetorical tendencies.[157]

The 37 metanarratives studied here, however, are not at all rich in gnomic statements. Three generalisations concern love, whether directly (4.68, 4.278) or indirectly (10.573) and belong to narratives told by female characters (the Minyeides, Venus). Since his days at the schools of rhetoric Ovid has been the erotic expert. Seneca (*Con*.2.2.10) has preserved for us one of the young Ovid's *controversiae*, which includes the generalisation: *sic senes amant* ("this is the way old men love"). The discovery of the hole in the wall that separates the houses of the two lovers Pyramus and Thisbe is explained by the unnamed Miyeid **[5]** as a manifestation of the special sensitivity of love: *quid non sentit amor?* (4.68 "what escapes love's notice?").[158] The form of a question has the advantage of involving the audience in the narration, albeit in a manipulative way. There is no parallel of content in the diegetic narrative; nor is there any precise formal parallel, as all other parenthetic rhetorical questions include *enim* and cannot be classified as generalisations. The story of Daphnis the shepherd (4.276-8) is the only tale rejected by Alcithoe **[7]** for which a minimum of information is given, enough to form a minimal narrative (what happened to whom for what reason).[159] It is concluded (*in speciem epimythii*) with a generalizing interpretative comment on the fierceness of indignation felt by deceived lovers: *tantus dolor urit amantes* (so great is the lovers' distress!).[160]

Finally, Venus **[22]**, reminding her audience of Atalanta's beauty (cf. 10.563) and filling out the customary details of heroic wooing, closes line 10.573 with a typical 'epiphonema': *tanta potentia formae est* ("so great is the power of beauty!"). Unlike the Minyeides' comments, Venus' glorification of beauty in her story is immediately applicable to the external reality of Orpheus' song **[21]**, which includes the tale of her

---

[157] For a balanced view on this aspect of Ovid's literary art see Galinsky 1975: 208 n.60.
[158] In a slightly different sense in *Ars* 2.648 *incipiens omnia sentit amor*.
[159] Cf. e.g. the minimalist definition of narrative in Toolan 1988: 7 as "a perceived sequence of non-randomly connected events."
[160] For such comments made by the primary narrator see 1.60, 440; 2.731; 4.448; 8.168.

love-affair with Adonis, a youth of exceptional beauty (10.515-24). This homology of herself and Adonis with Atalanta is made explicit by Venus in 10.580 [*corpus*] *quale meum, vel quale tuum, si femina fias* ("a body like mine or yours, if you were a woman"). Anderson's suggestion that the emphasis on beauty and the silencing of any other motive (e.g. monetary or political advantages to be gained through this marriage) are in accordance with epic norms of wooing is undoubtedly reasonable, although such comments on the power of beauty are more frequent in elegiac poetry, as Bömer reminds us.[161] Yet, it is also appropriate for Venus, the goddess who won the beauty contest judged by Paris, to emphasize beauty as a motive for love.

Besides common subject-matter, at least the first and third of these generalisations have a common function in narrative. They are used in order to justify something which may appear unlikely at first sight. In the unnamed Minyeid's tale the crack in the wall was there but nobody noticed it except the two young lovers. Venus has strived to present Atalanta as inimical to the idea of marriage (10.564-72). The insistence of her suitors can only be justified by the girl's stunning looks. The fourth example comes from the opening of king Anius' narrative about his daughters' transformation into doves **[27]**: *tanta homines rerum inconstantia versat* (13.646 "so fickle is human fortune"). This motif is used elsewhere in the *Metamorphoses* (3.131f.) as a bridging device on the diegetic level. The maxim's content is congenial to the poem's major theme of metamorphosis, i.e. the instability of bodily form. A fifth generalisation is attributed to Macareus **[32]**, who underlines the source of Circe's power: *tantum medicamina possunt* (14.285 "such is the power of magic drugs!"). In form these two generalisations are similar to those concerning love and beauty, beginning with a form of the demonstrative *tantus*. They are also used to justify surprising events: how a father of four children now lives alone, and the marvel of men's transformation into pigs in Circe's house.

The only generalisation that concerns gods is ascribed to Orpheus **[21]**. In the proem to his *carmen* he admits that *cedunt Iovis omnia regno*

---

[161] Anderson on 10.573-74 and Bömer *ad loc.*

(10.148 "all things bow before Jupiter's power").[162] Jupiter's kingship (he is *rex superum* "king of heavens" at 10.155, cf. 1.251) was famously challenged by the Giants (1.152), which is precisely the subject Orpheus is going to leave aside. Orpheus' parenthetical comment is certainly tainted with irony in the light of the story about Ganymede, a young man who cannot resist the Heavenly Father's power and will. It certainly proves Jupiter's unlimited power but leaves him wanting *maiestas*. For as the extradiegetic narrator comments at 2.846-47 of Jupiter's transformation into a bull in order to abduct Europe: *non bene conveniunt nec in una sede morantur / maiestas et amor* ("Majesty and love go ill together, nor can they long share one abode"). Yet, it is essentially the same explanation that the extradiegetic narrator offers for Callisto's unwilling surrender to Jupiter's lustful desire: *sed quem superare puella, quisque Iovem poterat?* (2.436-7 "but how could a girl overcome a man, and who could defeat Jupiter?"). It seems that both 'Ovid' and his intradiegetic alias 'Orpheus' would agree with E. Fantham that "sex was a privilege of power, not a disqualifier as it seems in our democracies."[163]

VI.7 Conclusions

This chapter was dedicated to the study of the four functions a narrator usually performs alongside the main function of telling a story: (a) directing, (b) communicative, (c) testimonial, and (d) ideological or interpretative. The oral nature and the short size of most metanarratives limit the intradiegetic narrators' directing function. Only Jupiter [1], the Crow [3], Leuconoe [6], Alcithoe [7], Calliope [11], Aeacus [15], Cephalus [16], Achelous [17], Nestor [26], and Diomedes [34] make comments on their narratives' internal organisation. Some of them express their concern to avoid wastage of time (*mora*). When time allows, (*ex*) *ordine referre* is considered the best kind of organising their narrative material, avoiding the excess of digressive details and the extreme

---

[162] The thought derives from VERG. *Ecl.* 3.60-61 (*Iovis omnia plena;/ ille colit terras, illi mea carmina curae* "all things are full of Jove; He cultivates the earth, my verses are his care"), in turn adapted from Arat.*Phaen.* 2-4, on which the Scholiasts comment: For, being pious (φιλόθεοι), all ancient people used to start by mentioning the gods, who were the source of all that is good for men.
[163] Fantham 1995: 54.

conciseness of summary. Some narrators introduce the topic of their narrative formally with a kind of title, while others signal the beginning of a narrative sequence with *primus*. Orpheus' **[21]** artistic narrative opts for a beginning *ab Iove*, while Aeacus **[15]** and Cephalus **[16]** present the two possibilities for a tragic plot (from misfortune into happiness and the reverse). The communicative function will be examined in greater detail in chapter 7.

The testimonial function, which concerns the narrator's attitude towards the story narrated, its provenance, veracity, authenticity and emotional impact, is more frequently performed than the directing. The emphasis lies on the narrator's memory and the story's authentication rather than the narrator's emotive response. Nestor **[26]** is clearly the most self-conscious intradiegetic narrator in this respect. When the narrator cannot prove the story in any other way, (s)he may invoke the narratee's knowledge. They normally take care to distinguish between the events they narrate as witnesses and those that they have learned from others, whom they usually name or describe as persons. On occasion, however, they have to resort to invocations of *fama* or acknowledge that access to absolute truth is impossible. Indeed, sometimes truth is so much like fiction that only faith in the narrator's credibility can validate the story.

The intradiegtic narrators' ideological function was described under three headings: First, judgment, which may take the obvious form of qualitative nouns (e.g. *nefas* and *populator*), adjectives and adverbs (e.g. *nequiquam*), but is also conveyed indirectly through allusions to previous literature and similes. On the whole judgement is negative: impiety, cruelty, and ignorance are the major causes of criticism. None of the exact words used seems to have particular links with Augustan discourse, although *audax* and *impius* were common in the late Republican political discourse. It is remarkable that some of the terms used like *inmanis, ferox*, and *simplex* are words with potential ambiguity as they can be used both for praise and blame. *Pietas*, a key-concept of Augustan discourse itself, is problematised in the tale of Myrrha **[21f]**. Mendacity is also another target for negative criticism, although the very concept is contested by the gods' assumption of false appearances to satisfy their lust or to save themselves, an idea hotly contested between the Pierides and the Muses **[9b]**. It seems, therefore, that rather than openly rejecting the values of the poet's contemporary society, intradiegetic narrators are used in order to present the ambiguities and contradictions inherent in Augustan discourse.

Explanations are sometimes presented as parentheses, so that the flow of narrative is not essentially interrupted. Two motives that recur in explanations are love and fate. In a regime that has collapsed the division between private and public even love can have political implications. This does not mean that these comments are not justified by such intratextual factors as the narrator's gender (female) and the stories' theme (love). Fate, on the other hand, is also prominent in the canonical Augustan epic, the *Aeneid*, referring to Rome's destiny of glory. In the intradiegetic narrators' explanations *fatum* becomes a cause of separation from loved ones and consequently of deeply personal suffering without a wider historical perspective.

The power of love is also prominent in the handful of generalisations employed in the 37 metanarratives. By contrast, fate is absent. Instead, cosmic order is conceived in terms of the instability of fortune (13.646) and Jupiter's supreme power (10.148). The latter is illustrated in its application to the area of love, not only creating a humorous effect with undertones of political subversiveness. For, as Wallace-Hadrill observes from a neo-historicist point of view rightly, though with some hyperbole, "the alert reader is (...) invited to take Jupiter as a mask for Augustus throughout" the *Metamorphoses*.[164] Feeney's observation that "it is a god-like prerogative to be beyond the limits of human behaviour, an insight which the *Metamorphoses* explicates more systematically than any other ancient poem"[165] is corroborated by Orpheus' generalisation and Lelex' proclamation in the introduction to his tale: *inmensa est finemque potentia caeli / non habet et, quiquid superi voluere, peractum est* (8.618-9 "The power of heaven is measureless, and knows no bounds; whatever the gods wish is at once achieved"). But are we justified to show absolute confidence in the views of two intradiegetic narrators in order to deduce Ovid's views in the *Metamorphoses* about divine and/or political power, especially when

---

[164] Wallace-Hadrill 1982: 28. Ovid's association of Jupiter and Augustus was foreshadowed in Segal 1969: 86 and Otis 1970: 133 and 145.
[165] Feeney 1991: 222.

(a) they themselves problematize their narrative authority (8.721-22, 10.302), and (b) the extradiegetic narrator/author defies Jupiter's power over his own work in the *sphragis* (15.871-2)?

VII Intradiegetic Narratees

VII.1 The Study of the Narratee

All narration, in whatever medium, of whatever complexity, whether it recounts real or fictional events, presupposes not only a narrator but also a narratee, i.e. someone directly addressed by the narrator. Being a integral part of the narrative situation, the narratee necessarily belongs to the same diegetic level as the narrator addressing him/her. In other words, an intradiegetic narrator (like the ones we studied in the previous chapter) does not address the actual reader of the *Metamorphoses* or even his extradiegetic substitute, the extradiegetic narratee. This means that we as readers cannot simply identify with these mythical narratees: our existence (like that of the extradiegetic narratee) is ignored by the intradiegetic narrators. We cannot interrupt Jupiter nor can we write to Byblis.

In the original *Discours du récit* Genette dedicated to the narratee a mere three pages towards the end of the chapter on voice.[1] In the *Nouveau Discours* he essentially adopts with pleasure Gerald Prince's detailed study which appeared soon after the publication of the original model.[2] A reconsideration of Prince's typology of the narratee was published by Mary Ann Piwowarczyk in 1976.[3] She expanded Prince's number of narratee signs and organised them in four basic categories: **identity**, **spatial and temporal location**, **status**, and **role**. Still, most narratological handbooks dismiss the narratee in a couple of pages.

With regard to the *Metamorphoses*, Michael von Albrecht pioneered the study of the extradiegetic addressee first with his dissertation and later with two papers, published both in German and French, on similes and other signs of the reader in the poem respectively.[4] Gianpiero Rosati examined the embedded narratives in Book 5 as a mirror for the poet's interaction with the reader,[5] while much of interest about the intradiegetic narratees can be found in the path-breaking papers

---

[1] Genette 1972: 265-67.
[2] Genette 1983: 90-93; Prince 1973 was integrated in Prince 1982: 16ff.
[3] This is missing from the bibliography in Genette 1983.
[4] Albrecht 1964, 1981a, and 1981b.
[5] Rosati 1981 [a paper I have been unable to see].

published by Betty Rose Nagle throughout the eighties.[6] The following discussion of intradiegetic narratees in the *Met.*, their perceptibility, their characteristics, and their function will be based on Prince's typology, like Wheeler's portrait of the extradiegetic narratee (1999: ch.4), and is the first systematic analysis of this constituent part of the narrative situation in the poem.

VII.2 Signals of the Narratee

The portrait of a narratee emerges above all from the narrative addressed to him/her. The intradiegetic narratee is part of the diegesis, i.e. the world of the narrative. This means that the first-level narrative may also contain some indications about his/her personality. For example, Argus is introduced as a hundred-eyed monster (1.625-27); this is precisely the characteristic Mercury as a narrator will try to overcome through the tale of Pan and Syrinx **[2]**. The Raven **[3]** is presented at greater length (2.534-41), so that we know the outcome of the Crow's effort to dissuade Phoebus' bird (2.544-45 *ales* / ... *Phoebeius*) from delivering the news about Coronis' adultery: the Raven is a *non exorabilis index* (2.546 "a pitiless informer") and has no time for false predictions (2.597 *vanum ... omen*). Pentheus **[4]** appears in the diegesis as a *contemptor superum* (3.514 "scoffer at gods") who laughs at the prophet Tiresias. So when the time comes to listen to Acoetes' story celebrating Bacchus' divinity, we are sure that he will be a resistant narratee, like the Raven earlier and Pirithous later in the poem. The Minyeides **[5]** are also presented as non-believers in Bacchus' *numen*. It is not surprising then that after the second sister's story there should be some discussion about the power of the gods, apparently as a reaction to the story they have just heard.

Minerva **[9]** makes her first appearance in the poem as one of the characters in the metadiegetic narrative of her ex-protegé, the Crow. Next, another group of story-tellers, the Minyeid sisters, have preferred to serve the virgin goddess by the hearth rather than celebrate the rites of Bacchus high on the mountains. Immediately before her visit to Helicon we followed the adventures of Perseus, another of Minerva's protegés and intradiegetic narrators of the poem. Her reaction recalls

---

[6] Nagle 1983, 1988a, 1988b, 1988c, 1989 [I have been unable to see the last one].

that of the divine audience of Jupiter's story about Lycaon in the Council of Gods of Book 1: "Some of the gods shouted their approval of Jupiter's words, and sought to increase his indignation" (1.244-45 *Dicta Iovis pars voce probant stimulosque frementi adiciunt*). Here again there is no reference to her pleasure or emotions; instead we learn that "she expressed her approval of the Muse's song and of their righteous indignation" (6.2 *carminaque Aonidum iustamque probaverat iram*).

The characters of a mythological poem like the *Met.* belong to the semiotic system of myth and literature. They have certain traditional traits, even though it is debatable to what extent this information is assumed or even required for a sufficient understanding of their role in the *Met.* Sometimes, however, the way in which an intradiegetic narratee is presented alludes to his position in myth. The reference to Pirithous **[17]** as *Ixione natus* is an example that will be analysed in detail in section 3 of this chapter. On the same occasion, Theseus **[18]** is said to have been "particularly moved" (8.725) by Lelex' story of Baucis and Philemon. The point of this remark will be lost for the reader who does not sense the literary allusion to the description of his reception by Hecale in Callimachus' epyllion named after his host.[7] Finally, Tlepolemus **[26]** is an Iliadic hero, who seems to have been resurrected by Ovid, first in *Ep.*1.19-20 and then in the *Met.* His intervention at the end of Nestor's account of the battle against the Centaurs could be illuminated by his behaviour in *Iliad* 5, where he is boasting about his lineage (638-42).

The intradiegetic signals capable of portraying the narratee are quite varied and one can easily distinguish several types that are worth discussing. First, they include all the passages in which the narrator (both extra- and intra-diegetic) refers directly to the narratee. Second, there are passages that describe the narratee implicitly: first person plural statements, questions, negations, comparisons, extratextual references. All these have been assembled and classified in **Table 1**.

---

[7] The allusion was noticed by Kenney 1986: xxviii.

Table 1: Implicit Signs of the Narratee

No.	Line(s)	Passage	Type
1	1.209	*(curam hanc dimittite)*	second-person address
1	1.214-15	*longa mora est, quantum noxae sit ubique repertum, / enumerare: minor fuit ipsa infamia vero*	metanarrative comment
3	2.564-65	*mea poena volucres / admonuisse potest, ne voce pericula quaerant*	indirect address (the narratee is a bird)
3	2.567	*–ipsa licet hoc a Pallade quaeras*	second-person address
3	2.571	*(ne me contemne)*	second-person address
3	2.589-90	*quid tamen hoc prodest, si diro facta volucris / crimine Nyctimene nostro successit honori?*	questions
4	3.661	*haud aliter, quam si siccum navale teneret*	comparison
4	3.682	*qualia dimidiae sinuantur cornua lunae*	comparison
4	3.685	*inque chori ludunt speciem*	comparison
5	4.122-24	*non aliter, quam cum vitiate fistula plumbo / scinditur et tenui stridente foramina longas / eiaculatur aquas atque ictibus aëra rumpit*	comparison
5	4.135	*aequoris instar*	comparison
6	4.178-9	*non illud opus tenuissima vincant / stamina, non summo quae pendet aranea tigno*	negation/comparison
7	4.331-33	*hic color aprica pendentibus arbore pomis / aut ebori tincto est aut sub candour rubenti,/ cum frustra resonant aera auxiliaria, lunae.*	comparisons
7	4.348-49	*non aliter, quam cum puro nitidissimus orbe / opposita speculi referitur imagine Phoebus*	comparison
7	4.354-55	*ut eburnea siquis / signa tegat claro vel candida lilia vitro*	comparison
7	4.362-67	*ut serpens, quam regia sustinet ales / sublimemque rapit (pendens caput illa pedesque / adligat et cauda spatiantes inplicat alas),/ utve solent hederae longos intexere truncos, utque sub aequoribus deprensum polypus hostem / continent ex omni dimissis parte flagellis*	comparison
7	4.375-76	*velut siquis conducat cortice, ramos / crescendo iungi pariterque adolescere cernit*	comparison

INTRADIEGETIC NARRATEES 229

8	4.793-94	*quoniam scitaris digna relatu,/ accipe quaesiti causam*	second-person address
9b	5.533-34	*—sed forsitan otia non sint,/ nec nostris praebere vacet tibi cantibus aures?*	question
11	5.429	*videres*	second-person
11	5.570-71	*ut sol, qui tectus aquosis / nubibus ante fuit, victis e nubibus exit*	comparison
12	5.605-6	*ut fugere accipitrem penna trepidante columbae,/ ut solet accipiter trepidas urgere columbas*	comparison
12	5.626	*quid mihi tunc animi miserae fuit?*	second-person address
12	5.626-29	*anne quod agnae est,/ siqua lupos audit circum stabula alta frementes,/ aut lepori, qui vepre lateens hostilia cernit / ora canum nullosque audit dare corpore motus?*	comparison & question
12	5.635	*citius, quam nunc tibi facta renarro*	second-person address & metanarrative comment
14	6.360	*quem non blanda deae potuissent verba movere?*	Question
15	7.520	*neu longe ambage morer vos*	metanarrative comment
15	7.521	*memori quos mente requiris*	second-person address
15	7.587	*templa vides contra gradibus sublimia longis*	second-person address
15	7.588-9	*quis non altaribus illis / inrita tura dedit?*	rhetorical question
16	7.694-95	*si forte magis pervenit ad aures / Orithyia tuas*	second-person address
16	7.732-33	*tu conlige, qualis in illa,/ Phoce decor fuerit*	second-person address
16	7.776-78	*non ocior illo / hasta nec exutae contorto verbere glandes / nec Gortyniaco calamus levis exit ab arcu.*	comparisons
17	8.579	*quoque minus spretae factum mirere Dianae*	second-person address
17	8.590	*ut tamen ipse vides*	second-person address
18	8.620	*quoque minus dubites*	second-person address
17	8.762-64	*haud aliter fluxit discusso cortice sanguis,/ quam solet, ante aras ingens ubi victima Taurus / concidit, abrupta cruor e cervice profundi.*	comparison
17	8.837-39	*utque rapax ignis non umquam alimenta recusant / innumerusque faces cremate et, quo copia maior / est*	comparison

		data, plura petit turbaque voracior ipsa est	
17	9.4	*triste petis munus*	second-person address
17	9.8-9	*nomine siqua suo tandem pervenit ad aures / Deianira tuas*	second-person address
17	9.17	*(nondum erat ille deus)*	negation
17	9.38	*aut captare putes*	second person
17	9.40-41	*haud secus ac moles, quam magno murmure fluctus / oppugnant*	comparison
17	9.46-49	*non aliter vidi fortes concurrere tauros,/ cum pretium pugnae toto nitidissima saltu / experitur coniunx: spectant armenta paventque / nescia, quem maneat tanti victoria tauri.*	comparison
17	9.78	*ceu guttura forcipe pressus*	comparison
20	9.327-8	*quid, si tibi mira sororis / fata meae referam?*	second person address
21	10.190-93	*ut, siquis violas riguoque papaver in horto / liliaque infringat fulvis horrentia linguis,/ marcida demittant subito caput illa gravatum / nec se sustineant spectentque cacumine terram*	comparison
21	10.220	*at si forte roges ...*	second person
21	10.284-85	*ut Hymettia sole / cera*	comparison
21	10.372-74	*utque secure / saucia trabs ingens, ubi plaga novissima restat,/ quo cadat, in dubio est omnique a parte timetur*	comparison
21	10.515-16	*qualia namque / corpora nudorum tabula pinguntur Amorum*	comparison
22	10.560	*forsitan audieris*	second person
22	10.562	*nec dicere posses*	second person
22	10.579	*quale meum, vel quale tuum, si femina fias*	second-person address & comparison
22	10.588	*Scythica non setius ire sagitta*	comparison
22	10.595-96	*haud aliter, quam cum super atria velum candida purpureum simulatas inficit umbras*	comparison
22	10.654	*posse putes*	second person
22	10.679	*neve meus sermo cursu sit tardior ipso*	metanarrative comment
22	10.681-82	*Dignane, cui grates ageret, cui turis honorem / ferret, Adoni, fui?*	question
21	10.734	*ut fulvo perlucida caelo / surgere bulla solet*	comparison
23	11.291-92	*forsitan ... putetis*	second-person address

INTRADIEGETIC NARRATEES 231

23	11.318-20	*quid peperisse duos et dis placuisse duobus / et forti genitore et progenitore Tonanti / esse satam prodest?*	question
23	11.330	*haud aliter quam murmura ponti*	comparison
23	11.334-36	*similisque iuvenco / spicula crabronum pressa cervice gerenti,/ qua via nulla ruit*	comparison
25	11.753	*adspicis*	second-person
26	12.191	*(tibi enim popularis, Achille)*	second-person address
26	12.193-95	*temptasset Peleus thalamos quoque forsitan illos,/ sed iam aut contigerant illi conubia matris,/ aut fuerant promissa, tuae.*	second person (reference to narratee's parents)
26	12.274	*veluti seges arida*	comparison
26	12.363	*armiger ille tui fuerat genitoris, Achille*	second person (reference to narratee's father)
26	12.440	*(scit tuus hoc genitor)*	second person (reference to narratee's father)
26	12.444	*signa vides*	second person
26	12.455	*nec tu credideris*	second person
26	12.461	*vulnera non memini*	negation
26	12.520-21	*veluti, quam cernimus, ecce,/ ardua si terrae quatiatur motibus Ide.*	comparison
26	12.548	*—quis enim laudaverit hostem?*	question
27	13.644-47	*non falleris, heros / maxime; vidisti natorum quinque parentem,/ quem nunc (...)/ paene vides orbum*	second person
27	13.647-49	*quod enim mihi filius absens / auxilium, quem dicta suo de nomine tellus / Andros habet, pro patre locumque et regna tenentem?*	question
27	13.656-7	*ne non ex aliqua parte vestram sensisse procellam / nos quoque parte putes*	second person
28	13.756	*si quaesieris*	second person
30	13.935	*sed quid mihi fingere prodest?*	rhetorical question
29	13.956-57	*hac tenus acta tibi possum memoranda referre, / hactenus et memini; nec mens mea cetera sensit.*	metannarative comment & second person
30	14.130-31	*nec dea sum (...) nec sacri turis honore / humanum dignare caput*	negation
30	14.131	*neu nescius erres*	second person
32	14.244	*mihi crede*	second person

32	14.246-47	*(neque enim finito Marte vocandus / hostis es, Aenea)*	second person & negation
33	14.322	*quam cernis*	second person
34	14.508	*si, volucrum quae sit dubiarum forma, requiris*	second person
35	14.759	*neve ea ficta putes*	second person
37	15.497	*fando aliquem Hippolytum vestras si contigit aures*	second person
37	15.499	*mirabere*	second person
37	15.527-9	*ossa gravem dare fracta sonum fessamque videres / exhalari animam nullasque in corpore partes, / noscere quas posses*	second person
37	15.530-31	*num potes aut audes cladi conponere nostrae, / nympha, tuam?*	second-person question

Complicity between narrator and audience may be promoted through **rhetorical questions** that acknowledge the audience's presence while at the same time imply that a certain response to the story is desired. Wheeler has counted eight audience-oriented rhetorical questions on the diegetic level of narration.[8] He also reports two basic strands in the interpretation of this phenomenon. On the one hand, critics like Galinsky and Solodow consider it (with reference to 1.400-401 *quis hoc credat, nisi sit pro teste vetustas?*) as a manifestation of Ovid's self-irony, as a means of eliciting the extradiegetic narratee's / reader's scepticism about the veracity of the myth.[9] On the other hand, von Albrecht,[10] suggests that through these questions (like through negative statements) the poet anticipates the disbelief of a critical audience, sharing with it a knowing smile and aesthetic detachment. Detaching himself from either interpretation, Wheeler tentatively argues for a third way of interpretation, which is bound, however, to the particular example from Book 1: Ovid's rhetorical question to the audience defines the appropriate frame of mind for the imaginative reception of the metamorphosis, i.e. the co-presence of fictional belief and disbelief.[11]

---

[8] Wheeler 1999: 105.
[9] Galinsky 1975: 178 and Solodow 1988: 71.
[10] Albrecht 1964: 213 cf. 1981b: 209-210
[11] Wheeler 1999: 106. Feeney 1991: 229-32 argues that both attitudes of belief and disbelief are inscribed in the poem as alternative options the reader can opt for.

With the exception of Glaucus' "but what good would it do me to invent this?" (13.935), the eight rhetorical questions in metanarrative do not concern the narrative's veracity or the narrator's authority. While self-irony is a strong possibility in the case of the extradiegetic narrator, it is clear that Glaucus himself cannot but intend his question to be answered negatively: Scylla should not doubt that Glaucus' story about the power of the herb he found on the beach. Glaucus' rhetorical question has a formal similarity with those used by two other intradiegetic narrators. The Crow (2.589-93) and Ceyx (11.318-20) also consider factors that could have been advantageous only to dismiss them. Finally, the Muse's question to Minerva is not strictly rhetorical, since Minerva takes the trouble to answer it. Essentially, however, it is a polite means of ensuring her narratee's attention, since she would like to repeat Calliope's song verbatim (unlike the opponents' entry which was presented mostly in summary). The Muse knows Minerva is a person of action (*O, nisi te virtus opera ad maiora tulisset* 5.269) and acts appropriately, making sure that her narrative will not be interrupted.[12]

Negation is another technique the poet uses to communicate with the audience. Irene de Jong (1987: 61-68) has examined its use in the *Iliad* as an aspect of the "interaction between primary narrator-focalizer and primary narratee-focalizee," i.e. on the diegetic level. She concluded that such negative statements are meant to contradict the narratee's expectations and/or create expectations (suspense); sometimes they contradict expectations of the characters in the story.[13] While admitting its allegiance to de Jong's work, Wheeler's discussion again revolves around a limited number of examples (1.89-101, 450-51 and 3.141-42), without taking advantage of de Jong's refined distinction between **negations with retrospective scope** and **negations with prospective scope**.[14] In metanarrative it is particularly rare. Nestor admits not

---

[12] Cahoon 1996: 50 considers the Muse's question an expression of "toadying deference towards those more powerful than themselves" in an effort to position her sisters and herself more securely. Surely, the Muses in general are rather toadying creatures, since their *raison d' être* is above all to praise the gods with their stories about them. I am not so sure as Cahoon, however, that they have a significantly lower position in divine hierarchy than Minerva (also a daughter of Zeus).
[13] De Jong 1987: 68.
[14] Wheeler 1999: 106 with n.28.

remembering the particular blows suffered by Caeneus' victims (12.461), and, anxious to prevent Aeneas from committing sacrilege, the Sibyl denies deserving divine honours (14.130-31). Both intradiegetic narrators' statements contradict the respective narratees' expectations of a detailed narrative and assumption that the Sibyl is a goddess. In other words, they are negations with retrospective scope. In the latter case, however, it also looks forward, to the Sibyl's narrative about her dealings with Apollo, which follows immediately. A third negation occurs in 4.178-9, but this is essentially a comparison, not a narrative possibility denied.

The **parenthesis** (*interiectio*) is a characteristic of Ovidian style that leaps to the modern reader's eye thanks to the use of brackets.[15] It has received exhaustive treatment by Michael von Albrecht (1964), who saw it as a comment addressed to the reader with a knowing wink.[16] Based on his own statistical data, Wheeler observed that "Ovid's characters use parenthesis more frequently than he himself does."[17] **Table 1** includes only four parentheses that also involve an address, a direct reference to the narratee or a question. Jupiter's reassuring statement (1.209) can be read as a disguised attempt at *captatio benevolentiae*: essentially he thanks his audience for their concern. The Crow's request to be respected as befits her former status as princess and sought-after bride (2.571) is part of her rhetoric of authority like the other two parentheses employed by the same narrator: *ipsa licet hoc a Pallade quaeras* (2.567), and *(nota loquor)* (2.570). Nestor's parenthesis referring to Achilles' (i.e. his main narratee's) father (12.191) is also part of an authenticating strategy, while his first aside to Achilles excites the interest of the "best of the Achaeans" and at the same time encourages the other members of the audience to seek further links between the hero of Nestor's story and the privileged narratee. By curious coincidence the last two examples of

---

[15] This is not identified as a sign of the narratee by Prince and rightly so, because it is not a category of the same order as the rest. It has been included here because (a) it was discussed by Wheeler with regard to the extradiegetic narratee and (b) because it is such an important feature of Ovidian narrative technique. Its ubiquitous use is also a familiar aspect of Jamesian narratorial organisation; see Aczel 1998: 483.
[16] Albrecht 1964: 209-15 and Solodow 1988: 54-55.
[17] Wheeler 1999: 102. His statistics include all character speech in direct discourse, not only metadiegetic narrative, though.

parentheses in **Table 1** express the narrators' thoughts on enemies. Nestor (12.548) considers it unthinkable that one could praise one's enemy, while Macareus (14.246-47) expresses a different view, namely that once hostilities are over enemies can be praised: *o iustissime Troum, / nate dea* (14.245-46).

Table 2: Parenthesis in Metanarrative

No.	Lines	Passage
1	1.209	*curam hanc dimittite*
3	2.567	*ipsa licet hoc a Pallade quaeras:/ quamvis irata est, non hoc irata negabit*
3	2.570	*nota loquor*
3	2.571	*ne me contemne*
4	3.600-1	*Aurora rubescere primo / coeperat*
4	3.630	*Bacchus enim fuerat*
4	*3.658-9	*nec enim praesentior illo est deus* (in non-narrative part)
4	3.687	*tot enim ratis illa ferebat*
5	4.68	*quid non sentit amor?*
6	4.178-9	*non illud opus tenuissima vincant / stamina, non summo quae pendet aranea tigno*
6	4.234-5	*neque enim moderatus in illa / Solis amor fuerat*
7	4.330	*nescit enim, quid amor*
7	4.363-4	*pendens caput illa pedesque / adligat et cauda spatiantes implicat alas*
9	5.273	*vetitum est adeo sceleri nihil*
9	5.280	*cognorat enim*
9	5.282	*imber erat*
12	5.585	*memini*
15	7.588	*Iuppiter illa tenet*
15	*7.660	*eurus enim attulerat* (voice of extradiegetic narrator)
16	7.690	*quis possit credere?*
16	7.722	*videor sensisse*
16	7.730-1	*sed nulla tamen formosior illa / esse potest tristi*
16	7.790	*mirum*
16	7.813	*recordor enim*

16	7.816	*sic me mea fata trahebant*
16	7.846	*me miserum!*
18	8.721	*neque erat, cur fallere vellent*
17	8.785-6	*neque enim Cereremque Famemque / fata coire sinunt*
17	8.798	*Caucason appellant*
17	8.809-10	*neque enim est accedere iuxta / ausa*
17	8.818	*noctis enim tempus*
17	*8.860	*nam stantem in litore vidi* (in directly reported speech)
17	9.17	*nondum erat ille deus*
17	9.53	*certum est mihi vera fateri*
20	9.330	*me pater ex alia genuit*
20	9.343	*namque aderam*
20	9.356-7	*namque hoc avus Eurytus illi / addiderat nomen*
21	10.148	*cedunt Iovis omnia regno*
21	10.214	*is enim fuit auctor honoris*
21	10.424	*sensit enim*
21	10.557	*et requievit*
22	10.562	*superabat enim*
22	10.573	*tanta potentia formae est*
23	11.293	*tanta est animi constantia*
23	11.316	*namque est enixa gemellos*
23	11.328	*o pietas!*
26	12.191	*tibi enim popularis, Achille!*
26	12.197	*ita fama ferebat*
26	12.200	*eadem hoc quoque fama ferebat*
26	12.232-3	*neque enim defendere verbis / talia facta potest*
26	12.305	*accepto tum vulnere tardius ibat*
26	12.372	*id quoque vix sequitur*
26	12.383	*nam vires animus dabat*
26	12.389	*stabat enim propior*
26	12.440	*scit tuus hoc genitor*
26	12.548	*quis enim laudaverit hostem?*
27	13.646	*tanta homines rerum inconstantia versat*
28	*13.843-4	*nam vos narrare soletis / nescio quem regnare Iovem*
28	*13.866	*sic se tibi misceat*
28	13.870	*nam cuncta videbam*

32	14.244-45	*procul hinc, mihi crede, videnda / insula, visa mihi!*
32	14.246-7	*neque enim finito Marte vocandus / hostis es, Aenea*
32	14.279	*et pudet et referam*
32	14.285	*tantum medicamina possunt*
33	14.406	*dictu mirabile*
33	14.421	*facit haec tamen omnia*
34	14.478	*velle puta*
35	14.695-6	*etenim mihi multa vetustas / scire dedit*
35	14.730-1	*nihil ultra lingua precari / sustinet*
35	14.742	*nam pater occiderat*
37	15.503	*indiciine metu magis offensane repulsae?*

In **Table 2** appear all 72 parentheses occurring in metanarrative, from which one case (7.660) at least should be excluded from consideration for the reason that it cannot be attributed to the voice of the intradiegetic narrator, but could only be uttered by Ovid, the extradiegetic narrator. Perhaps its location in the last line of Aeacus' narrative could explain this anomaly, although the only comparable case is a parenthesis near the beginning of metanarrative **[25]** (11.753 *ostendens spatiosum in guttura mergum*). I have only included it in the table because, unlike the latter case, it is not immediately perceptible that it is anomalous (Anderson, for example, is silent about it in his comment on the line). For, unlike the example from Book 11 it does not relate to the narrator's directing function but rather to the testimonial function, which is elsewhere frequently performed by intradiegetic narrators' parentheses: 2.567, 3.687, 5.585, 7.722, 7.813, 8.721, 9.53, 10.424, 12.197, 12.200, 12.440, 13.870. By contrast, there is only one other parenthesis attributable to an intradiegetic narrator's voice that refers to the story's setting, 3.600-1; but in this case the bracketed comment essentially rephrases the content of the first hemistich (*nox ubi consumpta est*) and does not refer to the narrator's actions while performing, surely only describable by someone outside the immediate narrative situation.

Most parentheses in the poem are manifestations of the narrator's ideological function. In the previous chapter we explored this from the narrator's point of view. But these asides are also revelatory of the narratee's projected character. As the narrator tries to explain the world of his characters and justify their thoughts and actions, (s)he makes certain assumptions about what the narratee knows and understands. For example a common feature of the explanatory parentheses used by the Minyeides in their narratives is the reference to love. This probably means that they assume everyone in their company accepts love as a powerful motive for action (4.234-5), which increases perceptiveness (4.68), while ignorance of it can create problems (4.330). Cephalus and the other Athenians visiting the court of Aeacus in Aegina are assumed not to know that the temple nearby is dedicated to Jupiter (7.588). Theseus and the other heroes at Achelous' dinner-party are supposed not to know that the Scythian mountain where Hunger has its abode is called Caucasos (8.798). Even exclamations like 7.790, 7.846, 11.328 are revelatory about the sensibilities of the narratees, who can apparently sympathise with the narrator's *pietas*, self-pity or awe.

But perhaps the most revelatory signals and at times the most difficult to grasp and describe in a satisfactory way are those called by Prince **over-justifications**. Any narrator more or less explains the world inhabited by his characters, motivates their acts, and justifies their thoughts (see previous paragraph). When these explanations and motivations are situated at the level of meta-language, meta-commentary, or meta-narration, they are over-justifications. Over-justifications always provide us with interesting details about the narratee's personality, even though they often do so in an indirect way; in overcoming the narratee's defences, in prevailing over his prejudices, in allaying his apprehensions, they reveal them. There are eight such over-justifications in the metanarratives under consideration. Jupiter **[1]**, Arethusa **[12]**, Aeacus **[15]**, Venus **[22]**, Diomedes **[34]**, and Vertumnus **[35]** are ascribed one each, while Glaucus **[29]** is credited with two (see **Table 1**). Almost all of them concern either the speed of narrated versus narrative time (i.e. the relationship between story and text) or the truth of the events reported (i.e. the story itself). Only Glaucus' second comment refers to memory as a source of narrative material. On the basis of these comments, one may assume that intradiegetic narratees in the *Met.* do not normally appreciate a long narrative –although Minerva, the birds, beasts and plants lulled by Orpheus, and the Achaeans who listen to Nestor's narrative evidently enjoy a song/narrative of considerable length. They are also suspicious of people who are trying to present false stories as true.

VII.3 Classification of Narratees

The intradiegetic narratee may play no other role in the narrative than that of narratee (e.g. the narratee of Conrad's *Heart of Darkness*). But (s)he might also play **other roles in diegesis**. It is not rare, for example, for him/her to be at the same time a narrator.

Table 3: Diegetic Roles of Narratees

No.	Narratee	Other Diegetic Role
1	Olympian Gods	Yes (including that of narrator)
2	Argus	Yes
3	Raven	Yes
4	Pentheus	Yes
5	Minyads and servants	Yes (including that of narrator)
6	Minyads and servants	Yes (including that of narrator)
7	Minyads and servants	Yes (including that of narrator)
8	Court of Cepheus in Ethiopia	Yes (including that of narrator —narrative summarized)
9	Minerva	Yes
10	Nymphs, Muses	Yes (including that of narrator for the Muses)
11	Nymphs, Pierides, other Muses	Yes (including that of narrator for the Pierides)
12	Ceres	Yes
13	Lydians	No
14	Anonymous Narrator of No. 13	Yes (including that of narrator)
15	Cephalus, sons of Pallas, sons of Aeacus	Yes (including that of narrator for Cephalus)
16	Phocus, sons of Pallas	Yes
17	Theseus, Pirithous, Lelex	Yes (including that of narrator for Pirithous and Lelex)

18	Pirithous, Achelous, Theseus	Yes (including that of narrator for Achelous)
19	Iole	Yes (including that of narrator)
20	Alcmene	Yes (including that of narrator)
21	Trees, birds, beasts	Yes
22	Adonis	Yes
23	Peleus and companions	Yes
24	Peleus and companions and Ceyx	Yes (including that of narrator for Ceyx)
25	An old man	No
26	Achilles and Achaeans	No
27	Anchises and Trojans	No
28	Scylla	Yes
29	Scylla	Yes
30	Aeneas	Yes
31	Macareus and Trojans	Yes (including that of narrator for Macareus)
32	Achaemenides and Trojans	Yes (including that of narrator for Achaemenides)
33	Macareus	Yes (including that of narrator)
34	Venulus	Yes
35	Pomona	Yes
36	Numa	Yes
37	Egeria	Yes

Although the *Met.* is a poem which moves through the ages and the mythic cycles, the narratees are rarely introduced merely in order to listen to a story and then disappear. They are normally characters involved in the events narrated on the diegetic level. In fact, almost half of them (17 out of 37, or 46%) also tell stories in the poem. For example, Scylla's role in the narrative situation is continually changing. Her role shifts from traditional narrative figure, to narrator (her story opens as she is telling Galatea and the other sea-nymphs about her rejected suitors), to narratee (she is dragged into becoming the audience for Galatea's triangle), to a character in another triangle.[18] With Glaucus as much as with Galatea, Scylla's narrative role is that of narratee. In both cases she is to some degree reduced to being an audience, when her curiosity is aroused.[19]

Another criterion of classification is **the degree to which the narratee-character is affected** and influenced by the narrative addressed to him/her. This is not unrelated to the third and last criterion proposed by Prince, i.e. whether the narratee-character represents from the narration someone more or less essential, more or less irreplaceable as a narratee. In *Heart of Darkness*, an example used by Prince himself, it is not necessary for Marlowe to have his comrades on the *Nellie* as narratees; in turn, they are not transformed by the story related to them.

With the exception of the Olympians **[1]**, Argus **[2]**, Minerva **[9]**, and Alcmene **[20]**, intradiegetic narratees in the *Met.* are not affected or otherwise influenced by the narrative they hear. Denis Feeney has perceptively observed that the typically human behaviour of the gathering of gods is wittily highlighted by their reaction. In previous divine councils (a standard epic feature), dissent is just as possible as a reaction as agreement.[20] Ovid holds back two key words to show that now the only competition is in degrees of acquiescence (1.244-5). In Argus' case, the tale of Syrinx has the unusual of effect of putting him to sleep before it is scarcely under way. But the price the sentinel pays for not listening to the tale attentively is much dearer than missing the end; it is his own death. It is commonly assumed that Argus dozes because he loses interest in Mercury's narrative.[21]

Argus is not the only poor listener in the *Metamorphoses*. In the first three books of the *Metamorphoses*, the narratorial audience is introduced to two more internal audiences (the raven and Pentheus) that fail to listen to or believe in the tales that they hear.[22] Both pay dearly for their disbelief: the former loses the beauty of its white plumage, while the latter is dismembered by his own mother. Betty Rose Nagle suggested

---

[18] Nagle 1988: 81.
[19] Nagle 1988: 82.
[20] Feeney 1991:200.
[21] See most recently Wheeler 1999: 1.
[22] Wheeler 1999: 81.

that all cautionary tales in the poem fail perhaps because the narratee knows the end and the motive, and so there is no suspense about the 'point'.[23]

A tale can also inspire its audience into action. After hearing about the punishment of the Pierides by the Muses, Minerva decides it is time that she took measures against those that showed contempt for her: *numina nec sperni ne sine poena nostra sinamus* (6.4). She flies to earth and makes Arachne fall into the trap of challenging her into competition. The action may take the form of another narrative. Besides the anonymous narrator of the story of Marsyas (6.383), we have Achelous' tale about Mestra and his own duel with Hercules, which are presented in corroboration of Lelex' thesis that the gods have the power to transform, expressed in the form of his narrative about Baucis and Philemon. Iole's story about her half-sister Dryope is also a reaction to the story told by Alcmene about her maidservant. But this stretches Prince's criterion to the limits of its inclusiveness.

Audiences in the *Met.* are not always responsive. In the first pentad Ceres, in the second the narratees of Aesacus and Cephalus, in the third Adonis, the narratees of Ceyx, the anonymous old-man from Trachis, the Sibyl, Galatea, Diomedes, and Pomona (i.e. 27% of the narratees) do not seem to be affected by the stories they hear. They are not even touched (as the heroes in Achelous' cave are by the river-god's first story or after hearing Lelex' version of 'Baucis and Philemon': 8.611, 725). Some of them depart immediately after the narration is finished (Ceres, Nereides, Venulus), but only Scylla's departure while Glaucus is still talking can be construed as an oblique indication of her reaction to his speech. Nonetheless, Glaucus has already finished his narrative and is now trying to woo her. So, Scylla's departure is not the result of the narrative itself, but rather of the conclusion Glaucus is trying to draw from it.

More often than not, the way an intradiegetic narratee is affected is temporary and passive. Touched (see previous paragraph) or moved to tears (like Alcmene), their reaction resembles closely that of Orpheus' sub-human audience: *silvas animosque ferarum / Threicius vates et saxa*

---

[23] Nagle 1988c: 43.

sequentia ducit (11.1-2).[24] Credulously believing in the story they hear (see Anderson's note on 7.611), they are carried away for a while, until reality breaks in, shattering the narrative enchantment.[25] Once the Thracian women manage to make a noise so loud that Orpheus' song is no longer audible, the bard is unable to control nature and he falls victim to women who are apparently insensitive to the charm of his art –in no way can they be described as narratees of Orpheus' song.

A third aspect of the narratee which may help with his/her classification is **whether (s)he is indispensable as an audience**. To put it differently, could the narrator have told the story to somebody else or is this particular narratee the only possible audience for the particular story? The Olympians **[1]**, for instance, are the only audience Jupiter could have for his story about Lycaon's outrage. First, because it would be hard for a human to sympathize with Jupiter's divine perspective. Besides, Jupiter's motive for telling the tale is to authorize the annihilation of the human race, and only the consent of his neighbours in the *Palatia caeli* will do to that end. For the same reasons, *mutatis mutandis*, the Crow's tale **[3]** is only suitable for another bird, though not specifically the Raven. Likewise, the Muse's account of Pyreneus' attempt to rape all nine sisters **[9]**, does not call for Minerva as an audience, but any chaste female would be suitable. On the whole, the intradiegetic narratees of the poem could not be called indispensable *per se*; they represent, however, a choice among other possible members of groups that share a minimum of the values or characteristics of the narrator.

An intradiegetic audience could be **limited to an individual or extend to a whole group of people**. Many of the metanarratives in the *Met.* are told to large audiences: Jupiter addresses the divine assembly; Calliope sings her hymn to Ceres in the presence of an audience including nymphs (as judges of the competition), the nine Pierides (the other contestants) and her eight sisters (as support group); Orpheus' shocking erotic tales are sung to a large group of animals, birds, and

---

[24] Barchiesi 1989: 73 observes that, ironically, Orpheus' audience is comprised of the only *natae* and *parentes* that naturally practice incest.
[25] For *credulitas* in connection with *movere* see *Am.*3.3.24 and *Pont.*1.1.43-44.

trees; and Nestor's mock-epic is told in the presence of many Achaean heroes, even though he singles out Achilles as his main addressee.

A final criterion, among those proposed by Prince, that is relevant to the intradiegetic narratees in the *Met.* is **the extent to which they are familiar** with the respective narrators and their tales, including the characters taking part in the action. It is evident from the table below that although none of the stories is known to the addressee for certain, (s)he is at least assumed to be familiar with the relevant gods. This is evident from the lack of introductory description each time a god is mentioned.

Table 4: Narratees' Familiarity with Metadiegesis

No.	Narratee	Familiar with Characters
1	Olympian Gods	Yes with Jupiter but not Lycaon
2	Argus	Probably with Pan
3	Raven	Possibly according to the Narrator
4	Pentheus	No
5	Minyads and servants	No
6	Minyads and servants	Yes with gods
7	Minyads and servants	No
8	Court of Cepheus in Ethiopia	Yes with Neptune
9	Minerva	Yes with Muses
10	Nymphs, Muses	Yes with gods
11	Nymphs, Pierides, other Muses	Yes with gods
12	Ceres	Yes with Arethusa
13	Lydians	Perhaps some in the audience know the narrator
14	Anonymous Narrator of No.13	Yes with Latona
15	Cephalus, sons of Pallas, sons of Aeacus	Yes with Jupiter and Aeacus
16	Phocus, sons of Pallas	Yes with Cephalus
17	Theseus, Pirithous, Lelex	Yes with Achelous
18	Pirithous, Achelous, Theseus	Yes with gods and Hercules
19	Iole	Yes with Alcmene

20	Alcmene	No
21	Trees, birds, beasts	?
22	Adonis	Yes with Venus
23	Peleus and companions	No
24	Peleus and companions and Ceyx	Yes (with the shepherds)
25	An old man	No
26	Achilles and Acheans	Yes with some of the heroes
27	Anchises and Trojans	Yes, Anchises with Anius' daughters
28	Scylla	No?
29	Scylla	No
30	Aeneas	Yes with both
31	Macareus and Trojans	
32	Achaemenides and Trojans	
33	Macareus	Yes with Circe
34	Venulus	Yes
35	Pomona	No
36	Numa	Yes with Hercules
37	Egeria	No

Already in 1961 W. C. Booth observed that "in every reading experience there is an implied dialogue among author, narrator, the other characters, and the reader. Each of the four can range, in relation to each of the others, from identification to complete opposition, on any axis of value, moral, intellectual, aesthetic, and even physical."[26] In the previous paragraph we explored the difference on the cognitive axis. Obviously a narratee who has taken part in the events narrated (no example of this in the *Met.*) or is familiar with the characters cannot have the same attitude as someone who has never even heard of them. The narratee can also be distanced from the narrator morally, intellectually or physically.

On the whole, intradiegetic narratees in the *Met.* match the narrators. In other words, a divine narrator normally relates a story to a divinity (e.g. Jupiter **[1]** to the whole of the Divine Assembly, the Muses **[9]** to Minerva), a hero to another hero or a heroic gathering (e.g. Aeacus to

---

[26] Booth 1983: 155

Cephalus **[12]**, Nestor to the Greeks in Troy –to Achilles in particular **[18]**), and a female narrator normally addresses a female audience, like the daughters of Minyas **[5-7]** who tell stories to each other and their handmaids, the Muses who address Minerva **[9]** or the local nymphs of Parnassus and the Pierides **[11]**, and Alcmene **[19]** who exchanges stories with Iole **[20]** about their familial sufferings. This is not, however, a rule with universal application in the poem.

Women of semi-divine (the Sibyl **[30]** and Canens **[33]**) or divine status (Venus **[22]**) are represented as telling stories to individual men, Aeneas, Macareus, and Adonis respectively. Adonis is very close to Venus physically: he is a man (10.523 *iam iuvenis, iam vir*) of superlative beauty comparable to that of Amor (10.515-18) and Venus herself (10.579). Yet, it is precisely his manly character, his *virtus* (10.709) that creates a moral gap (10.709 *stat monitis contraria*) between him and the goddess, who tries to keep her paramour away from hunting ferocious beasts, by telling him a story that proves her bad relations with lions in particular.[27] Venus does not seem to be unaware of this gap between her narratee's male/human and her own female/divine point of view. Her concluding phrase *ne virtus tua sit damnosa duobus* (10.707) epitomizes her own anti-heroic attitude as a lover.[28] For this reason she engages Adonis in the narrative from the outset with her second-person verbs (10.560 and 562) and pursues this strategy throughout her narrative (10.579, 654). Near the end of the tale she makes a most empathetic appeal to her narratee, inviting him to adopt her divine perspective and condemn a character's behaviour (10.681-82). Yet, she fails; boys will be boys.

In the case of Aeneas the situation is not so clear. There is certainly a huge gap of knowledge that separates the narratee from the narrator. On the other hand, he is superior to the Sibyl in terms of *virtus* (14.113 cf. 581 *Aeneia virtus*), which, as the Sibyl herself admits, is a key that opens all doors, even those of the Underworld. It is impossible, however, even to speculate whether this difference in gender and values between the two poles of the narrative situation is significant, as the narratee's

---

[27] Recent scholarship (Gauly 1992: 449 n.34 and Nagle 1988b: 116-17) has criticized the moral imposed by Venus on her narrative as unsuitable. Coleman 1971: 469 had already suggested that "the real moral of the story is that the goddess who rewards piety can also punish lapses from it."

[28] Anderson on 10.705-707.

reaction to the Sibyl's tale of youthful foolishness and female vanity is not recorded by the exradiegetic narrator. Discussing the episode in the context of Ovid's rewriting of the canonical Vergilian *Aeneid*, Solodow observed that "the Sibyl's resigned prophesying of her own disintegration seems intended as the very opposite of Virgil's confident prediction that Aeneas' descendants will one day rule the world."[29] Unlike his guide who would not sacrifice her virginity for the sake of *lux aeterna* (14.132), Aeneas gained eternal life (14.581-608) and enjoyed the divine honours (14.608), which she refused (14.130), thanks to his *virtus* (14.581), which he put in the service of the *fata* (13.624).

Although it may be reasonably assumed that the tale of Picus impressed Macareus enough to remember it and report it to Achaemenides, he does not describe his reaction to the tale as an audience. A further obstacle to our assessment of the narratee's importance for the narrative situation is created by the fact that we hear Picus' tale from the lips of the original narratee as he relates it to an audience, which is closer to him than he was to the maidservant of exotic Circe.

The reverse case, i.e. a man telling a story to a woman, can also be problematic. Scylla **[29]** is a reluctant narratee: she only agrees to listen to Glaucus when she feels she is at a safe distance from the enamoured god (13.912) and ceases to do so at the moment Glaucus finishes the story of his apotheosis and starts making verbal advances to her. Belonging to the same gender or species, however, does not guarantee a sympathetic hearing. Pentheus and the Raven think they have wasted their time listening to the stories of Acoetes **[4]** and the Crow **[3]** respectively, while Tlepolemus **[26]** reacts with undue indignation to Nestor's narrative about the battle against the Centaurs,[30] and Pomona **[35]** remains unmoved by the old woman's tale.

---

[29] Solodow 1988: 150.
[30] Nagle 1988d: 30 referring to Glenn 1986: 166.

VII.4 FUNCTION OF THE NARRATEES
VII.4.1 Function of Mediation
If "the most obvious role of the narratee is that of relay between the author and the reader(s)," [31] it follows that the most important function of the intradiegetic narratee is to mediate between the extradiegetic narrator and his narratee(s), and hence ultimately also between the author and his reader(s). Indeed, compared with the extradiegetic, the intradiegetic narratee occupies a privileged position, as (s)he is granted the power to speak, whether to ask a question of the narrator or to express his/her opinion.[32] Indeed this is so obvious that, despite the relative lack of interest in intradiegetic narratees in Ovidian scholarship, this particular function of theirs has been the focus of much published work since the early 1990s.

The critics' attention, however, seems to have been focused on a couple of narratees from Book 1, especially Argus, probably because their early appearance guarantees their programmatic significance.[33] Pirithous' disbelief in Book 8 has also attracted scholarly attention: both Feeney and Wheeler have discussed it,[34] reaching somewhat divergent conclusions as to its significance for the reader of the *Met.* For as Wheeler reminds us, the intradiegetic narratee's reaction need not represent the ideal reader's response; "internal audiences often dramatize responses that the narratorial audience cannot appprove."[35] In such cases, we might say that "the narratorial audience [i.e. extradiegetic narratee] is cued to differentiate its own response from that of the internal audience."[36] Alternatively, one could follow Feeney in accepting all narratees' reactions as options presented to the reader, who is exclusively responsible for his choice and does not have to make the same choice each time (s)he reads the text: "Readers tend to be either

---

[31] Prince in Onega 1980: 20.
[32] Wheeler 1999: 80.
[33] See Konstan 1991.
[34] Feeney 1991: 230-32 and Wheeler 1999: 168-71.
[35] Wheeler 1999: 80.
[36] This view was already expressed by Barchiesi 1989: 56.

Lelex or Pirithous."[37] He even suggests that a double vision (in this particular case both Lelex and Pirithous) might be the ideal response.[38]

Table 5: Reactions of the Narratees

No.	Narratee	Reaction
1	Olympian Gods	(belief —>) approval
2	Argus	sleep
3	Raven	disbelief
4	Pentheus	disbelief
5	Minyads and servants	—
6	Minyads and servants	dissent (belief and disbelief)
7	Minyads and servants	—
8	Court of Cepheus in Ethiopia	—
9	Minerva	—
10	Nymphs, Muses	—
11	Nymphs, Pierides, other Muses	— (the Pierides have accused the Muses of lying before the contest began, though)
12	Ceres	—
13	Lydians	—
14	Anonymous Narrator of No.13	belief assumed (since the narrative is reported by the narratee on a later occasion)
15	Cephalus, sons of Pallas, sons of Aeacus	—
16	Phocus, sons of Pallas	—
17	Theseus, Pirithous, Lelex	dissent (belief and disbelief)
18	Pirithous, Achelous, Theseus	moved
19	Iole	—
20	Alcmene	moved
21	Trees, birds, beasts	enchanted

---

[37] Feeney 1991: 230.
[38] Feeney 1991: 231.

22	Adonis	"moral" of the story ignored
23	Peleus and companions	—
24	Peleus and companions and Ceyx	Peleus unmoved
25	An old man	—
26	Achilles and Acheans	indignation (Tlepolemus)
27	Anchises and Trojans	—
28	Scylla	—
29	Scylla	—
30	Aeneas	—
31	Macareus and Trojans	—
32	Achaemenides and Trojans	—
33	Macareus	—
34	Venulus	—
35	Pomona	unconvinced (*nequiquam* 14.765)
36	Numa	—
37	Egeria	—

It is evident from the above table (a) that the responses of the audience are not meticulously reported by the extradiegetic narrator (in 23 out of 37 metanarratives it is not recorded), and (b) that the reported responses can be typified as [+/- belief] or [+/- emotion] (only the narratees of metanarratives **[21]** and **[26]** have a response that does not fit either binary antithesis). On two occasions, **[6]** and **[17]**, the reactions of the audience are mixed. As Boillat has observed, the Minyeides' summarized discussion about the possibility of metamorphosis and the power of the gods does not follow naturally from the *factum mirabile* (4.271) narrated by Leuconoe.[39] Clytie's transformation, in particular, to which the extradiegetic narrator's phrase most naturally refers, was not effected through divine power according to Leuconoe's metanarrative. The second dissension (this time among men) is also caused by the narration of a *factum mirabile* (8.611), but follows more naturally from Perimele's transformation through Neptune's intervention. It is also

---

[39] Boillat 1976: 130.

reported at greater length with the dissident narratee having a name (Pirithous).[40]

We have already referred to the critical discussion of this latter case. Feeney, who mentions the former in a footnote, observes that Ovid dramatizes in Lelex and Pirithous the divided belief that is necessary for reading fiction.[41] But this already implies that myth is literary fiction. So his admission that he succumbs to the allure of disbelief comes as no surprise.[42] A shortcoming of his argument is the neglect of the mythical context of these expressions of disbelief. It is in this respect that Wheeler's argument makes progress. He astutely observes that "in a poem noted for its amorality, it is striking how often incredulous characters are singled out as morally dubious."[43] Pirithous is introduced as a *deorum spretor* (8.612-13) and *Ixione natus* (8.613), i.e. as the son of one of the eternally damned of Greco-Roman myth. The Minyeides are also presented as despising a particular god, Bacchus, whose power has already been affirmed by the extradiegetic narrator's account of Pentheus' punishment for denying Bacchus' divinity, and will be affirmed once more in his account of the Minyeides' metamorphosis for the same reason.

VII.4.2 Function of Characterisation
Through the narrator's addresses to the narratee a certain relationship is developed or rather projected on the latter by the former. This projected relationship naturally reflects on the narrator's character. When the narrator is intradiegetic this function is maximised, as he also is a "character" on the diegetic level.

It is obvious, for instance, from Jupiter's **[1]** words addressed to the divine assembly that he wants to present himself as a powerful god, who is capable of taking care of any problem of disobedience that might arise (1.209).[44] He is also prone to exaggeration, in order to be more

---

[40] A blasphemous intervention as a way of keeping the symposium going is also used in Macr. 1.24.2, while a similar discussion occurs in Apuleius' *Metamorphoses* 1.2.20, on which see Winkler 1985: 27-33; the parallel was noticed by Sandy 1970: 469-70 n.14.
[41] Feeney 1991: 230 n.155.
[42] Feeney 1991: 232.
[43] Wheeler 1999: 169.
[44] The passages are quoted above in **Table 1** above.

persuasive (1.214-15). The Crow **[2]** is clearly an egocentric character (2.564 *mea*, 2.571 *me*, 2.590 *nostro*), who presents her own situation as a typical manifestation of universal truths. Acoetes **[3]** does not address his audience directly. Perhaps this is justified by the context of a trial before the city's supreme authority. It may also be indicative of the indirect way Acoetes is using to convert Pentheus to Bacchus' worship. Two of the similes he employs (3.661 and 682), however, clearly reinforce his self-presentation as a sailor, who knows about astronomy: *Oleniae sidus pluviale Capellae / Taygetenque Hyadasque oculis Arctonque notavi* (3.594-5 "I marked well the rainy constellation of the Goat, Taygete and the Hyades, and the Bears"). The third is appropriate for a celebrant of Bacchus: given the context it is highly probable that the word *chorus* denotes a bacchic chorus (Anderson thinks of a 'comic chorus' in particular), rather than generally a "band" or even a "troupe of dancers."[45]

Comparisons are also the only means of communication between the daughters of Minyas **[5-7]**. Perhaps we could deduce something about their character from the mere fact that they try to enhance the realities of e.g. death (4.122-4) and sex (4.362-7) with elaborate imagery. They are trying to escape from the confines of their Boeotian house through arcane tales set in the Orient, and use comparisons with things they cannot see inside their house (animals, birds, flowers, sea) and also a kind of science-fiction simile of bursting water-pipes. Perseus' **[8]** comment projects an image of a discerning narrator. The Muse **[9]** also shows deference to her distinguished narratee, which may even seem hypocritical to some readers. Calliope's song **[11]** is an entry in a contest and perhaps she feels it would be against the rules, or even unnecessary for a certain winner, to establish contact with her narratees: only one simile and a second-person singular verb which is incongruent with her plural narratees. Arethusa **[12]**, on the other hand, is clearly trying to elicit her narratee's sympathy with several apostrophes to her and similes, which both emphasize her self-representation as victim.

We have already had the opportunity to note the anonymous Lycian's **[14]** religiosity, which is introduced by the second-level narrator **[13]** and

---

[45] On the origins of the image see R. Kannicht on Eur.*Hel.*1454. For the kind of dance implied by *lasciva* see *Copa* 1-3 and MART. 6.71.1-2.

reflected in his own apostrophe about Latona's sweet words (6.360). Aeacus **[15]**, Cephalus **[16]**, and Achelous **[17]** are all trying to create an atmosphere of familiarity with their narratees in similar contexts of hospitality. Cephalus addresses his privileged narratee, Phocus, by his name, and all of them are trying to relate their stories to knowledge the narratees possess (7.521) or are likely to possess (7.694-5, 9.8-9), as well as to objects that can be seen right there (7.587, 8.590). It is perhaps indicative of Achelous' *inmanitas* that four out of the five similes he uses refer either to raging natural elements (fire at 8.837-9, water at 9.40-1) or to a bull (8.762-4 and 9.46-9), an animal into which he himself was transformed during his fight with Hercules but also famous for its ferocity: *sic quoque devicto restabat tertia tauri / forma trucis: tauro mutatus membra rebello* (9.80-81 "So he overcame me in this guise too; but there remained my third shape, that of a fierce bull. I therefore transformed myself into a bull, and as such renewed the fight.")

Orpheus **[21]**, on the other hand, uses similes that draw their subject-matter from the world of his audience: a flower has its stem broken (10.190-3), and a huge tree wavers, waiting for the last blow of the axe (10.372-4). As both similes involve suffering, perhaps the narrator is trying to elicit his audience's sympathy by appealing to traumatic experiences they may have had. Venus **[22]**, the third-level narrator in Orpheus' song, uses apostrophes to her narratee and lover Adonis to introduce an erotic element: a comparison with pictures of naked Cupids, a complimentary reference to her lover's extraordinary beauty. Their intimacy is evident from the frequency of Venus' references to Adonis, even by name (10.682). Nestor **[26]** also calls Achilles twice by name, distinguishing him from the other Achaeans who are listening to his story, probably paying honour in this way to the hero of the day (Achilles has just killed Cygnus). The same honour is paid by Macareus **[32]** to Aeneas, whom he no longer considers an enemy. Ceyx **[23]**, on the other hand, addresses his audience of *Peleus comitesque* (11.290) in the plural (11.292).

Anius **[27]** is also a host who is trying to create an atmosphere of intimacy at the beginning of his narrative with frequent references to his narratee. Glaucus **[29]**, on the other hand, is desperately trying to persuade Scylla that the story of his transformation into a sea-god with a fish-tail is true. Naturally, because he thinks that she will be impressed and succumb to his desire. The same preoccupation with narrative authority is evident in Diomedes' story of his companions' transformation into swans **[34]**. Obviously he does not want his narratee, the Latin ambassador Venulus, to think that he is lying about his inability to help them fight the Trojan invaders. The Sibyl **[30]** is portrayed as someone who is humble enough to admit that she is not a goddess (14.130-1) and apparently considers knowledge as very important (14.131). Finally, Hippolytus' **[37]** addresses to his narratee, the widowed Egeria, betray a self-important character (cf. his proud disclosure that he is a minor *numen* at 15.545-6), who thinks it is likely that the Latin nymph Egeria has heard the story of a young Athenian prince, and indeed considers his story of death and resurrection more painful than Egeria's loss of her husband. Apparently, he is too self-centered to realise that resurrection "reverses the tragic view and makes tragedy impossible."[46]

VII.4.3 Other Functions

Prince also observes a few other functions a narratee may perform: (a) highlighting, elucidating or refuting a theme, which may or may not be related to the narrative instance; (b) furthering the narrative; and (c) clarifying the moral attitude of the narrator. We have already seen in section 3.2 above that a narratee often becomes a narrator. Another way in which the narratee contributes to propelling forward the narrative is by being curious to listen to stories. We have seen in chapter 4 section VIII (p.131) that this is a common motivation for Ovidian metanarrative. We have also had the opportunity to discuss various themes reflected in the intradiegetic narrators' addresses to their narratees, like fictionality (p.235), authority (p.189-90), and the failure of propaganda that uses mythical ideology (p.202, 206-7).

VII.5. Conclusions

This chapter attempted to analyse the narratees of the 37 metanarratives in the *Met.* according to the model developed by Gerald Prince. First, we examined the evidence, explicit and implicit, offered by the narrators,

---

[46] Sewell 1959: 50 on Christianity.

both extradiegetic and intradiegetic, which could help the reader create a portrait of the narratees. As the characters of the poem are mythical and historical figures they also carry a certain semiotic load, which can be supplied from the reader's own knowledge; but a thorough research of this issue would require a separate treatment.[47] All major types of signals identified by Prince are used in one or another of the metanarratives: rhetorical questions, negation, and comparison are all there, however rare they may be (e.g. negation). Completely absent are first-person plural statements, which are used only by the extradiegetic narrator.[48] A characteristic of Ovidian style which also permeates the metanarratives is the use of parenthesis. These asides are not only manifestations of the narrator's interpretative function but also indications of the narratee's cognitive, emotive, etc. qualities. In this respect the most revelatory of the parentheses are those called by Prince 'over-justification'. We found 8 such comments on the act of narrating. Almost all of them concern either the relative speed (or duration) of the narrative or the truth of the events reported. Projected on to the narratees, these statements imply that the poem's characters do not like wasting their time listening to long narratives of labyrinthine structure, or narratives that are not about true stories.

Second, the narratees were classified according to the various criteria suggested by Prince. Although the *Met.* is a poem which moves through the ages and the mythic cycles, the narratees are rarely introduced merely in order to listen to a story and then disappear. They are normally characters involved in the events narrated on the diegetic level. In fact, almost half of them (17 out of 37, or 46%) also tell stories in the poem. Only a few among the intradiegetic narratees are affected or influenced by the narrative they hear. Argus is not the only poor listener in the *Met.*, but he is paradigmatic because he pays for his inability to listen through a narrative with decapitation. Minerva, on the other hand, is almost unique in being inspired to action by the story she has listened to. More frequent is a passive reaction of the narratee, like bursting into tears, or telling a story in his/her turn, in order to thank or challenge the narrator of the story (s)he has listened to. A few of the metanarratives are

---

[47] For a study of **[3]** along these lines see Keith 1992: 9-37.
[48] See Wheeler 1999: 103-5.

represented as public performances in front of several narratees. These are not always indispensable as individuals. On the whole, they represent a choice among other possible members of groups that share a minimum of values or characteristics with the narrator. This means that the narratee is morally and emotionally close to the narrator. The fact that the metanarratives are generally mythological stories in which the gods play some role means that although most of the narratees are supposed to be unfamiliar with them, the divine characters involved are known.

Finally, the various functions of the narratees were examined, in particular (a) their role as mediators between the extradiegetic narrator and his narratees, and ultimately between the author and his readers, and (b) their role as mirrors for the narrators. Although the responses of the intradiegetic audiences are not meticulously reported, when they are they normally concern the narratee's belief in the story and whether (s)he was moved or not. Peleus' **[24]** lack of emotional reaction to Onetor's report does not pose a problem for the reader; it is explained away by the extradiegetic narrator himself: "remembering the crime he had committed, he realized that the Nereid whose son he had killed was inflicting these calamities upon him" (11.380-1). By contrast, the narratees that show disbelief have attracted more critical attention. Their reaction is generally considered to inscribe in the text the possibility that the actual reader may dismiss the poem as pure fiction. It is important to supplement this observation with the fact that these resisting narratees are usually punished and singled out as morally dubious. *Caveat lector.*

VIII Conclusions

"Rumours of the death of narratology have been greatly exaggerated. Recently we have witnessed a small but unmistakable explosion of activity in the field of narrative studies."[1] In David Herman's view, from whose introduction to recent collection of narratological essays the previous quotation is drawn, this renaissance is the result of the recontextualisation of classical models of narratological research and the adaptation of various philosophical, political, literary and interdisciplinary perspectives: feminist, Bakhtinian, deconstructive, reader-response, psychoanalytic, historicist, rhetorical, computational, etc. In other words, "structuralist theorizing has evolved into a plurality of models for narrative analysis,"[2] and 'narratology' has become 'narratologies'. An overview of the main developments and problems of three particular 'narratologies' (marxist-historicist, Bakhtinian, and feminist) was outlined in Chapters I and V.

This process of evolution is irreversible, and we have tried to be open to the advantages of ideological critique and feminism (or gender studies) for our understanding and appreciation of metanarrative in the *Metamorphoses*. Yet, it is evident from the overall structure of the dissertation that in essence we have remained loyal to the structuralist model proposed in 1972 by Gérard Genette. For, as Scott Richardson argued a decade ago, "one virtue of a structural approach to a narrative is the opportunity it provides for comparison with others."[3] Another advantage is the clarity of description made with categories which are antithetically and therefore clearly defined. So, this analysis not only provides another perspective on the *Metamorphoses* but also data that ultimately could be used for a comparative historical poetics of (meta)narrative in Latin and European literature.

Stories "shape the process of life. It is through stories that our social selves, which are our real selves, are actually produced."[4] As we saw in chapter 4, intradiegetic narrators in the *Metamorphoses* tell stories for a

---

[1] Herman 1999: 1.
[2] Herman 1999: 1.
[3] Richardson 1990: 199.
[4] Cupitt: ix.

host of reasons: to support a plan of action, to put someone to sleep and then to death, to take part in a competition, to make someone yield to their erotic desire, etc. But above all, stories are told, often exchanged, to while away time, i.e. for entertainment. An obvious consequence of telling stories for their own sake is that they are normally fairly detailed accounts. Of course, this does not explain why Ovid would have us read these accounts in the narrators' *ipsissima verba*, rather than merely alluding to the stories, as he does, for instance, in the case of the stories embroidered on Minerva's and Arachne's tapestries (6.87-100, 103-26).

The traditional, functionalist view of metadiegetic narrative considers it a convenient means of filling gaps in the primary narrative (*completing analepsis*) with the added advantage of preserving the continuity of primary narrative. This is Heinze's exclusive and Fusillo's partial interpretation of metadiegetic narrative in the *Aeneid* and the *Argonautica* respectively.[5] But whatever interpretative validity and adequacy it may have for poems with the vigorous unity of the *Aeneid*, it seems unsuitable for the *Metamorphoses*, a poem that continually frustrates the reader's expectation for linear progression. A modified version of this theory, proposed by Boillat, is more appealing.[6] He argues that metanarrative in the *Met.* is a convenient way of including stories that had not been inscribed in the traditional chronology of myth. This explanation has the double advantage of taking into account the particularity of the *Met.* as a *Kollektivgedicht* and hinting at the function of metanarrative in the poem as a live demonstration of the processes that created the mythographic tradition of Graeco-Roman culture.

If metadiegetic narrative contributes to any concept of time in the *Met.*, it is a vague sense of achrony, at least until we get to the Trojan war, in the aftermath of which lie the origins of Roman history.[7] In fact, the metadiegetic narratives examined in this dissertation contribute to distorting preconceptions about narrative temporality in a further way.

---

[5] Heinze 1993: 307 and Fusillo 1985: 73.
[6] Boillat 1976: 119-20.
[7] Solodow 1988: 35, a view anticipated in Ahl 1985: 292: "Ovid's genius in the *Metamorphoses*, as in the *Fasti* –his other experiment in expanding small units of time into eternity– lies in creating a causality without time: the purest myth." *Contra* Boillat 1976: 116, who argues that genealogy, when we can reconstruct it, gives the impression that time flows. For stimulating observations on time in the *Met.* see Nolan 1990: 36-37.

Their production requires and indeed constitutes some sort of *scene* in terms of narrative speed, which results in dilation of narrative time at unexpected moments, like one night during the Bacchic festival some time after Pentheus' *sparagmos* or during the reception in Achelous' cave after the hunt of the Calydonian boar. Not to mention Orpheus' performance (10.148-739) which takes up more narrative time than, say, the events between Aeneas' and Romulus' apotheoses, which span several generations (14.609-804).

Focusing on this tension between scenes and vectors, P. Gros suggested his own alternative theory about the effect of inserted narrative (rather than metadiegetic narrative in particular), which he considered analogous to that of the contemporary sanctuaries-museums of the *Urbs*, a pleasure which would soon efface the more austere, if not more ambitious, plans of the new imperial regime.[8]

More interesting and more apposite in the context of an enquiry into narrative poetics seems S. Rimmon-Kenan's thesis that to turn the characters-objects of narration into narrative subjects is "to question the separation between reality and narration, and to suggest that there may be no reality apart from its narration, [that] texts reflect nothing but their own textuality, resulting in infinite regress, (...) and tautology: "a text is a text is a text.""[9] Metadiegesis is certainly a reflexive gesture with metanarrative potential. Through his use of fictive narrators and audiences, Ovid, the extradiegetic narrator, "persistently and programmatically emphasises the process of storytelling which produced the mythological tradition in which he works."[10] It is within this theoretical context that the brilliant ideas put forward in Barchiesi 1989 seem to achieve their full potential as an accurate portrayal of the Ovidian experimentation with metadiegesis in the *Metamorphoses*. Examining the narratives of Achelous **[14]**, Orpheus **[16]** and Pythagoras, he argues that internal narrators are not differentiated by an

---

[8] Gros 1981: 366: "Cette tension, sourdement entretenue, entre des images et des vecteurs, constituait, à n' en pas douter, la source principale du plaisir de celui qui entrait dans les sanctuaires-musées de l' *Urbs*; la lecture des *Métamorphoses* nous restitue, au moins en partie, la saveur de ce plaisir, que devaient très vite faire oublier les desseins plus austères sinon plus ambitieux du nouveau régime impérial."
[9] Rimmon-Kenan 1992: 31.
[10] Nagle 1988c: 46.

individual narrative style and lexical particularities; their distinctiveness lies in the type of narrative that they represent.[11]

Our research has confirmed that internal narrators mirror the extradiegetic narrator (Ovid) in more than one way. It has been frequently noted in the previous chapters that, irrespective of the age, gender or status of the individual narrator, the text of their narration exhibits the same interest in aetiology and etymology as well as many of the mannerisms of presentation that are evident in the primary narrative. Brief similes, apostrophe, and catalogue are employed to tell a story in which the forces of love, pity, fate and revenge provide the causative links. Similes, a figure which brings to the foreground the narrator and may involve implicit judgement of the events narrated, even occasionally reflect the reality of Augustan Rome rather than that of the narrating persona (e.g. 4.121-24). Love, Ovid's area of expertise and chief concern throughout his poetic life, is frequently the subject not only of the stories but also of the narrators' comments: 4.68 (*quid non sentit amor?*), 330 (*nescit enim quid amor*), 5.396 (*usque adeo est properatus amor*) and 400 (*tantaque simplicitas puerilibus adfuit annis*). Ovid's intradiegetic *alter egos* even share his self-consciousness (cf.5.207-8 *nomina longa mora est media de plebe virorum/ dicere*). They also make several metanarrative comments, primarily concerning narrative time and its relation to narrated time: 1.214-15 (*longa mora est, quantum noxae sit ubique repertum, / enumerare*), 5.462-3 (*quas dea per terras et quas erraverit undas / dicere longa mora est*), 635 (*citius, quam nunc tibi facta renarro*), 10.679 (*neve meus sermo cursu tardior ipso*).

And yet, given the limited variety of narrative styles and types that could be convincingly employed by the extradiegetic narrator 'Ovid', the use of internal narrators gave our poet the opportunity to present his readers with an encyclopaedia of narrative forms, as they could be accommodated in hexameter verse. Thus the *Met.* become not only a universal chronicle *ab origine mundi / ad mea tempora* (1.3-4), but also a history of narrative forms and contexts from Olympus to Italy, from

---

[11] Pythagoras' speech, which illustrates the genre of didactic hexameter poetry (cf. 15.479 *instructo pectore*) was not examined in this dissertation because it does not conform with the notion of narrative that has prevailed in our choice of material, even though it contains some narrative sections, like the succession of the four seasons (15.201-13).

Palatia caeli (1.176) to "the deep woods that grow in the valley of Aricia" (15.488), from Homer's *Odyssey* and Lucilius' *Satires* to Vergil's *Aeneid*.[12]

A story told well is a story told in the traditional manner. In metadiegetic narrative Ovid used the norms of established forms of narrative, like the hymn, the messenger-speech, and the novel(la), and story-types, like call, miracle, foundation, epic battle, home-coming, and single-combat. But this medley of narrative forms and patterns would certainly be far less interesting if Ovid had not ingeniously ascribed each one of them to an appropriate character. By this I mean a character whose literary history has been connected with a particular type of story. Jupiter **[1]** had previously appeared in the same narrative role in *Odyssey* 1 and Lucilius' *Satire* 1.1, the Crow **[3]** in Callimachus' *Hecale*, Acoetes **[4]** in Euripides' *Bacchae*, Achaemenides in Vergil's *Aeneid* and Orpheus **[16]** in Phanocles' *Erotes*. That this was not intended as a ubiquitous means of authentication is suggested by the last case: the civilizing mission ascribed to Orpheus by Horace (*Ars* 391-98), i.e. to prevent humans from primitive promiscuity and relations *more ferarum*, is parodied, as Ovid's Orpheus sings to an audience of animals on a theme that cannot harm **them** morally.[13]

Polyphony, however, is a concept developed by Bakhtin to describe the complex ideology of Dostoievsky's novels. Our analysis has shown that intradiegetic narrators in the *Met.* do not normally engage in ideological dialogue with the extradiegetic narrator, with each other or with their narratees. At times they may adopt perspectives determined to a certain extent by their gender, age or class, but, on the whole, they do not offer a coherent and consistent alternative voice. Perhaps, it is not irrelevant that, unlike Dostoievsky's characters, intradiegetic narrators in the *Met.* generally have a fleeting presence in the poem.

To conclude, it seems that Ovid, the author, is intent on continually reminding us that "he has created the world of the poem, he has brought it into existence and shaped it, just as in the earlier *Heroides* he had "not overcome his reductive tendency to violate the intimacy of the autodiegetic mode with his wit, interrupting the reader's process of

---

[12] See Galinsky 1996: 262.
[13] Barchiesi 1989: 73.

sympathetic rediscovery of the events narrated."[14] Galinsky's rapprochement of the extradiegetic narrator of the *Met.* with the pantomime-dancer, who "performed the most diverse roles with changing masks" may not be a sufficient interpretation of the narrators' multiplicity in the poem but is certainly an illuminating analogy.[15]

---

[14] Solodow 1988: 73 and Verducci 1985: 31.
[15] Galinsky 1996: 265; to his parallels add the fact that Pythagorean philosophy also figures among the subjects represented in pantomime, see Athen.*Deipn.*1.36.21.

Bibliography

The references to works of ancient authors conform to the system of *LSJ* and *OLD*, while individual books of the Holy Bible are abbreviated according to *The Holy Bible containing the Old and New Testaments with the Apocryphal/Deuterocanonical Books. New Revised Standard Version (Anglicized Edition)*, Oxford 1995. The titles of journals are abbreviated as in *L' Année Philologique*. The fragments of Greek epic poets are numbered according to M. Davies, *Epicorum Graecorum Fragmenta* (Göttingen 1988), and quotations from Ovid's *Metamorphoses* are from W. S. Anderson's Teubner edition (Stuttgart and Leipzig 1993[5]). Quotations in Latin are italicised while quotations in modern languages are put in double inverted commas. The stories are individually and continuously numbered so that they can be easily referred to in bold figures within square brackets, e.g. **[1]**.

General Works and Collections of Material

ANRW   H. Temporini & W. Haase, *Aufstieg und Niedergang der römischen Welt*, Berlin/ New York 1972-

CAGN   B. P. Reardon, *Collected Ancient Greek Novels*, Berkeley-Los Angeles- London 1989

DNP   H. Cancik & H. Schneider (eds.), *Der Neue Pauly Enzyklopädie der Antike*, Stuttgart-Weimar 1996-2003

EV   *Enciclopedia Virgiliana*, Roma 1984-1991

FGrH   F. Jacoby (ed.), *Die Fragmente der griechischen Historiker*, Berlin/Leiden 1923-1969

HE   A. S. F. Gow & D. L. Page (eds.), *The Greek Anthology. Hellenistic Epigrams*, 2 vols, Cambridge 1965

H-S   J. B. Hofmann & A. Szantyr, *Lateinische Syntax und Stilistik*, München 1965

LIMC   *Lexicon Iconographicum Mythologiae Classicae*, Zürich-München 1981-

LSJ   H. G. Liddell, R.Scott, R. McKenzie, P. G. W. Glare, H. S. Jones (eds.), *A Greek-English Lexicon with Revised Supplement*, 9th edition, Oxford 1940

OLD	P. G. W.Glare (ed.), *Oxford Latin Dictionary*, Oxford 1982
PMG	D. L. Page, *Poetae Melici Graeci*, Oxford 1974
RE	A. Pauly, G. Wissowa *et al.*, *Real-Encyclopädie der classischen Altertumswissenschaft*, Stuttgart 1893-1980
SH	P. J. Parsons & H. Lloyd-Jones, *Supplementum Helenisticum*, Berlin 1983
TGF	B. Snell *et al.*, *Tragicorum Graecorum Fragmenta*, Göttingen 1971-
TLL	*Thesaurus Linguae Latinae*, München 1900-

Commentaries on Ovid's Metamorphoses

W. S. Anderson, *Ovid's Metamorphoses. Books 1-5 Edited, with Introduction and Commentary*, Norman and London 1997

W. S. Anderson, *Ovid's Metamorphoses. Books 6-10 Edited, with Introduction and Commentary*, Norman 1972

F. Bömer, P. Ovidius Naso, *Metamorphosen: Kommentar*, Heidelberg 1969-1986

M. Haupt & O. Korn, *P. Ovidius Naso, Metamorphosen* Unveränderte Neuausgabe der Auflage von R.Ehwald, korrigiert und bibliographisch ergänzt von M.von Albrecht, Dublin/Zürich 1966

A. S. Hollis, *Ovid Metamorphoses VIII*, Oxford 1970

A. D. Melville (transl.), *Ovid's Metamorphoses*, Introduction and Notes by E. J. Kenney, Oxford 1986

J. J. Moore-Blunt, *A Commentary on Ovid's Metamorphoses II* [Classical and Byzantine Monographs 3], Uithoorn 1977

G. M. H. Murphy, *Ovid Metamorphoses XI*, Oxford 1972

Commentaries on Other Works

T. W. Allen, W. R. Halliday, and E. E. Sikes, *The Homeric Hymns*, edited with a Preface, Apparatus Criticus, Notes, and Appendices, Oxford 1936

R. G. Austin, *P. Vergili Maronis Aeneidos Liber Primus*, with a commentary, Oxford 1971

R. G. Austin, *P. Vergili Maronis Aeneidos Liber Secundus*, with a commentary, Oxford 1964

R. G. Austin, *P. Vergili Maronis Aeneidos Liber Quartus*, edited with a commentary, Oxford 1955

R. G. Austin, *P. Vergili Maronis Aeneidos Liber Sextus*, with a commentary, Oxford 1977

C. Carey and R. A. Reid, *Demosthenes: selected Private Speeches*, Cambridge 1985

M. Coffey and R. Meyer (eds.), *Seneca: Phaedra*, Cambridge 1990

M. Edwards, *The Iliad: A Commentary. Vol.V: Books 17-20*, Cambridge 1991

C. J. Fordyce, *P. Vergili Maronis Aeneidos Libri VII-VII*, with a Commentary, introduction by G. P. Walsh, edited by John D. Christie, Oxford 1977

P. Hardie (ed.), *Virgil: Aeneid Book IX*, Cambridge 1994

S. J. Harrison, *Vergil: Aeneid 10*, with Introduction, Translation, and Commentary, Oxford 1991

B. Hainsworth, *The Iliad: A Commentary, Volume III: books 9-12*, Cambridge 1993

R. L. Hunter, *Eubulus: The Fragments*, edited with a commentary, Cambridge 1983

R. Janko, *The Iliad: A Commentary, Volume IV: books 13-16*, Cambridge 1992

R. Kannicht, *Euripides: Helena*, herausgegeben und erklärt, Band II: Kommentar, Heidelberg 1969

E. J. Kenney (ed.), *Apulleius: Cupid and Psyche*, Cambridge 1990

R. G. M. Nisbet and M. Hubbard, *A Commentary on Horace Odes, Book I*, Oxford 1970

R. G. M. Nisbet and M. Hubbard, *A Commentary on Horace Odes, Book II*, Oxford 1978

R. M. Ogilvie and Sir I. Richmond (eds.), *Cornelii Taciti, De Vita Agricolae*, Oxford 1967

M. C. J. Putnam, *Tibullus: A Commentary*, Norman, Oklahoma 1973

O. Skutsch, *The Annals of Q. Ennius*, edited with introduction and commentary, Oxford 1985

R. D. Williams, *Virgil: Aeneid III*, Edited with a Commentary, Oxford 1962

R. D. Williams, *Virgil: Aeneid V*, Edited with a Commentary, Oxford

1960

Other Works

N. Abercrombie – B. Turner, "The Dominant Ideology Thesis," *British Journal of Sociology* 1978, pp.151-155

R. Aczel, "Hearing Voices in Narrative Texts," *NLH* 29 (1998) 467-500

J.-M. Adam, *Les Textes: Types et prototypes. Récit, Description, Argumentation, Explication et Dialogue*, Paris 1997

C. F. Ahern, Jr., "Ovid as vates in the proem to the Ars Amatoria," *CPh* 85 (1990) 44-48

F. Ahl, *Metaformations: soundplay and wordplay in Ovid and other classical poets*, Ithaca NY 1985

M. von Albrecht, *Die Parenthese in Ovids Metamorphosen und ihre dichterische Funktion* [Spudasmata 7], Hildesheim 1964

M. von Albrecht, "Les comparaisons dans les Métamorphoses d' Ovide," *BAGB* 1981, 24-34 = "Zur Funktion der Gleichnisse in Ovids Metamorphosen," in H. Görgemanns & E. A. Schmidt (eds.), *Studien zum antiken Epos, Franz Dirlmeier und Viktor Pöschl gewidmet* [Beiträge zur klassischen Philologie, 72], Meisenheim am Glan 1976, pp. 280-90

M. von Albrecht, "Ovide et ses lecteurs," *REL* 59 (1981) 207-15 = "Dichter und Leser –am Beispiel Ovids," *Gymnasium* 88 (1981) 222-35

M. von Albrecht, *Roman Epic: An Interpretative Introduction* [Mnemosyne Supplements 189], Leiden-Boston-Köln 1999

R. Alden-Smith, "Ov.Met.10.475: An Instance of 'Meta-allusion'," *Gymnasium* 97 (1990) 458-60

L. Alfonsi, "Phanoclea," *Hermes* 81 (1953) 379-83

G. Allwood, *French Feminisms: Gender and Violence in Contemporary Theory*, London 1998

W. S. Anderson, "The Orpheus of Virgil and Ovid: *flebile nescio quid*," in John Warden (ed.), *Orpheus: The Metamorphoses of a Myth*, Toronto-Buffalo-London 1982

W. S. Anderson, "Lycaon: Ovid's deceptive paradigm in

Metamorphoses 1," *ICS* 14 (1989) 91-101

J. L. Austin, *How to do Things with Words*, Oxford 1962

C. L. Babcock, "Si certus intrarit dolor: A reconsideration of Horace's fifteenth Epode," *AJPh* 87 (1966) 400-19

M. Bakhtin, *The Dialogic Imagination: Four Essays*, ed. M. Holquist, trans. C. Emerson and M. Holquist, Austin,Texas 1981

M. Bakhtin, *Speech Genres and Other Late Essays*, ed. C. Emerson and M. Holquist, trans. V. W. McGee, Austin, Texas 1986

M. Bal, "Sexuality, Semiosis, and Binarism: A Narratological Comment on Bergen and Arthur," *Arethusa* 16 (1983) 117-35

M. Bal, "Tell-Tale Theories," *Poetics Today* 7 (1986) 555-64

M. Bal, *Narratology: Introduction to the Theory of Narrative*, Second Edition, Toronto - Buffalo - London 1997

G. Baldo, "Il codice epico nelle *Metamorfosi* di Ovidio," *MD* 16 (1986) 109-31

A. Barchiesi, "Voci e istanze narrative nelle Metamorfosi di Ovidio," *MD* 23 (1989) 55-97

A. Barchiesi, "Discordant Muses," *PCPS* 37 (1991) 1-21

A. Barchiesi, *The Poet and the Prince: Ovid and Augustan Discourse*, Berkeley- Los Angeles- London 1997 [=*Il poeta e il principe: Ovidio e il discorso augusteo*, Roma 1994]

A. Barchiesi, "Endgames: Ovid's *Metamorphoses* 15 and *Fasti* 6," in D. H. Roberts, F. M. Dunn and D. Fowler (eds.), *Classical Closure: Reading the End in Greek and Latin Literature*, Princeton NJ 1997, pp.181-208

A. Barchiesi, "Poeti epici e narratori," in G. Papponetti (ed.), *Metamorfosi: Atti del Convegno Internazionale di Studi (Sulmona, 20-22 Novembre 1994)*, Regione Abruzzo 1997, pp.121-41

A. Barigazzi, "Cornacchie nell' *Ecale* di Callimaco," *Prometheus* 17 (1991) 97-110

A. Bartenbach, *Motiv- und Erzählstruktur in Ovids Metamorphosen: das Vehältnis von Rahmen- und Binnenerzählung im 5. 10. und 15. Buch von Ovids Metamorphosen* [Studien zur klassischen Philologie, 52], Frankfurt am Main 1990

R. Barthes, *S/Z*, Paris 1970 (= trans. Richard Miller, New York 1974)

S. de Beauvoir, *La Vieillesse*, Paris 1970

R. Beck, "Mystery, Aretalogy and the Ancient Novel," in G. Schmeling (ed.), *The Novel in the Ancient World* [Mnemosyne Supplements 159], Leiden 1996, pp.131-150

A. L. T. Bergren, "The *Homeric Hymn to Aphrodite*: Tradition and Rhetoric, Praise and Blame," *ClAnt* 8 (1989) 1-41

E. J. Bernbeck, *Beobachtungen zur Darstellungsart in Ovids Metamorphosen* [Zetemata 43], München 1967

B. Bilinsky, "Elementi Esiodei nelle 'Metamorfosi' di Ovidio," in *Atti del Convegno Internazionale Ovidiano II*, Roma 1959, pp.101-23

E. Block, "Narrative Judgment and Audience Response in Homer and Vergil," *Arethusa* 19 (1986), 155-69.

A. L. Boegehold and A. C. Scafuro (eds.), *Athenian Identity and Civic Ideology*, Baltimore 1994

R. Böhme, *Das Prooimion, eine Form sakraler Dichtung der Griechen*, Buehl 1937

M. Boillat, *Les Métamorphoses d' Ovide: Thèmes majeurs et problèmes de composition* [Publications Universitaires Européennes. Série XV Philologie et littérature classiques Vol.8], Berne/Francfort a.M. 1976

M. Bonfanti, *Punto di vista e modi della narrazione nell' Eneide*, Pisa 1985

W. C. Booth, *The Rhetoric of Fiction*, Second Edition, Chicago 1983

J. L. Borges, *Fictions*, ed. by Anthony Kerrigan, London 1998

E. L. Bowie, "Greek Table-Talk before Plato," *Rhetorica* 11 (1993) 355-73

C. M. Bowra, "Aeneas and the Stoic Ideal," in S. J. Harrison (ed.), *Oxford Readings in Vergil's* Aeneid, Oxford-New York 1990, pp.363-77 [reprinted from *G&R* 3 (1933/4) 8-21]

C. M. Bowra, *Heroic Poetry*, London 1952

K. Bradley, *Slavery and Society at Rome*, Cambridge 1994

T. Breitenstein, *Recherches sur le poème Mégara*, Copenhague 1966

J. N. Bremmer, "The Old Women of Ancient Greece," in J. Blok (ed.), *Sexual asymmetry. Studies in ancient society*, Amsterdam 1987, pp.191-205

M. M. Brewer, "A Loosening of Tongues: From Narrative Economy to

Women Writing," *MLN* 99 (1984) 1141-61

S. Brownmiller, *Against Our Will: Men, Women and Rape*, New York 1975

L. Cahoon, "Let the Muse sing on: Poetry, Criticism, Feminism, and the case of Ovid," *Helios* 17 (1990) 197-231

L. Cahoon, "Calliope's Song: Shifting Narrators in Ovid, Metamorphoses 5," *Helios* 23 (1996) 43-66

A. Cameron, *Callimachus and His Critics*, Princeton 1995

W. A. Camps, *An Introduction to Virgil's Aeneid*, Oxford 1969

E. Cantarella, *Bisexuality in the Ancient World*, trans. C. Ó Cuilleanáin, New Haven and London 1992

A. Carter, *The Sadeian Woman: an exercise in cultural history*, London 1979

A. Della Casa, "L' uso del termine poeta a Roma nell' età augustea," in L.Belloni, G.Milanese and A.Porro (eds.), *Studia classica Johanni Tarditi oblata*, Milano 1995, pp.51-62

V. Castellani, "Two Divine Scandals: Ovid Met.2.680ff. and 4.171ff. and his sources," *TAPhA* 110 (1980) 37-50

M. Cave, "Bakhtin and Feminism: The Chronotopic Female Imagination," *Women's Studies* 18 (1990) 117-27

S. Chatman, *Story and Discourse: Narrative Structure in Fiction and Film*, Ithaca 1978

S. Chatman, "On Deconstructing Narratology," *Style* 22 (1988) 9-17

J. R. Clarke, *Looking at Lovemaking: Constructions of Sexuality in Roman Art 100 B.C. – A.D. 250*, Berkeley 1998

J. J. Clauss, "The Episode of the Lycian Farmers in Ovid's Metmorphoses," *HSPh* 92 (1989) 297-314

D. Cohn, "The Encirclement of Narrative: on Franz Stanzel's *Theorie des Erzählens*," *Poetics Today* 2 (1981) 157-182

R. Coleman, "Structure and Intention in the *Metamorphoses*," *CQ* 21 (1971) 461-477

G. B. Conte, *The Rhetoric of Imitation: Genre and Poetic Memory in Virgil and Other Latin Poets*, transl.C.P.Segal, Ithaca 1986

D. Cornell, *Beyond Accommodation: Ethical Feminism, Deconstruction and the Law*, London 1991

D. Cornell, *The Philosophy of the Limit*, London 1992.

P. Courcelle, "Antécédents autobiographiques des Confessions du Saint Augustin," *RPh* 31 (1957) 23-51

A. Crabbe, "Structure and content in Ovid's Metamorphoses," *ANRW* 2.31.4 (1981) 2274-2327

M. M. Crump, *The Epyllion from Theocritus to Ovid*, Oxford 1931

P. Culham, "Decentering the Text: The Case of Ovid," *Helios* 17 (1990)161-170

J. Culler, "Problems in the Theory of Fiction," *Diacritics* 14 (1984) 2-11

D. Cupitt, *What is a Story?*, London 1991

L. C. Curran, "Rape and Rape Victims in the Metamorphoses," in J. Peradotto and J. P. Sullivan (eds.), *Women in the Ancient World: The Arethusa Papers*, Albany 1984, 263-86 [originally published in *Arethusa* 11 (1978) 213-41]

H. Dahlmann, "Vates," *Philologus* 97 (1948) 337-53

J. D'Arms, "The Roman Convivium and Equality," in O. Murray (ed.), *Sympotica. A Symposium on the Symposion*, Oxford 1990

N. G. G. Davis, *Studies in the Narrative Economy of Ovid's Metamorphoses*, [unpublished PhD Diss.] University of California 1969

I. J. F. de Jong, *Narrators and Focalizers. The Presentation of the Story in the Iliad*, Amsterdam 1987

I. J. F. de Jong, *Narrative in Drama. the Art of the Euripidean Messenger-speech* [Mnemosyne Supplement 116], Leiden 1991

I. J. F. de Jong and J. P. Sullivan (eds.), *Modern Critical Theory and Classical Literature* [Mnemosyne Supplement 130], Leiden 1994

I. J. F. de Jong, *Mnemosyne* 51 (1998) 463-466: review of Doherty 1995

J.-F. Deniau, *Un héros très discret*, Paris 1989

J. Derrida, *Of Grammatology*, trans with preface by G. C. Spivak, Baltimore and London 1976

J. Derrida, *Dissemination*, trans. with intro. and additional notes by B. Johnson, London 1981

M. Detienne, *The Creation of Mythology*, trans. M. Cook, Chicago and London 1986

M. Detienne & J. Svenbro, "The Feast of the Wolves, or the Impossible City," in M. Detienne & J.-P. Vernant (eds.), *The Cuisine of Sacrifice among the Greeks*, trans. P. Wissing, Chicago & London 1989, pp.148-163

K. Dickson, *Nestor. Poetic Memory in Greek Epic* [A. B. Lord studies in oral tradition 16], New York & London 1995

N. Diengott, "Narratology and Feminism," *Style* 22 (1988) 42-51

M. Dippel, *Die Darstellung des trojanischen Krieges in Ovids Metamorphosen (XII,1-XIII,622)* [European University Studies Series XV, Vol. 46], Frankfurt a.M.-Bern-N.York-Paris 1990

J. Döring, *Ovids Orpheus*, Basel-Frankfurt a.M. 1996

H. Dörrie, "Der verliebte Kyklop. Interpretation von Ovid, met.13,750-897," *AU* 12 (1969) 75-100

L. E. Doherty, *Siren Songs: Gender, Audiences, and Narrators in the Odyssey*, Ann Arbor 1995

O. S. Due, *Changing Forms: Studies in the Metamorphoses of Ovid*, Copenhagen 1974

T. Eagleton, *Ideology: An Introduction*, London - New York 1991

C. Edwards, *The Politics of Immorality in Ancient Rome*, Cambridge 1993

B. Egger, "Women and Marriage in the Greek Novels: The Boundaries of Romance," in J. Tatum (ed.), *The Search for the Ancient Novel*, Baltimore and London 1994, pp. 260-280

C. C. Esler, "Horace's Old Girls: Evolution of a Topos," in Falkner 1989: 172-82

T. M. Falkner & J. de Luce (eds.), *Old Age in Greek and Latin Literature*, Albany 1989

E. Fantham, "Rewriting and Rereading the Fasti: Augustus, Ovid, and Recent Scholarship," *Antichthon* 29 (1995) 42-59

D. C. Feeney, *The Gods in Epic: Poets and Critics of the Classical Tradition*, Oxford 1991

D. C. Feeney, "*Si licet et fas est*: Ovid's Fasti and the Problem of Free Speech under the Principate," in Powell 1992: 1-25.

D. Feeney, *Literature and Religion at Rome: cultures, contexts and beliefs*,

Cambridge 1998

A. Fehn, I. Hoesterey, and M. Tatar (eds.), *Neverending Stories: Toward a Critical Narratology*, Princeton NJ 1992

B. Fenik, *Typical Battle Scenes in the Iliad. Studies in the Narrative Techniques of Homeric Battle Description* [Hermes Einzelschriften 21], Wiesbaden 1968

M. I. Finley, "The Elderly in Classical Antiquity," *G&R* 28 (1981) 156-71, [reprinted in Falkner 1989: 1-20.]

R. K. Fisher, "The Concept of Miracle in Homer," *Antichthon* 29 (1995) 1-14

W. Fitzgerald, *Slavery and the Roman literary imagination*, Cambridge 2000

B. L. Flaschenriem, "Speaking of Women: 'Female Voice' in Propertius," *Helios* 25 (1998) 49-64

A. Florin, "Narratology and the Study of the Narrating Instance," in Wahlin 1996: 9-22

H. P. Foley, *The Homeric Hymn to Demeter*, Princeton NJ 1994

P. M. C. Forbes Irving, *Metamorphosis in Greek Myths*, Oxford 1990

A. Ford, *Homer: The Poetry of the Past*, Ithaca and London 1992

M. Foucault, "Truth and Power," in P. Rabinow (ed.), *The Foucault Reader*, New York 1984, pp.51-75 [first published in Italian in A. Fontana - P. Pasquino (eds.), *Microfisica del potere: interventi politici*, Torino 1977, and in English trans. by F. Edholm as "Truth and power: an iterview with Michel Foucault," *Critique of Anthropology* 4 (1979) 131-137]

R. Fowler, *Literature as Social Discourse: The Practice of Linguistic Criticism*, London 1981

D. Fowler, "Deviant Focalisation in Virgil's *Aeneid*," *PCPhS* 36 (1990) 42-63

D. Fowler, "Narrate and Describe: the Problem of Ecphrasis," *JRS* 81 (1991) 25-35

D. Fowler, "Postmodernism, Romantic Irony, and Classical Closure," in de Jong-Sullivan 1994: 231-56

J.-M. Frécaut, "Humour et imaginaire dans un épisode des *Métamorphoses* d' Ovide: Les paysans lyciens (VI, 313-381), *Latomus* 43 (1984) 540-53

B. R. Fredericks, "*Tristia* 4.10: Poet's Autobiography and Poetic Autobiography," *TAPA* 106 (1979) 139-54

N. Friday, *Forbidden Flowers: More Wome's Sexual Fantasies*, London 1994

P. Friedländer, "Das Proömium von Hesiods Theogonie," *Hermes* 49 (1914) 1-16

M. Fusillo, *Il tempo delle Argonautiche. Un' analisi del raconto in Apollonio Rodio* [Filologia e Critica 49], Roma 1985

M. Fusillo, "Textual Patterns and Narrative Situations in the Greek Novel," *Groningen Colloquia on the Novel* 1 (1988) 17-31

M. Fusillo, *Il romanzo greco. Polifonia ed Eros*, Venezia 1989. [trans. in French by M. Abrioux as *Naissance du Roman*, Paris 1991]

G. K. Galinsky, "Hercules Ovidianus (*Metamorphoses* 9, 1-272), *WS* 6 (1972) 93-116

G. K. Galinsky, *Ovid's Metamorphoses: An Introduction to the Basic Aspects*, Berkeley and Los Angeles 1975

K. Galinsky, *Augustan Culture: An Interpretive Introduction*, Princeton NJ 1996

M-K. Gamel, "Baucis and Philemon: Paradigm or Paradox," *Helios* 11 (1984) 117-31

M. Gardiner, *The dialogics of critique: M. M. Bakhtin and the theory of ideology*, London and New York 1992

B. M. Gauly, "Ovid, Venus and Orpheus über Atalanta und Hippomenes: zu Ov.met. 10,560-707," *Gymnasium* 99 (1992) 435-454

C. Geertz, "Religion as a Cultural System," in M. Banton (ed.), *Anthropological Approaches to the Study of Religion*, London 1966, 1-46

C. Geertz, *The Interpretation of Cultures*, New York 1973

G. Genette, *Figures III*, Paris 1972

G. Genette, *Narrative Discourse*, trans.J.E.Lewin, Oxford 1980

G. Genette, *Nouveau Discours du récit*, Paris 1983

G. Genette, *Narrative Discourse Revisited*, trans.J.E.Lewin, Ithaca 1988

A. Gibson, *Towards a Postmodern Theory of Narrative*, Edinburgh 1996

A. Gibson, "Ethics and Unrepresentability in *Heart of Darkness*," in Andrew Gibson and Robert Hampson (eds.), *Conrad and Theory*, Amsterdam and Atlanta 1997, pp.113-37

W. Ginsberg, *The Cast of Character: The Representation of Personality in Ancient and Medieval Literature*, Toronto/Buffalo/London 1983

E. M. Glenn, *The Metamorphoses: Ovid's Roman Games*, Lanham Md, New York, and London 1986

B. K. Gold, "But Ariadne Was Never There in the First Place," in Rabinowitz 1993: 75-101

S. Goldhill, "The Great Dionysia and Civic Ideology," in J. J. Winkler and F. I. Zeitlin (eds.), *Nothing to Do with Dionysos?*, Princeton 1990, pp. 97-129

P. Gordon, "The Lover's Voice in *Heroides* 15: or, Why is Sappho a Man?," in Hallett 1997: 274-91

A. Grafton, *The Footnote: A curious history*, London 1997

F. Graf, *Greek Mythology: An Introductin*, trans. by T. Marier, Baltimore and London 1993

A. H. F.Griffin, "Philemon and Baucis in Ovid's Metamorphoses," *G&R* 38 (1991) 62-74

S. Griffin, *Pornography and Silence: culture's revenge against nature*, London 1981

S. Gubar, "Representing Pornography: Feminism, Criticism, and Depictions of Female Violation," *Critical inquiry* 13 (1987) 712-741

F. Guizzi, *Augusto: La Politica della Memoria*, Roma 1999

K. J. Gutzwiller and A. N. Michelini, "Women and Other Strangers: Feminist Perspectives in Classical Literature," in J. E. Hartman and E. Messer-Davidow (eds.), *(En)Gendering Knowledge: Feminists in Academe*, Knoxville 1991, pp.66-84

J. Haarberg, "Lycaon's impious and Ovid's rhetorical strategy. A note on the Lycaon episode in Met.1," *SO* 58 (1983) 111-15

M. Halbwachs, *La Mémoire Collective*, Paris 1950

L. Coser (ed.), *Maurice Halbwachs: On Collective Memory*, Chicago 1992

J. P. Hallett, "The Role of Women in Roman Elegy: Counter-Cultural Feminism," *Arethusa* 6 (1973) 103-124 [reprinted in J. Peradotto and J. P. Sullivan (eds.), *Women in the Ancient World: The Arethusa Papers*, Albany 1984, pp.241-62]

J. P. Hallett, "Feminist Theory, Historical Periods, Literary Canons, and the Study of Greco-Roman Antiquity," in Rabinowitz 1993: 44-72

J. P. Hallett & Marilyn B. Skinner (eds.), *Roman Sexualities*, Princeton 1997

M. Halm-Tisserant, *Cannibalisme et Immortalité. L' enfant dans le chaudron en Grèce ancienne*, Paris 1993

D. M. Halperin, *Before Pastoral: Theocritus and the Ancient Tradition of Bucolic Poetry*, New Haven and London 1983

P. Hamon, "Text and Ideology: For a Poetics of the Norm," *Style* 17 (1983) 95-121

P. Hamon, *Texte et Idéologie*, Paris 1984

P. Hamon, *Du Descriptif*, Paris 1993

A. Hardie, *Statius and the Silvae.Poets, Patrons and Epideixis in the Graeco-Roman World* [ARCA 9], Leeds 1983

P. Hardie, "Ovid's Theban History: The First Anti-*Aeneid*?" *CQ* 40 (1990) 224-35

P. Hardie, "The Speech of Pythagoras in *Metamorphoses* 15: Epmedoclean *Epos*," *CQ* 45 (1995) 204-14

P. Hardie, "Metamorphosis, Metaphor, and Allegory in Latin Epic," in Mary Beissinger, Jane Tylus, and Susanne Wofford (eds.), *Epic Traditions in the Contemporary World: The Poetics of Community*, Berkeley, Los Angeles, London 1999, pp. 89-107

J. Hargreaves (ed.), *Sport, Culture and Ideology*, London 1982

B. Harries, "Causation and the Authority of the Poet in Ovid's *Fasti*," *CQ* 39 (1989) 164-185

R. Heinze, *Ovids elegische Erzählung* [Berichte der Sächsischen Akademie zu Leipzig. Philologisch-historische Klasse 71.7], Leipzig 1919

R. Heinze, *Virgil's Epic Technique*, transl. by H. and D. Harvey and F.

Robertson, pref. by A.Wlosok, London 1993

J. Hemker, "Rape and the Founding of Rome," *Helios* 12 (1985) 41-47

G. L. Hendrickson, "The Memoirs of Rutilius Rufus," *CPh* 28 (1933) 153-175

D. Herman (ed.), *Narratologies: New Perspectives on Narrative Analysis*, Columbus 1999

S. E. Hinds, *The Metamorphosis of Persephone: Ovid and the Self-conscious Muse*, Cambridge 1987

S. E. Hinds, "*Arma* in Ovid's *Fasti*," *Arethusa* 25 (1992) 81-153

I. Hoesterey, "Introduction," in: Fehn-Hoesterey-Tatar 1992: 3-14

H. Hofmann, "Ovid's *Metamorphoses: Carmen Perpetuum, Carmen Deductum*," *Papers of the Liverpool Latin Seminar* 5 (1985) 223-42

A. W. J. Holleman, "Ovidii Metamorphoseon Liber XV 622-870 (carmen et error?)," *Latomus* 28 (1969) 42-60

N. Holzberg, "Ovids 'Babyloniaka' (Met.4.55-166)," *WS* 101 (1988) 265-77

N. Holzberg, "*Ter quinque volumina* as *carmen perpetuum*: The Division into Books in Ovid's *Metamorphoses*," *MD* 40 (1998) 77-98

K. Hopkins, "Novel Evidence for Roman Slavery," *P&P* 138 (1993) 3-27

N. Hopkinson (ed.), *A Hellenistic Anthology*, Cambridge 1988

R. A. Hornsby, "Horace on art and Politics (*Ode* 3.4)," *CJ* 58 (1962/63) 97-104

G. O. Hutchinson, *Hellenistic Poetry*, Oxford 1988

L. Irigaray, *This Sex Which Is Not One*, trans. By C. Porter, with C. Burke, Ithaca 1985

N. M. Jacobs, "Gender and Layered Narrative in *Wuthering Heights* and *The Tenant of Wildfell Hall*," *Journal of Narrative Technique* 16 (1986) 204-19

H. Jacobson, *Ovid's Heroides*, Princeton 1974

S. L. James, "From Boys to Men: Rape and Developing Masculinity in Terence's *Hecyra* and *Eunuchus*," *Helios* 25 (1998) 31-47.

F. Jameson, *The Political Unconscious: Narrative as a Socially Symbolic Act*,

London 1981

M. Janan, "The Book of Good Love? Design and Desire in *Metamorphoses* 10," *Ramus* 17 (1988) 110-137

M. Janan, "'There beneath the Roman ruin where the purple flowers grow': Ovid's Minyeides and the feminine imagination," *AJPh* 115 (1994) 427-48

R. Janko, "The Structure of Homeric Hymns: A Study in Genre," *Hermes* 109 (1981) 9-24

A. Jardine, *Gynesis: Configurations of Women and Modernity*, Ithaca, NY 1985

H. D. Jocelyn, "'Poeta' and 'vates': concerning the nomenclature of the composer of verses in republican and early imperial Rome," in L. Belloni, G. Milanese and A. Porro (eds.), *Studia classica Johanni Tarditi oblata*, Milano 1995, pp.19-50

P. J. Johnson, "Constructions of Venus in Ovid's Metamorphoses V," *Arethusa* 29 (1996) 125-49

W. R. Johnson, "Vertumnus in Love," *CPh* 92 (1997) 367-375

C. Jouanno, "Sur un topos romanesque oublié: Les scènes de banquets," *REG* 109 (1996) 157-84

S. Kaempf-Dimitriadou, *Die Liebe der Götter in der attischen Kunst des 5. Jahrhunderts v. Chr.*, [Antike Kunst Beiheft 11], Bern 1979

Ε. Γ. Καψωμένος- Γρηγόρης Πασχαλίδης (επιμ.), *Η Ζωή των Σημείων. Τρίτο Πανελλήνιο Συνέδριο Σημειωτικής (Ιωάννινα 26-29 Οκτωβρίου 1989)*, Θεσσαλονίκη 1996

A. M. Keith, *The Play of Fictions: Studies in Ovid's Metamorphoses Book 2*, Ann Arbor 1992

D. F. Kennedy, "'Augustan' and 'Anti-Augustan': Reflections on Terms of Reference," in Powell 1992: 26-58

D. F. Kennedy, *The Arts of Love: Five Studies in the Discourse of Roman Love Elegy*, Cambridge 1993

D. Kienast, *Augustus: Prinzeps und Monarch*, 3. durchges. und erw. Auflage, Darmstadt 1999

J. T. Kirby, "Mimesis and Diegesis: Foundations of Aesthetic Theory in Plato and Aristotle," *Helios* 18 (1991) 113-128

Hans Kloft, "Aspekte der Prinzipatsideologie im frühen Prinzipat," *Gymnasium* 91 (1984) 306-26

D. Knecht, review of Newman 1967 in *AC* 37 (1968) 303

P. E. Knox, *Ovid's Metamorphoses and the Traditions of Augustan Poetry* [Cambridge Philological Society Supplementary Vol.11], Cambridge 1986

P. E. Knox, "Pyramus and Thisbe in Cyprus," *HSPh* 92 (1989) 315-28

H. Koller, "Das kitharodische Prooimion," *Philologus* 100 (1956) 159-206

D. Konstan, "The Death of Argus, or What Stories Do: Audience Response in Ancient Fiction and Theory," *Helios* 18 (1991) 15-30

D. Konstan, *Sexual Symmetry. Love in the Ancient Novel and Related Genres*, Princeton NJ 1994

P. Kretschmer, "Mythische Namen 11.Triptolemos," *Glotta* 12 (1923) 51-61

J. Kristeva, "Word, Dialogue and the Novel," in *Desire in Language: A Semiotic Approach to Literature and Art*, ed. L. S. Roudiez, trans. T. Gora, A. Jardine and L. S. Roudiez, New York 1980

A. Ph. Lagopoulos, "Semiotics and History: A marxist approach," *Semiotica* 59 (1971) 215-44

A. Ph. Lagopoulos, "Über die Möglichkeit einer materialistischen Soziosemiotic," *Zeitschrift für Semiotik* 10 (1988) 9-17

A. Ph. Lagopoulos, "Materialist Social Semiotics Versus Semiotics," in Καψωμένος-Πασχαλίδης 1996: 485-95

S. S. Lanser, *The Narrative Act: Point of View in Prose Fiction*, Princeton 1981

S. S. Lanser, "Toward a Feminist Narratology," *Style* 20 (1986) 341-63

S. S. Lanser, "Shifting the Paradigm: Feminism and Narratology," *Style* 22 (1988) 52-60

S. S. Lanser, *Fictions of Authority. Women Writers and Narrative Voice*, Ithaca and London 1992

S. S. Lanser, "Sexing the Narrative: Propriety, Desire, and the Engendering of Narrratology," *Narrative* 3 (1995) 85-94

S. S. Lanser, "Queering Narratology," in Mezei 1996: 250-61

J. Latacz, *Kampfparänese, Kampfdarstellung und Kampfwirklichkeit in der Ilias, bei Kallinos und Tyrtaios* [Zetemata 66], München 1977

D. Lateiner, "Nonverbal Behaviors in Ovid's Poetry, primarily *Metamorphoses* 14," *CJ* 91 (1996) 225-53

E. W. Leach, "Ekphrasis and the Theme of Artistic Failure in Ovid's *Metamorphoses*," *Ramus* 3 (1974) 102-42

F. Lechi, "Testo mitologico e testo elegiaco. A proposito dell' exemplum in Properzio," *MD* 3 (1979) 83-100

M. Leigh, "Wounding and Popular Rhetoric at Rome," *BICS* n.s.2 (1995) 195-212

P. Lejeune, *Le pacte autobiographique*, Paris 1975

L. H. Lenz, *Der homerische Aphroditehymnus und die Aristie des Aineias in der Ilias*, Bonn 1975

F. Létoublon, *Les lieux communs du roman. Stéréotypes grecs d' aventure et d' amour* [Mnemosyne suppl.123], Leiden/New York/Köln 1993

S. C. Levinson, *Pragmatics*, Cambridge 1983

J. H. W. G. Liebeschuetz, *Continuity and Change in Roman Religion*, Oxford 1979

S. Lilja, *Homosexuality in Republican and Augustan Rome* [Commentationes Humanarum Litterarum 74], Helsinki 1983

B. Lincoln, "The Rape of Persephone: A Greek scenario of women's initiation," *HThR* 72 (1979) 223-35

S. H. Lindheim, "I am dressed, therefore I am?: Vertumnus in Propertius 4.2 and in Metamorphoses 14.622-771," *Ramus* 27 (1998) 27-38

Θ. Λίποβατς - Ν. Δεμερτζής, *Δοκίμιο για την Ιδεολογία*, Athens 1998[2]

V. Longo, *Aretalogie nel Mondo Greco. I Epigraphie Papiri*, Genoa 1969

N. Loraux, *The Experiences of Tiresias. The Feminine and the Greek Man*, trans. P.Wissing, Princeton NJ 1995

M. Lowrie, *Horace's Narrative Odes*, Oxford 1997

J. de Luce, "'O for a Thousand Tongues to Sing": A Footnote on Metamorphosis, Silence, and Power," in M. de Forest (ed.), *Woman's*

Power, Man's Game. Essays on Classical Antiquity in honour of Jon K. King, Wanconda IL 1993, pp.305-21

W. Ludwig, *Struktur und Einheit der Metamorphosen Ovids,* Berlin 1965

R. O. A. M. Lyne, "Ovid's Metamorphoses, Callimachus and l'art pour l' art," *MD* 12 (1984) 9-34

R. O. A. M. Lyne, *Further Voices in Vergil's* Aeneid, Oxford 1987

R. MacMullen, "Roman Attitudes to Greek Love," *Historia* 31 (1982) 484-502

I. Marahrens, *Angefochtene Verse und Versgruppen in den Metamorphosen. Beiträge zu Ovids Sprache und Kompositionskunst,* Diss. Heidelberg 1971

M. Marcovich, "Phanocles ap. Stob. 4.20.47," *AJPh* 100 (1979) 360-6

F. Martínez-Bonati, Don Quixote *and the Poetics of the Novel,* trans. By Dian Fox, Ithaca and London 1992

I. McEwan, *Enduring Love,* London 1997

B. McHale, "Free Indirect Discourse: a survey of recent accounts," *Poetics and Theory of Literature* 3 (1978) 249-87.

H. Meyer, *Hymnische Stilelemente in der frügriechischen Dichtung,* Diss. Köln 1933

K. Mezei (ed.), *Ambiguous Discourse: Feminist Narratology & British Writers,* Chapel Hill & London 1996

F. J. Miller, "Some Features of Ovid's Style: II The Dramatic Element," *CJ* 15 (1919/20) 417-35

A. M. Miller, *From Delos to Delphi: A Literary Study of the Homeric Hymn to Apollo* [Mnemosyne Suppl. 93], Leiden 1986

W. W. Minton, "The Proem-Hymn of Hesiod's *Theogony,*" *TAPhA* 101 (1970) 357-77

C. H. Moore, "Prophecy in the Ancient Epic," *HSCPh* 32 (1921) 99-175.

G. W. Most, "The Stranger's Stratagem. Self-disclosure and Self-sufficiency in Greek Culture," *JHS* 109 (1989) 114-133

N. W. Musgrove, *Narrative Experimentation in Ovid's 'Metamorphoses', Books 12-14,* PhD Diss., The Univ. of N. Carolina at Chapel Hill 1991

K. S. Myers, *Ovid's Causes: Cosmogony and Aetiology in the Metamorphoses,*

Ann Arbor 1994

B. R. Nagle, "Byblis and Myrrha. Two incest narratives in the 'Metamorphoses'," *CJ* 78 (1983) 301-15

B. R. Nagle, "A Trio of Love-Triangles in Ovid's Metamorphoses," *Arethusa* 21 (1988) 75-98

B. R. Nagle, "Two Miniature *Carmina Perpetua* in the *Metamorphoses*: Calliope and Orpheus," *GB* 15 (1988) 99-125

B. R. Nagle, "Erotic Pursuit and Narrative Seduction in Ovid's *Metamorphoses*," *Ramus* 17 (1988) 32-51

B. R. Nagle, "Ovid's Reticent Heroes," *Helios* 15 (1988) 23-39

B. R. Nagle, "Ovid's *Metamorphoses*: A Narratological Catalogue," *SyllClass* 1 (1989) 97-125

G. Nagy, *The Best of the Achaeans: Concepts of the Hero in Archaic Greek Poetry*, Baltimore and London 1979

W. Nelles, *Frameworks: Narrative Levels and Embedded Narrative* [American University Studies: Sr. 19, General Literature; Vol. 33], New York 1997

R. Neuberger-Bonath, "Die Rolle des Sklaven in der griechischen Tragödie," *C&M* 31 (1970) 72-83

C. Newlands, "The Simile of the Fractured Pipe in Ovid's Metamorphoses 4," *Ramus* 15 (1986) 143-53

J. K. Newman, *The Concept of Vates in Augustan Poetry* [Collection Latomus 88], Bruxelles 1967

E. Norden, *Agnostos Theos*, Leipzig 1913

G. Nugent, "This Sex Which Is Not One: De-constructing Ovid's Hermaphrodite," *differences* 2 (1990) 160-85

J. Ober, *Mass and Elite in Democratic Athens: Rhetoric, Ideology, and the Power of People*, Princeton 1989

J. J. O'Hara, *Death and Optimistic Prophecy in Vergil's* Aeneid, Princeton, NJ 1990

S. Onega and J. A. García Landa (eds), *Narratology: An Introduction*, London and New York 1996

P. O'Neill, *Fictions of Discourse: Reading Narrative Theory*, Toronto -

Buffalo - London 1994

U. Olsson, "The Greatest Story Ever Told: Some Remarks on the Voice of Narratology," in Wahlin 1996: 81-94

I. Opelt, *Die lateinischen Schimpfwörter und verwandte sprachliche Erscheinungen*, Heidelberg 1965

B. Otis, *Ovid as an Epic Poet*, Cambridge 1970[2]

S. G. Owen, "Ovid's use of the simile," *CR* 45 (1931) 97-106

E. Pais, "L' autobiographia ed il processo di P. Rutilio Rufo," in *Ricereche sulla Storia e sul Diritto Publico di Roma. Dalle Guerre Puniche a Cesare Augusto*, Roma 1918, pp.35-89

R. Palla, "Appunti sul makarismos e sulla fortuna di un verso virgiliano," *SCO* 33 (1983) 171-192

E. Paratore, "L' influenza delle Heroides sull' episodio di Biblide e Cauno nel L.ix delle Metamorfosi ovidiane," in *Studia Florentina A. Ronconi sexagenario oblata*, Roma 1970, pp.291-309

W. Parks, *Verbal Duelling in Heroic Narrative. The Homeric and Old English Traditions*, Princeton NJ 1990

A. Parry, "The Two Voices of Vergil's *Aeneid*," *Arion* 2 (1963) 66-80; reprinted in S. Commager (ed.), *Virgil: A Collection of Critical Essays*, Englewood Cliffs, NJ 1966, pp.107-23

H. Parry, "Ovid's *Metamorphoses*: Violence in a Pastoral Landscape," *TAPhA* 95 (1964) 268-282

H. Parry, "The Homeric Hymn to Aphrodite: Erotic *Ananke*," *Phoenix* 40 (1986) 253-264

Γ. Πασχαλίδης, Η Ποιητική της Αυτοβιογραφίας, Αθήνα 1993

T. Pavel, "Between History and Fiction: On Dorrit Cohn's Poetics of Prose," in Fehn-Hoestery-Tatar 1992: 17-28.

C. O. Pavese, "L' Inno Rapsodico: Analisi Tematica degli Inni Omerici," *AION (filol.)* 13 (1991) 155-178

J. Peradotto, *Man in the Middle Voice: Name and Narration in the Odyssey* [Martin Classical Lectures n.s.1], Princeton,N.J. 1990

C. A. Perkins, "Ovid's Erotic Vates," *Helios* 27 (2000) 53-61

L. A. Perraud, "Amatores exclusi: Apostrophe and Separation in the

Pyramus and Thisbe Episode," *CJ* 79 (1983/84) 135-39

H. Peters, *Symbola ad Ovidii artem epicam cognoscendam*, Diss. Göttingen 1908

I. L. Pfeijffer, "The Image of the Eagle in Pindar and Bacchylides," *CPh* 89 (1994) 305-317

C. R. Phillips, "Rethinking Augustan Poetry," *Latomus* 42 (1983) 780-818

G. Piccaluga, *Lykaon: un tema mitico* [Quaderni di SMSR 5], Roma 1968

R. Pichon, *De Sermone Amatorio apud Latinos Elegiarum Scriptores*, Paris 1902

M. A. Piwowarczyk, "The Narratee and the Situation of the Enunciation: A Reconsideration of Prince's Theory," *Genre* 9 (1976) 161-177

A. Powell (ed.), *Roman Poetry & Propaganda in the Age of Augustus*, London 1992

L. Pratt, *Lying and Poetry from Homer to Pindar: Falsehood and Deception in Archaic Greek Poetics*, Ann Arbor 1993

G. Prince, "Introduction à l'étude du narrataire," *Poétique* 14 (1973) 178-196 [translated into English as G. Prince, "Introduction to the Study of the Narratee," in J. P. Tompkins (ed.), *Reader-Response Criticism: From Formalism to Post-Structuralism*, Baltimore and London 1980, pp.7-25]

G. Prince, "Le discours attributif et le récit," *Poétique* 35 (1978) 305-13

G. Prince, *Narratology: the form and function of narrative*, The Hague 1982

G. Prince, "On Narratology: Criteria, Corpus, Context," *Narrative* 3 (1995) 73-84

G. Prince, "Remarks on Narrativity," in Wahlin 1996: 94-106

P. Pucci, *Hesiod and the Language of Poetry*, Baltimore 1977

N. Sorkin Rabinowitz and A. Richlin (eds.), *Feminist Theory and the Classics*, New York and London 1993

N. Sorkin Rabinowitz, *Anxiety Veiled: Euripides and the Traffic in Women*, Ithaca and London 1993

W. H. Race, *The Classical Priamel from Homer to Boethius*, Leiden 1982

W. H. Race, "Aspects of Rhetoric and Form in Greek Hymns," *GRBS* 23 (1982) 5-14

W. H. Race, "How Greek poems begin," *YClS* 29 (1992) 13-38

O. Rank, *The Incest Theme in Literature and Legend. Fundamentals of a Psychology of Literary Creation*, trans. G. C. Richter, Baltimore and London 1992

R. Reitzenstein, *Hellenistische Wundererzählungen*, Leipzig 1906 (repr. Darmstadt 1974)

A. Rich, *Of Woman Born*, 10th ed., London 1986

N. J. Richardson, *The Homeric Hymn to Demeter*, Oxford 1974

S. Richardson, *The Homeric Narrator*, Nashville, Tenessee 1990

A. Richlin, *The Garden of Priapus*, New York & London 1983

A. Richlin (ed.), *Pornography and Representation in Greece and Rome*, New York 1992

A. Richlin, "Reading Ovid's Rapes," in Richlin 1992: 158-79

S. Rimmon-Kenan, *Narrative Fiction: Contemporary Poetics*, London and New York 1983

C. C. Rohrer, "Red and White in Ovid's *Metamorphoses*. The Mulberry Tree in the tale of Pyramus and Thisbe," *Ramus* 9 (1980) 79-88

G. Rosati, "Il racconto dentro il racconto. Funzione metanarrativa nelle 'Metamorfosi' di Ovidio," *MCSN* 3 (1981) 297-309

G. Rosati, *Narciso e Pigmalione. Illusione e spettacolo nelle Metamorfosi di Ovidio*, Firenze 1983

P. W. Rose, "Ideology in the *Iliad*: Polis, Basileus, Theoi," *Arethusa* 30 (1997) 151-199

V. Rosivach, "Anus: Some Older Women in Latin Literature," *CW* 88 (1994) 107-17

D. A. Russell and M. Winterbottom (eds.), *Ancient Literary Criticism. The Principal Texts in New Translations*, Oxford 1972

M.-L. Ryan, "Cyberage Narratology: Computers, Metaphor, and Narrative," in Herman 1999: 113-41

R. M. M. Sáez, "El tema symposiaco en la poesía latina, de Horacio a Marcial, I: Los elementos externos del simposio," *Myrtia* 6 (1991)

129-147

C. Salles, *Lire à Rome*, Paris 1992

G. N. Sandy, "Petronius and the tradition of the interpolated narrative," *TAPhA* 101 (1970) 463-76

H. Saussy, "Writing in the *Odyssey*: Eurykleia, Parry, Jousse, and the opening of a letter from Homer," *Arethusa* 29 (1996) 299-338.

R. Schlaifer, "Greek Theories of Slavery from Homer to Aristotle," *HSPh* 47 (1936) 165-204

U. Schmitzer, "Meerstille und Wasserrohrbruch: über Herkunft, Funktion und Nachwirkung der Gleichnisse in Ovids Erzählung von Pyramus und Thisbe (met.4,55-166)," *Gymnasium* 99 (1992) 519-45

A. Scobie, "Storytellers, Storytelling, and the Novel in Graeco-Roman antiquity," *RhM* 122 (1979) 229-259

C. P. Segal, *Landscape in Ovid's Metamorphoses: A Study in the Transformations of a Literary Symbol* [Hermes Beiheft 23], Wiesbaden 1969

C. Segal, "Art and the Hero: Participation, Detachment, and Narrative Point of View in *Aeneid* 1," *Arethusa* 14 (1981) 67-83

C. Segal, "Senecan Baroque: The Death of Hippolytus in Seneca, Ovid, and Euripides," *TAPhA* 114 (1984) 311-25

C. P. Segal, "Pyramus and Thisbe: Liebestod, Monument, and the Metamorphosis in Ovid, Beowulf, Shakespeare and Some Others," *AFLNice* 50 (1985) 387-99

C. Segal, *Pindar's Mythmaking: The Fourth Pythian Ode*, Princeton NJ 1986

C. Segal, *Orpheus: The Myth of the Poet*, Baltimore and London 1989

C. Segal, "Philomela's web and the pleasures of the text: Reader and violence in the *Metamorphoses* of Ovid," in de Jong-Sullivan 1994: 257-80

R. Sewell, *The Vision of Tragedy*, New Haven 1959

A. Shapiro, "Eros in Love: Pederasty and Pornography in Greece," in Richlin 1992: 53-72

A. R. Sharrock, "The Love of Creation," *Ramus* 20 (1991) 169-82

E. Showalter, "A Criticism of Our Own: Autonomy and Assimilation in Afro-American and Feminist Literary Theory," paper presented at the School of Criticism and Theory, Dartmouth College, Hanover, N.H., June 1986

P. Simpson, *Language, Ideology and Point of View*, London and New York 1993

P. Sinclair, *Tacitus the sententious historian: a sociology of rhetoric in* Annales *1-6*, University Park, Pennsylvania 1995

L. M. Slatkin, *The Power of Thetis. Allusion and Interpretation in the Iliad*, Berkeley and Los Angeles 1991

M. Smith, "Prolegomena to a Discussion of Aretalogies, Divine Men, the Gospels and Jesus," *JBL* 90 (1971) 174-199

S. C. Smith, "Remembering the Enemy: Narrative, Focalization, and Vergil's Portrait of Achilles," *TAPA* 129 (1999) 225-262

J. B. Solodow, *The World of Ovid's Metamorphoses*, Chapel Hill/London 1988

E. Souriau, *L'Univers Filmique*, Paris 1953

C. A. Sowa, *Traditional Themes and the Homeric Hymns*, Chicago IL 1984

Dale Spender, *Man Made Language*, London 1980

G. C. Spivak, "Displacement and the Discourse of Woman," in Mark Krupnik (ed.), *Displacement: Derrida and After*, Bloomington 1983, pp.169-95

F. K. Stanzel, *Theorie des Erzählens*, 3., durchgesehene Auflage, Göttingen 1985 [English trans. by Charlotte Goedsche as *A Theory of Narrative*, Cambridge Mass. 1984]

E. Stehle, "Sappho's Gaze: Fantasies of a Goddess and a Young Man," in E. Greene (ed.), *Reading Sappho: Contemporary Approaches*, Berkeley - Los Angeles - London 1996, pp. 193-25 [first printed in slightly different form in *differences* 2 (1990) 88-125]

G. Steiner, "Ovid's *Carmen Perpetuum*," *TAPhA* 89 (1958) 218-36

D. T. Steiner, *The Tyrant's Writ: Myths and Images of Writing in Ancient Greece*, Princeton 1994

K. Stendhal, *Paul among Jews and Gentiles and Other Essays*, Philadelphia 1976

B. E. Stirrup, "Techniques of Rape: Variety of Wit in Ovid's *Metamorphoses*," G&R 24 (1977) 170-184

W. Stroh, "Ovids Liebeskunst und die Ehegesetze des Augustus," *Gymnasium* 86 (1979) 323-352

W. Suerbaum, "Die objektiv und die subjektiv erzählende Göttin. Bericht Dianas von der Jugend Camillas (Verg.Aen.XI 535-586) und die Erzählung der Venus von Hippomenes und Atalanta (Ovid.met. 10, 560-707)," *WJA* 6a (1980) 139-160

R. Swinburn, *The concept of miracle*, London 1970

J. Tambling, *Narrative and Ideology*, Milton Keynes & Philadelphia 1991

R. J. Tarrant, "The Silence of Cephalus: Text and Narrative Technique in Ovid, Metamorphoses 7.685ff.," *TAPhA* 125 (1995) 99-111

A. Robinson Taylor, *Male Novelists and Their Female Voices: Literary Masquerades*, Troy 1981

Φ. Τερζάκης, *Τα ονόματα του Διονύσου: Προαναγγελίες μιας διαρκώς ματαιούμενης έλευσης*, Αθήνα 2000

W. G. Thalmann, *Conventions of Form and Thought in Early Greek Epic Poetry*, Baltimore and London 1984

W. G. Thalmann, *The Swineherd and the Bow: Representations of Class in the Odyssey*, Ithaca and London 1998

R. Thomas, *Oral Tradition and Written Record in Classical Athens*, Cambrindge 1989

M. J. Toolan, *Narrative: A Critical Linguistic Introduction*, London and New York 1988

Α. Τζούμα, *Η Διπλή Ανάγνωση του Κειμένου*, Athens 1991

Α. Τζούμα, "Απορητική Προσέγγιση στην Κοινωνιοσημειωτική της Αφήγησης," in Καψωμένος-Πασχαλίδης 1996: 438-52

B. Uspensky, *A Poetics of Composition*, Berkeley 1973

E. Valette-Cagnac, *La lecture à Rome: Rites et pratiques*, Paris 1997

J.-P. Vernant, *Mortals and Immortals: Collected Essays*, F. I. Zeitlin (ed.), Princeton NJ 1991

L. Vinge, *The Narcissus Theme in Western European Literature up to the Early 19th Century*, Lund 1967

F. Vinteuil, "Ordre et violences," *Cahiers du Féminisme* 83 (1985) 8-10

C. Wahlin (ed.), *Perspectives on Narratology: Papers from the Stockholm Symposium on Narratology*, Frankfurt a. M. 1996

K. Wall, *The Callisto Myth from Ovid to Atwood: Initiation and Rape in Literature*, Kingston 1988

A. Wallace-Hadrill, "The Golden Age and Sin in Augustan Ideology," *P&P* 95 (1982) 19-36

A. Wallace-Hadrill, "Propaganda and Dissent? Augustan Moral Legislation and the Love-Poets," *Klio* 67 (1985) 180-184

A. Wallace-Hadrill, "Time for Augustus: Ovid, Augustus and the *Fasti*," in M. Whitby, P. Hardie & M. Whitby (eds.), *Homo Viator: Classical Essays for John Bramble*, Bristol 1987, pp.221-230

A. Wallace-Hadrill, "Rome's Cultural Revolution," *JRS* 79 (1989) 157-64

G. B. Walsh, *Varieties of Enchantment. Early Greek Views of the Nature and Function of Poetry*, Chapel Hill and London 1984

J. Walters, "Invading the Roman Body: Manliness and Impenetrability in Roman Thought," in J. P. Hallett and M. B. Skinner (eds.), *Roman Sexualities*, Princeton NJ 1997, p.29-43

R. R. Warhol, *Gendered Interventions: Narrative Discourse in the Victorian Novel*, New Brunswick 1989

L. Watson, *The Curse Poetry of Antiquity* [ARCA 26], Leeds 1991

M. Weber, *Die mythologische Erzählung in Ovids Liebeskunst. Verankerung, Struktur und Funktion* [Studien zur klass.Philol. 6], Frankfurt a.M./Bern 1983

S. M. Wheeler, *A Discourse of Wonders: Audience and Performance in Ovid's Metamorphoses*, Philadelphia 1999

L. P. Wilkinson, *Ovid Recalled*, Cambridge 1955

G. Williams, "Poetry in the Moral Climate of Augustan Rome," *JRS* 52 (1962) 28-46

G. Williams, *Technique and Ideas in the Aeneid*, New Haven and London 1983

C. A. Williams, "Greek Love at Rome," *CQ* 45 (1995) 517-39

C. A. Williams, *Roman Homosexuality*, Oxford 1999
J. J. Winkler, *Auctor & Actor. A Narratological Reading of Apuleius's Golden Ass*, Berkeley/Los Angeles/London 1985
J. J. Winkler, *The Constraints of Desire*, New York and London 1990
C. Wirszubski, "*Audaces*: A Study in Political Phraseology," *JRS* 5 (1961) 12-22
M. Wyke, "The Elegiac Woman at Rome," *PCPS* 33 (1987) 153-78
M. Wyke, "Written Women: Propertius' *Scripta Puella*," *JRS* 77 (1987) 47-61
M. Wyke, "Mistress and Metaphor in Augustan Elegy," *Helios* 16 (1989) 25-47
M. Wyke, "Taking the Woman's Part: Engendering Roman Love Elegy," *Ramus* 23 (1994) 110-28
P. Zanker, *The Power of Images in the Age of Augustus*, trans. by A. Shapiro, Ann Arbor 1988
F. I. Zeitlin, *Playing the Other: Gender and Society in Classical Greek Literature*, Chicago and London 1996

GENERAL INDEX

Aczel, A. 104
aetiology 47, 76, 78, 167, 174, 175, 178, 213, 260
Ahl, F. 161
Albrecht, M. von 205, 212, 225, 234
amor 214, 260
anachronism 98, 99
anachrony 42, 43, 47, 53, 54, 67
  complete 45
  external 45, 124
  heterodiegetic 21, 47
  homodiegetic 21, 47
  incomplete 45
  internal 45
  mixed 45
  partial 45
analepsis 43, 45, 46, 48, 53, 54, 67, 258
  complete 46, 54
  external 45, 54, 124
  homodiegetic 47, 48, 53
  internal 45, 46
anaphora 65
Anderson, W. S. 47, 77, 163, 164, 188, 191, 237
androcentrism 147, 154
Apollodorus 46
Apollonius of Rhodes 17, 19, 45, 80, 258
apostrophe 19, 183, 198, 210, 253
Apuleius 168
aretalogy 167
Aristotle 121, 168, 170
  Poetics 185
art 153, 155, 162
asyndeton 54
audacia 204
Augustus 18, 24, 26, 43-46, 85, 156, 157, 193, 199, 201, 205, 206, 211, 216, 218, 223
  art 200
  legislation 24
  Res Gestae 200, 204
authentication 116
author 45, 52, 62, 76, 99, 104, 138, 149, 156, 224, 245, 248, 256
  female 31, 34

implied 100
male 32, 155
authority 33, 34, 55, 92, 95, 105, 118, 121, 159, 160, 187, 193-96, 198, 224, 233, 234, 252, 254, 255
  male 155

Bakhtin, M. 18, 26-28, 258
  chronotope 140
Bal, M. 14-19, 70, 88, 137, 138, 202
Baldo, G. 189
Barchiesi, A. 29, 105
Bartenbach, A. 125
Barthes, R. 122, 196
beginnings 64, 67
  ab Iove 184
  Priamel/praeteritio 184
Bergren, A. 158
Bilinsky, B. 146
Block, E. 197
Boegehold, A. L. 23
Boillat, M. 46, 47, 125, 251, 258
Bömer, F. 155, 182, 189, 208, 220
Booth, W. C. 182
Borges, J. L. 72
Brewer, M. M. 137
Brownmiller, S. 150

Cahoon, L. 138, 206
Callimachus 29, 129, 175, 178, 184, 227, 261
canon 138, 216
catalogue 182
Carter, A. 152
Catullus 32, 143, 165
Cave, M. 140
Cervantes, M. de 27, 99
Cestius 219
Chariton 62
Chatman, S. 13-15, 182, 197, 199
Chopin, K. 140
Cicero 52, 120, 138, 142, 167-69, 184, 205
class 139, 141, 142, 144, 156, 176
Clauss, J. J. 175
closure 123, 137, 160
  happy end 62, 147
  tragic end 215

unhappy end 209
comment 16, 22, 94, 169, 172, 174, 180-82, 184, 185, 187-89, 191, 194, 195, 196, 199, 202, 203, 208-10, 213, 214, 216, 218, 220-23, 234, 237, 238, 252
  ideological 202
  metannarrative 55
  premonitory 203
  testimonial 193
competition 146, 157, 177
Conrad, J. 239, 241
Conte, G. B. 17, 23, 24, 216
Cornell, J. 136
Crabbe, A. 207
Culham, P. 34
Culler, J. 141
culture 17, 196, 205, 219
curiosity 122, 129
Curran, L. C. 149, 152, 155

De Jong, I. J. F. 15-18, 30, 37, 38, 54, 108, 110, 112, 124, 233
deconstruction 14, 20, 136, 155, 258
deixis 98, 115, 133
Demosthenes 189
Derrida, J. 20, 104
description 19, 43, 46, 48-50, 54, 56-58, 60, 61, 65, 66, 92, 95, 97, 110, 151, 175, 176, 184, 188, 190, 197, 214, 227, 244
desire 147, 149, 150, 154, 155, 162, 206, 213, 214, 217, 221
  female 156
  illicit 165
  imperialist 157
  male 177
  sexual 166
dialogism 18, 27
dialogue 82, 138
  dramatic 80
diegesis 35, 42, 43, 45, 62, 66, 67, 70, 71, 73, 88, 103, 118, 121-25, 156, 218, 226, 232, 233, 239, 241, 252, 256, 258, 260
Diengott, N. 138, 140, 141
discourse 16, 39, 43, 48, 49, 115, 116, 122, 180, 199
  amatory 33
  attributive 108, 110-12, 115, 132
  (directly) reported 64, 71, 73, 74, 76, 77-82, 84, 85, 90, 100, 108, 130, 136, 209, 216, 234, 236
  Augustan 202, 211, 223
  female 136, 143, 177
  free indirect 25, 37, 71, 79
  hegemonic 142
  indirect *see* transposed
  masculine 147
  mimetic 51
  narrated 130
  narratized 51, 71, 72, 81, 85, 100
  non-narrative 180
  oral/written 104
  patriarchal 142
  pseudo-direct 83
  quasi-legal 166
  referential 21
  reported 71, 73, 100, 117, 139, 215, 249
  summarized 85
  transposed 49, 71, 73, 74, 76, 100, 130
distance 39, 45, 69-71, 73, 100
doctus 112
Doherty, L. E. 30, 144, 145
Döring, J. 166
Dörrie, H. 160
Dostoyevsky, F. 27, 261
dream 35, 84
duration 13, 38, 42, 45, 48, 49, 70, 238, 255
  slow-down 55, 57, 59

Edwards, C. 165
ellipsis 48, 50, 58, 60, 68, 110
Ennius 24, 84
escapism 146
ethics 155
Euripides 54, 55, 64, 78, 80, 82, 97, 98, 171-73, 175, 178, 261
events (narrated) 21, 42-45, 48-56, 60, 68, 69, 73, 88, 93-95, 98, 100, 101, 111, 112, 130, 172, 180, 192-95, 215, 217, 221, 223, 255

repeated 51
exemplum 122, 124, 126, 128
explanation 56, 76, 161, 165, 192, 196, 202, 212, 213, 215, 217, 221, 223
extent 42, 45, 46, 53, 67
eye-witness 192, 193

fantasy 138, 151, 164
  female 150
  homoerotic 155
  male 150
fata 215, 216, 247
Feeney, D. C. 23, 200, 224
feminism 14, 30-32, 34, 40, 136-39, 141, 142, 149, 151, 156, 176, 258
Fenik, B. 56
fiction(ality) 40, 191, 222, 255
Finley, M. 23
Fitzgerald, W. 171
focalisation 13, 18, 22, 25, 39, 69, 70, 75, 77, 87-89, 92, 98, 100, 103, 130, 139
  deviant 18
  external 88, 89
  fixed 88
  internal 39, 48, 88, 92-95, 97, 98, 101
  male 143
  multiple 88
  perceptual 93
  variable 26, 88, 89
  zero 39, 89, 90
focalized 89
focalizee 233
focalizer 22, 26, 88-90, 92, 84, 95, 233
Foley, H. P. 158
formalism 14
Foucault, M. 195
Fowler, D. 17, 28, 25
Fowler, R. 196
frequency 13, 38, 42, 51, 52, 55, 64, 67, 68, 75, 83, 101, 209
function (of narratee) 254
function (of narrative)
  explanatory 121
  formal 122, 123
  hermeneutic 122, 123
function (of narrator) 40
  directing 237
  ideological 19, 182, 195-98, 202, 222, 238
  testimonial 182, 185, 193, 194, 195, 222, 237
Fusillo, M. 17, 19, 47, 258

Galinksy, G. K. 63, 165, 232, 262
García Landa, J. A. 14
Gardiner, M. 20
gaze 34, 93
  male 147
gender 13, 32, 33, 40, 87, 93, 130, 137-42, 153, 156, 160, 161, 247, 248, 258, 260, 261
  feminine 66, 137, 146, 147, 218, 223
  masculine 136, 137, 147
  studies 136
generalisation 182, 218-20, 224
Genette, G. 12, 13, 15, 17, 19, 21, 22, 24, 27, 34, 35, 38, 39, 43, 45, 47-49, 67, 69-72, 87, 89, 103, 118, 121, 123, 132, 182, 185, 195-97, 199, 225, 258
genre 29, 57, 62, 64, 68, 141
  autobiography 82, 117-20, 130
  choral lyric 184
  comedy 27, 62, 154, 177
  didactic 28, 29, 260
  drama 33, 82, 172
  elegy 32, 129, 132, 142, 143, 173, 208, 220
  epic 15, 17, 23, 27-30, 35, 43-45, 47, 48, 64, 80, 83, 85, 94, 97, 101, 105, 106, 129-31, 143, 145, 152, 163, 164, 170, 176, 192, 197-99, 203, 207, 209, 213, 216, 218, 220, 223, 241, 244
  epigram 78
  epitaph 87, 107
  hymn 57, 117, 124, 157, 244, 261
  novel 27, 137, 140, 141, 261
  romance 62, 83, 147
  satire 27

Gibson, A. 69, 103, 104, 136
Gildenhard, I. 81
Gold, B. K. 32, 142
Goldhill, S. 23
Goldmann, L. 21
Gordon, P. 154
Graecism 190
Gros, P. 259
Gutzwiller, K. 32
gynesis 31, 34

Haarberg, J. 91, 124, 188
Hainsworth, J. B. 52, 182
Hallet, J. 32, 143
Hamon, P. 22
Hardie, P. 44
Harries, B. 121
Harrison, S. J. 209
Haupt, M. 47
Heinze, R. 77, 199, 258
Hemker, J. 150
Herman, D. 258
Hesiod 146, 147
   Theogony 157
   Works and Days 217
Hinds, S. 23, 57
historiography 46
historicism 20, 258
history 17, 25, 28, 38, 42, 44, 45, 105, 110, 120, 137, 193, 218, 258, 260, 261
Hoesterey, I. 14
Holzberg, N. 63, 83
Homer 15-17, 19, 28, 46, 52, 56, 57, 60, 63, 64, 68, 73-75, 80, 85, 87, 97, 108, 115-17, 131, 138, 142, 144, 146, 169, 171, 182, 192, 194, 197-99, 214, 217, 218
   Homeric Hymn to Aphrodite 158, 217
   Homeric Hymn to Demeter 57, 158
   Homeric Hymn to Dionysos 80, 82, 173, 203
   Homeric Hymn to Hermes 84
   Iliad 15, 16, 35, 37, 56, 73, 75, 77, 80, 90, 91, 94, 97, 106, 108-10, 123-25, 159, 192, 227, 233
   Odyssey 15, 28, 30, 35, 36, 46, 80, 94, 106, 123, 129, 131, 143, 146, 168, 171, 173, 184, 189, 191, 261
Horace 25, 105, 132, 143, 201
   Ars 261
   Odes 157
humanitas 206, 211
humour 27, 52, 59, 175, 207, 210
Hyginus 188

ideology 18-23, 25, 40, 136, 139, 141, 151, 176, 195, 196, 199, 202, 255, 261
   aristocratic 142, 146, 176
   Augustan 199-201
   male 33, 142, 150, 155, 176, 177
   of the conquered 150
   patriarchal 34
imitation 191
incest 165, 188, 190, 205, 206
interpretation 182, 212, 214
intertextuality 30, 175, 178, 174, 178, 194, 210, 227, 261
Irigaray, L. 145
irony 188, 232, 233
iterative (narrative) 51, 61, 64-68, 82, 101

Jacobs, N. M. 161
Jacobson, H. 95, 189, 190
Jakobson, R. 19
James, H. 88
James, S. L. 154
Jameson, F. 20
Janan, M. 155, 156
Jardine, A. 31, 34, 136, 137, 142
judgement 22, 182, 191, 196, 197, 202, 203, 205-7, 210, 211, 222

Kaempf-Dimitriadou, S. 153
Keith, A. 36
Kleist, H. von 61

Lagopoulos, A. 20
Lanser, S. 34, 136-38, 140, 141
Latacz, J. 56, 97, 183
letters 35, 106, 107, 130, 132
level (of narration) 100, 103, 116-

18, 122, 123, 129, 130, 140, 225, 226
  primary 43, 74, 76, 77, 108, 220
  second 34, 36, 55, 77, 79, 117, 117, 253
  third 55, 73, 77, 117, 118, 214, 253
  fourth 73, 77
Lindheim, S. 161
linearity 43, 47
Livy 25, 193, 204
Longus 83, 191, 214
Lucan 44
Lucilius 29, 261
Ludwig, W. 46
Lyne, R. O. A. M. 198, 199

Martínez-Bonati, F. 99
McEwan, I. 96
McHale, B. 71
Marxism 20, 21
memini 95, 189, 190, 195, 235
memory 96, 105, 109, 178, 184, 185, 191, 192, 195, 239
  communal 167
messenger-speech 54, 55, 64, 172-75, 261
metalepsis 21
metaphor 103
metaphysics 136, 137
metapoetics 175, 191
Mezei, K. 139, 141
Michelini, A. N. 32
Miles, G. 151
mimesis 11, 69-72, 100, 138
mirum 194
mise en abyme 21
misogyny 154, 163, 165, 177
modernism 28, 32, 66
monologue 78
  interior 25, 78
  exteriorized 79
mora 181, 182
Most, G. W. 82, 119, 120, 173
motif
  aristeia 170, 190, 193
  battle 56, 85, 87, 97, 183, 261
  exclusus amator 82

locus amoenus 95
makarismos 131
paraklausithyron 82, 209
primus 97, 183
sphragis 105, 109, 224
Myers, K. S. 174
myth 20, 185, 188, 189, 191, 193, 195, 202, 212, 219, 220, 227, 232, 251, 258

Naevius 24
Nagle, B. R. 160, 226, 242
narratee 11, 19, 39, 40, 48, 55, 58, 67, 68, 73, 105, 110, 111, 117, 120, 122, 123, 131, 133, 155, 156, 177, 178, 183, 185, 189, 191, 193, 195, 202, 212, 219, 220, 225-27, 233, 234, 238, 239, 241-43, 246-49, 251-55
  divine 227
  extradiegetic 62, 93, 110-12, 121, 130, 225, 232, 234, 249
  female 30, 145, 146, 148
  intradiegetic 40, 121, 122, 225-27, 239, 241, 243, 244, 246, 248, 256
  male 145
  non-human 163
  primary 99
  reluctant 247
  resistant 226
  signals of 227
narration 12, 18, 21, 26, 36, 43, 48-50, 58, 61, 65, 68, 69, 71, 75, 82, 90, 94, 107, 113, 117, 122, 131, 139, 169, 180, 182, 183, 185, 188, 189, 191-93, 195, 202, 212, 214, 219, 220, 225, 241, 243, 251, 259, 260
  autodiegetic 63, 64, 120, 140, 149, 173, 261
  dramatic 16, 70
  heterodiegetic 140
  homodiegetic 121, 140, 173
  intradiegetic 35, 123, 129
  oral/written 51, 69, 83, 171, 180
  subsequent 107, 132
  third-person 79, 116, 207

zero-degree 89
narrative situation 192, 225, 226, 238, 247
narrativity 66, 180
narrator 11, 15, 19, 22, 27, 33, 35, 39, 40, 42-44, 46, 48, 49, 51, 53, 55, 56, 58-64, 68-75, 77, 79, 83, 87, 90, 91, 96, 97, 100, 103, 105, 106, 108, 110, 111, 116-18, 120, 122, 124, 130, 132, 140, 141, 144, 147, 151, 160, 162, 176, 177, 182-85, 189, 192, 194, 196-98, 202, 205, 206, 209, 212-15, 217, 220, 222, 225, 227, 232, 234, 238, 239, 241, 242, 245, 247, 252, 253, 256
    aged 120, 139, 142, 166-70, 166, 170, 178
    anonymous 172
    artistic 101
    biased 188
    credible 53, 122
    divine 101, 118, 121, 144, 246
    extradiegetic 15, 26, 28, 36-38, 60, 67, 85, 93, 98, 99, 101, 105, 107-12, 117, 118, 122, 123, 126, 130, 132, 143, 154, 170, 182, 183, 191, 205, 207, 212, 221, 224, 233, 237, 248, 250, 251, 255, 256, 259, 260, 262
    female 30, 40, 118, 120, 142-47, 153-56, 160, 246
    heterodiegetic 15, 62, 73, 92, 118, 119, 121, 174
    homodiegetic 39, 62, 73, 93, 95, 101, 118, 119, 192
    human 94, 144, 145, 216
    identification of 108, 116
    intradiegetic 28, 36, 37, 39, 40, 47, 48, 54, 67, 68, 84, 90, 93, 98, 101, 106, 108-11, 117-19, 123, 125, 131, 132, 140, 143, 159-62, 167, 171, 172, 176-78, 180, 183, 185, 194, 200, 203, 210, 211, 216-18, 221-26, 233, 234, 237, 244, 252, 253, 255, 258, 260, 261
    intrusive 199, 203
    male 30, 32, 150

    perceptible 16, 182, 183
    professional 183
    reliable 141, 187, 188, 222
    rustic 175
    slave 171
    self-conscious 16, 72, 96, 111, 180, 191, 192, 197, 260
    unreliable 94, 170
Nelles, W. 37, 122
neo-historicism 223
nequiquam 209
Newlands, C. 62
Nicolaus the Sophist 61
Nigidius Figulus 45
novelty 184
Nugent, G. 143
nymphs 50, 51, 53, 59, 64, 65, 83, 92, 107, 130, 144-46, 152, 241, 244, 246

Ober, J. 23
Ollson, U. 103
omniscience, *See* focalisation, zero
Onega, S. 14
orality 11, 33, 35, 132, 142, 167, 176, 178, 197, 222
order 13, 16, 21, 42, 52, 182
ordine 52, 182
over-justification 238, 255
Ovid 25, 29, 31, 36, 39, 44, 46, 47, 49, 52, 53, 54, 56, 57, 60, 62, 64, 66-68, 70, 74, 75, 77, 80, 82, 84, 91, 93, 97-101, 104, 105, 108, 109, 112, 115, 117, 118, 121, 123, 129, 131, 132, 138, 143, 145, 146, 149-54, 157, 159-62, 165, 167, 173-75, 182, 201, 203, 206, 212-17, 219, 221, 223, 224, 232, 234, 247, 251, 258, 261
    Amores 165, 189, 208
    Ars Amatoria 24, 150, 164, 189
    Fasti 121, 130, 151, 181
    Heroides 106, 132, 190, 206, 227, 261
    Tristia 120

pantomime 161
paralipsis 141

parenthesis 93, 95, 191, 209, 212-14, 219, 221, 223, 234, 235, 237, 238, 255
parody 29, 63, 190
patriarchy 31, 34, 136, 140, 147, 149, 156-60, 177
pause 16, 48, 49, 54, 55, 61-64, 68
  descriptive 61, 64
pederasty 163, 164, 177
Peradotto, J. 121
Perraud, L. A. 65, 83
person 103, 141
Peters, H. 36, 54
Phanocles 261
Phillips, C. R. 25, 200
philosophy 44, 151, 204, 262
phonocentrism 103
Piccaluga, J. 91, 188
piety 93, 168, 170, 205-7, 212, 246
Pindar 193
Piwowarczyk, M. A. 225
Plato 70
  Laws 163
  Republic 11, 206
pleasure 131, 160, 167, 191, 227, 259
  masochistic 151, 156
  private 156
  sadistic 58, 151, 156
  sadomasochistic 177
  sexual 163, 164
poetics 139
polyphony 26-28, 30, 261
Porcius Latro 219
pornography 151, 152, 156
postmodernism 31, 69, 104, 107, 136
post-structuralism 20, 34, 196
power 191, 196, 199, 201, 202, 213, 216, 217, 219-21, 223
pragmatics 139
prayer 72, 73, 78, 81, 84, 216
predictive (narrative) 119
Prince, G. 108, 138-41, 225, 226, 238, 241, 254, 255
proem 57, 105, 118, 123, 125, 131, 145, 164, 165, 183, 184, 221
prolepsis 43, 54, 109

Propertius 29, 32, 33, 142, 143, 170, 175
prophecy 43-45, 109, 132
Proust, M. 13, 28, 69, 70
pseudo-iterative (narrative) 66-68
psychoanalysis 150, 151, 258
Pucci, P. 84

Quintilian 53

Rabelais 27
Rabinowitz, N. 30, 31
rape 147-55, 159-61, 177
reach 45
reader 18, 19, 30, 33, 40, 48, 62, 67, 88, 89, 99, 112, 121, 122, 125, 130, 132, 149, 156, 160, 162, 165, 189, 206, 216, 225, 227, 232, 233, 246, 248, 255, 256, 258, 261
  alert 223
  male 151
repetition 51, 52, 83, 207
repetitive (narrative) 52, 67
reportability 180
representationalism 69
Rich, A. 159
Richlin, A. 143, 151-53, 161
Richardson, S. 15-17, 19, 38, 73, 117, 197, 214, 218, 258
Rimmon-Kenan, S. 13, 182, 259
Rosati, G. 225

Sade, Marquis de 152
Sandy, G. N. 129
Sappho 93, 96
Scafuro, A. C. 23
scene 39, 48-51, 56, 57, 60, 64, 67, 82, 111, 118, 171, 190, 259
scholia 184
Segal, C. 162, 163, 215
semiotics 11, 12, 20-22, 31, 138, 180
Seneca 64, 219
sententia 24, 218, 219
Servius 182
sexuality 141, 158, 161, 163, 165, 177
Sharrock, A. 217

Showalter, E. 139
silence 111, 112, 133, 145, 152, 158
simile 49, 61-64, 98, 101, 148, 210, 211, 225, 252, 253, 260
simultaneous (narrative) 119
singulative (narrative) 51, 65-67
sociology 23, 40
Solodow, J. B. 46, 98, 125, 232
song 52, 54, 57, 75-79, 91, 101, 104, 107, 109, 111, 112, 116, 118, 131, 142, 146, 153, 157, 158, 161-64, 178, 182-84, 189, 191, 217, 220, 227, 233, 239, 243, 253
Sophocles 138, 172
Souriau 34
span 45
speech 16, 37, 39, 50, 71-81, 83, 85, 87, 100, 110-12, 124, 151, 152, 159, 171, 173, 209. *See also* discourse
deprivation of 106
one-word 209
speech-act theory 111
speed. *See* duration
Spender, D. 140
Spivak, G. C. 142
Stanzel, F. K. 13
Stehle, E. 93
Steiner, G. 189
Stirrup, B. E. 149
story 12, 15, 16, 19, 26, 28, 30, 34, 35, 38, 42-48, 51-58, 60-67, 72, 75, 76, 88, 90, 93, 95, 100, 101, 103, 105, 115, 116, 118, 121-23, 125, 126, 132, 147, 151, 160, 161, 165, 168, 169, 173, 180, 185, 195-97, 202, 210, 219, 227, 232, 238, 246, 250, 256
Stroh, W. 24
structuralism 13, 14, 21, 132, 136, 138, 140, 258
summary 16, 39, 48-51, 55-58, 60, 64-68, 70, 71, 75, 115, 130, 182, 222, 233
symposium 111, 130

teleology 44, 61, 121
tense 103

imperfect 65, 68
perfect 65
present 65
Terence 154
text 11-13, 16, 19, 21, 22, 26, 29, 33, 35, 37, 39, 42, 43, 61, 66, 77, 83, 88, 100, 103, 104, 107, 122, 132, 137, 140, 141, 180, 190, 198, 210, 219, 238, 256, 259, 260
Thalmann, W. G. 171
Theocritus 160
Tibullus 165
transition 53, 56, 57, 65, 82, 126, 185
transvestism 161, 177
tyrannus 206
Tzouma, A. 21

Uspensky, B. 25
utilitas 53
variatio 51, 67, 123
vates 105, 108, 109, 114, 115, 132
Vergil 25, 105, 132, 138, 142, 197, 199, 201, 203, 205, 216
Aeneid 18, 23, 29, 44, 46, 47, 63, 80, 97, 107, 129, 131, 143, 145, 174, 198, 199, 201, 208, 210, 214, 216, 218, 223, 247, 258, 261
Eclogues 164
Georgics 98
Vinteuil, F. 149
violence 148-51, 153, 159
virtus 247
vocare 73
voice 11, 13, 16, 18, 19, 27, 33, 34, 36, 37, 39, 40, 103, 104, 109, 112, 118, 120, 132, 140, 145, 151, 152, 180, 182, 198, 218, 225, 237, 261
usurpation of 98

Wall, K. 153
Wallace-Hadrill, A. 23, 24, 223
Walsh, G. B. 116
Walters, J. 164
Warhol, R. 34, 136, 137, 139, 141
Weber, M. 23
Wheeler, S. M. 37, 226, 232-34, 251

Wilamowitz, U. von 79
Williams, G. 165, 199
Woolf, V. 141
Wyke, M. 32, 33

Zanker, P. 200
Zeitlin, F. 33, 160

κατὰ κόσμον 52, 182
πρῶτος 183. *See also* motif, *primus*